THE HISTORY OF BROADCASTING
IN THE UNITED KINGDOM
VOLUME I

THE BIRTH OF
BROADCASTING

THE HISTORY OF BROADCASTING
IN THE UNITED KINGDOM

VOLUME I

THE BIRTH OF BROADCASTING

BY

ASA BRIGGS

LONDON
OXFORD UNIVERSITY PRESS
NEW YORK TORONTO
1961

Oxford University Press, Amen House, London E.C.4

GLASGOW NEW YORK TORONTO MELBOURNE WELLINGTON
BOMBAY CALCUTTA MADRAS KARACHI KUALA LUMPUR
CAPE TOWN IBADAN NAIROBI ACCRA

PRINTED IN GREAT BRITAIN

This History is dedicated to

LORD REITH

Managing Director of
The British Broadcasting Company
and
First Director-General of
The British Broadcasting Corporation

PREFACE

THIS volume is intended to be the first of a three-volume history of broadcasting in the United Kingdom. In writing it I have had extremely generous help from everyone whom I have consulted within the BBC. I have had the fullest access to all surviving archives, and I have benefited greatly from a number of interviews and conversations. The record I present and the conclusions I have reached are, however, entirely my own. Outside the BBC I am deeply grateful for the friendly and invaluable co-operation of Lord Reith, who has placed at my disposal his private papers and his extremely full and informative Diary. The use of this unique source has greatly enlivened the writing of this history.

I am also grateful to a number of other people and organizations too numerous to name in detail. Among them are Major Basil Binyon and Captain Peter Eckersley, who figure prominently in the history itself. The late Sir Arthur Fleming, Mr. Gladstone Murray, and Mr. Leonard Crocombe filled in a number of gaps. The Publicity Department of the Marconi Company kindly allowed me access to early papers relating to broadcasting from Chelmsford, Writtle, and 2LO; and Associated Electrical Industries (Manchester) Ltd. and Standard Telephones and Cables Ltd. also provided me with useful information. I have also been able to make use of relevant Post Office archives and certain other official papers, and I would particularly like to thank Mr. E. C. Baker of the G.P.O.

It would be invidious to single out people within the BBC, but four people have worked very closely with me: Mr. D. H. Clarke, with his wide experience and knowledge, has assisted me at every stage; Mr. R. L. W. Collison, the Librarian, Miss M. S. Hodgson, the Archivist, and Miss E. Sawyers, my secretary, helped me to organize and pursue the whole enterprise. My friend Mr. J. Trenaman read the manuscript, and gave me valuable expert advice.

ASA BRIGGS

The University of Leeds
July 1961

CONTENTS

LIST OF ILLUSTRATIONS

The author would like to acknowledge with thanks the kind permission given to reproduce
illustrations belonging to individuals and corporate bodies.

I

INTRODUCTION

BROADCASTING AND SOCIETY

———————

Listen in, Virginia,
To someone who is feeling blue;
Listen in, Virginia,
'Cause every word is meant for you;
Anybody, everybody, 'way down there,
I don't care who they be;
Somethin's doing, somethin's brewin' in the air,
So please tune up on me.

One of the first songs with a wireless theme. Words and music by
HARRY PEASE

Introduction

BROADCASTING AND SOCIETY

THIS volume is concerned largely with four years in the history of the BBC. In 1922 the BBC first came into existence. At that time the initials meant nothing to most people: they even meant nothing to John Reith, who became the BBC's first General Manager. By the end of 1926 the initials made up one of the most familiar combinations of letters in the country. Yet throughout the whole of these four formative years the initials did not stand for what they stand today. The agency which brought broadcasting to this country was not a public body but a business enterprise. The C in BBC stood not for 'Corporation' but for 'Company'.

The British Broadcasting Company came into existence only after tough commercial bargaining, first between competitive wireless interests and second between the wireless interests as a whole and the Post Office. During the course of these discussions it seemed on more than one occasion that the outcome would be two broadcasting companies instead of one. Even when these battles were over, new ones began. As a new concern the BBC had to struggle hard against more powerful established interests, particularly the press, which in many ways was then at the peak of its public power. It was easy at first for press magnates to dismiss the claims of the BBC by branding it as an 'ordinary commercial enterprise', to point to the fact that 'the people who are at the back of it are not philanthropists, they are business-men'.[1] In fact, the BBC was never an 'ordinary commercial enterprise'. By Post Office ruling, its dividends were restricted to 7½ per cent. By the will of its chief and greatest administrator, Reith, it set out from the start to act as a 'public service'. In the first four years of its history, although it was technically a business concern, it made no profits out of broadcasting beyond the return of 7½ per cent. on capital nor did it concern itself primarily with the interests of either radio manufacturers or the

---

[1] *Lord Riddell to H. Hirst, 10 Feb. 1923. [An * in front of a footnote means that the letter or document cited is in the BBC Archives.]

manufacturers of anything else. In the last months of its existence its directors connived at their own extinction and did not
seek to interfere with the constitutional rearrangements which
transformed the BBC from a Company to a Corporation on
1 January 1927. Indeed, Reith himself was one of the main
advocates of the change, which corresponded to the lessons he
had drawn from his own broadcasting experience.

There is a temptation to treat the events and policies of these
four years as sufficient in themselves, to paint an intimate
portrait rather than to fill in part of a much bigger canvas. This
is not so much because the Company was then a relatively small
and intimate concern, but because so much of interest happened
during the four years. A Company was formed and grew, but
with that formation and growth something happened both to
British society and to British government. Broadcasting itself
ceased to be a toy, an amusing novelty, an affair of 'stunts' (we
would now call them 'gimmicks') and surprises: it became an
institution. It affected people's ways of thinking and feeling, and
their relations with each other. No history of the BBC—not even
a history of the Company—can be a business history alone. It
must be a history at different levels—first, perhaps, the history
of the inner life of the organization and the strategic decisions
its leaders made, but second, and always of equal importance,
the history of the changing place of the organization in society.
During the four years with which this volume is concerned
there is a strong element of personal history also. Reith did not
make broadcasting, but he did make the BBC. He commanded
during the four years in the same way that a captain com-
mands a ship. As he himself has written, he had no sealed orders
when he started his journey. He was journeying out into the unknown.[1] His own diary has been used freely in this book: it is
fuller and far more revealing than any conventional log book.
Quite enough happened—both spectacular and routine—
during the four years from 1922 to 1926 to fill a bulging volume
of narrative record. Yet the temptation to dwell on the four
years in isolation has been resisted in this study. Reith had no
sealed orders, but he had a ship. There was much shipbuilding
between the end of the nineteenth century and 1922. What

[1] See below, p. 69.

ended with an institution began with an invention or rather a cluster of radio inventions and innovations discovered in all parts of the world. The relationship between technical invention and economic and social change is a fascinating theme in itself: as far as this study is concerned, it is the prelude to all that went afterwards.

Neither inventors nor business men, however, had an early idea of the social significance of what they were doing. Nor did the prophets. One of the first of them, Sir William Crookes, a chemist and a physicist, tried in 1892 to peer not into the mists of the future but into what he recognized was thick fog. 'Rays of light', he wrote, 'will not pierce through a wall, nor, as we know only too well, through a London fog; but electrical vibrations of a yard or more in wavelength will easily pierce such media which to them will be transparent. Here is reached the bewildering possibility of telegraphy without wires, posts, cables or any of our present costly appliances. Granted a few reasonable postulates the whole thing becomes well within the realms of possible fulfilment.'[1] These lines were written four years before Marconi arrived in Britain; they were concerned with telegraphy not with telephony, with the known as much as with the unknown. Marconi more than anyone else showed that 'reasonable postulates' and business initiative did not belong to two separate segments of life. He and the Company which he founded play an important part in the story not only of wireless telegraphy but of broadcasting. Before the BBC was, they were.

We have become so used to the language of 'mass communications' that a leap of the imagination is needed to understand the sequence of events between 1896, the year when Marconi arrived in London, and 1922, the year when the BBC was founded. What now looks massive and dominant in our society was then tentative and experimental. The term 'mass communication' itself is misleading not only because it rests on social fallacies about the 'masses' but because it confuses transmission and communication.[2] Leaving such modern confusions on one side,

[1] Sir William Crookes, 'Some Possibilities of Electricity', in *The Fortnightly*, Feb. 1892.
[2] See Raymond Williams, *Culture and Society* (1958), pp. 310–11.

wireless—even wireless telephony—was thought of for years as an instrument of private rather than of public communication: the idea of its being used to 'feed' or to 'serve' a whole community was foreign.

Only with the help of hindsight can we fit radio into the bigger story of what is loosely called 'mass culture'. And in the four years with which this volume is largely concerned Reith and his colleagues did not try to fit it in at all. This was of

MUSIC BY ELECTRIC TELEGRAPH.

(From *Punch*, 1850)

I

fundamental importance. Radio in Britain might have been integrated into the market complex as it was in the United States. There had, after all, been 'omens of change for many years' on both sides of the Atlantic. 'The appetite for entertainment had been growing, and the machinery for duplicating the printed page, the phonograph record, and eventually the motion-picture film brought quantity production into this field.'[1]

The BBC accepted the techniques, but resisted many of the values which often went with them. Reith and his colleagues

[1] G. Seldes, *The Public Arts* (New York, 1956), p. 2; A. Briggs, 'Mass Entertainment: The Origins of a Modern Industry' (The Joseph Fisher Memorial Lecture, University of Adelaide, 1960).

had values of their own, which themselves demand careful scrutiny. They believed that interest in education, the growth of public libraries, and the diffusion of knowledge were just as active forces in a democratic society as the drive for 'superior entertainment'. They did not hesitate to oppose tendencies which are now thought to be 'inevitable' tendencies of our age, and sought neither to drift with the tide of 'mass culture' nor, in the modern idiom, to treat people as 'masses' and 'manipulate' them. Wireless to them was an instrument of public good, not a means of handling people or of 'pandering to their wants'. The controllers had a choice: they tried to make it responsibly. They necessarily made it, of course, in terms of their own background and philosophies. Sometimes a broad contrast was drawn at the time between the 'elevating' work of the broadcasters and the 'debasing' work of other agencies of 'mass transmission' —for example, the cinema.[1]

Reith and his colleagues emphasized on many occasions that it had been their endeavour 'to give a conscious social purpose to the exploitation of this medium'.[2] Of course, it was a medium which could never be treated in isolation. All the so-called 'mass media' interact on each other: all had certain features in common. The press, which might have tried to direct radio, remained suspicious or aloof. The cinema, which in America had links with radio, followed a different line of development. In the meantime the clientèle of each of the media grew. For all their differences, what cinema and radio had in common during this period was the transition from novelty to acceptance. Between 1922 and 1926 Reith and his colleagues saw broadcasting begin to pass from the first flush of novelty to the phase of acquiescence. 'People turned from its wonder to a more prosaic, but more fruitful consideration of its potentialities as an instrument of social well-being.'[3]

During the four years from 1922 to 1926 almost all the later developments of radio were anticipated if not fulfilled. The content of programmes was thought out as carefully and as

[1] A. H. Morse, Radio: Beam and Broadcast (1925), p. 78. The same point was made in a letter from John Murray, the publisher, to Reith, 19 Sept. 1924. This letter is in Lord Reith's possession.
[2] Speech to the retiring Directors and the Governors-designate, 16 Dec. 1926.
[3] J. C. W. Reith, Memorandum of Information on the Scope and Conduct of the Broadcasting Service (1925), p. 21.

imaginatively as it has ever been since. Only constitutional limitations—limitations, for example, on 'controversial' broadcasting—prevented more from being done. One feature of programme policy has dominated the history of British broadcasting ever since. The BBC did not interpret its task as the provision of entertainment alone: to supply entertainment by itself was thought of as the betrayal of a trust. 'Education' in the broadest sense was thought of as an equally important objective. 'I think it will be admitted by all', Reith wrote in 1924, 'that to have exploited so great a scientific invention for the purpose and pursuit of entertainment alone would have been a prostitution of its powers and an insult to the character and intelligence of the people.'[1] There was a sharp divergence at this point with the history of the cinema.

Reith often took time on his journey to think what other people might have done had they been placed in the same position as he was. It usually made him shudder. 'I wonder if many have paused to consider the incalculable harm which might have been done had different principles guided the conduct of the service in the early days.'[2] Reith's remark remains a pertinent invitation to further reflection. Deep reflection, of course, can hardly be limited to the experience of the four years from 1922 to 1926, yet in 1926 itself, at the close of the 'early years' of broadcasting, both Reith's pride and fears were widely shared. His demand that the broadcasting medium should be used for other purposes besides entertainment emerged unscathed from the inquiry into the future of broadcasting undertaken by the Crawford Committee.

So too did the idea of a 'monopoly' in broadcasting, for the Crawford Committee, almost the whole of the press, and an overwhelmingly large majority of parliamentary opinion in 1926 were agreed that there should be 'unified control'. The problem is interesting but complicated, in that between 1922 and 1926 discussions about 'monopoly' usually began with a consideration of technical factors and ended with a discussion of social and administrative factors. On the technical side, the Post Office used its tremendous power to insist on 'unified

[1] J. C. W. Reith, *Broadcast Over Britain* (1925), p. 17.
[2] Ibid., p. 31.

control'. On the social and administrative side Reith himself was the chief spokesman.

The word 'monopoly' itself was very loosely used. In 1922 and 1923 the BBC was at some pains to argue that it was not a monopoly. By this, it did not mean that it denied that it was exercising 'unified control': it meant rather that membership of the British Broadcasting *Company* was open to any manufacturer who wished to join. In other words the BBC asserted that it was not a monopolistic combine of the biggest radio firms who had supplied the greatest amount of capital. In 1926 this distinction was no longer drawn and the case for monopoly was stated without equivocation. The case against monopoly was never very effectively put at this time.

By far the most interesting contributions to the debate on monopoly were made in 1923 during the hearings of the Sykes Committee, the first official committee to investigate broadcasting. A fascinating document survives, the draft of a working paper of this committee, which asks all the right questions without giving any of the answers. It is headed 'Questions Concerning Scheme that would be recommended if Government had free hand with no Commitments', and the first part of it deserves to be quoted almost in full:

(1) (a) Should broadcasting be entrusted to one organization only, or to more than one?

(b) If to more than one, should the service at each centre be thrown open to tender?

(c) Should a system be aimed at under which the wireless societies would provide and pay for the broadcast programme?

(d) Is it agreed that eight stations are sufficient to meet the needs of the country?

(e) Is it considered that the public needs would best be met by one central station, which would broadcast a programme simultaneously through a number of relay stations?

(f) In the event of the adoption of the system referred to in (e), is it considered that, in view of the narrow band of wavelengths required, the hours of broadcasting could be extended to cover the whole day? If a system of separately operated stations is retained, is it desirable and practicable to extend the hours, and if so to what extent?

(2) If broadcasting is entrusted to one organization only, should it be to a Government Department, or to a Company working under a Government licence?

(3) If the latter, should the Company's operations be controlled— or advised on—by a Committee representing various 'interests'? If so, what should be the Committee's functions and its relation to licensing authority? Should it undertake censorship and to what extent? Should it exercise any financial supervision?

(4) About what annual revenue would the Company require to give satisfactory service?

(5) Should licences be dispensed with for receiving purposes and enforced only for transmission?

(6) Should Company derive its revenue from:
   (a) a fixed share of receiving licence fees and, in addition, royalties on apparatus, as at present; or
   (b) a fixed share of receiving licences only; or
   (c) a fixed share of receiving licence fees and of licence fees payable by manufacturers and dealers; or
   (d) any other source?[1]

For the most part this document speaks for itself. Although it was a draft prepared only a few months after regular broadcasting had begun, it is not without relevance nearly forty years later. The context in which it was prepared will be discussed fully in this volume, along with the answers which were given by the BBC and other bodies to its leading questions. Only a few glosses are necessary at this point. The 'narrow band of wavelengths' was thought to be a technical limiting condition of all early broadcasting development. It drove the Post Office to press for monopoly before the BBC came into existence, and it was the cause of many disputes between different contestants in the 'battle of the ether'. The 'eight stations' were the original eight stations which supplied the country's needs. The 'hours of broadcasting' were still severely restricted. At first they consisted only of two or three sessions in the evening, for example from 6.30 to 7.30, 8 o'clock to 9 o'clock, and 9.30 to 10 o'clock; occasionally from 5 o'clock to 5.30. The first morning and afternoon programmes began in March 1923—the morning programmes were dropped later—and as late as 1925 the London programmes did not start until 1 o'clock, with an interval from

[1] *'Questions Concerning Scheme that would be recommended.'

2 o'clock until 3.15. The 'income from licence fees' was shared from the start with the Post Office, and the system of collecting royalties on apparatus, which was adopted when the Company was formed, was dropped completely at the Company's request in 1924. When it was dropped, the close connexion between the radio manufacturing industry and broadcasting was inevitably weakened, although it was never destroyed.

'Control' and 'finance' were the two major practical questions in early broadcasting history. As the author of one of the first textbooks of radio economics put it in 1925—'from the point of view of public policy and broadcasting the two fundamental issues affecting the quality of radio service are—who shall control and how? and who shall pay and how? These are not isolated problems, but are closely connected.'[1] This was an American textbook, and its writer paid tribute to the superior way in which the British had answered both questions. Reith himself was more satisfied about the answer to the first question than to the second. Given that the main—almost the exclusive—source of BBC revenue should be derived from licences, why should the Post Office hold back a greater share of licence revenue than was necessary to cover administrative expenses? Throughout the whole of the period covered in this volume, broadcasting was arbitrarily and inequitably financed. Leaving on one side the needs of capital development, which were met out of revenue, the cost of programmes rose with the provision of a more regular service. 'It is stated', one of the technical magazines commented in 1924, 'that Great Britain is the only country which so far has produced a satisfactory solution of the financial problems involved in broadcasting. . . . The problem has been solved, but only just solved.'[2] More than two years later, after the Crawford Committee had finished its deliberations and the government had accepted its main conclusions, the most that Reith could say was 'financial offer slightly improved. . . but still inadequate'.[3]

The first calculations about radio economics were based on the assumption that there would be 200,000 receiving licences

---

[1] H. L. Jome, *Economics of the Radio Industry* (Chicago, 1925), p. 239.
[2] *The Engineer*, 27 June 1924.
[3] Diary, 20 Sept. 1926.

during the first year of working and that annual expenditure on the operation of the whole 'system' would be about £160,000. With the development of additional 'relay stations', the extension of transmitting hours, and the continued increase in the cost of programmes, these calculations were completely upset. By the spring of 1925 the estimated expenditure had increased to £445,000, and a year later it had leapt to £600,000. In the last year of the old Company the Postmaster-General restricted the revenue of the BBC to £500,000, 'presumably', as Reith generously put it, 'because of possible trouble in securing Parliamentary acquiescence in the enforcement of revenue collection for a concern which does not appear to be altogether under public control'.[1] It was his hope that the new Corporation would be more successful than the old Company had been in 'developing the full potentialities of the service'.

The growth of expenditure mirrors the growth of the organization. At the end of 1922 the BBC had a total staff of four: at the time when Reith prepared his evidence for the Crawford Committee it had a staff of 630.[2] It is always a mistake to conceive of the BBC as a vast monolithic organization:[3] between 1922 and 1926 it was only beginning to create a 'machine'. There were many tendencies making for increased 'departmentalization', certainly for increased formality, but Eric Maschwitz was doubtless right when he referred to the 'village' atmosphere of Savoy Hill when he joined the organization in 1926.[4] When Maurice Gorham was appointed to the BBC staff in June 1926, he still did not know quite what to expect. 'The portrait of the prim official with a black hat and a rolled umbrella, or the fraightfully naice young man with a military moustache, had not yet crept into the cartoons.' He soon found that his colleagues were 'a mixed lot, using the phrase literally and with no disparagement'. His gossipy account of the Savoy Hill of the mid-twenties makes it abundantly clear that whatever else the BBC was, it was never monolithic.[5]

There were many comings and goings during the period

[1] *Memorandum of Information*, p. 16. See also, for details of finance, Appendix III.
[2] For further details see below, p. 200.
[3] T. R. Fyvel, 'The BBC Image', in *Encounter*, Dec. 1959.
[4] E. Maschwitz, *No Chip on My Shoulder* (1957), p. 58.
[5] M. Gorham, *Sound and Fury* (1948), pp. 11, 15.

between 1922 and 1926. This story begins with the 'pioneers', the men who already knew a great deal about radio long before the BBC was founded—Peter Eckersley stands out among them —and it ends with the entry into the organization of a number of young men and women who were to play a most important part in the future of the BBC, men and women who, if they scarcely figure in this volume, must necessarily figure in the next. Broadcasting cannot be dealt with anonymously. Whatever may be true of the history of government departments, the history of the BBC, by the very nature of the tasks with which the BBC is concerned, is a history not only of an organization but of individuals. Reith is not the only individual who deserves to be treated in these terms. The content of radio—and its sense of style—is always determined by a large number of people reaching their decisions independently. They are, and were, as Gorham wrote, 'a mixed lot'. It required a man of the stature of Reith to hold them together.

Of course, some of the pioneers themselves were already drawing a distinction between the 'old informal days' and the 'age of organization'.[1] As early as September 1923, indeed, a writer in the *Radio Times* nostalgically contrasted Savoy Hill and the old premises in Magnet House, from which the first BBC broadcasts were made:

Those were hectic but happy times. A whole crowd of us were herded together in one small room; all but the general manager, who had a cupboard to himself, so small that he had to sit like an Oriental at a bazaar. 'Uncle Arthur' and 'Uncle Caractacus' would be 'broadcasting' at different 'phones a yard apart. Captain Eckersley would be dictating a highly technical letter and an intensely humorous burlesque at the same time. That is probably the origin of simultaneous broadcasting. Then the 'phones would be ringing all over the place with all sorts of queries. . . .[2]

At a later date Savoy Hill in its turn would be nostalgically contrasted with Broadcasting House. The temptation to romanticize usually proves irresistible.

Certainly there is an element of nostalgia in many of the reminiscences of the 'listeners' of the early 1920s. The programmes may be forgotten, but the memory of the cat's whisker

[1] See below, p. 204.   [2] *Radio Times*, 28 Sept. 1923.

and the first crystal set remains. Some listeners still claim that it gave 'the purest reception'. Others recall buying their first valve set. As *The Radio Year Book* for 1925 extravagantly put it, 'when we first get the wireless set from the shop there comes the first thrilling moment when the set is to be operated and the family delighted with music. This, like the wedding day and the first ride on a bicycle, gives a thrill such as we seldom feel in this unromantic age.'[1]

What is less frequently remembered is the debate about the likely social effects of broadcasting, which has much in common with the recent debate about the likely social effects of television.[2] Broadcasting, it was claimed, would not only keep people away from the concert halls, it would stop them from reading books. It would encourage contentment with superficiality. 'Instead of solitary thought', the headmaster of Rugby complained, 'people would listen in to what was said to millions of people, which could not be the best things.'[3] Radio would make people passive. It would produce 'all-alike girls'.[4] At the same time it would strengthen the forces making for healthy domesticity.[5] 'Charmed by the voice', husbands would stay at home in the evenings. Children would find a new source of daily satisfaction, shared no doubt by their mothers. 'At 5.57 the procedure is something like this. Marshal children to their appointed places; settle heated disputes of the "these are my headphones" order; proceed to enjoy the Children's Hour.'[6]

Of course, every opinion expressed on these subjects generated counter-opinions. There would be more reading of books and certainly more buying of music. 'In five years' time', wrote one famous musical scholar in October 1923, 'the general *musical public* of these islands will be treble or quadruple its present size.'[7] The opportunities for education far outweighed the perils of superficiality. There would be less passivity, not more, as 'minds were opened and horizons widened'. This would be particularly true of the village: radio, indeed, might bring with it a renais-

---

[1] Leslie Baily, BBC programme, *Scrapbook for 1925*.
[2] See my article 'The Image and The Voice', in *Twentieth Century*, Sept. 1959.
[3] Quoted in the *Daily Telegraph*, 23 Oct. 1926.
[4] *Evening Chronicle*, 23 Dec. 1926.
[5] *Radio Times*, 16 July 1926, 'Radio in the Changing Home'.
[6] Ibid., 30 Nov. 1923.
[7] Ibid., 19 Oct. 1923.

sance of rural life.[1] On the other hand, why claim that radio made for domestic bliss or the sharing of family chores? The truth was that people were always quarrelling about the use of headphones or the choice of programmes. There had even been one or two 'wireless divorces'. As for children, were they not in danger of being contaminated, lulled into 'listening'—for a long time the word was used in inverted commas—instead of learning to fend for themselves? Everything always ended eventually with a question mark.

Lord Riddell, a voluble but on the whole reasonably friendly critic of broadcasting, conveniently catalogued many of the leading questions in December 1923. His article was significantly called 'Modern Witchcraft'.

What effect is radio going to have on life? (By the way I do not like the description 'wireless': why describe a thing as a negation?) Are people going to read less? Are they going to talk less? Are they going to be better or worse informed? Are they going to the theatre and music less? Are those who reside in rural districts going to be more or less satisfied? Who can tell? . . . So far as the present generation is concerned I believe that those accustomed to read and who like reading will continue to read whether they use the radio or not. But what about the next generation brought up on radio? Are they going to prefer information through the medium of the ear to that through the medium of the eye?[2]

Few people have had the chance to choose. The eye has it. Already before the date at which this volume ends, John L. Baird had demonstrated television in January 1926. Three years before that a listener had written to the *Radio Times* suggesting that it would not be long before football cup ties would be televised: they had not even been broadcast at that stage. 'It is not too much to prophesy', he went on, 'that within ten years "television" will be as far advanced as wireless telephony is today.'[3] In retrospect the 'wireless revolution' and the 'television revolution' are twin halves of the same revolution in 'multiple transmission', a social and cultural revolution comparable in its consequences to the revolution in printing in the fifteenth century. Revolutions in communication always bring

[1] Ibid., 'When Radio Came to the Village', 17 Sept. 1926.
[2] Ibid., 21 Dec. 1923.
[3] Ibid., 19 Oct. 1923.

with them controversial social consequences.[1] There are not only struggles with existing interests but shifts of attitudes and opinions.

During the few months preceding the transfer of power from the British Broadcasting Company to the British Broadcasting Corporation there was the first general stocktaking of the effects of the introduction of 'the voice'. Effectively from that date the first big debate was closed. There was plenty of criticism of programmes still to come and many lively tussles about the personality of Reith and the constitution of the BBC, but broadcasting itself, to quote Lord Clarendon, the first Chairman of the Board of Governors of the new BBC, was 'an established and accepted institution'.

These were some of the results of the stocktaking. Entertainment thrived, as did the entertainment industry. The main challenge to the theatre was coming from the cinema, not from the BBC. The press was not losing its hold on the public. It was a pressman, Sir Robert Gray, who wrote in the *Radio Times* in July 1926 that 'supposing that listeners receive a larger service of news it does not follow that the press will suffer to any appreciable extent'.[2] The sale of books was increasing, and more than one local librarian in his annual report referred to wireless as a 'new ally . . . creating and deepening the interest of the public in the higher forms of literature'.[3] The beginning of a popular revolution in musical appreciation was generally conceded. Conclusions about the effects of radio on children and the home were remarkably similar to recent conclusions about the effects of television. It all depended on the children and on the home. In any case, these problems were not taken quite so seriously. After all, these were the 1920s, and a well-drawn cartoon caught the mood. A fashionably dressed lady is leaving her nurse in charge of the one child in the large nursery. 'Let the little darling listen to the Children's Hour,' she is saying, 'and then when he's had his supper, the Radio Dance Band can play him to sleep.'[4]

---

[1] There are few general surveys of revolutions in communication. See, however, two books by the late Professor H. A. Innis, a Canadian scholar of distinction in this field—*Empire and Communications* (1950) and *The Bias of Communication* (Toronto, 1951).   [2] *Radio Times*, 9 July 1926.
[3] Ibid., 23 July 1926. The quotation is from the annual report of the Librarian at Lincoln.   [4] Ibid., 3 Sept. 1926.

This was the comment of a fashionably dressed lady. Not all listeners, of course, fell into this category. The 1920s were hard times. There were never less than a million unemployed, and many people could not afford to buy a wireless set. At the time of the General Strike in 1926 there was a great deal of communal

WHAT IS HOME WITHOUT A RADIO?
Mother (to nurse): "Let the little darling listen to the Children's Hour, and then, when he's had his supper, the Radio Dance Band can play him to sleep."

2

listening. There were also parts of the country—some of the mining villages, for example—where wireless sets were relatively rare. The remarkable fact is that by the end of 1926 there were more than two million licence-holders. This was only the 'core' of the listening public. Leaving on one side the families of the licence-holders, there were thousands of other people who 'dropped in' to listen. A certain number of superior people thought, of course, that it was the right thing to do *not* to have a wireless set. Reith has described one of them in his diary. 'Lots of people to lunch today, including a freak professor from Oxford, who did not like telephones or wireless. I soon disposed of him.'[1]

Early licence figures are notoriously unreliable, but the figures are given below. In the right-hand column, for purposes of comparison, are set out the figures for combined radio and

[1] Diary, 8 Jan. 1925.

television licences during the first five years of post-war television. The comparison shows that the wireless audience grew faster in the early 1920s than the television audience during the period after the end of the Second World War. By the end of 1926, after four full years of broadcasting, there were over two million listeners: it was not until 1953, after six years of regular post-war television, that the number of television viewers passed the two million mark. At the same time the number of holders of television licences was increasing more rapidly in the fifth year of television than the number of holders of wireless licences in the fifth year of wireless. The television audience more than doubled between March 1950 and March 1951. The number of wireless listeners did not double even between December 1924 and December 1926.[1]

Year (31 December)	Number of wireless licences	Number of wireless and television licences	Year (31 March)
1922 .	35,744*	14,560	1947
1923 .	595,496	45,564	1948
1924 .	1,129,578	126,567	1949
1925 .	1,645,207	343,882	1950
1926 .	2,178,259	763,941	1951

* This figure is not strictly comparable with the rest.

Unfortunately it is not possible to break down these figures further either by area or by social class. Both exercises would be interesting and revealing. Radio manufacturers, however, occasionally gave a clue as to the way the 'great audience' of radio was created. The early 'enthusiasts' came from all sections of the population: they were said to be particularly strongly recruited from the grammar schools. The purchase of wireless sets was somewhat different. In August 1922 *The Morning Post* reported that people 'of all classes' were asking for advice about wireless sets, and concluded that there was every indication that broadcasting would become as popular in London as in New York.[2] A few months later, however, there were complaints that

---

[1] In the last year before post-war television (1946) there were 10,395,551 holders of wireless licences. At the end of March 1959 there were 9,255,422 holders of combined wireless and television licences.

[2] *The Morning Post*, 17 Aug. 1922.

the 'boom was not up to expectation'.[1] There were no 'roaring twenties' in Britain as there were in the United States, and the price of a wireless set represented for large numbers of employed people several weeks' wages. 'Receiving sets have been pur-

3. Model of 1925

chased in the first place', one large radio concern reported in 1923, 'by middle-class and lower middle-class people, and the sale of sets is spreading more slowly among the working classes.'[2] When Reith wrote his book *Broadcast Over Britain* in 1924, he reported that continuous lines of aerials were to be seen in the great towns: there were large numbers of aerials also 'in the most inaccessible and remote regions of the country'.[3] People of 'every order of social class' were listening, and even those who did not listen were influenced by those who did. 'Broadcasting is much too big a thing to be ignored for long. Sooner or later it

[1] *Westminster Gazette,* 9 Jan. 1923.
[2] Metropolitan-Vickers Electrical Company, Ltd., *Research Department Report on the Development of Radio Broadcasting in Great Britain* (Oct. 1923), p. 16.
[3] Reith, *Broadcast Over Britain* (1925), pp. 79–80.

will cross all paths. It has crossed most already. It will eventually force itself on the attention of any who may have succeeded for a time in overlooking it.'[1]

This is a point which has been made by many subsequent writers on broadcasting, indeed on the agencies of 'mass transmission' in general. 'The effect of the public arts cannot be escaped by turning off the radio or the television set. . . . Neither our indifference nor contempt gives us immunity against them.'[2]

Before turning in more detail to the story of how broadcasting began and of how the 'great audience' was built up, it is helpful, perhaps, to provide a simple but sturdy chronological framework. The main dates are not well known, although more than one general historian has been tempted to take the closing date of this volume—the foundation of the British Broadcasting Corporation—as a pivotal date in twentieth-century British history. Marconi arrived in England in 1896. The Marconi Company was founded in 1897. The first 'broadcast' of music and speech was made by an American, R. Fessenden, in 1906. There were no 'triode' valves in use until about 1912. In December 1916 the American Radio and Research Corporation was broadcasting concerts two or three times a week. A ban imposed on 'amateur' radio in Britain on the outbreak of war in 1914 was not lifted until 1919. The first well-known American broadcasting station, KDKA, Pittsburgh, went on the air with regular broadcasts in 1920. During the same year regular concerts began to be broadcast in Europe from The Hague. Also in 1920—in February—the Marconi Company began to broadcast from Chelmsford. Later in the year the Post Office withdrew permission for these broadcasts to be made. On 14 February 1922 the first regular broadcast service in Britain was started from Writtle: it was organized by the Experimental Section of the Designs Department of the Marconi Company. Their London station, 2LO, began its broadcasts later in the same year on 11 May. In the meantime talks between the radio manufacturers and the Post Office had started on 18 May with a view to forming a broadcasting syndicate. The BBC was born

[1] *Broadcast Over Britain*, p. 78.
[2] G. Seldes, *The Great Audience* (1951), p. 4.

during the course of these talks. Its first programmes were broadcast on 14 November 1922, although the Company was not formally registered until 15 December 1922 and did not receive its Licence from the Post Office until 18 January 1923.

This bare list of basic dates will be given meaning in the pages which follow. Between 1923 and 1926 there were two official government inquiries which culminated in two basic Reports— that of the Sykes Committee, which was appointed in April 1923 and published its Report in August 1923, and that of the Crawford Committee, which was appointed in the summer of 1925 and published its Report in March 1926. On 14 July 1926 the Postmaster-General, Sir William Mitchell-Thomson (later Lord Selsdon), announced in the House of Commons that the government accepted the main recommendations of the Crawford Committee and proposed to set up by Royal Charter a British Broadcasting Corporation. The Charter was granted for a ten-year period from 1 January 1927.

None of these dates should be taken in isolation. The 1890s, when Marconi arrived in Britain, was a decade of considerable social transformation; the First World War was a period of quickened technical and economic progress in the radio industry, and valves were used for signalling before they were used for broadcasting. In terms of the history of the 'mass media' it is an interesting coincidence that Lord Northcliffe bought the *Daily Mail* in 1896, the year when Marconi first demonstrated his wireless inventions to a leading Post Office engineer, and died in 1922, the year when the BBC was founded.

The four years which followed from 1922 to 1926 were themselves extremely interesting years in the history of British politics and British society. The Coalition government broke up in 1922, and the first item in the programmes of the new BBC was a broadcast of election results: a Labour government came into power for the first time in the following year. In 1926 there was Britain's only general strike. Broadcasting, of course, made its début with these big events not in the background but in the foreground of people's consciousness. What could be heard in the background was the beating of drums, the blaring of saxophones, and the rhythms of the Charleston.

The motto at the beginning of this Introduction is a verse from one of the first popular songs with a wireless theme. Here is

another, which was designed to be taken a little less seriously.
It appeared in the *Radio Times* just before Christmas 1923:

> You've set my valves a-throbbing,
> My headpiece is a whirl,
> So turn your ear piece to me, love,
> My wondrous wireless girl.[1]

[1] *Radio Times*, 21 Dec. 1923.

II

THE WONDER OF WIRELESS

―――――

'I always feel that's a miracle', said a friend
waving towards a chattering box in the corner.

P. P. ECKERSLEY
The Power Behind the Microphone (1941), p. 14

1. Discovery and Prophecy

'Every student of science', wrote James Clerk-Maxwell, the distinguished Victorian physicist, 'should be an antiquary of his subject.' Most writers on the history of wireless have shared his opinion. Some of them have been content to go no farther back in time than 1888 when Heinrich Rudolf Hertz demonstrated experimentally the creation and communication of electromagnetic waves, or to 1864 when Clerk-Maxwell himself showed theoretically—without apparatus—that the creation and communication of such waves was possible. Other writers have begun the story of wireless two centuries earlier with the revolution in physics and the theories of Christian Huyghens.

Very few have started with the popular hero of wireless history, Guglielmo Marconi, who in 1896 filed an application for his first wireless patent in London. It consisted of a sensitive tube-like receiver or 'coherer' connected to an earth and an elevated aerial. Marconi had arrived in London a few months earlier, and had been given an introduction to the Engineer-in-Chief of the Post Office, Sir William Preece, himself a pioneer of telephones and a keen experimenter with primitive wireless apparatus. Marconi was content to prove to Preece that he could transmit signals for a hundred yards. They were signals, of course, not words, least of all programmes. No one foresaw the possibilities of wireless telephony. No one foresaw either that what was originally conceived of as a method of private communication would ultimately be thought of as an instrument of mass transmission, that it would be considered not as a technique but as a 'medium'.

For many years, however, progress was fitful and only intermittently spectacular. After signals sent out from Poldhu in Cornwall in 1901 were successfully received in St. John's, Newfoundland, a distance of just over 2,000 miles away, Marconi 'for the first time felt absolutely certain that the day would come when mankind would be able to send messages without wires not only across the Atlantic but between the furthermost parts of the earth'.[1] But he was certainly not thinking of broadcasts.

[1] Recorded message by Marconi. Leslie Baily, BBC programme, *Scrapbook for 1901*.

What he had demonstrated—in face of scepticism and even opposition from distinguished scientists—was that radio waves could travel beyond the horizon. The social horizon was still obscure. It was not until fifteen years later that the first of the prophets of broadcasting, an ambitious young American, David Sarnoff, predicted 'a plan of development which would make radio a "household utility" in the same sense as the piano or phonograph'.[1] Sarnoff was still well ahead of his times. Even on the technical front it was possible for a knowledgeable writer nearly ten years later to complain that 'the evolution of radio has been characterized by comparatively few original inventions of outstanding merit and commercial ability; and by fewer still that, for one reason or another, have found any practical application until they were about ten years old. Moreover, the borrowings from other arts have been all too few and tardy.'[2]

A critical examination of the process of invention in radio history can never be narrowly antiquarian. Historians of wireless must concern themselves with developments on an international front: they must continually stretch their range of reference. They must always move from a consideration of technical discoveries to an examination of economic and social consequences. By reason of the nature of their subject they are called upon to exercise both their analytical and their imaginative powers. How far was the end implicit in the beginning? When did the history of wireless lead into the history of broadcasting? The internationalism of the inventive process in wireless history was the necessary prelude to the nationalism which has expressed itself in the creation of broadcasting institutions. Few other institutions reveal more clearly the differences between national traditions, national ways of life, and national policies. The initial internationalism was expressed quite simply in the varied nationalities of the leading inventors. During the formative years between the experiments of Hertz and those of Marconi, important discoveries were made by Oliver Lodge, an Englishman, Edouard Branly, a Frenchman, A. S. Popoff, a Russian, and Giuseppe Righi, an Italian. It was Branly who developed coherers, the tube-like containers carrying loose

---

[1] See G. L. Archer, *History of Radio to 1926* (New York, 1938), pp. 110 ff.
[2] A. H. Morse, op. cit., p. 17.

particles which would respond to the currents set up by the Hertzian waves. In his first experiments Marconi used both coherers of this type and a form of oscillation devised by Righi. Lodge anticipated Marconi in transmitting and receiving signals at distances of up to sixty yards, and was the first person to experiment with 'the tuned circuit', a means of controlling the wavelength of a receiver by adjustments to coils of wire. Without the introduction of tuning devices, signals from different radio transmitters would have been bound to interfere with each other, and Marconi, who eventually in 1911 acquired Lodge's 'master patent' of 1897, was quick to see its significance.

Radio invention remained an international process in the years of continued technical development from the late 1890s to 1914. The wave-trains set up by the original wireless spark transmitters used by the first inventors were not continuous. They consisted of groups of waves following each other in rapid succession. Before radio-telephony—speech by wireless—could be perfected, some method had to be found of producing waves that were continuous and consistent in form. In 1902 Valdemar Poulsen, a Dane, developed a means of producing continuous waves by 'arc transmission': it had already been thought of by an Englishman, William Duddell, two years before. It was an American, however, R. A. Fessenden of the University of Pittsburgh, who in 1902 first used wireless waves to carry the human voice—over a distance of one mile. On Christmas Eve in 1906 he succeeded in transmitting both speech and music over a distance of several hundred miles.

Early that evening wireless operators on ships within a radius of several hundred miles sprang to attention as they caught the call 'CQ CQ' in morse code. Was it a ship in distress? They listened eagerly, and to their amazement heard a human voice coming from their instruments—someone speaking! Then a woman's voice rose in sound. It was uncanny! Many of them called to officers to come and listen; soon the wireless rooms were crowded. Next someone was heard reading a poem. Then there was a violin solo; then a man made a speech, and they could catch most of the words. Finally, everyone who had heard the programme was asked to write to R. A. Fessenden at Brant Rock, Massachusetts—and many of the operators did. This was the first broadcast in history.[1]

[1] A. F. Harlow, *Old Wires and New Waves* (1936), p. 462. See also the *Radio World*, 28 May 1932.

In the same year the Marconi Wireless Telegraph Company of America hired as an office boy, at a wage of 5½ dollars a week, David Sarnoff, who was then fifteen years old. Eventually he was to become as commanding a figure in American broadcasting as J. C. W. Reith in Britain. The inventors of apparatus were to give way to the organizers of a new medium.

The transition from wireless to broadcasting would not have been practicable without the development of the valve, variously described as 'the Cinderella of electrical science', 'the magic lamp of radio', 'the truest "little giant" in all history', and the greatest invention since fire, the lever, and the wheel. In 1904 J. A. Fleming, Professor of Electrical Engineering of University College, London, experimented with the first thermionic two-electrode valve or diode. His experiments spanned the past and the future. In the background were Edison and the exploitation of light; in the foreground were Lee de Forest and the exploitation of sound. The full significance of Fleming's experiments was not appreciated at the time, and it was an American, Lee de Forest, who by inserting a third electrode into Fleming's valve, thereby making it a triode, took 'the most important single step in the whole development of radio communication'.[1] Yet the full significance of de Forest's invention was not realized either, and the two inventors quarrelled about British and American patents instead of exploring the revolutionary implications of their discovery.

The multi-electrode valve enabled much more sensitive wireless receivers to be made and permitted radio-telephone messages to be picked up at far greater distances than had previously been thought possible. It was applicable at one and the same time both to transmitting and receiving circuits. It contained within itself all the potential force of broadcasting.[2] But the range of its potentialities was not appreciated until the First World War. It was paradoxical that it was only when the international communications system was severed that the development of valves was rapid. The British firms which made valves during the First World War provided the nucleus of the firms which after the war took up broadcasting.[3] All this was round the corner. Before 1914 almost all the books on radio described it as a universal technique which might be universally controlled. Their

[handwritten letter, left column:]

discovery. I have found a method of rectifying Electrical oscillations. that is, making the flow of Electricity all in the same direction. so that I can detect them with an ordinary mirror galvanometer. I have been receiving signals on an aerial with nothing but a mirror galvanometer and my device. but at present only in a laboratory

[handwritten letter, right column:]

scale. This opens up a wide field for work. as I can now measure exactly the effect of the transmitter. I have not mentioned this to any one yet as it may become very useful

Yours very sincerely

J. A. Fleming.

4. A Fleming Letter of 1904

writers were as optimistic about constructing 'circles around the world' as their predecessors had been about the international electric telegraph during the middle of the nineteenth century. Inventors might quarrel, but the world was one. It was thought to be a portent when de Forest broadcast from the Eiffel Tower in Paris in 1908.

The word 'radio' was beginning to be used more widely between 1908 and 1914 not only among scientists but among 'a motley group of people, mostly boys and young men, working all alone on crude apparatus in the isolation of their own homes'.[4] Most of them were still preoccupied with radio-telegraphy; their language was the morse code. From the most

---

[1] *Radio Broadcast*, Aug. 1922.

[2] G. W. O. Howe, 'The Genesis of the Thermionic Valve', in *Thermionic Valves, 1904–1954* (1954), p. 13; S. R. Mullard, 'The Development of the Receiving Valve', in *The Proceedings of the Institution of Electrical Engineers* (1935).

[3] See S. G. Sturmey, *The Economic Development of Radio* (1958), p. 35.

[4] G. L. Archer, op. cit., p. 100. It was a term, however, which was popularized in America. Many of the British pioneers resented the use of the word 'radio', and even after the war some radio engineers preferred to be called 'wireless engineers'.

brilliant to the least talented, they all shared the sense of wonder in the experiments they were carrying out. It was J. A. Fleming himself who, in 1911, wrote in a new illustrated wireless magazine *The Marconigraph* that 'no familiarity with the subject removes the feeling of vague wonder with which one sees a telegraphic instrument, merely connected with a length of 150 feet of copper wire run up the side of a flagstaff, begin to draw its message out of space and print down in dot and dash on paper tape the intelligence ferried across thirty miles of water by the mysterious ether'.[1]

Businessmen also thought of radio in terms of dot and dash: their interest centred on what might be described as its private use, as a means of point-to-point communication. They saw it as an adaptable and profitable substitute for communication by cable. The limit of their vision was not the radio station with large numbers of scattered listeners but a network of radio communications across deserts and oceans which would dispense with 'the use of copper wires, gutta percha coverings and iron sheathings' They thought and talked in proud capital letters about 'Telegraphy Without Connecting Wires'.[2]

The cable companies were too well established to be seriously worried about the threat of competition from wireless. It is true that when the Marconi Wireless Telegraph and Signal Company was founded in 1897, with an initial capital of £100,000, 'there was a great flutter in the dove-cots of telegraphy and holders of the many millions of telegraph securities, and those interested in the allied industries, began to be alarmed for the safety of their property. Mysterious paragraphs about the New Wireless or Space Telegraphy, as it was variously called, kept appearing in the papers.'[3] More sober investors, however, grumbled about 'speculation'. 'The public will be well advised to keep clear of this concern', wrote *The Investors' Review*; 'Signor Marconi's ingenious ideas do not seem to have made much headway, and it would be interesting to learn what the government officials reported about them.'[4] Despite successful experiments in the use of radio in naval manœuvres, the linking of

[1] *The Marconigraph*, vol. i, No. 1, Apr. 1911.
[2] Professor Ayrton, Lecture on Submarine Telegraphy at the Imperial Institute, 15 Feb. 1897.
[3] J. J. Fahie, *A History of Wireless Telegraphy* (1899), p. 1.
[4] *The Investors' Review*, 7 Oct. 1898.

Britain and the Continent by radio, and the interchange of signals across the Atlantic, no dividends were paid by the Marconi Company until 1911. The more conservative commentators remained extremely cautious, claiming, in the words of one of the first technical authorities on radio, that 'the unbounded potentialities of the new telegraphy have been whittled down ... to small ... proportions', so that 'those interested in the old order can sleep in peace and can go on so doing for a long time to come'.[1]

With imagination and courage, Marconi and his competitors were not interested in the old order even though they could not yet see clearly the shape of the new. Despite all its difficulties, the company which Marconi had set up successfully crossed the frontier between science and business during the early years of the twentieth century. The frontier had to be crossed at this stage if further progress was to be made, and it was not an accident that after the end of the First World War the company was later to take the lead in broadcasting also.

Marconi himself had two indispensable and exceptional qualities which enabled him to blaze a trail in radio history. First, he could see the technical relevance of other people's work as well as his own. He turned when a very young man to the 'scrap heap of unrelated discovery' and found there just what he wanted. 'He did not so much invent as adapt the work of others to a specific purpose.'[2] He freely admitted this himself. His first patent was described modestly as 'improvements in transmitting electrical impulses and signals and in apparatus therefor'.[3] 'By availing myself of previous knowledge', he wrote later, 'and working out theories already formulated I did nothing but follow in the footsteps of Howe, Watt, Edison, Stephenson and other illustrious inventors. I doubt very much whether there has ever been a case of a useful invention in which all the theory, all the practical applications and all the apparatus were the work of one man.'[4] Second, he could see business openings when many other radio pioneers had seen only intricate and fascinating laboratory problems. This second quality

[1] Fahie, op. cit., p. xii.
[2] P. P. Eckersley, *The Power Behind the Microphone* (1941), p. 26.
[3] Patent No. 12039, 2 June 1896.
[4] *Chapters of Marconi History* (unpublished): 'Guglielmo Marconi and the Invention of Wireless'.

was noted as early as 1898 in *The Electrician*. 'All the essential features of signalling by Hertzian waves', it was explained, 'were really outlined in scientific laboratories long before any idea of utilising them for commerce had occupied prominent attention. ... All honour is due to Signor Marconi for having been the first to bring prominently forward the possibility, and indeed the eminent practicability of using Hertzian waves for telegraphy between two places not connected by an electrical conductor.'[1] Marconi came to Britain in the first place because he believed that, with a large mercantile marine, it would be a profitable market for his discoveries. For all his occasionally highly romantic talk, he was driven by powerful and compelling economic incentives.

Between 1898 and 1911 not only did he achieve important new triumphs, but the Marconi Wireless Telegraph and Signal Company established a commanding position in international business, including a virtual monopoly in Great Britain, Italy, and Canada.[2] It paid no dividends, but its capital increased from £100,000 to £1,000,000.[3] In 1910 Godfrey (later Sir Godfrey) Isaacs became its managing director. He was to be one of the key figures in the negotiations leading up to the formation of the British Broadcasting Company in London twelve years later. Many of the people on the technical side of the Marconi Company were also to be numbered among the pioneers. Captain H. J. Round, a clever, keen, and affable engineer, who became the head of its research department, was carrying out his first experiments with radio-telephony in New York in 1906, when he succeeded in transmitting speech and gramophone records over a distance of four miles. He has described how these experiments were continued in Britain before 1914 both in London and at Chelmsford, the company's main works.[4] They were given a further impetus in 1913 when a German scientist, A. Meissner, demonstrated that the triode valve could generate continuous high-frequency oscillations when it was connected to an external

[1] *The Electrician*, 14 Oct. 1898.
[2] In 1900 it changed its name to Marconi's Wireless Telegraph Company. In the same year the Marconi's International Marine Communication Company was founded. In 1899 the Marconi Wireless Telegraphy Company of America was incorporated.
[3] The figures are given in H. L. Jome, op. cit., p. 26.
[4] See *World Radio*, 21 Oct. 1932.

circuit arranged to cause it to react upon itself. C. S. Franklin of the Marconi Company carried out similar parallel demonstrations. In 1913 and 1914 there were several transmissions of speech and music from Marconi House in London, and the 'broadcasts' were sometimes picked up a hundred miles away. At the same date 'wireless telephone sets' were being manufactured at Chelmsford. They had a working radius of thirty miles, but they were capable of being heard on sensitive apparatus over much greater distances.

Because of the interplay of invention and enterprise the period from the late 1890s to 1914 was characterized by conflict and litigation as well as by technical development. 'To the casual observer it might well have seemed that the great inventive geniuses of this period were of pirate blood and that they boldly seized one another's ideas without regard to consequences.'[1] As usually happens in such circumstances, questions of piracy and patents went together. The Marconi Company held key patents. The same question arose which had stirred inventors, business men, and the general public in the Industrial Revolution of the eighteenth century. Were these patents in the public interest?

The Marconi Company protested vigorously against the recommendations of the International Radio Telegraphic Convention held in Berlin in 1906.[2] Its representatives feared that their valuable patent rights would be prejudiced or infringed. Opinions were divided as to the merits of the company's case. It was Sir William Preece—the man who had welcomed Marconi to Britain and had paid many striking tributes to his work,[3] —who gave evidence before a select committee that 'the whole effort of the operations of the Marconi Company has been to check and really stop the growth of wireless telegraphy as a con-

[1] Archer, op. cit., p. 81.

[2] An earlier International Convention had been held in 1903. At neither Convention was there any talk of broadcasting, although wireless was clearly defined almost for the first time as 'the transmission of signals by electric energy between two points which are not connected by a wire or other metallic conductor . . . in connexion with instruments employing the Hertzian waves'. See J. Erskine Murray, *A Handbook of Wireless Telegraphy* (1907), p. 1.

[3] In a lecture delivered at the Royal Institution in June 1898 Preece attacked those critics who said that Marconi 'has done nothing'. 'Columbus', he remarked, 'did not invent the egg, but he showed how to make it stand on its end and Marconi has produced, from known means, a new electric eye more delicate than any known electrical instrument and a new system of telegraphy which will reach places hitherto inaccessible.'

venience to navigators as well as a commercial undertaking'.[1]
Marconi himself, speaking like Wedgwood, Arkwright, and
Boulton before him, counter-claimed that if the Convention
were ratified, it would 'so to say, wrap up a new science in iron
swaddling clothes . . . and may tend very seriously to impede the
scientific progress of the art'.[2] Marconi's relations with the Post
Office had deteriorated within a few months of his arrival, and
in 1912, when the Marconi Company was for a brief moment
in the forefront of British politics, the Secretary of the Post
Office remarked correctly that 'for years we have been fighting
the Marconi Company. We have had years of struggle with
them.'[3]

The arguments used in 1906 and 1912 are indirectly relevant
to the history of broadcasting, but neither Preece and those
who felt like him, nor Cuthbert Hale, who preceded Isaacs as
managing director of the Marconi Company, at this stage
thought of radio in terms of broadcasting. They thought of wireless as the International Radio Telegraphic Convention thought
of it, simply as a device for carrying out a select list of tasks—
notably communication between ships, between sea and land,
and between lighthouses, outlying islands, and the mainland.[4]
Even when they turned from radio-telegraphy to radio-telephony, they still thought entirely in terms of 'point-to-point
communication', messages addressed to specific stations from
specific stations.

So long as they continued to think in these restricted terms,
they not only failed to see the opportunities of broadcasting,
but thought of it as a positive nuisance. The fact that confidential point-to-point messages could be picked up by other
listeners was their chief drawback. An almost equally important
drawback was interference. 'The main defect which was first
found in the working of wireless telegraphy', the Select Committee on the Radio Telegraphic Convention concluded, 'resulted in part from inability to control direction. As every
receiving station within range of the transmitting centre would

[1] *Report of the Select Committee to Consider the Report of the Radio-Telegraphic Convention signed at Berlin* (1907), p. 227.
[2] Ibid., p. 200.
[3] *Report of the Select Committee on Marconi's Wireless Telegraph Company Ltd.* (1913),
p. 234.
[4] The tasks are well set out in A. F. Collins, *Manual of Wireless Telegraphy* (1906).

read all the messages sent from that centre, it was not possible
for more than two stations in a given area to interchange signals
at a given time without mutual interference.'[1] The problem of
interference was to linger long after the advent of broadcasting,
but it was after all the central idea of broadcasting that large
numbers of receiving sets within range of a transmitting station
could pick up all the messages sent out from that station. The
fears expressed by the select committee were shared by most
early technical writers on radio.

There still remain cross interferences [wrote one of them] of which
I fear we can never be rid, and therefore we can never use the system
in a network of lines which criss-cross, recross and overlap each other
in all ways and directions. The various waves of electricity would so
interfere with each other . . . that the result would be chaos. Therefore wireless telegraphy can only be used in lines removed from each
other's disturbing influences, as in sparsely populated countries and
undeveloped regions.[2]

To have restricted the use of radio to 'undeveloped regions'
would have been like using the telephone only as an internal
instrument within the home, as some of the first prophets
of the telephone suggested, in order to link the dining-room
and the servants' quarters. The blindness of almost all the
prophets makes a most interesting theme in the history of the
application of science and technology to life. Only Oliver (later
Sir Oliver) Lodge and R. A. Fessenden had an early glimmer of
light. 'It might be advantageous', Lodge said, 'to "shout" the
message, speaking broadcast to receivers in all directions, and
for which the wireless system is well adapted, seeing that it is so
inexpensive and so easily and rapidly installed, such as for army
manœuvres, for reporting races and other sporting events, and
generally for all important matters occurring beyond the range
of the permanent lines.'[3]

Lodge's vision just encompassed broadcasting, as we understand it; he was the first man in this country to realize that what
other people thought of as disadvantages might well be advan-

[1] *Report of the Select Committee to Consider the Report of the Radio-Telegraphic Convention*, p. iv.
[2] Fahie, op. cit., p. 259.
[3] *Report of the Select Committee to Consider the Report of the Radio-Telegraphic Convention*.

tages in disguise. It was only during the First World War that this realization dawned on other people too.

In the meantime radio had established itself. Laymen already recognized that it was not an entity in itself, but a force that could be used, that electro-magnetic waves travelling in space were amenable to further exploitation. Public imagination was stirred by the successful way in which it was used during the *Titanic* disaster in 1912 or even in the arrest of Dr. Crippen in 1910. Technically it had reached a stage, as Preece told the 1907 Select Committee, where 'it was not dependent upon scientific discovery from day to day'. When pressed by a member of the committee to state whether this stage, like the existing stage in cable telegraphy, was a 'state of perfection', Preece prudently replied, 'It has reached a practical stage; I will not say that it is quite perfection.'[1]

2.   From Radio-Telephony to Broadcasting

THE First World War harnessed the new powers of wireless to the needs of the separate armies, navies, and intelligence services. The value of wireless for such a purpose had long been recognized. Before 1900 Marconi had demonstrated his apparatus for both the British and Italian navies, and during the Boer War his company had negotiated a contract for the supply and manning of six wireless stations for use at the front in South Africa. A few days before the declaration of war in 1914 the great naval review off Spithead was dispersing when a wireless signal from Whitehall diverted every vessel to its war station. The Germans also had not been inactive, particularly in the few years before 1914. Their construction a few months before war broke out of a large wireless station—indeed what was then the most high-powered wireless station in the world—at Nauen, about twenty miles from Berlin, showed that they appreciated the value of the new means of communication. When war was imminent they were able to contact the scattered and vulnerable

[1] *Report of the Select Committee to Consider the Report of the Radio-Telegraphic Convention*, p. 229.

ships of the German mercantile marine; when war was declared they were able at once to begin broadcasting military and naval communiqués. The long association between radio and propaganda had begun.

Counter-measures were quickly taken. The Admiralty took over control of production at the Marconi Works, while a wireless interception service was immediately started at Chelmsford. 'The interception of enemy wireless propaganda rapidly became a very considerable business. Marconi operators, bound to secrecy, worked in shifts day and night throughout the entire $4\frac{1}{2}$ years, the relieving operator taking up his duties before the man relieved ceased work, so that not a single dot or dash was missed.'[1] The man who wrote these words, Arthur Burrows, spent several months collecting, editing, and distributing to several government departments the wireless propaganda of the Central Powers. He was to be the first Director of Programmes of the British Broadcasting Company, and later the first secretary of the International Broadcasting Union.

Other men who were to figure prominently in post-war radio and broadcasting were actively concerned with wireless during the war. H. J. Round, who had been engaged in the Marconi experimental 'broadcasts' of 1913 and 1914, was employed with a group of assistants in operating wireless direction-finding stations on the east coast. It was he and his assistants who reported unusual signals from the principal wireless ship in the German fleet on the eve of the Battle of Jutland. Peter Eckersley, who was to become the first of the post-war 'broadcasters' and later the first Chief Engineer of the British Broadcasting Company, was a wireless equipment officer in the Royal Flying Corps. He first heard of the thermionic valve in 1915 when he attended a training school, where Major C. E. Prince, a Marconi engineer since 1907 and another pioneer of radio, was one of the lecturers. He has described vividly how but for the thermionic valve the wireless signals of the German fleet would never have been audible on the eve of Jutland.[2] Another of his 'first ever' stories relates to Prince. One day he stood beside Prince and heard him speak into a microphone, ' "Hullo, Furnivall. If you can hear me now it will be the first time speech has ever been communicated

---

[1] A. R. Burrows, *The Story of Broadcasting* (1924), p. 25.
[2] Eckersley, op. cit., p. 32.

to an aeroplane in flight. Dip if you are hearing me." The aeroplane, lumbering along at fifty miles an hour, gave an obedient lurch.'[1]

In Eckersley's view the war was chiefly important in radio history because it gave a great fillip to the rapid industrial development of the thermionic valve. Although the work of the 'amateurs' was abruptly brought to a halt with the beginning of hostilities and all wireless stations were commandeered by their respective governments, there was a sustained pressure not only to develop the valve but to use it for new tasks. It was still often a crude instrument which had to be teased into life by warming its 'pip' by lighted matches. Its very limitations, however, were a spur to organized research which went on while the war was in progress. Perhaps just as important as the stimulus given to the development of the valve during the war was the stimulus given to people. Many soldiers, sailors, and airmen first learned of wireless between 1914 and 1918 not as a mystery but as an art. Courses of radio instruction were given at Marconi House in the Strand, and later at the Crystal Palace. The pupils who attended them were often to be found among the most enthusiastic wireless 'amateurs' of the post-war years. Although most of them were more knowledgeable about radio-telegraphy than about radio-telephony, they had heard something at least about the new 'voice' experiments which were being carried out. There are even stories of gramophone records being played over military wireless stations in the trenches of France.

For the United States the years from 1914 to 1918 were crucial in the story of radio. Since the United States did not enter the war until 1917, there was opportunity to continue peacetime experiments unhindered. De Forest introduced a young lady singer to his 'amateur' listeners: she has been described as the 'Original Radio Girl'. When he led her to the crude microphone in his workshop he is reputed to have said, 'You are about to become the first woman ever to sing for people and continents invisible.'[2] De Forest also transmitted election results during the presidential election of 1916.[3] In the meantime the American

[1] Eckersley, op. cit., pp. 33–34. For a pre-war assessment of the use of wireless in aeroplanes, see *Flight*, 20 Apr. 1912: 'The more one thinks about the use of aeroplanes for military purposes, the more apparent does the importance of successfully employing wireless for transmitting messages become.'
[2] Archer, op. cit., p. 133.   [3] Ibid., p. 134; *New York Times*, 8 Nov. 1916.

Telephone and Telegraph Company, working together with the Western Electric Company, startled the world in October 1915 by transmitting speech and music from the United States naval station at Arlington to the Eiffel Tower 3,800 miles away. On this occasion 300 transmitting and modulating valves were employed.[1]

On the outbreak of war with Germany, the United States government followed the lead of other belligerents in taking over all wireless stations in the United States and banning all 'amateur' wireless activities, but research and experiments continued. As in Britain, a large number of new 'radio schools' increased the ranks of the knowledgeable. The official wireless station at New Brunswick was the most powerful in the world, and battleships in all parts of the world were said to be able to pick up its call sign. 'Even portable wirelesses in the trenches could tune in to it, and it kept the American soldier in touch with home events and with public opinion in the United States.'[2]

In a sense, organized broadcasting grew naturally out of these war-time developments. The surprise is that there were still so few people who saw its possibilities. David Sarnoff in America, as has been noted, was one of them.

A radio telephone transmitter having a range of say twenty-five to fifty miles [he wrote in 1916] can be installed at a fixed point where instrumental or vocal music or both are produced. The problem of transmitting music has already been solved in principle and therefore all the receivers attuned to the transmitting wave length should be capable of receiving such music. The receiver can be designed in the form of a simple 'Radio Music Box' and arranged for several different wave lengths, which should be changeable with the throwing of a single switch or pressing of a single button.

Sarnoff did not stop at what we now call the 'wireless set'. He went on to describe the potential radio audience, a large number of people all receiving simultaneously from a single transmitter. He even forecast the kind of programmes which would attract this new audience—broadcasting of events of national importance, concerts, lectures, and baseball scores. Modestly

[1] Burrows, op. cit., p. 45.
[2] Archer, op. cit., p. 138.

he added that 'there are numerous other fields to which the principle can be extended'.[1]

On this side of the Atlantic Burrows also was successful in peering even farther into the future.

5. A 1925 'Radio Music Box'

There appears to be no serious reason why before we are many years older, politicians speaking, say, in Parliament should not be heard simultaneously by wireless in the reporting room of every newspaper office in the United Kingdom. . . . The same idea might be extended to make possible the concert reproduction in all private residences of Albert Hall or Queen's Hall concerts, or the important recitals at the lesser *rendez-vous* of the music world. . . . Such departures would expose us, of course, to all sorts of logical but unwelcome developments. There would be no technical difficulty in the way of an enterprising advertisement agency arranging for intervals in the musical programme to be filled with audible advertisements, pathetic or forcible appeals—in appropriate tones—on behalf of somebody's soap or tomato ketchup.[2]

Burrows in Britain looked farther into the future than Sarnoff

[1] Archer, op. cit.., pp. 110 ff.
[2] *Yearbook of Wireless Telegraphy and Telephony* (1918), p. 958.

in the United States, for Sarnoff did not reconcile himself to the arguments for commercial broadcasting until the late 1920s. In looking forward, however, Burrows was also looking back. Given the likely transition from radio to broadcasting, he realized that a prophet had to take into account not only technical but social forces. Broadcasting would never be left to the scientists. He turned back therefore to the previous thirty or forty years of history and selected a number of elements in British history which would help to shape the use of the new invention. Today we can see them more clearly still—the attitude of government; the power of the press; the strength of business—particularly business in so-called 'consumer goods', those which were bought over the counter and, as the market was extended, were advertised for all the world to buy; the organization of entertainment, both local and national; and, not least in importance, the level of education of the potential radio audience. Given the transition from radio to broadcasting, all these became factors to take into the reckoning.

The first of them—the attitude of government—obviously requires much further attention. So long as the war lasted, the official attitude was the same in all sovereign states. Radio should be restricted for military reasons. But what was to happen when it ended? All kinds of differences in traditions and political processes became relevant. So too did economic and social pressures. The social factors shaping broadcasting had independent histories of their own, and it is easy in retrospect to see that the 1890s, when critical radio discoveries were being made, were also a critical decade in the development of what have come to be called 'mass communications' as a whole. Individuals were being conceived of (artificially but often profitably) in large numbers as 'masses': local differences were being ironed out. The national press was beginning to establish new empires. In 1896, the same year that Marconi arrived in Britain, Alfred Harmsworth launched the *Daily Mail*. During the first twelve months of its existence its daily sale averaged 202,000; at the end of three years it had reached more than 543,000. The 'new order' in journalism was duly established—with enormous and unpredicted social consequences—and it has been correctly said that during the 'Fashoda crisis' of 1898 'for the first time Fleet Street went to Downing Street'.

Mass reading-publics and mass markets tended to go together, and the 1890s were years of unprecedented development both for the industries which made consumer goods and for the advertising business. The various aspects of growth were associated. Without advertising in popular national newspapers the mass production of 'branded goods' would have been impossible. Without advertising revenue the publication of cheap daily newspapers would have been impossible.[1] Without a higher standard of living there would have been a severe limit to the growth both of the press and of the consumer goods industries. The goods and the advertisements were being specially prepared for 'the ordinary man', as he was beginning to be called. Indeed, more than one suggestion was made in the 1890s that the new century around the corner would be his for the taking. Of course, the 'ordinary man' would have to be entertained as well as educated. Popular music hall was at the height of its appeal in the 1890s, but again there were portents of the shape of things to come. In the same year that Marconi arrived in Britain and Harmsworth launched the *Daily Mail*, the first moving-picture show was given in London.

In one obscure branch of entertaining there were intimations of 'broadcasting' before 1900. In view of recent attention paid to 'wire broadcasting' they are of more than antiquarian interest. It was in relation to the telephone, not in relation to wireless, that the idea of scattering 'sound-at-a-distance' was first mooted. It was of the telephone not of wireless that a distinguished engineer, Frank Gill, a prominent figure in the 1922 talks leading up to the inauguration of broadcasting in Britain, wrote that 'telephony has some of the properties both of the letter and of the newspaper: it can be clothed with privacy, given to one individual only, or it can be broadcast to millions simultaneously'.[2]

In some towns and cities of Britain the practicability of the telephone as a technical instrument was first demonstrated by

---

[1] There was talk in 1894 of using advertising to subsidize the American gramophone record business. 'Nobody will refuse', it was claimed, 'to listen to a fine song or concert piece or an oration—even if it is interrupted by a modest remark "Tartar's Baking Powder is Best".' Quoted by W. Abbot and R. L. Rider, *Handbook of Broadcasting* (4th edn., New York, 1957), p. 387.

[2] Preface to F. G. C. Baldwin, *The History of the Telephone in the United Kingdom* (1925).

the transmission of music, frequently organ music, from a 'distant source', and in 1892 performances at the Lyric Theatre in London and theatres and concerts in Birmingham, Liverpool, Manchester, and other places were transmitted 'with entire success' to an Electrical Exhibition at the Crystal Palace.[1] Ten years before this experiment, a Hungarian, Theodore Puskas, had demonstrated a 'telephoned newspaper' at an Electrical Exhibition in Paris, and his son went on to introduce a regular newspaper of this type in Budapest.[2] In 1894 an Electrophone Company was formed in London to provide 'listening facilities', including four pairs of headphones and an answering-back 'hand microphone' for every subscriber. Musical performances, public lectures and addresses, and church services were 'electrophoned'. The service was neither a technical nor a business success: after twelve years of activity sounds were still distorted and there were only 600 subscribers. In its restricted way, however, it pointed to the existence not only of a potential demand for diffused entertainment but of a wide range of available 'programmes'.[3]

Between the late 1890s and the end of the First World War the electrophone was of little importance in this country, but the tendencies to reshape society were producing a new pattern in national life. The 'ordinary man' (as culturally 'weighted' a term as the word 'masses') had begun to assert his social claims, and there was no shortage of agencies in society which were seeking to satisfy or to exploit them. 'The breaking down of barriers which formerly existed between class and class and group and group'[4] was an acknowledged social fact. It was the war itself which had produced the final jolt, and inevitably it left many social vacuums to fill.

Broadcasting was of the greatest possible importance in relation to this changing social pattern. It arrived at a time when many different social forces were converging. Would it augment and accelerate the tendencies described above or would it seek

[1] Ibid., pp. 266–7. The first of these 'transmissions' was in 1883.

[2] See J. Erdoess, 'Le Journal Téléphonique de Budapest', in *Radiodiffusion*, Oct. 1936. For a recent appraisal, see P. Adorjan, 'Wire Broadcasting', in the *Journal of the Royal Society of Arts* (1945), pp. 511–14.

[3] Baldwin, op. cit., p. 267.

[4] A contemporary phrase quoted by F. W. Hirst, *The Social Consequences of the War to Great Britain* (1934), p. 75.

to counteract and check them? Would the values of its sponsors
and organizers be the values of the market, the values of tradi-
tional authority, or some new values related, however loosely
and inadequately, to the advent of democracy? Would it mould
or would it merely distract? The questions were basic, although
in 1918 there was no one to ask them. Burrows implied that the
control of broadcasting might shape its content, but he did not
say so clearly. Ironically, David Sarnoff did not draw out of

6. 'Punch' anticipates broadcast entertainment, 1878.

relevant American experience the elements which were to
fashion the shape of broadcasting there. He continued as late
as 1924 to dream of broadcasting by endowment 'similar to that
enjoyed by libraries, museums, and educational institutions'.[1]
Burrows for his part did not anticipate the forging of instruments of public control in Britain, instruments which in 1926
were to shape the first Charter of the British Broadcasting
Corporation.

The forging of the instruments is one of the main themes of
this volume. Before the instruments could be forged, however,
there had to be organized broadcasting. The immediate post-
war initiative was taken by commercial concerns as it had been
before the war, and on this side of the Atlantic the Marconi

[1] Archer, op. cit., p. 342.

Company led the way. In March 1919 a wireless telephony transmitter, with a power of $2\frac{1}{2}$ kilowatts, was installed at Ballybunion in Ireland, and under the direction of H. J. Round successful transmissions were made to America. The voice of a well-known Marconi engineer, W. T. Ditcham, was the first European voice to be heard by wireless on the other side of the Atlantic, and the achievement was looked upon at the time as 'something almost uncanny'.[1] The comparatively long wavelength of 3,800 metres was used.

The success of the Ballybunion experiment led to the building of a 6-kilowatt transmitter at Chelmsford, which employed the large Marconi Works aerial suspended between two 450-foot masts. The new station was used chiefly for tests of speech and transmission over long distances, but G. W. White, one of the engineers assisting Round and Ditcham, also organized short transmissions of musical items. Two assistants from the Marconi Works played the cornet and the oboe, one of the research engineers played a one-string fiddle, and White himself, whenever possible, played the piano. Sometimes vocalists were 'dragged in to help'[2] and Miss W. Sayer undoubtedly had the distinction of being the first British radio soprano. Godfrey Isaacs told her that she was helping to make history, but she insisted on referring to wireless as 'this punch and judy show'.[3] Impromptu though the Chelmsford concerts were and unimpressive though some at least of the artists were, they soon had their 'fans', and appreciative letters were received from places as far away as Madrid and Rome.

Experimental work with this 6-kilowatt station established a standard Marconi transmitter for commercial purposes. It could be used both for telegraphy and telephony, and some of the transmitters were exported to other countries, including 'undeveloped' countries like China. A subsidiary company, the Chinese National Wireless Company, was organized. When the success of the Chelmsford experiments was assured, the 6-kilowatt station was replaced by a station of even greater power, 15 kilowatts. Between 23 February and 6 March 1920 two daily programmes were 'broadcast' from this transmitter on a wavelength of 2,500 metres. Each programme lasted for half an hour,

---

[1] *The Essex Chronicle*, 24 Jan. 1946.   [2] *World Radio*, 21 Oct. 1932.
[3] W. T. Ditcham. Leslie Baily, BBC programme, *Scrapbook for 1920*.

and consisted of news, musical items, and gramophone records. The 2,500-metre wavelength was the same as that employed at Poldhu for telegraphically transmitting news to ships. A large part of the first British 'listening audience' consisted, therefore, of sailors miles away from their homes.

One of the more general purposes of the Chelmsford experiments was to discover whether or not the public would be interested in wireless. A considerable number of people were, notably the so-called 'amateurs'.[1] They were even prepared to listen intently each night to Ditcham reciting the names of the main British railway lines and their London termini, hardly an inspiring subject.

It was not only the Marconi Company which was interested in public reactions. Some pressmen were also concerned for two reasons—first, they realized, sometimes dimly, that radio might become either a dangerous competitor or a profitable subsidiary; and second, they appreciated the news value of 'radio stunts' themselves. Tom Clarke, the assistant of Lord Northcliffe, the outstanding newspaper magnate, had been a signals officer during the war, and in 1919 and 1920 he established good relations both with Burrows and with the amateur 'listeners-in'. A *Daily Mail* reporter was sent out in 1919 to roam Hampstead Heath to listen for messages transmitted from Chelmsford, and later a second reporter was sent to the coast by train with a portable wireless receiver in his baggage. As he listened-in, he was given instructions to get out at the next station and report to headquarters. 'These things', Clarke has noted, 'seemed sheer wizardry in those days.'[2] On one Saturday in May 1920 the *Daily Mail* included two columns of news 'collected by wireless telephone', and printed several enthusiastic reports about a 'Voyage of Wireless Discovery' which Marconi was planning in his yacht *Electra*.[3] A 'permanent wireless receiving station' was soon afterwards installed in the *Daily Mail* office.[4]

Northcliffe himself was somewhat suspicious of these first wireless experiments, but this did not deter him from conceiving a brilliant idea for publicity. He suggested that a special *Daily*

[1] See below, pp. 50–58.
[2] See T. Clarke, *My Northcliffe Diary* (1931), pp. 149–51.
[3] *Daily Mail*, 12, 13, 14 Apr.; 29 May; 19 June 1920.
[4] *Wireless World*, 26 June 1920.

Mail broadcast should be planned with 'only one artist . . . the world's very best', Dame Nellie Melba. On 15 June 1920 Dame Nellie travelled down to Chelmsford for what she told reporters was 'the most wonderful experience of my career'.[1] In the presence of a distinguished audience, including Godfrey Isaacs and Northcliffe's friend, Sir Campbell Stuart, Dame Nellie sang in English, Italian, and French. She began with a 'long silvery trill', which she described as her 'hello to the world', and ended with 'God Save the King'. Melba's voice was heard by listeners all over Europe, and at places as far away as St. John's, Newfoundland. At Christiania the signals were so strong that an operator at a wireless station some distance from the town relayed the music by telephone to the principal newspaper offices. In Paris a phonograph record of the broadcast was made in the radio operations room below the Eiffel Tower, while in the London office of the *Daily Mail* a press audience listened and admired. There were not enough headphones to go round. 'Melba's girl secretary was there. Her eyes nearly came out of her head as she heard the nightingale voice in "Addio" from *La Bohème*. "It is Melba!", she cried in astonishment.' 'I think', adds Clarke, 'she had not believed us up to that moment.'[2]

The Melba broadcast was a turning point in the public response to radio. It caught people's imagination. 'It was a wonderful half-hour,' proudly proclaimed a special correspondent of the *Daily Mail*, 'Art and Science joined hands, and the world "listening-in" must have counted every minute of it precious.'[3] Later writers, seeing the event in historical perspective, echoed the original verdict. 'The renown of the singer, the world-wide attention which was given to her performance, the great distances at which good reception was obtained, all combined to give to the Melba Concert the atmosphere of a great initiation ceremony, and the era of broadcasting for the public amusement, of which this was an ideal example, may be said to have completed its preliminary trials and to have been definitely launched on its meteoric career from this date.'[4]

[1] *Daily Mail*, 16 June 1920. Dame Nellie had made one of the first popular gramophone records in 1904, when the London press was invited to a recorded concert at the Hotel Metropole. See R. Gelatt, *The Fabulous Phonograph* (1956), p. 85.
[2] Clarke, loc. cit.   [3] *Daily Mail*, 16 June 1920.
[4] See H. M. Dowsett, *Wireless Telephony and Broadcasting* (1925), ch. ii.

There was a brief period of further experiment before the 'meteoric career' of broadcasting was brought to a temporary halt. The Marconi Company continued its 'demonstrations', and the *Daily Mail* and the *Daily News* encouraged further experiments in co-operation between radio and the press.[1] There was no shortage of publicity. A 'wireless demonstration lorry' attracted the public at home,[2] while far away one Marconi concert was heard in its entirety at a British aerodrome in Northern Persia, much to the astonishment of the commanding officer and the members of his staff.[3] Lauritz Melchior, the Danish operatic singer, broadcast from Chelmsford, creating an early 'technical hitch' by imagining that the louder he sang the easier it would be for his Danish friends to hear him. Finally, after 'news' tests had been carried out in co-operation with the Press Association and frame aerials with multi-valve amplifiers had been constructed in newspaper offices in Sheffield, Preston, Newcastle, and Belfast, a bold attempt was made to associate the new power of wireless with the Imperial Press Conference at Ottawa in July and August 1920. Wireless transmitting and receiving sets were installed in the *Victorian*, the ship which was carrying the British Press delegation to Canada. As a practical demonstration of their effectiveness arrangements were made for the reception of music, news, and 'messages' from Chelmsford and Poldhu, while each evening the *Victorian* broadcast short gramophone concerts to other ships at sea. Among the passengers was Lord Burnham, president of the Empire Press Union, who exchanged messages by 'wireless telephone' with the Prime Minister of Canada.

All these 'broadcasts' were arranged 'by kind permission of the Post Office'. By the Wireless Telegraphy Act of 1904 all transmitters or receivers of wireless signals had to have a licence, the terms and conditions of which were laid down by the Post Office. In 1920 the Marconi Company held a general licence 'to conduct experimental telephony transmission', but on each occasion that a major experiment was carried out special permission had to be granted. There is a sheaf of letters in the Post

---

[1] *The Times*, 20 July 1920; *Wireless World*, 7 Aug. 1920. There were also experiments with the foreign Press including tests of wireless link-up with Scandinavian newspaper offices.

[2] *Wireless World*, 10 July 1920.

[3] *Chapters of Marconi History* (unpublished): 'The Birth of British Broadcasting'.

Office archives granting or withholding this permission. Of course, the Post Office was by no means a completely free agent. It had to watch over British interests in international commercial wireless, but more particularly it had to take account of Armed Services' opinion as represented in the Wireless Telegraph Board, the most important Services committee concerned with wireless, and the Wireless Sub-Committee of the Imperial Communications Committee. On this latter body there were influential civilian as well as Service representatives.

It became increasingly apparent in the autumn of 1920 that the Marconi Company broadcasts were being criticized in official circles on the grounds that 'they were interfering with important communications'.[1] According to one report the Melba broadcast was deplored because it represented a 'frivolous' use of a 'national service'.[2] The Financier reported in August 1920 that 'opinion among airmen is practically united against a continuance of the "concerts" given to the world at large by the Chelmsford wireless station. A few days ago the pilot of a Vickers Vimy machine . . . was crossing the Channel in a thick fog and was trying to obtain weather and landing reports from Lympne. All he could hear was a musical evening.'[3] According to these critics, wireless, which was ideally equipped to be the 'servant of mankind', was being treated as 'a toy to amuse children'. Many of the criticisms were from high-ranking officers in the Army, Navy, and Air Force, including members of the Wireless Telegraph Board itself. A colonel protested against the Melchior broadcast: it 'jammed aircraft communication'.[4] The link-up with foreign press services was also deplored. 'Do you agree that trials of this nature, which are obviously "stunts" and not calculated to advance the science in any way, should not be permitted, more especially if they are to be carried out with a Continental country?'[5] Commander (later Captain) Loring, the Post Office Inspector of Radio Telegraphy, was anxious to keep a balance. 'Experiments . . . ought not to be handicapped in any way unnecessarily, but on the other hand

[1] Eckersley, op. cit., p. 38.
[2] B. L. Jacob and D. M. B. Collier, Marconi, Master of Space (1936), p. 123.
[3] The Financier, 25 Aug. 1920. A copy of this comment was sent to the Post Office.
[4] Letter to the Secretary, the G.P.O., 11 Sept. 1920.
[5] Memorandum of 13 Sept. 1920.

I think we have been very considerate towards the constant applications which the Marconi Company have made to us for permission to demonstrate—often on grounds which are obviously more propaganda than scientific.'[1]

Pressure from the Services and uneasiness in the Post Office staff were sufficiently strong in the autumn of 1920 to lead to the imposition of a ban on the Chelmsford broadcasts. The Postmaster General told the House of Commons on 23 November that 'it was found that the experiments caused considerable interference with other stations, and for the present the trials have been suspended'.[2] A few weeks before that, in somewhat different language, the *Wireless World* had written cryptically of 'Chelmsford's inability to transmit speech'.[3]

3. Amateurs and Professionals

THE end of the Marconi experiments did not mark the end of broadcasting even in the short run. By the summer of 1920 there were large numbers of wireless 'amateurs' whose enthusiasm for wireless could not easily be contained within a mesh of bureaucratic regulation. It was their enthusiasm, indeed, which filled the gap between the cessation of the Marconi Company's experiments and the authorization of short regular broadcast programmes of words and music in January 1922. The authorization itself was largely their doing. The Postmaster-General rescinded his veto on broadcasting in response to a petition drawn up in December 1921 and signed by representatives of sixty-three wireless societies with over 3,000 members.

We would point out [the petition stated] that it is telephony in which the majority of our members are chiefly interested, this being the most recent achievement in wireless and that for which, for moderate distances at all events, improvements such as avoidance of distortion, and the production of really articulate loudspeakers and

---

[1] E. 8658, Post Office Archives.
[2] *Hansard*, vol. 135, col. 204, 23 Nov. 1920.
[3] *Wireless World*, 16 Oct. 1920.

such like, are most required. It is therefore, primarily, to serve the scientific purpose of improving the receiving arrangements that we desire to have telephony included.[1]

The emphasis on 'scientific purpose' in the petition was in keeping with the avowed objectives and outlook of the Wireless Society of London, which had been founded before the war—in July 1913—in West Hampstead, and in October 1922 was to change its name to that of the Radio Society of Great Britain.[2] It was the Wireless Society of London which convened two important conferences of 'amateur' wireless societies in February 1920 and March 1921. At the first of these, held in the Library of the Royal Society of Arts, the chairman of the Wireless Society of London, F. H. Hope-Jones, reported that there appeared to be twenty wireless societies in the country at that time, of which fifteen were willing to become affiliated to the Wireless Society of London. The fifteen included clubs and societies in Manchester, Sheffield, Bristol, Plymouth, Brighton, Southport, and Derby; the five that were not affiliated included the Birmingham Wireless Association, which was associated with the nineteenth-century Birmingham and Midland Institute.

Hope-Jones added that since the war there had been a remarkable burst of interest in wireless in many parts of the country. Some of the enthusiasts were content to dabble with simple crystal sets, unreliable and exasperating though they might be; others, a small minority, were both knowledgeable and lavishly equipped some with six- and seven-valve receivers. Quite apart from the pleasures of home listening there were pleasures in building wireless sets as an agreeable and active hobby combining science and craftsmanship.

The speakers at the conference confirmed the increase in public interest and went on to describe the various 'problems' that worried them. The wireless experimenter could never be a completely solitary creature, living to himself: he worked within his home, but he always needed the co-operation of others. Various speakers suggested that an amalgamation of wireless societies would be useful; so, too, would an annual conference of representatives from different districts. Even more useful,

[1] *Wireless World*, 21 Jan. 1922.
[2] Meetings of the R.S.G.B. were numbered consecutively with those of the Wireless Society of London: they did not start with a new sequence of numbers.

however, would be a relaxation of government restrictions. The crippling terms of D.O.R.A.—the Defence of the Realm Act— held back home experiments which might be as far-reaching in the history of wireless as commercial research carried out within business laboratories. Above all, could not limitations on the ownership of receiving apparatus be amended or removed altogether?

Loring of the Post Office spoke at this meeting. He said that there was no intention of imposing any unnecessary restrictions on amateurs, but that the Post Office was the 'custodian of naval, military and civil interests', all of which were making increasing demands on it. Everybody, soldier, business man, or amateur, was working in the same 'laboratory', and it was necessary, therefore, to restrict the operations of the experi- menters by making sure that they were all 'fit to use the appa- ratus' and would not interfere with 'the super-sensitive receivers of public stations'. In these circumstances 'the policy of the Post Office was not yet stereotyped'. The provisions of D.O.R.A. would be gradually relaxed, and in the meantime wireless re- ceiving licences would be issued freely 'to all approved persons, with exceptions as regards the use of valves in certain limited areas'. Transmitting sets with a power of ten watts or less would be licensed 'wherever this can be done without interference with Government installations, to approved applicants who can satisfy the Post Office that their qualifications, apparatus, knowledge of the subject and objects, are sufficiently good to justify the grant'.

This 'offer' allowed for a very substantial measure of Post Office discretion, and Loring made it clear first that licences would not be issued for mere 'purposes of inter-communication' and second that licences for stations with more than 10-watt power would be granted only in 'special cases' after not only the Post Office but other departments had scrutinized the applica- tion. Restrictions would be placed on the use of transmitting sets—both restrictions of wavelength and hours of working— but special permits would be provided (given due notice) 'for specific tests of apparatus on any power and wavelength over and above the conditions of the licence'.

Wireless was thus to be treated not as a personal pleasure but as a 'definite object of scientific research or of general public utility'.[1] The neat distinction, however, was impossible to draw in practice. The 10-watt 'amateurs' were unwilling to experiment in words only: they spoke in music. With their one seventy-fifth of horse-power at their disposal, they were sometimes able to achieve remarkable results. 'The telephony could often be heard at very considerable distances, and the number of tests requiring the assistance of gramophone records seemed somehow to increase week by week.'[2] Apart from their own 'programmes'—they still did not think in these terms—they were able to listen to regular Sunday-night concerts from The Hague, which first went on the air in May 1920.[3] At a meeting of the Wireless Society of London in 1920, B.T.H. (British Thomson-Houston) displayed a radio receiver which could be installed in the home for about £30 and which could receive both The Hague and Paris.[4]

'Science' and 'art' often went together. By the time that the second conference of wireless societies was held in March 1921, the Post Office had issued 150 amateur transmitting licences and 4,000 receiving licences.[5] All the successful applicants had to be 'men of good character' as well as men of curiosity. Some of their testimonials survive. 'It gives me great pleasure to recommend Mr. Harold Butler as an Honest, Hardworking and Industrious Man', one of them reads in almost eighteenth-century language. 'Having known him since he was born, I also know his Parents as most Industrious People. I know Butler is very intelligent among Machinery, and I should take a great interest in his success concerning Wireless Telegraphy.'[6]

There was usually at least one 'wireless enthusiast' in every village—if not by 1921, certainly very soon afterwards. These enthusiasts came from all walks of life, and although it is tempting to try to sketch their qualities in one common profile, they were really men of diverse gifts united only in a common enthusiasm. Some of them passed into the radio business either as salesmen or manufacturers. A few were given jobs by the Marconi Company. P. P. Eckersley himself had been a keen

[1] There is a full report of this meeting in *Wireless World*, 3 Apr. 1920.
[2] Burrows, op. cit., p. 57.   [3] *The Times*, 30 Jan. 1922.
[4] *Electrical Review*, 6 Feb. 1920.
[5] *Wireless World*, 16 Apr. 1921.
[6] I owe this reference, written by a Wokingham councillor, to the kindness of the late Mr. Butler's daughter, Mrs. Miller.

experimenter while still a schoolboy at Bedales. So too was his brother, T. L. Eckersley, who experimented before him. 'Returning home from school,' P. P. Eckersley has written, 'I found our playroom filled with lovely and exciting instruments. There were Induction Coils to make fat sparks, Leyden jars, long black rods of ebonite wound with green silk-covered wire, X-ray tubes and galvanometers. The things, their touch and shape, gave me a sensual pleasure and made me want to understand what they were for.'[1] The war pushed him firmly forward from science into radio, as it did scores of other people: the post-war world propelled him still further forward into the Marconi Company.

One interesting individual profile of an 'experimenter' who remained an 'amateur' has been provided by William Le Queux, the popular novelist.[2] He claimed that he was 'one of the earliest experimenters in the field of radio telegraphy' in Britain. As a young man he had taken over Marconi's flat in Leghorn after the young inventor had just left it. From that time onwards he had 'dabbled' with radio in his 'spare time', 'possessing various sets, coherers, magnetic and electrolytic detectors, and various crystals'. In 1911 he had set up a spark station on the cliffs between Cromer and Sheringham and with the permission of the Admiralty had transmitted news each night to the Cross Sands lightship in the North Sea. After the war ended he turned to long-distance radio telephony. Along with two other enthusiasts he set up Station ZAZ at Guildford. 'I gave up my profession as a novelist and devoted my whole time to my laboratory until it became a mass of apparatus and a great tangle of wires.' One of his broadcasts of nursery rhymes was picked up in Manchester, another in Aberdeen. 'At last I had succeeded in establishing a station which transmitted speech and music over long distances on low power. Then I commenced to inaugurate nightly gramophone concerts and talks to amateurs, all of which was greatly appreciated as the first attempt to broadcast, badly modulated and uncertain though it was.'

Given men like Le Queux, wireless could never be treated austerely as a 'definite object of scientific research or of general public utility'. Yet the increase in the number of experimental

[1] Eckersley, op. cit., p. 27.
[2] See *Radio Times*, 21 Dec. 1923. See also his book *Things I know about Kings, Celebrities and Crooks* (1923).

licences provided by the Post Office after the first conference of wireless societies did not satisfy the Wireless Society of London and its affiliates. They stood for a principle. 'Their first and constant duty', they often reiterated, 'is to urge the granting of Receiving Licences with complete freedom. They hold that every Englishman is entitled to hear what is going on in his aether provided his listening apparatus does not annoy his neighbours. Any tendency to restrict such freedom as the Postmaster-General has already accorded is bound to cause serious apprehension.'[1] The constant reiteration of this principle was as important in the circumstances of 1921 and 1922 as the principle itself: in a sense even the Post Office itself—or at least some leading people in it—welcomed it, for it was a principle untainted by 'commercialism', which from the start the Post Office feared.

When the second conference also suggested 'the possibility of regular telephone transmission from a high-power station to include all matters of interest to amateurs, and to be on different definite wavelengths for calibration purposes', Loring replied on behalf of the Post Office 'that this proposal had better come from the Wireless Society of London than from a company. There were several companies, and they would want similar treatment.'[2] Perhaps the old fear of the Marconi Company obtruded at this point.[3]

Fear of 'commercialism' was not the only reason for attention being paid to the amateurs' case. The Post Office included men who were themselves 'experimenters' of proven enterprise and established reputation. They had a natural and often profound interest in the work of the amateurs, as described each week, for example, in the pages of the *Wireless World*. There were also people on the Wireless Sub-Committee of the Imperial Communications Committee who shared this approach. Sir Henry Norman, its chairman, went out of his way to state the amateurs' point of view, sometimes in face of serious opposition. He said clearly in the autumn of 1920 that he wanted to give the amateur every chance of doing something nationally useful and

---

[1] Extract from the report of L. McMichael (for and on behalf of the Wireless Society of London) of his interview at the General Post Office, 16 Apr. 1921.
[2] *Wireless World*, 16 Apr. 1921.
[3] See above, p. 34.

to remove any unnecessary restrictions on his efforts.[1] Indeed, before the suspension of the Marconi Company broadcasts in 1920, the Post Office proposed a 'free hand' in licences up to 50 watts, and the 10-watt licences were eventually granted. Sir Henry Norman himself was one of the first people to take out one of these experimental licences.

Despite these signs of mutual understanding, there were months of fruitless negotiation between amateurs and the Post Office concerning an extension of radio facilities. The negotiators were not interested in the establishment of a regular broadcasting service as such. Nonetheless there was an obvious community of interest between amateurs and commercial companies at least in the endeavour to secure permission for regular broadcasts from a high-power station. A representative of the Marconi Company was present at the 1921 wireless societies' conference. He told the representatives present that the Marconi Company had applied for a temporary licence to carry out 'a somewhat humbler programme for amateurs than was suggested in the agenda'—a half-hourly transmission each week. The Post Office had replied that it required 'some very good evidence that such a programme would really be welcomed by amateurs'. The amateurs agreed to support the Marconi Company's application, and at last, in August 1921, the company was allowed to broadcast special calibration signals for a period of half an hour a week for amateurs. Permission to broadcast wireless telephony was still refused.

The delay in 1921 suggests that quite apart from Services' pressure an attempt was still being made by the Post Office to distinguish between 'useful' wireless telegraphy and 'frivolous' wireless telephony. The first was held to be legitimate; the second was 'unscientific'. There was some justification for the distinction in that the president of the Wireless Society of London, Major Erskine Murray, had himself remarked at the second wireless societies' conference of 1921 that 'C. W. [continuous wave] and the rest of the programme is very much more important than telephony, although the latter, perhaps, is more amusing.' Many of his fellow amateurs did not agree. They were more anxious than ever to mix 'science' and 'amusement'.

[1] Minutes of the 18th Meeting of the Wireless Sub-Committee of the Imperial Communications Committee, 7 Oct. 1920.

Wireless World records their mood. In June 1921 it included a report of the use of a 'Marconi wireless telephone set to transmit the result of the Derby': a photograph of the lorry used, with the operator's position behind the driver's seat, antedates by about ten years the BBC's first outside broadcast vans.[1] In August 1921 there was an account of a demonstration of wireless telephony as part of an entertainment in aid of St. Dunstan's Hospital for the Blind.[2] In September and October 1921 there were appeals for financial assistance to maintain the musical concerts broadcast from The Hague.[3] Letters began to appear demanding regular broadcasts from 'a British Station such as Chelmsford, which would give us a concert once a week and perhaps half an hour's news a day with our breakfast'.[4] One of them, from the Portsmouth and District Wireless Association, specifically asked for Chelmsford to imitate The Hague. It added that 'a short transmission of telephony, if only for a few minutes daily . . . would be greatly appreciated and would, undoubtedly, do much to further amateur work, and increase enthusiasm in the amateur hobby'.[5]

In the light of these expressions of opinion it is not surprising that the representatives of sixty-three wireless societies who drafted their petition to the Post Office in December 1921 stated unequivocally that 'it is telephony in which the majority of our members are chiefly interested'. The petition was presented to Loring and de Wardt of the Post Office on 29 December at St. Martin's-le-Grand. It voiced 'a national resentment that public services such as wireless time and telephony should be left to our neighbours to provide, and that permission to transmit weather reports, news and music by wireless telephony should be refused to companies competent and willing to do so without interference with the defensive services of the country'.[6]

A fortnight elapsed, and on 13 January the Marconi Company was officially informed that the Postmaster-General 'had consulted the other Authorities concerned and he now author-

---

[1] *Wireless World*, 25 June 1921.
[2] Ibid., 20 Aug. 1921. Further reports of wireless concerts in aid of St. Dunstan's are given in *Wireless World*, 17 Sept. 1921. The concerts were 'broadcast' from the Soho works of the Marconi Instrument Company Ltd.
[3] Ibid., 3 Sept., 26 Nov. 1921.
[4] Ibid., 1 Oct. 1921.
[5] Ibid., 25 Oct. 1921.
[6] Ibid., 21 Jan. 1922.

izes you to include within the weekly period of half-an-hour already authorized a programme of 15 minutes' telephony (speech and music) in the transmission from your Chelmsford station for the benefit of the Wireless Societies'.[1] On the same day the wireless societies were informed. They could regard the decision, limited though it was, as a major victory. It was, of course, to produce far-reaching results which the amateurs did not anticipate and not all of which they were to welcome.

The first Marconi broadcast took place on 14 February 1922. It was made not from Chelmsford itself but from a hut at Writtle a few miles away. And it was at the Writtle station that the 'nucleus of the "brains trust" of the technical side of British broadcasting'[2] could be found: a group of lively, intelligent, and extremely versatile young men. In an enterprise that was at once 'constructive and gay', they guaranteed the future of broadcasting in Britain.

4. The American Boom

ONE of the talks given to the Wireless Society of London on the eve of the Postmaster-General's authorization of limited Marconi Company broadcasts was by an American visitor, P. F. Godley. He vividly described what was happening to broadcasting on the other side of the Atlantic.

Some of the largest organizations, the General Electric Company and the Westinghouse Company, [he explained] are installing in our principal cities broadcasting radiophone stations, and at this moment there are daily concerts and about every other day gramophone concerts and operas, the artists performing before the microphone. On Sunday, almost everyone within range of one of those stations has the privilege of listening to a sermon from one of our best pastors in the country, together with the music by the choir, and an organ solo. And the thing is only just starting.[3]

He added what seemed to him to be the 'moral': the attitude of

[1] Marconi Company Archives.   [2] Eckersley, op. cit., p. 39.
[3] *Wireless World*, 10 Dec. 1921.

the British Post Office was 'deplorable'. Britain procrastinated while the United States forged ahead.

Both the lecture and the developments it described came at the right time in relation to the story of broadcasting in Britain. To the pressure of amateurs and the energies of the Marconi Company was added the direct influence of the 'broadcasting boom' in the United States. 'Serious broadcasting', H. J. Round has written, 'did not arrive until the situation in America forced the hands of the authorities here to allow it.'[1]

Not only the American lead in broadcasting but the kind of broadcasting pattern which took shape there had considerable impact on the sequence of events in Britain. Eventually the British and American broadcasting systems were to be so completely different—one based on a concept of 'public service', the other fully integrated into the business system—that in all controversies about the place of radio in society they were to be taken as the two chief contrasting types.[2] In their birth and infancy, however, they were not so distinct as they have since become. In both countries there were the same pressures and the same outspoken advocates of common ideas and comparable institutions. It was Sarnoff who in June 1922 anticipated J. C. W. Reith by arguing that 'considered from its broadest aspect [sic] . . . broadcasting represents a job of entertaining, informing and educating the nation, and should therefore be distinctly regarded as a public service'. He went on to urge the creation of a 'Public Service Broadcasting Company or National Broadcasting Company', which would include on its Board of Directors not only business men but 'a few men from outside, prominent in national or civic affairs'.[3]

Sarnoff's failure to achieve this early vision was not immediately apparent either to Americans or their critics. What was immediately apparent, however, and historically of great significance, was that for technical rather than social reasons the experience of American broadcasting in 1921 and 1922 could not easily be taken as a model on this side of the Atlantic. America's lead in time was envied in Britain and quickened the

[1] Marconi Company Archives.

[2] See C. A. Siepmann, *Radio, Television and Society* (New York, 1950), Part I.

[3] Letter to E. W. Rice, 17 June 1922. Quoted by G. L. Archer, *Big Business and Radio* (New York, 1939), p. 31.

pace of development in Britain, but the use made by American broadcasters of their lead served as a warning rather than an example.

When the war ended two Bills were introduced into Congress, each tending to perpetuate the war-time government monopoly of all wireless communications. At once the American amateurs, more numerous than the British, and tidily and compactly organized in the National Wireless Association, attacked the idea of government monopoly as 'high handed and unjustified'.[1] Commercial interests were just as angry at the implied threat to the system of private enterprise, and there was a rapid counter-stroke. While the Secretary of the Navy was still extolling war experience, the Radio Corporation of America was founded in October 1919.

The new organization was a product of American national-ism, and among its articles of incorporation was the rule that 'no person shall be eligible for election as a director or officer of the Corporation who is not at the time of such election a citizen of the United States'. The international era of radio was formally brought to a close. The Corporation emphasized its 'American-ism' by criticizing British attempts to secure 'a substantial monopoly of world communication' and by acquiring the American interests of the British Marconi Company. Soon afterwards it gained control of the stations and assets of the American Marconi Company. Its first president was E. J. Nally, former vice-president and general manager of the American Marconi Company, and its first commercial manager was David Sarnoff.[2]

Neither Nally nor Sarnoff lacked faith in the future. The Radio Corporation of America was concerned primarily with commercial traffic, the sale of wireless apparatus, and marine radio engineering, but broadcasting had a place in this struc-ture of interests. Sarnoff was sure that his 'music box' would not only sell but would transform the daily life of millions of Americans: he anticipated that the Radio Corporation of America would sell a million 'music boxes' within three years. Some of his business rivals shared this faith. Harry P. Davis, the

[1] *Wireless Age*, Jan. 1919.
[2] The fullest contemporary statement of the American position is the *Report of the Federal Trade Commission on the Radio Industry*, Dec. 1923.

vice-president of the Westinghouse Company, for example, en-thusiastically encouraged experiments in broadcasting carried out by Dr. Frank Conrad, one of his engineers, in the spring of 1920.

Efforts . . . to develop radio telephony as a confidential means of communication [he believed] were wrong, and . . . instead its field is really one of wide publicity, in fact, the only means of instan-taneous collective communication ever devised. . . . Here was an idea of limitless opportunity if it could be 'put across'. . . . The natural fascination of its mystery, coupled with its ability to anni-hilate distance, would attract, interest, and open many avenues to bring happiness into human lives.[1]

Broadcasting was thus deliberately recognized as being more important than point-to-point communication.

It was Westinghouse, not the Radio Corporation of America, which led the way in organizing regular broadcasts in the United States. Dr. Frank Conrad's broadcasting station in Pittsburgh (KDKA), the direct successor of an experimental station first registered in the monthly bulletin of the Department of Com-merce in August 1916, was the first broadcasting station in the world. Its experimental transmissions were so popular that a local store began selling receiving sets to people who wished to listen. The result was a great extension of programmes. KDKA broadcast election results in November 1920 and by the end of the year had put on the air not only gramophone-record programmes but its own 'station band'; in January 1921 it broadcast its first church service and an after-dinner speech by Herbert Hoover. In August 1921 it broadcast a sports com-mentary on a baseball match, the Davis Cup competition, and a prize fight.

The Radio Corporation of America did not open its first broadcasting station until December of that year—it lasted for only a year—but in the meantime several other stations had been started. Nine went on the air in September 1921, 12 in October, 9 in November and 9 in December. In the first few months of 1922 the numbers increased dramatically—26 in January, 14 in February, 27 in March, and 88 in April. By the first of May there were 219 registered radio stations in the United States, broadcasting news bulletins, weather and market

[1] Quoted by Archer, *History of Radio*, pp. 199–200.

reports, concerts, lectures, and commentaries on outside events. In the month of May itself 99 new stations were started.[1]

'The rate of increase in the number of people who spend at least a part of their evening in listening-in is almost incomprehensible', a writer noted in the first issue of *Radio Broadcast* which appeared in that month.

To those who have recently tried to purchase receiving equipment, some idea of this increase has undoubtedly occurred, as they stood perhaps in the fourth or fifth row at the radio counter waiting their turn, only to be told when they finally reached the counter that they might place an order and it would be filled when possible. . . . The movement is probably not even yet at its height—it is still growing in some kind of geometrical progression. . . . It seems quite likely that before the movement has reached its height, before the market for receiving apparatus becomes approximately saturated, there will be at least five million receiving sets in this country.[2]

By the end of 1924 there were 530 American radio stations.[3] The dimensions of the American 'radio boom', as it began to be called, were making even Sarnoff's enthusiastic prophecies seem cautious and pessimistic. The manufacturers of radio transmitters, receivers, and accessories were in much the same position, as *Radio Broadcast* pointed out, that munition makers were when war broke out. 'Before the dealers knew what had happened, their shelves were empty. . . . Then as always experimenters set to work. In different cities all kinds and types of transmitters were created by radio shops, departmental stores, newspapers, furniture stores and similar companies. Anything that would speak was called a broadcasting station.'[4] The number of retail radio dealers had risen to 15,000 by the end of 1922.[5] From 1921 to 1923 the rate of increase in the radio manufacturing industry greatly exceeded that even in the flourishing automobile industry.[6] Sceptics talked of 'the novelty of radio

[1] Archer, *History of Radio*, p. 241. For a different set of figures, see H. L. Jome, op. cit., p. 70.

[2] *Radio Broadcast*, May 1922.

[3] Union Internationale de Radiophonie, *Monthly Bulletin*, No. 193, Feb. 1942, pp. 50–51.

[4] *Wireless World*, 9 Sept. 1922.

[5] *Annual Report* of the Board of Directors of the Radio Corporation of America for the Year ended 31 Dec. 1922.

[6] Jome, op. cit., p. 77, gives a graph of rates of growth in the automobile, phonograph, sporting goods, and radio industries in relation to all American industries.

wearing off', but in the words of a writer in the *Scientific American*, 'broadcasting has become so popular and its possibilities are so great that it can never become obsolete'.[1] As Sarnoff had predicted, from being an 'attic experiment' radio became a 'household utility'.

Almost from the start broadcasting in America was thought of as a 'mass communication'.[2] The 'lively arts', which sustained popular entertainment in America—the only 'arts' that really 'belonged' to America—were quickly turned into the mass media:[3] neither indifference nor contempt gave Americans immunity from them.[4] Initially, however, radio was not thought of as a medium for advertising. The first 'commercial' went on the air on 28 August 1922—ten minutes of station WEAF's radio time sold to a real-estate developer—yet not only Sarnoff but Herbert Hoover, the Secretary of the Department of Commerce, was opposed to advertising. At the first American Radio Conference in 1922 he stated that it was 'inconceivable that we should allow so great a possibility for service . . . to be drowned in advertising chatter'.[5]

High-minded opposition to advertising in the United States did not destroy the practice, largely because no reasonable alternative means of securing revenue for broadcasting companies was ever proposed. The methods later adopted in Britain—licensing and raising a levy on the sale of broadcasting receiver sets—were opposed by powerful interests and unpopular with the public. As a result 'driblets of advertising, most of it indirect . . . but still unmistakable' were 'floating through the ether every day. Concerts are seasoned here and there with a dash of advertising paprika.' 'More of this sort of thing', it was accepted,

[1] A. C. Lescarboura, 'The Gentle Art of Radio Broadcasting', in *Scientific American*, June 1922.

[2] The term was used in Oct. 1921 when the business order for the equipment of station WJZ (Newark) asked for 'the installation of a radio telephone for mass communication' (quoted Archer, *History of Radio*, p. 217).

[3] G. Seldes, *The Seven Lively Arts* (New York, 1957 edition), p. 10. This fascinating book, first published in 1924, was one of the first books to concern itself with what is now often called 'mass culture' and its problems. In a later book, *The Public Arts* (1936), Seldes further developed his terminology. 'The lively arts and the mass media are two aspects of the same phenomenon which I now call the "public arts".'

[4] G. Seldes, *The Great Audience* (1951), p. 4.

[5] Quoted by C. A. Siepmann, *Radio's Second Chance* (New York, 1946), p. 140. There were four important American Radio Conferences in 1922, 1923, 1924, and 1925.

'may be expected. And once the avalanche gets a good start, nothing short of an Act of Congress . . . will suffice to stop it.'[1]

As late as September 1925 a Congressman stated that he was about to introduce a Bill into Congress to abolish all advertising by radio,[2] but by then the mood had changed. *Radio Broadcast*, which had begun by criticizing the pressure of advertisers and the effects of advertising on broadcast programmes, itself capitulated. It went so far as to concede that 'the public will never get something for nothing, and so if they are to get a good musical program without paying a cent for the artists, it will probably be necessary to listen to the donor of the hour's entertainment'.[3] The process was rationalized: in retrospect it even seemed as if 'the commercial was needed to integrate radio completely into our everyday business of living'.[4]

This was a later verdict. During the first years of broadcasting experience it was not distaste for American advertising which influenced the first British critics of American broadcasting, but alarm at the 'chaos of the ether' in the United States. The multiplicity of radio stations and the scarcity of wavelengths led to interference and overlapping, 'a jumble of signals' and a 'blasting and blanketing of rival programmes'. Even in America itself, despite its tradition of free enterprise, there was pressure for government 'policing of the ether'.[5] The government's powers, which were based on an Act of 1912, were quite inadequate to control the new medium. A few Americans were even tempted to look with approval on the British Post Office.

The very speed of development in the United States was given as a reason for governmental action. 'The automobile was not an overnight development. It became an important factor in our transportation scheme. The radiophone, on the other hand, was developed into an everyday nation-wide convenience overnight.'[6] Radio 'traffic laws' were necessary. At the first National Radio Conference, held in February and March 1922, 'the general opinion was that radio communication is a public utility and as such should be regulated and controlled by the Federal Govern-

---

[1] *Radio Broadcast*, Nov. 1922.
[2] Archer, *History of Radio*, p. 363.
[3] *Radio Broadcast*, Oct. 1925.
[4] Seldes, *The Lively Arts*, p. 11.
[5] *Scientific American*, Aug. 1922.   [6] Ibid.

ment in the public interest'.[1] There was a difference of opinion, however, about what form the 'traffic laws' should take, amateurs arguing vehemently with representatives of commercial interests, and commercial interests becoming more and more divided amongst themselves.

Behind the problem of the 'chaos of the ether' there were all kinds of division of outlook. The struggle for wavelengths was a symptom of a more basic struggle. The reasons for the multiplicity of radio stations were economic rather than technical. The 'boom' induced established business men and would-be business men to turn to radio as a field of profitable investment. Often their businesses were 'not founded on logic', certainly not on long-term logic. 'While the radio boom persists, a few companies can well afford to maintain the radiophone broadcasting stations, but sooner or later other arrangements will have to be made.'[2] From the start the 'big radio men' had a considerable advantage over the smaller men, and in the short run as well as the long run the mortality rate of radio stations was high. Between the middle of March and the end of April 1923, 42 stations gave up their 'franchises'; in May 1923 there were 26, and in June 50.[3] The total number of new stations established and licensed up to August 1924 was 1,105: the total of discontinuances during the same period was 572. In other words, a little more than half the stations dropped out.[4] It is not surprising, therefore, that writers on radio should quickly discern tendencies making for 'nation-wide chains of broadcasting systems'.[5] The first 'network' broadcasts were in 1923 when WEAF linked up with stations as far away as Boston, Pittsburgh, and Chicago,[6] and by the summer of 1924 Hoover himself was expressing the opinion that broadcasting would eventually be organized into 'six or seven great national circuits'.[7]

The American radio industry as a whole was 'poorly financed, lacked direction, and suffered from tendencies to over-production'.[8] There was as much rivalry between makers of sets as there was between promoters of stations, and the thorny question of

[1] Ibid., June 1922: G. C. Davy, 'Uncle Sam and Radio'.
[2] Ibid.   [3] Archer, *History of Radio*, p. 312.
[4] Jome, op. cit., p. 71.   [5] *Scientific American*, Dec. 1922.
[6] Archer, *History of Radio*, p. 313; *Big Business and Radio*, p. 65.
[7] Ibid.   [8] *Scientific American*, Aug. 1922.

patents preoccupied both. The Radio Corporation of America, in particular, was the subject of many bitter attacks. When it embarked on a test case to protect its alleged patent rights in the winter of 1923, there were many complaints that 'should the injunction which is sought by the Radio Corporation be granted, it seems that every manufacturer in the country would be put out of business—excepting, of course, the Radio Corporation itself. It seems that a monopoly of the most grinding sort is the object of this firm.'[1] A few months later a Report of the Federal Trade Commission attacked the power of RCA 'to stifle competitors in the manufacture and sale of receiving sets, and to prevent all radio apparatus from being used for commercial radio broadcasting stations'.[2] The spokesmen of RCA were not content to defend: they counter-attacked with vigour and determination. David Sarnoff, in particular, was 'an indomitable fighter for any cause to which he set his face—and his iron jaw'.[3] He came to believe that the future of broadcasting rested on a 'few super-stations supported by the industry itself'.

As late as 1925 American broadcasting was still in a state of turmoil. Its internal conflicts were unresolved and attempts by the government to apply external pressure had failed. The Wireless Act of 1912 was the only Act on the statute book, and it contained no provisions for the regulation of an industry which did not really come into existence until almost ten years after the Act had been passed. Hoover's attempts to guide the industry into harmonious agreement reached an impasse, and 'radio broadcasting was in danger of destroying itself by the mad scramble of selfish interests'.[4] Even the question of who should pay the bills of radio broadcasting was still not finally settled. There were 5½ million wireless sets in the United States, nearly half the total number in the world, but they did not guarantee smooth and easy reception. You might 'pick up' 346 stations, but you might have difficulty in hearing one properly.[5]

It was not until the end of 1926 and the spring of 1927 that the constitutional pattern of American broadcasting took shape. In September 1926 the National Broadcasting Company of

---

[1] *Radio Broadcast*, Mar. 1923.   [2] Archer, *History of Radio*, p. 326.
[3] Ibid., p. 361.   [4] Ibid., p. 370.
[5] At the Radio Exhibition in Chicago in 1926 a lady who won the title 'Champion Woman Listener of the United States' had 'picked up' 346 American stations.

America was incorporated, the first of the giant broadcasting concerns; a few months later Congress at last passed a Radio Act and a Federal Radio Commission of five members met for the first time in March 1927. By then broadcasting in Britain had been fully institutionalized, and the Charter of the British Broadcasting Corporation was already a few months old.

Hoover could argue optimistically at the fourth Radio Conference that 'we are bringing a lusty child out of swaddling clothes without any infant discases',[1] but his remarks were much too cheerful to correspond to the facts. The fact that American experience served as a warning throughout the whole of this period is apparent in almost all the writings on radio on this side of the Atlantic. Burrows, for example, wrote in 1924 that 'it is an ill-wind that blows no one any good. Irritating though it had been for those who were alive to the possibilities of broadcasting to remain inactive whilst the subject was being freely discussed throughout the world, the American experience provided a valuable lesson. It showed the dangers which might result in a diversely populated country of a small area like our own if the go-as-you-please methods of the United States were copied.'[2] In 1926 Hamilton Fyfe, who had just visited the United States, wrote an article in the *Radio Times* on 'The Way they Live in America': it was mainly factual, but it emphasized that 'our programmes are decidedly of better quality'.[3] By then the argument had shifted. Concern for technical control was giving way to concern for standards and taste.

During the critical months of 1920 and 1921 when Britain was still lagging behind in pace of development, two British visitors of particular interest and importance crossed the Atlantic to find out what was happening there. The first was Godfrey Isaacs. He went there in November 1920. The second was F. J. Brown, an assistant secretary at the Post Office, who spent the winter of 1921–2 in the United States.[4] It would be an exaggeration to say that the former went to study business 'development'

---

[1] *Proceedings of the Fourth National Radio Conference*, 9–11 Nov. 1925 (Washington, 1926), p. 1.

[2] Burrows, op. cit., p. 56.

[3] *Radio Times*, 26 Nov. 1926.

[4] He later wrote a number of interesting articles about his visit. See 'The Story of Broadcasting in England' in *Radio Broadcast*, June 1925, and 'Broadcasting in Britain' in *London Quarterly Review*, Jan. 1926.

and the latter governmental 'regulation', but both visits produced results. Isaacs came back convinced of the need for British
business to strengthen its initiative in radio development; Brown
came back with a dossier of valuable information gleaned from
talks with American broadcasting interests and meetings of
Hoover's first Radio Conference, which Brown had attended as
an observer.[1]

This conference recommended *inter alia* that 'the Secretary of
Commerce should assign to each radio telephone broadcasting
station a permissible power based on the normal range of the
station' and that specific wavelengths should also be allocated.
It further recommended that 'direct advertising in radio broadcasting service be absolutely prohibited'. Brown listened and
learned. It is not difficult to detect the advice he gave about the
'lessons' in a reply made by the Postmaster-General to a question in the House of Commons in April 1922.

It would be impossible to have a large number of firms broadcasting. It would result only in a sort of chaos, only in a much more
aggravated form than that which arises in the United States, and
which has compelled the United States, or the Department over
which Mr. Hoover presides, and which is responsible for broadcasting, to do what we are now doing at the beginning, that is, to lay
down very drastic regulations indeed for the control of wireless
broadcasting.[2]

5. Writtle and its Rivals

IN one sense, of course, American broadcasting had the effect
of a stimulus. It proved beyond doubt not only that broadcasting was technically possible but that large numbers of
people were interested in it, people who might know nothing at
all about science. In opening a new station of the Radio Corpora-

---

[1] The report of this Conference was published by the U.S. Bureau of Navigation,
Department of Commerce, *Radio Service Bulletin*, No. 62, 1 May 1922.
[2] *Hansard*, vol. 152, col. 1869, 3 Apr. 1922.

tion of America in May 1923 Owen D. Young, the company's chairman, rightly claimed that broadcasting had appealed to the imagination of large numbers of people more than any other scientific development of the age: 'its ultimate effect on the educational, social, political and religious life of the country', he went on, 'is quite beyond our ability to prophesy'.[1] After thirty years of technical progress the social implications of wireless still remained exciting but uncertain. Everything was still 'new'. The first pioneers of broadcasting in Britain also shared this feeling of adventure into the unknown, of always being able, as one of them put it, to do things for the first time.[2] J. C. W. Reith was to couple the sense of adventure with a deep-rooted sense of responsibility, but he too shared the excitement of moving into what he called 'uncharted seas'. 'There were no sealed orders to open', he wrote in 1925. 'The commission was of the scantiest nature. Very few knew what broadcasting meant; none knew what it might become. A broadcasting service was expected, and had to be initiated and developed. We had to do it.'[3]

The members of the designs department at Writtle approached their new assignment to 'broadcast' a weekly half-hour 'programme' for amateurs with no sense of what the future was to contain. The first members of the Marconi Company to work at Writtle had moved there in 1920. Their numbers grew, but when the first 'broadcast' went on the air on 14 February 1922 they were still a bright young team with R. D. Bangay in charge and P. P. Eckersley the head of the experimental section. They were primarily interested in technical development, an activity which is usually carefully hidden away from the eyes and ears of the public. Eckersley himself has admitted that he and his colleagues were not 'particularly sorry' when the Post Office ordered the Chelmsford experimental 'broadcasts' to stop in 1920. The Chelmsford station had been too close to Writtle, and 'it interfered with reception tests'. The new 'call' in 1922 was interpreted mainly as a request to do another job of work—a job that would cut into spare time and for which no new funds were provided. The staff felt, not without reason, that

[1] Quoted Archer, *History of Radio*, p. 304.
[2] C. A. Lewis, *Broadcasting from Within* (1924), p. 1.
[3] J. C. W. Reith, *Broadcast Over Britain* (1925), p. 23.

they would be blamed if things went wrong but hardly noticed if things went right.[1]

Rather 'light-heartedly', therefore, the basic apparatus was put together on the spot. H. L. Kirke, later to be the head of the BBC's Research Department, and B. N. MacLarty, later to be head of the Design and Installation Department, built the transmitter, under Eckersley's direction, on a laboratory bench. Two field-station masts, 110 feet high, supported the aerial. An ex-army petrol-driven generator supplied the power. The microphones were of the carbon type such as are used in telephones. The whole enterprise was, as one of the research team has called it, 'an engineer's do'.[2] Moreover the first 'broadcasts' were technically unsatisfactory.

Even when the technical difficulties had been overcome, the 'programmes' themselves were formal and stereotyped. Gramophone records were the staple fare, and the first spoken comments were borrowed from the language of wireless telegraphy. 'Hullo CQ Hullo CQ This is Two Emma Toc, Writtle calling.' The Post Office insisted on a three-minute break—hardly a natural break—after each three minutes of transmission. What could have been done in such circumstances even by a 'programme executive'?

It was Eckersley's genius which transformed this unpromising situation. He was a brilliant engineer, but he was also, by accident, something quite different—a born entertainer. One evening, instead of playing all the gramophone records which his London office had provided, he began to talk. 'A certain ebullience, which often overcomes me when I have an audience, prompted a less formal attitude towards the microphone than was customary.'[3] The ebullience was appreciated, and a fan mail of fifty or more postcards asked him unanimously to 'do it again, we like it'. So began a remarkable series of programmes from the young men of Writtle, some of which were later to be developed in regular form by the BBC. The keynote was informality. R. T. B. Wynn, one of Eckersley's staff and later Chief Engineer of the BBC, has well described the early mood.

Some time on Tuesday afternoon the piano would be trundled

[1] Eckersley, op. cit., pp. 38 ff.
[2] Information collected for *London Calling*, 10 Oct. 1946.
[3] Ibid., p. 42.

into the hut, and we would receive a bunch of records—most of which were usually rejected as too highbrow! Programme planning was done at the 'Cock and Bull' up the road, about half an hour beforehand. We had artistic ambitions—for example we put on *Cyrano de Bergerac*, the first play ever to be broadcast in this country. I well remember our sitting around a table in my digs, reading our scripts (my part was to produce rustling leaves) with spoons held to our mouths in simulation of the hand microphones we had to use. There were more players than microphones, so much of the rehearsal consisted of practising the passing of a spoon from one to another at the right moment without dropping it. But our star was Eckersley. He'd go up to the microphone, and apparently without effort, be spontaneously funny for ten minutes at a time. He talked to our listeners as if he'd lived next door to them for years, and they loved it.[1]

The programmes once included a 'night of grand opera' pro-vided by one person—Eckersley himself. He not only sang the arias, but provided his own mock interruptions.

Always at the end of the half-hour programme there was a 'theme song'. Its words were improvisations on the theme of 'parting' and it was sung by Eckersley in a high tenor voice with an accompaniment vamped on an old piano.

Dearest, the concert's ended, sad wails the heterodyne.
You must switch off your valves, I must soon switch off mine.
Write back and say you heard me, your 'hook up' and where and how,
Quick! for the engine's failing, goodbye, you old low-brow.[2]

In such ways were the radio amateurs entertained as well as educated, and in such ways engineers were transformed into script writers and producers. The relative remoteness of Writtle was an advantage rather than a disadvantage at this stage, as was the shortage of funds. The former made for a feeling of 'esprit de corps'—for intimate and spontaneous gaiety; the latter forced the staff at Writtle to fall back on their own resources. Occasionally singers would go down to Writtle and sing from the studio. They were met at Chelmsford station, after being told beforehand that a Marconi Company repre-sentative would greet them just outside the ticket barrier and could 'be identified as the wearer of a black velours hat and a

[1] *London Calling*, 10 Oct. 1946.
[2] Eckersley, op. cit., p. 43.

navy-blue coat'.[1] On arriving at Writtle they would be given a 'try out' of their songs, and on leaving they were paid a nominal honorarium of £1.

Even this small cost was counted heavy in relation to the projected expenditure on broadcasting, and most of the Writtle programmes, like the apparatus, were 'home-made'. This was the primitive age of British broadcasting. It could not last, but for a brief time it enjoyed its own *élan* and it cast a powerful spell on the first British radio 'public'. The final programme from Writtle went on the air on 17 January 1923. Characteristically its farewell to its listeners included a toast drunk in water which was promoted to champagne by the sound of a pop gun.[2] By January 1923 BBC programmes had been on the air for several weeks.

Writtle was not the only station to go on the air in 1922 before the British Broadcasting Company was founded. Shortly after the first Writtle broadcast, permission was received by the Marconi Company to broadcast direct from London, from an experimental station at Marconi House in the Strand. The venture was to be strictly experimental: the first transmitting set was contained in a teak cabinet and housed in the small cinema theatre on the top floor of Marconi House. There were two desks, three telephones, a piano, a few music stands, and 'a signalling lamp which is alight when the station is operating' in this first broadcast 'studio', the walls and ceilings of which were draped with butter muslin. The first microphones were of the carbon granule type used in telephones. Occasionally the cinema was required for its original purpose, and the broadcasting team then had to work in the dark or watch demonstration films that they had seen many times before.[3] There were frequent arguments within the company as to where equipment should be stored and how often the cinema was to be placed at the broadcasters' disposal.[4]

Permission from the Post Office was at first hedged round with every kind of irksome qualification. The first 'broadcast' from 2LO, as the new station was known, was transmitted on 11 May, but early operations were tightly bound by red tape. At

[1] Letter of 10 Apr. 1922. Marconi Company Archives.
[2] Eckersley, op. cit., p. 46.
[3] L. Stanton Jefferies, 'Soap Box', in *The Popular Wireless Weekly*, 5 Oct. 1935.
[4] Letters exchanged by Burrows and R. H. White, 20 and 21 June 1922. Marconi Company Archives.

A.A.CAMPBELL SWINTON.
ELECTRICAL ENGINEER.

Telegraphic Address.
"DUNAMIS, LONDON."

TELEPHONE №2165.

66, Victoria Street,
London, S.W.

March 30 th 1896.

Dear Mr Preece.

I am taking the liberty of sending
to you with this note a young Italian of the name
of Marconi, who has come over to this country
with the idea of getting taken up a new system of
telegraphy without wires, &t which he has been
working. It appears to be based upon the use of
Hertzian waves, and Oliver Lodge's coherer, but
from what he tells me he appears to have got
considerably beyond what I believe other people
have done in this line.

It has occurred to me that you
might possibly be kind enough to see him and hear
what he has to say and I also think that what he
has done will very likely be of interest to you.

Hoping that I am not troubling you too
much.

Believe me,

Yours very truly,

A.A.C. Swinton

W.H.Preece Esq. C.B.

Guglielmo Marconi
101 Westport R?
Bayswater Bologna

7. Marconi's Introduction to Britain

8. The Writtle Pioneers

Left to right. Standing: B. N. MacLarty, H. L. Kirke, R. T. B. Wynn, H. J. Russell: *Seated:* F. W. Bubb, Noel Ashbridge, P. P. Eckersley, E. H. Trump, Miss E. M. Beeson

9. The Melba Microphone

Photo: G. E. Brant

10. An Early Wireless Receiving Set, assembled 1922–3

11. An Early Wireless Transmitter, 2 MT, Writtle, 1921

first no musical sounds could be broadcast: only speech was permitted. The power of the station was limited to 100 watts. The times of broadcast transmission were severely restricted to not more than one hour a day either between 11 o'clock and 12

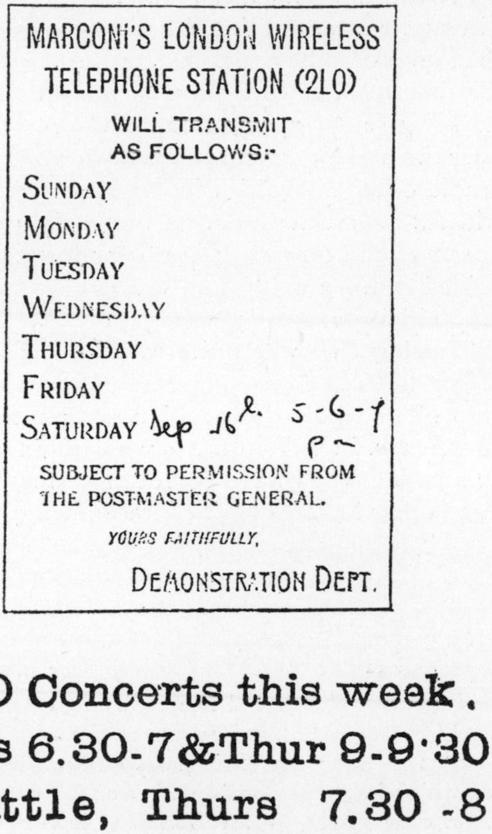

MARCONI'S LONDON WIRELESS
TELEPHONE STATION (2LO)

WILL TRANSMIT
AS FOLLOWS:-

SUNDAY

MONDAY

TUESDAY

WEDNESDAY

THURSDAY

FRIDAY

SATURDAY Sep 16th. 5-6-7 p.m.

SUBJECT TO PERMISSION FROM
THE POSTMASTER GENERAL.

YOURS FAITHFULLY,

DEMONSTRATION DEPT.

2LO Concerts this week.
Tues 6.30-7 & Thur 9-9·30
Writtle, Thurs 7.30 -8

12. Invitations to listen, 1922

o'clock in the morning or between 2 o'clock and 4 o'clock in the afternoon. At the end of every seven minutes' transmission there had to be a three-minute interval during which the 'operator' was enjoined to listen on his wavelength for official messages to tell him if for some reason the programme could not go on. No such messages were ever received, and this absurd regulation may be compared with the 'red flag' rule imposed on early motorists.[1]

[1] A letter of 7 Sept. 1922 to Burrows from R. H. White of the Independent

Many of these restrictions were either removed or relaxed during the early summer of 1922. Music was soon broadcast as regularly as speech, and from 24 June onwards 'concerts'— 'musical evenings'—were broadcast by small 'ensembles'. These became the staple broadcasting fare. Both songs and instrumental items were conventional and stereotyped, particularly after it had soon become apparent that the approval of listeners invariably increased in direct proportion to the familiarity of what was being sung or played. Duets were technically 'impossible under the present system of microphones',[1] and there were innumerable other difficulties in presenting particular instruments without too much distortion. Some of the notes appended by engineers to the typescript evening programmes have candid pencilled comments—'Piano was like sitting right under a very tinny old instrument'; 'tenor quite unrecognizable, last note of "Passing By" was quite m.f. instead of p.p.'; 'fiddle sounded just like oboe or concertina';[2] 'not a soft note in the whole show. The whole transmission was almost too bad to be borne on the ears. I tried to tone down without effect as directly I got the metallic tone away everything seemed 100 miles off.'[3] There were other hazards besides transmitting difficulties.

With the singer facing the piano it becomes necessary for the M.C. who is checking the singing to go right round in front of her, using the long lead to the head phones for this purpose. This practice has two defects:

1. That other artistes have a most unfortunate habit of tripping over the 'phone leads and nearly breaking the M.C.'s neck.
2. That before the M.C. can return to the switches at the end of an item the singer has often passed a remark on her performance which becomes audible all over the country. With fresh artistes every night we are bound to have these asides unless the switches are immediately at hand to the M.C.[4]

The humour of early broadcasting was somewhat played down at 2LO. Burrows himself was a cautious man, extremely anxious to please, and his superiors also were determined to 'say

Research Department (Marconi Company Archives) stressed that the broadcasts still had to conform to this G.P.O. regulation.

[1] Letter of 18 Oct. 1922. Marconi Company Archives.
[2] Notes on a broadcast of 1 Nov. 1922. Marconi Company Archives.
[3] No date. Marconi Company Archives.
[4] Burrows to R. H. White, 18 Dec. 1922. Marconi Company Archives.

nothing which might offend any one'. Yet on two occasions at least Burrows was chided for introducing 'contentious matter' into a broadcast. Once the *Daily Herald* had complained that 'Marconi House was being used for political purposes' by broadcasts being sent out favourable to municipal reform candidates in London; on another occasion there were complaints about the reading of extracts from *The Times* which discussed the situation in Egypt and Ireland.[1]

The decision to play safe was determined entirely by Burrows and the Marconi Company: it was not influenced, as it was later, from 'above', when the same question confronted the BBC. As it was, 2LO was drawn into the discussion of 'responsibility' months before the BBC was founded. The 'frolic' of Writtle was replaced by the 'seriousness' of 2LO, and Burrows was not very happy when on Tuesday evenings 2LO had to close down so that the voices of Writtle could be heard loud and clear. The removal of the restriction on the power of 2LO added to its influence. So long as it was a 100-watt station, it could not be heard consistently outside a thirty- or forty-mile radius. Soon after it opened, however, its power was increased to $1\frac{1}{2}$ kilowatts. This meant that it could now be heard in many parts of the country. By the autumn of 1922, when the BBC was formed and took over the station, 2LO had a 'public' of about 30,000 licensed 'listeners-in' and a total audience of about 50,000 people, including wireless enthusiasts as far away as the Shetland Islands. Even its three-minute breaks had met with some signs of approval. 'You will be pleased to hear how much I have enjoyed your news of the air race', wrote one lady listener. 'I have enjoyed equally the three-minute intervals, which have given me time to reach the kitchen and baste the joint for dinner.'[2]

Not all 2LO's programmes were of the 'musical evening' type. The very first broadcast on 11 May, arranged at the suggestion of the *Daily Mail*, consisted of a 'running commentary' (the term was not yet used) on the prize fight at Olympia between Kid Lewis and Georges Carpentier. The first radio story was read by Pett Ridge of the *Daily News* in September. The suggestion came from the *Daily News* itself and was proclaimed as 'a first attempt here to do anything like the

[1] Letter of 1 Nov. 1922. Marconi Company Archives.
[2] Burrows, op. cit., pp. 60–61.

"Bed-time Stories" we have heard so much about from America'.[1]

On the evening of 7 October 1922 the Prince of Wales broadcast

13. A Royal Broadcast

an address to boy scouts, scattered throughout the country, who had not been able to attend a national rally held at the Alexandra

[1] The Assistant Editor of the *Daily News* suggested to Burrows that 'I do not think you would consider it an extravagant advertisement of the *Daily News* for us merely to announce at the beginning and the end that Mr. Pett Ridge would read one of the series of *Little Tales* from the *Daily News*, which he himself has written'. Letter of 4 Sept. 1922. Marconi Company Archives.

Palace that afternoon. This was the first royal occasion in the history of broadcasting, and it was stage-managed with efficiency and deference. A rehearsal was held at York House, at which the chief engineer of the Post Office was also present, and at the Alexandra Palace rally the Prince spoke to the 50,000 scouts assembled there through a similar microphone to that which he later used in his evening broadcast. The arrangements for amplification at the Alexandra Palace were generally thought to be superior to those ever made before: 'this was the first occasion on which so great a number of persons had been able to hear simultaneously and clearly in the open air the voice of a member of the Royal Family'.[1] The broadcast itself was regarded as an unqualified success. In all parts of Britain wireless societies organized 'listener-in' groups of boy scouts. The Prince was presented with a 'brief popular description of the principles underlying wireless telegraphy and broadcasting', a souvenir booklet, and a wireless receiving set, and Burrows was presented with the typescript of his preliminary announcement of the Prince's speech and a royal autograph.

Programmes of this kind were given the utmost possible publicity in the Press, particularly in the *Daily Mail*. The question of publicity for 'routine' programmes was, however, a little more complicated. At first there were no announcements, and the mention of Marconi House was expressly forbidden by the Post Office. Postcards were sent by the company advising registered listeners of forthcoming attractions. Later a few newspapers began to advertise programmes, the *Daily Mail* again leading the way. A few provincial newspapers, notably the *Liverpool Courier*, were quick to see the interest of the new medium, and the news editor was informed by telephone of the programmes a day before they went on the air. Burrows, a former journalist himself, enjoyed co-operating with the Press and established particularly close relations with the specialized wireless journals. At the end of 1922 there were four of them— *Wireless World*, *Amateur Wireless*, *The Popular Wireless Weekly*, and *The Broadcaster*.

Public broadcasts, however, represented only one side of the Marconi Company's work in the spring and summer of 1922.

[1] This account is based on a bundle of letters from the Marconi Company Archives.

'Demonstrations' were also arranged for the benefit of special audiences gathered together by outside bodies—most frequently hospitals and wireless societies—at garden parties or fêtes. Each of these transmissions was specially planned with the interests of the audience in mind, and Marconi Company engineers

Do You Want to Know Anything About

BROADCASTING?

A SPECIAL DEMONSTRATION OF

WIRELESS TELEGRAPHY & TELEPHONY
will take place

ON THURSDAY, JUNE 22ND,
at the

CENTRAL HALL, HIGH STREET, PECKHAM.

SPEECH and MUSIC will be sent out by MARCONI'S
and several other Stations and made audible to all.

Short Descriptions will be given by those who already possess
Wireless Apparatus, and there will also be a large collection of
different types of instruments.

Would you like to hear about Wireless from a Woman's View?

THE EVENING
will be spent in explaining the action of Wireless Instruments briefly
and then

Demonstrating on Actual Broadcast Signals
Both Speech and Morse.

You will have an opportunity of examining many instruments
and of asking questions.

This Demonstration is being held under the auspices of the Wireless and
Experimental Association at

THE CENTRAL HALL, HIGH STREET, PECKHAM
THURSDAY, JUNE 22ND, 1922.

ADMISSION, 5d. and 9d.   *Refreshments.*
J. BRYANT, 9, South Street, Greenwich, S.E. 10

14. A wireless demonstration

installed and handled the necessary receiving apparatus. Post Office authorization had to be granted for each individual broadcast, and sometimes it seemed to be given or withheld somewhat arbitrarily.[1] A complete list still survives of the 'demonstration' broadcasts given between 1 July and 21 December 1922. One of them—complete with cornet and piccolo solos—was arranged at Burrows's house in Wood Green.[2] The sponsoring bodies included Hampstead Garden Suburb, the

[1] Letter of 22 Mar. 1922. Marconi Company Archives.
[2] 24 Nov. 1921. Marconi Company Archives.

Chichester Red Triangle Club, Cardiff Y.M.C.A., St. Peter's Church, Tooting, University College, London, and the National Association of Supervising Electricians. Small fees were charged, along with incidental expenses which, as was carefully explained by Burrows, could 'probably be reduced a little if you are able to provide our demonstrator with two fully charged six-volt accumulators of forty ampere-hour capacity, as the railway companies have developed an unhappy knack of charging heavily for these'.[1] Burrows was the impresario at most of these 'demonstrations', often following up the display of the wonder of wireless by delivering 'a popular chat, lasting about twelve minutes'.[2] His services as an outside speaker were much in demand late in 1922, and he always took the opportunity to dwell on the 'romance of the new medium'.[3]

Throughout the whole life of the pre-BBC 2LO Burrows was the chief influence. Amiable, good-tempered, a little fussy, somewhat lacking in incisiveness and humour, easy to caricature, he was to be the first Director of Programmes of the BBC, known familiarly to thousands of people as 'Uncle Arthur'. Already when the BBC was founded he knew what broadcasting was. He had anticipated its development and he was familiar with its problems. On the technical side of radio he was not an expert, but his letters in 1922 reveal that he was already aware of two important considerations bearing on radio technique. First, good acoustics were indispensable to good broadcasting. The Marconi House cinema was heavily draped, but broadcasts from it often sounded as if they were coming from 'an empty room or a long corridor with polished walls'. Justice was never done even to his favourite set of tubular bells. 'It is evident to me', he concluded, 'that we have to face immediately several problems requiring solution by acoustical rather than electrical experts.'[4] Second, improved control of modulation by the engineers was a necessity, particularly if music were to be broadcast at all effectively. 'No two engineers have the same idea of musical balance and not being on the spot it is difficult for them to say whether the amount of piano coming through is

[1] Letter of 7 Sept. 1922. Marconi Company Archives.
[2] Letter of 7 July 1922. Marconi Company Archives.
[3] For an account of one of his addresses see *London Rotarian*, 6 Sept. 1922.
[4] Letter of 30 June 1922 to Colonel Simpson, Joint General Manager. Marconi Company Archives.

correct or not.'[1] A new relationship was necessary between the M.C. or producer and the engineer.

The quality of broadcasting was always of special importance to Burrows during these experimental months. He thought that his own voice was particularly well adapted to the new medium: he carefully looked around for people and instruments with what he felt was the same quality. He also scanned American radio magazines to find out what was happening there. 'We note from several photographs of American broadcasting stations', he remarked, for example, in one letter, 'that not one of them uses a conical horn to the transmitter [microphone] but that with one exception a small hollow cylinder is employed.'[2]

On non-technical matters he was quick to appreciate the need for adequate staff with qualifications other than those in engineering. As early as January 1922 he wrote to H. W. Allen, the joint manager of the Marconi Company, that broadcast concerts should be conducted 'in what I will term professional style as distinct from the Engineers' Programme work with which we have been hitherto accustomed'.[3]

Garden Fête

In aid of the
ARTHUR PEARSON
MEMORIAL FUND
(Registered under the Blind Persons Act, 1920)

at

St. JOHN'S LODGE (Inner Circle),
Regent's Park, N.W.

(ST. DUNSTAN'S HEADQUARTERS), on

FRIDAY and SATURDAY
JULY 7th and 8th, 1922

H.R.H. THE

Duke of Connaught, K.G.

will open the Fête on the First Day at 3 p.m., and

Dame Margaret Lloyd George
on the Second Day at 2.30 p.m.

Grand Theatrical Entertainment by leading Stars	Marconi Demonstration of Broadcasted Music	Crystal Gazing and Character Delineation
Dancing in the Grecian Garden	Monster Lucky Tub	Countless other Attractions
STRING BAND OF H.M. COLDSTREAM GUARDS		THE ST. DUNSTAN'S BLIND ORCHESTRA

Gates Open 2.30 p.m. First Day, and 2 p.m. Second Day

Admission - 5s. First Day ; 2s. 6d. Second Day

Tickets may be obtained from the Fête Secretary, St. John's Lodge, Regent's Park, N.W., or at St. Dunstan's Sales Depot, 155 Regent St., W.; or you can pay at the Gate on the Day

Adams (Printers) Ltd., Springdale Road, Stoke Newington, N.16

15. Wireless at a Fête

He stressed at the same time the value of broadcasting as a medium not only for music but for the transmission of news. In June 1922 he pressed for the appointment of a musical director, 'having not necessarily wireless experience but technical tendencies, sufficient grace of manner to make himself at home with well-known artists, and what is equally important an excellent

---

[1] Burrows to R. H. White, 18 Dec. 1922. Marconi Company Archives.
[2] Letter of 30 June 1922. Marconi Company Archives.
[3] Letter of 31 Jan. 1922. Marconi Company Archives.

telephone voice'.[1] He would also have to know something about the business side of music. As a result of Burrows's initiative L. Stanton Jefferies, already employed on the business side of the Marconi Company, was appointed Musical Director of the Company in the late summer of 1922. It seemed 'an extraordinary situation', almost Gilbertian, to be musical director of a wireless company, particularly when told to make sure that the artistes were either not paid or were given only nominal sums, but Jefferies greatly enjoyed his new work.[2]

Burrows was always in the background. 'Now that we are commencing to pay artistes nominal fees', he wrote to Jefferies in November 1922, 'I am satisfied that the time has come when we should dictate to them in a diplomatic way what style of song it is in the interests of all that they should sing. It has to be brought home to these people that they must adapt their artistry to the limitations of the wireless circuit if they hope to create the most favourable impression upon their vast audience.' He added that the vast audience had 'but a low proportion of persons who habitually attend the Albert, Queen's and Wigmore Halls and such other places of high-class musical entertainment'. In its broadcasts the Marconi Company should include a large number of items 'of a really popular character' but it should also try to 'lift' the public above its 'present standard of musical appreciation'.[3]

A few weeks before Christmas 1922, after the BBC had been formed, Burrows wrote to Isaacs, the managing director of the Marconi Company, 'respectfully to submit for your consideration' a statement relating to the future of broadcasting as a whole.[4] He began by setting out arguments relating to the urgent need for a bigger broadcasting staff. He and his colleagues, he pointed out, had worked for between eleven hours and seventeen hours a day during the previous few weeks. They were overwhelmed by the magnitude of their commitments. At the outset most of them, including Burrows himself, had been members of the staff of the publicity department of the Marconi Company. They had had to combine office work with the daily

---

[1] Burrows to H. W. Allen, 23 June 1922. Marconi Company Archives.
[2] See L. S. Jefferies, loc. cit.
[3] Burrows to Jefferies, 29 Nov. 1922.
[4] Burrows to Isaacs, 3 Dec. 1922.

operations of a broadcasting station. A specialist broadcasting staff was indispensable to the infant BBC if it was to do its work properly. Moreover, artistes would have to be paid regular fees for their performances and money would have to be set aside for equipment. Even his favourite 'tubular bells' had had to be hired by 2LO because the cost of buying them—between £17 and £20—was considered exorbitant. Burrows also asked Isaacs about his own position in relation to the Marconi Company and the new BBC. Could he continue to play a 'dual role'?

This last inquiry was answered soon afterwards when Burrows was appointed Director of Programmes of the BBC. He plunged himself into his new duties with enthusiasm. A few days later he wrote to Jefferies, 'For wireless to succeed everything must go with a bang, there must be no periods of silence in which one is compelled to listen to morse signals heterodyned by the carrier wave. Your programmes must be prepared beforehand down to the last detail and must be adhered to except in the case of the absence of an artiste, and the artiste must be ready to take up the running.' If any one had done the running in 1922, it was Burrows himself. While Writtle improvised, he ran round and round trying 'to drill everyone into a routine at the earliest possible moment'.[1]

The Marconi Company did not have a complete monopoly of British broadcasting in 1922.[2] Two other firms, each with American associations, were particularly anxious to stake their independent claims. The first was Metropolitan-Vickers in Manchester, the second Western Electric in Birmingham.

The Metropolitan-Vickers Electrical Company, now Associated Electrical Industries (Manchester) Ltd., was the successor of British Westinghouse, which had been founded by George Westinghouse, the promoter of the American company of the same name, in 1899.[3] The company's works were in Trafford

---

[1] Burrows to Jefferies, 11 Dec. 1922.

[2] Nor did it seek to encourage listeners not to listen to the concerts from The Hague. Announcements were sometimes made that 2LO was closing down 'in order that it may not interfere in any way with the Dutch concert'. Letter of 3 Aug. 1922. Marconi Company Archives.

[3] There is a jubilee history, *1899–1949. Metropolitan-Vickers Electrical Co. Ltd.* (1949). I have been able, however, to make use of valuable archive material in the following section.

Park at Manchester, and were primarily concerned with the manufacture of heavy electrical equipment and steam turbines. Valves were produced for the first time during the war, according to specifications set out by the Admiralty Signal School at Portsmouth and by Captain Round. A. P. M. (later Sir Arthur) Fleming, head of the research department, was largely responsible for the development of research activities at Trafford Park and he was keenly interested in radio. In 1921 he visited America, studying the radio station at Detroit, the Pittsburgh station set up by the American Westinghouse Company, and factories producing cheap radio equipment. On his return to Britain, and with the full approval of his managing director, Captain R. S. Hilton, he opened an experimental transmitting station with a power of 50 watts in the company's research department. The departmental conference room was converted into a studio; it was connected by festoons of wire to a tiny transmitter-room under a staircase. More wires led to a cage-type aerial slung between the top of the water tower and the top of the main building.[1] A smaller transmitting and receiving station was built in Fleming's home at Hale six miles away.

In addition to being managing director of Metrovick, Captain Hilton was a director of the Radio Communication Company which was formed after the end of the war and was entirely engaged in the marine radio business. For this and other reasons —not least the tremendous power of the Marconi Company— the two concerns decided to pool their patents and to reach an agreement about the sale and manufacture of radio receivers.[2] In February 1922 Fleming visited the factories of the Radio Communication Company: a few weeks later Basil Binyon, a director of the Radio Communication Company, visited Trafford Park. On 30 March 1922 Fleming and Binyon together went to see F. J. Brown of the Post Office, who had just returned from his American visit. They discussed without commitment the possibilities of a new broadcasting enterprise, and the following day Fleming formally wrote to Brown asking for permission to carry out broadcasts, including 'music, speeches, recitals and such news as you may permit'.

[1] Notes written by J. S. P. Paton of the Metropolitan-Vickers Research Department. A.E.I. (Manchester) Ltd. Archives.
[2] *Electrical Review*, 2 June 1922.

The arguments used had been carefully rehearsed with Binyon and likely objections had been taken into account. Some of the notes of these discussions still survive. Various 'reasons for broadcasting' were set out. It was deliberately stated that this was 'not a blatant advertising scheme' and that although the 'build-up of a market for sets' was important, 'broadcasting forms a most important social activity and should not be prevented, though it may be necessary to impose some limits'. Reference was made to educational broadcasts in the United States, and a cryptic but telling note was added in pencil: 'Moscow soon'.[1]

In his formal letter Fleming took up some of these points. He referred to the successful broadcasts of the American Westinghouse Company, the opportunities for research and technical development which experience of a British broadcasting station would provide, the possible market for radio sets which all radio manufacturers would share, and the likely canalization of amateur interest and enthusiasm. The last of these, he argued, would diminish 'the disturbing activities [of amateurs] in connection with the transmission of radio signals which at present is done from a large number of different centres'. He said that his company wished to erect two broadcasting stations, each with a power of 3 kilowatts, one in Manchester and one in Slough. They would broadcast each weekday between 4 and 5 o'clock in the morning and 7.30 and 10 o'clock in the evening. On Sundays they would broadcast for shorter periods 'in order to suit the public demand for church services or special music'. The hours would be the same for each of the stations, but the wavelengths would be sufficiently different to avoid mutual interference. Fleming assured the Post Office that his company would employ its facilities 'to the best public interest'. It would produce and supply receiving sets and would be prepared 'to undertake the initial licensing and registration of such apparatus'. He remarked that he was sure that if permission were granted 'a similar public demand for broadcasting will arise in this country' as had already arisen in the United States.[2] If the Post Office granted permission to a number of stations, he hoped

---

[1] Typewritten notes, *Broadcasting, Case for G.P.O.* A.E.I. (Manchester) Ltd. Archives.

[2] The letter is printed in full in *A.E.I. News*, Feb. 1948.

that there would be no 'geographical allocation of areas' but instead a limitation on the days of working for each group of stations and the preparation of an agreed schedule of hours.

The Post Office received one other application for permission to broadcast in March, five applications in April, and fifteen in May.[1] The Metropolitan-Vickers application, therefore, was treated as one of a group. The reply in each case was that 'the ether is already full'. Almost immediately, therefore, the Metrovick application was quickly caught up in the negotiations between the radio manufacturers and the Post Office which led up to the formation of the BBC and which are described in detail in the next chapter.

Experimental but regular broadcasts were made from the Manchester Metrovick station 2ZY, the first of them on 16 May. Official broadcasts did not start until 15 November, the day after the BBC had officially taken charge of national broadcasting. A month before this, however, a 700-watt transmitter had been built and installed at Trafford Park by the Radio Communication Company. Power was subsequently steadily increased to $1\frac{1}{2}$ kilowatts.

As at Writtle, the men running the new Manchester station were members of the staff of the 'development' department. The man in charge of the design and operation of the station was H. G. Bell, later chief engineer and manager of the Stretford and District Electricity Board. Major Buckley was concerned with technical arrangements in the studio, and he experimented effectively with new and more sensitive types of microphones. At first, carbon granule microphones were used—of the kind employed by 2LO—but, at a later date, experiments were made with 'photophone' instruments employing the principle of reflecting light on to a selenium cell. The 'photophones' greatly improved the quality of reception of music, but their large dimensions were a great disadvantage. Further experiments continued with electromagnetic microphones with oil or grease damping. Improvements in transmission were always associated with developments in the construction of receivers, and an experimental laboratory was set up at Trafford Park which in the autumn of 1922 produced a marketable Cosmos crystal type radiophone for £4. 10s. A few months later the

[1] Post Office Archives.

price had fallen to £3. 10s., and a two-valve cabinet receiving
set was priced at £26. 10s.

A long, interesting, and informative research department
Report was prepared by Metropolitan-Vickers and concluded
in July 1923. It is entitled *Report on the Development of Broadcasting at the Temporary Manchester Station* and it demonstrates
both the sheer volume of radio experiments carried out by the
company in 1922 and 1923 and the rapid progress made. Many

16. A Wireless Cabinet

of the problems which were worrying Burrows and Marconi
House were absorbing the energies of research engineers at
Manchester. Experiments were being carried out not only with
microphones and receiving sets but with studio design and
arrangement, the balance of sound between different instruments and persons in broadcasts of music, and what was called
in the Report 'control'—microphone switching and modulation
control and inter-communication between the studio and the
transmission room.

Part VII of the Report was concerned with 'programmes'. It
stated in the very first sentence that between March and August
1922 all available printed programmes of American broadcasting stations, and in particular of the four Westinghouse
stations, were being studied in detail at Trafford Park. The

main conclusions drawn were that musical programmes should be carefully 'segregated into distinct types so that the public would know beforehand on what nights to expect programmes to suit certain tastes', that gramophone records could be used in educational as well as entertainment programmes,[1] that reliable information on 'live' subjects—that is questions of the moment—should be given by lecturers of standing from universities and other places, that news should always be up to date, and that children's programmes should be both popular and educational.

Throughout the whole Report the claims of education were taken very seriously. In music as much as in words it was anticipated that 'the standard of broadcast programmes should be much higher than that of the American transmission'. Finally it was suggested that there should be a 'weekly printed programme for one or more British broadcasting stations'. It should contain photographs of personalities as well as details of the broadcasts of the coming week and space should always be reserved for listeners' letters, opinions gathered from 'the unseen audience'. 'No pains should be spared to make such a publication of the best possible quality, both in artistic design, careful layout . . . printing and quality of paper used.'[2]

The last of these suggestions anticipated by a few months the first appearance of the *Radio Times*. Its formulation in such clear-cut terms demonstrates how quickly ideas on broadcasting began to crystallize once experience had been acquired. The experience was, of course, far wider than that of either Manchester or Pittsburgh. By July 1923 the BBC was a going concern and 2ZY was part of its network.

Metropolitan-Vickers, in association with the Radio Communication Company, was almost the only large-scale concern able to compete with the Marconi Company in the radio development of 1922. Among the reasons given by Fleming in 1922 for the inauguration of broadcasting by the Metropolitan-Vickers Company was 'to give us a popular standing as a radio power'. Questions of power were to dominate the talks between the radio companies which led up to the formation of the BBC. In these talks, however, another large concern was represented

[1] Reference was made to a recent book by Percy A. Scholes, *How to Listen* (1923).
[2] A.E.I. (Manchester) Ltd. Archives.

—the Western Electric Company. It entered the British field after both the Marconi Company and Metropolitan-Vickers had established their positions, but it had already played an important part in the development of American broadcasting. Indirectly it represented the manufacturing side of the power-ful 'Bell' group of America.

It was not until October 1922 that the Western Electric Company assembled adequate 500-watt transmitting apparatus in a third-floor laboratory at Oswaldestre House in Norfolk Street, London. On 8 November 1922 Frank (later Sir Frank) Gill, the president of the Institution of Electrical Engineers and a key figure in the 1922 commercial talks, broadcast an appeal from this station (2WP) on behalf of the combined campaign of the King's Fund and the London hospitals.[1] In some respects the new station was better equipped than its rivals to broadcast music. The Western Electric Company of America had devised a microphone with a stretched steel diaphragm which would receive the highest notes of a soprano without causing any blurring.[2] It was this microphone which was used by 2WP. 'Your microphone is grand,' delighted listeners wrote to the Western Electric office, 'your carrier wave is almost undetectable and beautifully smooth.'

Before competitive rivalry could be pushed very far, however, the British Broadcasting Company was formed, and Gill under-took to transfer the Western Electric equipment lock, stock and barrel to Birmingham, which it was intended would be one of the first provincial stations. The equipment was dismantled and dispatched in steam lorries to the Midlands. Broadcasting from 5IT, the new Witton studio in the works of the General Electric Company, began on the evening of Wednesday 15 November. The first item on the programme was a concert, and from 11 o'clock onwards general election results were broadcast. There was a rush of congratulations and many favourable press com-ments that everything had been accomplished without a hitch. The broadcasts had been received in Copenhagen and Paris as well as the Midlands.[3] Behind the scenes, however, things had

---

[1] R. Appleyard, 'How Broadcasting Reached the Midlands' (typescript of 1924 in the Archives of Standard Telephones and Cables Ltd. Standard Telephones and Cables Ltd. was the successor of Western Electric); A. E. Thompson, 'The Silver Jubilee of Broadcasting', in *Standard News*, June 1948.

[2] Burrows, op. cit., p. 65.   [3] The *Birmingham Gazette*, 8 Jan. 1923.

not been so calm. Because of dense fog the steam lorries arrived in Birmingham a day late. On the evening of the first broadcast overheating developed in the motor-generator set and A. G. L. Mason, one of the engineers, had to spend the whole evening in the basement with a grease gun.

The story of 5IT is soon bound up with the bigger story of the BBC. By the time that the Company was founded, enthusiasm was as great in the provinces as in London. Regional and civic pride were being harnessed as well as curiosity. Ten days before the 5IT studio was opened, a wireless demonstration from London was arranged for the citizens of Bristol by the Marconi Company. Sir William Noble, a member of the Broadcasting Committee and one of the first Directors of the BBC, spoke to Bristol from Marconi House. The Lord Mayor of Bristol, Alderman Cook (later Sir Ernest Cook), spoke from Bristol, recalling how as a young man he had helped Graham Bell in explaining the telephone to the citizens of Bristol. The Lord Mayor Elect of London replied from the Guildhall. In three London halls 830 people, each with headphones, heard the experimental broadcasts. The chairman in one of the halls was F. J. Brown of the Post Office.[1]

To mix metaphors, all waves were crossing on this occasion. There was a certain symbolism in this. November 1922 was the month when the BBC nominally took over control of the air. But the future was still uncertain. The guests of the Lord Mayor of Bristol heard only morse signals when they were desperately longing to hear the spoken word. The future of the BBC was even less certain than the future of broadcasting. Would it be able not only to profit from the experience of the past but to ensure that broadcasting became an established and universally recognized service? Before the question can be considered at all, the steps leading up to the formation of the BBC must be examined one by one.

[1] There is a good account of the occasion in the *Western Daily Press and Bristol Mirror*, 30 Jan. 1945.

III

THE FORMATION OF THE BRITISH BROADCASTING COMPANY 1922

=====

The really vital point of control seems to have caused little comment or suggestion so far. Yet, on the assumption that the public takes eagerly to the new method of communication, it is a matter of supreme importance that the judges of what is to be communicated should command a good name.

Manchester Guardian, 15 August 1922

1. The Post Office Proposes

F. J. BROWN was the Post Office official most directly concerned with the organization of broadcasting. The chief permanent official, Sir Evelyn Murray, the secretary of the Post Office, had been appointed to this position just after the outbreak of war in 1914. He remained there until 1934 and exercised an important if often negative influence after the BBC had been formed.[1] He took the chair at the first conference on 'wireless telephony' held at the Post Office on 18 May 1922, and intervened on several occasions during the talks between the commercial companies which followed this meeting. He had no interest in broadcasting, however, and months later told Reith that concerts were 'not his line'. It was Brown who steered the negotiations and served as the leading spokesman of the Post Office point of view.

He was the Post Office representative on the Imperial Communications Committee, and it was his visit to the United States in the spring of 1922 which provided the requisite background of information and experience to enable the Post Office to evolve a broadcasting policy.[2] He told the Sykes Committee in 1923 that he had been 'in the thick of the whole business of broadcasting from its inception' and that the first document relating to broadcasting in the Post Office archives was a letter he had written from Washington early in 1922 describing what was happening on that side of the Atlantic. Like Reith, he was both a member of the Sykes Committee and a leading witness. Later in the proceedings, a fellow member of the Sykes Committee suggested bluntly that if official etiquette were swept on one side Brown was 'the official policy of the Post Office'. Modestly—and correctly—Brown replied 'No, I am not.'[3] He was always correct, but his own evidence before the Committee

---

[1] Murray wrote a useful account of the work of the Post Office in a book with that title published in 1927.

[2] See above, pp. 67–68.

[3] *Oral evidence of F. J. Brown before the Sykes Committee, 3 May 1923.

went far to substantiate his fellow member's assertion. Until his retirement from the Post Office in 1925 he was one of the leading figures in the history of broadcasting.

Of course, the technical side of broadcasting demanded expert knowledge and the Post Office could draw on the services of engineers of considerable experience. E. H. Shaughnessy of the Engineering Department of the Post Office served as Post Office spokesman at meetings of radio societies and experimenters. The engineering department had been founded in 1870 when the telegraphs were taken over by the Post Office, and Shaughnessy belonged to a distinguished family of telegraph engineers.[1] One of its chief officers in 1922 was F. G. Loring who had the title of Inspector of Wireless Telegraphy. Brown worked closely with these men. On the legal side R. W. (later Sir Raymond) Woods, the Post Office Solicitor, appointed to his post in 1921, was responsible for safeguarding the interests of the Post Office in the drafting of licences and agreements.

The office of Postmaster-General was political, and the department over which he presided was by no means outside the range of political controversy during the 1920s. During the crucial period from 1921 to 1924 when broadcasting was born there were no fewer than seven Postmasters-General. Such political mobility was somewhat exceptional. The next Postmaster-General—Sir William Mitchell-Thomson—remained in office from 1924 to 1929, and there were only seven Postmasters-General in the whole twenty years which followed Mitchell-Thomson's appointment. The chopping and changing of 1921 to 1924 was, however, a source of difficulty at more than one point in the early history of broadcasting.

The six men who held the post had different temperaments, inclinations, and sometimes policies. The first of them—F. G. Kellaway—was journalist turned politician, and it was he who guided the talks between the commercial companies which culminated in the foundation of the BBC in 1922. He lost his seat at the general election of that year, and was succeeded as Postmaster-General in the new Conservative government by Neville Chamberlain. Kellaway went on to become deputy chairman of the Marconi Company, and it was Chamberlain

[1] H. Robinson, *Britain's Post Office* (1953), p. 221.

who signed the first agreement with the BBC. After a few
months, however, he was succeeded by Sir William Joynson-
Hicks in March 1923. The contrasting temperaments of these
two men were responsible for significant shifts in the official
approach to broadcasting in its infancy.[1]

Temperament has usually been more significant than political
persuasion in this particular office, and Vernon Hartshorn,
Postmaster-General from January to November 1924 in the
first Labour government, has been described by Reith as not
much interested in broadcasting: 'there were few dealings
with him'.[2] His successor, Sir William Mitchell-Thomson, introduced an element of permanency. He stayed at his post for
$4\frac{1}{2}$ years, considerably longer than his five predecessors put
together.

The legal powers of the Postmaster-General to concern himself with broadcasting derived from two pieces of legislation
passed in very different circumstances. The 1869 Telegraph
Act gave the Postmaster-General the exclusive privilege of
transmitting telegrams within the United Kingdom, and a
year later the telegraphs were taken over by the Post Office.
The 1904 Wireless Telegraphy Act extended the Postmaster-
General's powers to control wireless telegraphy. It was the first
Wireless Act in the world, and laid down that no person should
establish a wireless telegraph station or 'instal or work any
apparatus for wireless telegraphy' without first securing a
licence from the Postmaster-General. A further clause stated
that 'every such licence shall be in such form and for such
period as the Postmaster-General may determine, and shall
contain the terms, conditions, and restrictions on, and subject
to which the licence is granted'.

When wireless telephony developed, the Postmaster-General
regarded it as a natural extension of wireless telegraphy in the
same way that in 1904 he had regarded wireless telegraphy as
a natural extension of line telegraphy. Moreover, he and his
legal advisers regarded the 1904 clause relating to licences as
binding both on the senders of wireless messages and the
receivers of them. Transmission included both sending and
receiving. This contention was attacked in some sections of the

[1] See below, pp. 155 ff.
[2] *Into the Wind* (1949), p. 96.

press,[1] but Woods told the Sykes Committee that the Post-master-General had no doubts about his powers under this heading.[2] The basic difference between non-experimental telegraphy and non-experimental wireless telephony—that the former, like other Post Office services, served separate individuals, while the latter diffused 'identical noises to all and sundry'[3]—was not clearly drawn by the Post Office in 1922.

Once it had been taken for granted that broadcasting was the proper concern of the Post Office, it followed that it was also the proper concern of the Imperial Communications Committee. This important committee was an offshoot of the Committee of Imperial Defence, which had been founded in 1904, by a coincidence in the same year that the Wireless Telegraphy Act was passed. The Imperial Communications Committee included representatives of the Admiralty, the War Office, and the Air Ministry, as well as of the Treasury, the India Office, the Foreign Office, the Colonial Office, and the Board of Trade. The Post Office, therefore, was merely one interest represented at this level of policy-making. On 3 April 1922 Kellaway announced in the House of Commons—in answer to a question —that the whole question of broadcasting was being referred to the Imperial Communications Committee 'in order that the views of the other Departments concerned may be obtained as early as possible'.[4] The crucial question was that of wavelengths. How would it be possible to allocate the limited number of wavelengths available between commercial broadcasting stations, experimenters, ships at sea, wireless telegraphy companies, and, above all, the Services? The Wireless Telegraph Board had, as we have seen, very strong views about the prior rights of the last of these claimants.[5]

On 5 April 1922 the Wireless Sub-Committee of the Imperial Communications Committee considered at length the whole question of broadcasting, including the petition from the Wireless Society of London.[6] It was at this meeting that Brown, just back from America, explained to his fellow members what he

[1] For an early example of press criticism on this point, see The Aberdeen Free Press, 19 Aug. 1922.
[2] *Oral evidence of R. W. Woods before the Sykes Committee, 2 May 1923.
[3] Robinson, op. cit., p. 241.
[4] Hansard, vol. 152, col. 1869, 3 Apr. 1922.
[5] See above, p. 49.   [6] See above, p. 57.

thought were the lessons of American experience. He told them of the 'chaos' of wavelengths in the United States and of the work of the Hoover Committee, the meeting of which he had attended.[1] He clearly outlined what the Post Office believed should be the essentials of British policy. Facilities should be given to *bona fide* radio manufacturing companies to broadcast music and educational matter.[2] The broadcasting of news, however, should be treated quite separately and should be further considered with great care. The same was true of 'advertising' matter. A scheme should be devised to avoid 'clashing' of wavelengths.

The sub-committee went on to draft a provisional plan. It envisaged the granting of licences for broadcasting on one single wavelength—440 metres. The power of each station was to be restricted to $1\frac{1}{2}$ kilowatts. The broadcasting of all advertising matter was to be prohibited. No matter was to be broadcast for which payment was received. The broadcasting of news not already printed was to be prohibited except by special permission. Broadcast matter was to be limited to music, educational and religious subjects, and entertainment. The hours of broadcasting were to be restricted to those between 5 o'clock and midnight. Government communiqués were to be distributed if and when required. Any arrangements made between the Post Office and commercial firms were to be provisional so that they could be altered, if necessary, in the light of experience.

This was hardly a manifesto for broadcasting. It represented a combination of caution and obstinacy, typical of relationships between an autocratic concessionaire and an objectionable licensee. Not only did it severely restrict the content of broadcasting, but it limited it to one single wavelength. This latter proposal implied either that there should be only one broadcasting agency—this first alternative was not explicitly stated—or that a limited number of broadcasting stations in various parts of the country would have to agree on a system whereby

[1] See above, p. 68.
[2] On this and on later occasions the emphasis on *bona fide* radio manufacturers ruled out such other applicants for broadcasting rights as newspapers and retail stores. The *Daily Mail* had mooted the idea of a *Daily Mail* broadcast service in conjunction with the Marconi Company (see T. Clarke, op. cit., p. 874). Frederick Marquis (later Lord Woolton) and Louis Cohen of Lewis's called at the Post Office to inquire about broadcasting. P.O. Archives 22,310/25.

they could share the single wavelength by each broadcasting on different days and at different times. American broadcasting had blundered into chaos: British broadcasting was to be forced into a strait-jacket. In reaching these conclusions the Wireless Sub-Committee reflected the views of the Services as it had done on previous occasions in its history.[1]

A further meeting of the sub-committee was held on 26 April 1922. By then the Post Office had received a spate of letters from radio companies and other bodies asking for permission to engage in broadcasting.[2] By invitation the two most important of the companies—the Marconi Company and Metropolitan-Vickers—were represented at the meeting.

Colonel Simpson, the representative of the Marconi Company, stated formally, as he had stated informally before the meeting, that the idea of one single wavelength was unsatisfactory. Instead, a band of wavelengths should be allotted to broadcasting. To be successful radio companies would need the largest possible audiences and the best hours for broadcasting would be between 7 o'clock and 11 o'clock in the evening. A. P. M. Fleming, representing Metropolitan-Vickers, agreed, adding that lunch-time and tea-time would also be profitable times, particularly in the industrial areas. Both Simpson and Fleming were then specifically asked—and it was historically a most important question—whether the various companies interested in the possibility of broadcasting could not join together for transmission purposes. They would thereby not only facilitate the allocation of wavelengths but would save unnecessary costs. Simpson replied that the companies had had no time to get together and co-operate. They were already being hurt by foreign competition, and they wished to know as soon as possible when they could start regular broadcasting. The Post Office would directly benefit from early action since it would be in a position to levy receivers' licences. Simpson suggested 5s. as an appropriate figure for each licence on the grounds that a higher figure would represent too high a proportion of the cost of the set.

In answer to a further question—and this time it was his answer rather than the question which was historically important —he said that if a wavelength band of 350 to 400 metres were allotted to broadcasting, probably six to eight broadcasting stations, each of 2 kilowatts, would be required to cover the whole of Great Britain. At this point Brown gave the blessing of the Post Office to Simpson's suggestion, adding that the Post Office had already received applications for transmitting stations from six firms of 'excellent standing'. He proposed that the Post Office should call a meeting of applicants to discuss the 'co-operative working of stations'.

After the representatives of the Marconi Company and the Metropolitan-Vickers Company had withdrawn, the Wireless Sub-Committee agreed to new proposals for presentation to the Imperial Communications Committee. They were not identical with Simpson's, but they followed the same lines. A wavelength band of 350 to 400 metres would be allocated to broadcasting. Transmitting licences would cost £50 and would only be granted to British companies. The site of each station would have to be approved by the Post Office. Receivers' licences should cost 10s. A suggestion of Simpson's that there should be some restriction of wavelengths on British receiving sets was not approved, the sub-committee holding that it was not possible to prevent the public listening to other wavelengths if it desired to do so. Lastly the Post Office, as Brown had suggested, was to be asked to arrange a meeting of companies at an early date and in the meantime was to communicate to all interested companies the conditions relating to broadcasting which had been agreed to at this and the earlier meeting.[1]

In the House of Commons on 1 May 1922 Sir Henry Norman, Liberal member of parliament for Blackburn, Vice-Chairman of the Imperial Communications Committee and Chairman of the Wireless Sub-Committee, asked the Postmaster-General in what was clearly a prearranged question what decisions had been arrived at concerning 'the broadcasting of musical, instructive and entertaining matter by wireless telephony'. Kellaway replied that he intended to make a full statement on the subject when he introduced the Post Office estimates the following week.[2] Accordingly, on 4 May Kellaway made what was the first full statement on broadcasting in the House of Commons.

[1] The above account is based on BBC Archives, supplemented by the record of the Wireless Sub-Committee of the Imperial Communications Committee.
[2] *Hansard*, vol. 153, col. 995, 1 May 1922.

He began with America and the Post Office's impression (*via* Brown) of the American 'chaos'. 'I hope', he added, 'that we shall be able to learn from the experience of the United States.' The proposals of the Wireless Sub-Committee would be accepted by the government. A limited number of 'radio-telephone broadcasting stations' would be licensed. The country would be divided into areas centred upon London, Cardiff, Plymouth,[1] Birmingham, Manchester, Newcastle, Glasgow or Edinburgh (but not both) and Aberdeen, and one or more broadcasting stations would be allowed in each of these zones. Only British firms which were *bona fide* manufacturers of wireless apparatus would be allowed to broadcast. The power of each station would be limited to $1\frac{1}{2}$ kilowatts and the hours from 5 o'clock to 11 o'clock, except on Sundays when they would be unlimited.

It is impossible [Kellaway stated] and it would not be in the interests of wireless if I granted all the applications that have been made to me for the rights of transmission. What I am going to do is to ask all those who apply—the various firms who have applied—to come together at the Post Office and co-operate so that an efficient service may be rendered and that there may be no danger of monopoly and that each service shall not be interfering with the efficient working of the other.[2]

This statement reflected clearly if not very precisely the kind of considerations which influenced the Post Office in 1922. The very imprecision of language is itself an indication of a certain lack of precision of mind. The phrase 'efficient service' meant that the Post Office was expressing an interest, however vague, in the content of broadcasting. Later in his statement Kellaway added that 'there will be certain regulations in regard to the character and classes of news which these agencies will be allowed to transmit, but on that head I have not yet come to a final decision'. When a member called out 'Who will be the censor?', Kellaway did not directly reply. He noted, however, that 'the possibilities of this service are almost unlimited'. 'In the United States of America it was suggested that some arrangement might be made by which speeches of members of

---

[1] For technical reasons Bournemouth was substituted for Plymouth at a later date. A relay station was opened in Plymouth, however, in March 1924.

[2] Ibid. col. 1600, 4 May 1922.

Congress might be radiated, and I can foresee a time when perhaps on this table a receiver will be properly concealed so as not to jar the aesthetic sense of members, and their eloquence will be transmitted to those of their constituents who are prepared to pay for the cost.'

This was prophecy—what was intended to be appropriately funny ministerial prophecy—not a development of the case for control of content. Yet a year later during the hearings of the Sykes Committee Brown took very seriously the question 'Had the Post Office in view [early in 1922] that it should be able to censor the programmes or news issued by the BBC?' 'No,' he replied, 'I do not think the idea of controlling the news entered our minds—at all events we did not regard it as a very practical thing—but certainly we did want to be able to exercise some sort of control over the nature of the programmes as a whole. If the ether was to be occupied, we hoped that it would be worthily occupied. We tried to word the Licence in such a way as to give us some right of objecting.'[1]

The wording of the Licence will be considered later.[2] Kellaway's initial statement, however, referred to two other considerations which influenced the Post Office—anxiety to avoid the danger of monopoly and to achieve technical efficiency. The use of the term 'monopoly' in the formulation of the first objective was plainly restricted. It meant at most that the Post Office was unwilling to allow control of broadcasting to pass into the hands of one existing commercial company, the Marconi Company being the most obvious 'danger', or perhaps of a group of companies. It certainly did not mean that the Post Office wished to see in existence several broadcasting companies. The statement should be set alongside Brown's remark concerning the 'six firms of excellent standing' at the Wireless Sub-Committee: it should also be set against the evidence of Brown and Woods before the Sykes Committee the following year.[3]

The reference to the 'efficient working' of the system reflects what was perhaps the chief concern of the Post Office. There was 'not room' in Britain, as the Postmaster-General put it in a debate later in 1922,[4] for too many broadcasting agencies. It was

[1] *Oral evidence of F. J. Brown before the Sykes Committee, 3 May 1923.
[2] See below, pp. 127 ff.   [3] See below, pp. 166 ff. See also above, p. 9.
[4] *Hansard*, vol. 157, col. 1951, 4 Aug. 1922.

better that the various interests should agree than that they should compete. It was Shaughnessy, not Brown, who referred to this element in Post Office policy—again a little vaguely—in his evidence before the Sykes Committee:

If they were prepared to license people, then you would have a very large number of firms asking for permission probably, and some of them might be sufficiently wealthy to put up decent stations—most of them would not—you would have a very great difficulty in acquiescing, you could not acquiesce in all demands. And then you would have the difficulty of selecting the firms which the Post Office thought were most suitable for the job, and, whatever selection is made by the Post Office, the Post Office would be bound to be accused of favouring certain firms. So that the solution of the problem seemed to be to make all the firms get together to form one Company for the purpose of doing the broadcasting.[1]

Kellaway did not say that he favoured one company in his speech of 4 May. Had he done so, he might even at that stage have provoked a discussion on what the word 'monopoly' really meant. If his criteria were to be operative, however, first there would have to be discussion between the various commercial firms and then there would have to be agreement. One point was certain. Kellaway had no desire that the Post Office should manage broadcasting itself. Nor apparently had his permanent officials. He told the House categorically a few weeks later on 16 June, 'I do not regard it as desirable that the work should be done by the Government, and I do not contemplate a condition of things under which the Post Office will be doing this work.'[2]

There were only two interesting references to broadcasting in the debate on the Post Office Estimates which followed Kellaway's statement of 4 May. Sir Douglas Newton thought that 10s. for a licence would be far too high: 'the service rendered would be virtually nothing'. Sir Henry Norman dwelt at length on the possibilities of broadcasting, anticipating Reith in comparing it with 'embarking on an uncharted and very extensive sea'. He said that those members of parliament who had laughed when Kellaway referred to the political implications of broadcasting would not always be laughing. 'I think one may say not merely as a matter of opinion but with the confidence

[1] *Oral evidence of E. H. Shaughnessy before the Sykes Committee, 14 June 1923.
[2] *Hansard*, vol. 155, col. 774, 16 June 1922.

with which one announces a certain fact, that before much time
has elapsed, at times of political crises the Prime Minister on the
one hand, and the leader of the Opposition on the other will be
addressing hundreds of people in the country simultaneously by
means of wireless telephony.' He hoped that the Post Office
itself would contemplate the organization of broadcasting,
perhaps using its new wireless station at Northolt 'to undertake
this service'. 'At first', he exclaimed, 'broadcasting will only
bring into tens of thousands of homes in the land music and entertainment, and perhaps some instruction. Later development
will enlarge its scope and give to this telephony a national
character for which the State will have to be responsible.'[1]
The contrast between the perspectives of Newton and those of
Norman is immense and startling. Yet it was Newton who
represented the overwhelming majority opinion early in 1922.

Norman developed his arguments in two important articles in
The Times a few days after the debate.[2] They revealed a somewhat different approach to that in his statement in the House
of Commons. This was the first occasion on which *The Times*
had dealt at length with broadcasting. The chain of argument
followed that of the Wireless Sub-Committee. Indeed, this was
now beginning to be the established sequence. The premise was
American experience. This was described and criticized: 'the
result is naturally confusion, congestion, mutual interference,
and "jamming" '. Britain was recommended to proceed 'with
caution', to avoid 'thoughtless haste', to move 'step by step'.
In the first instance only *bona fide* manufacturers should be
allowed to broadcast. 'Of course, every big retail house would
like to shout the merits and low prices of its taffetas and tulles,
its shirts and shoes. There is no room for this.' None the less,
Norman did not envisage a monopoly. Each company would
announce its own service 'and there will be a natural rivalry to
furnish the most attractive programmes, since hearers may
conclude that the firm supplying the best entertainment in the
clearest manner is most likely to make good apparatus'. It would
be necessary for the companies 'to arrange among themselves,

[1] Ibid., vol. 153, col. 1600, 4 May 1922.
[2] *The Times*, 8 and 9 May 1922. The articles were called 'Wireless for All', the
first being sub-titled 'Rapid American Progress' and the second 'The British
Plans'.

subject to the approval of the Postmaster-General, how they will share the sites, the time and the wave-lengths'. What Norman did envisage, as he had done in his House of Commons speech, was the early entry of the State into the field. 'In three months the new Post Office wireless station at Northolt will be ready with a powerful valve equipment, and this will doubtless be used for broadcasting official matter.' Such matter would not include the news. Still less should the news be considered appropriate business for commercial companies. 'Commercial broadcasting will, therefore, necessarily consist of music and songs, spoken entertainment, dance music, lectures, sermons, and such-like popular non-controversial matter.'

The argument was repeating itself, but it was being stretched farther and farther at the edges until it raised issues which are still debatable nearly forty years later. This was the first time (several months before the BBC came into existence) that the adjective 'non-controversial' was used in this context. Norman was following in the footsteps of the prophets who had preceded him when he concluded his articles with the sentence—'of the possibilities of broadcasting one can speak with diffidence, since no man can foresee them all'. It was when he contemplated the form and content of a broadcasting service that he was wandering into new regions of argument. In retrospect it is extraordinary how many of the basic issues of broadcasting were discerned, however dimly, months before Reith left engineering for broadcasting, months even before the BBC was founded.

There was thus in existence the outline of a 'plan' before the manufacturers met at the invitation of the Post Office to consider the position. Both the Post Office and the Wireless Sub-Committee of the Imperial Communications Committee had ideas about the shape of things to come. There was one brief flicker of controversy in May 1922 which had little to do with the ultimate outcome. On 17 May, at the first full meeting of the Imperial Communications Committee since the April talks of the Wireless Sub-Committee, it was reported that the Post-master-General had decided against the wishes of the Wireless Sub-Committee to accept Colonel Simpson's proposal[1] and to issue regulations restricting the type of wireless receiving

[1] See above, p. 99.

apparatus. The Postmaster-General wished, on Murray's advice, to limit the simple form of receiving licence to wireless sets capable of receiving only 'a band of waves reasonably close to that allowed for broadcasting—the object being to discourage the use by the ordinary public (as distinct from experimenters and serious amateurs) of receiving sets capable of receiving practically all wavelengths'.[1] The reasoning behind this restriction was circular. 'Wireless communication admittedly cannot be kept secret, but this seems to be no reason for making it easy for the general public to listen to everything that is passing in the ether.' The Wireless Sub-Committee did not accept this reasoning, but Brown reported to the Imperial Communications Committee that while the Postmaster-General had carefully considered the views which the Sub-Committee had expressed, he had come to the conclusion that the arguments on the opposite side were more weighty. That they were in fact less weighty is almost irrelevant. What is relevant is that one day before the manufacturers met at the General Post Office, the Postmaster-General had asserted his freedom of action. The Post Office entered the talks in a position of great strength.

It was Murray who presided over this important meeting and revealed to the assembled manufacturers the extent of their freedom to negotiate. He told the twenty-eight representatives of commercial interests who were present[2] that the Post Office preferred 'co-operation' to competition. Already in the letter of invitation sent out to them the Post Office had set out certain technical limitations on broadcasting—on power ($1\frac{1}{2}$ kilowatts), on hours, on wavelengths, on content, and even on station drill.[3] These points were elaborated at the meeting. The manufacturers argued both about 'co-operation' and about the restrictions the Post Office intended to impose. Some firms suggested two broadcasting groups sharing areas and times; one advocated 'simultaneous broadcasting'. One large firm pressed for 'competition'; another claimed that competition does not always succeed and tried to forestall criticism by maintaining

[1] Memorandum from Murray. Post Office Archives 22,310/25.
[2] For the names of the twenty-eight and the interests they represented, see Appendix I.
[3] Letter of 15 May 1922. Twenty-four firms were invited. Post Office Reference 34,609/22. Would-be broadcasters were told that every station should begin its programmes 'Hello, Hello. Here message for all stations [sic] from . . .'

that lack of competition was not necessarily a monopoly. No firm queried the Postmaster-General's ban on advertising, but several challenged his ban on the broadcasting of news which had not previously been published. In the Post Office letter inviting the business representatives, he had told them that there should be no broadcasting of news which had not previously been published in the press without the special permission of the Postmaster-General.[1] Murray was asked why the press should enjoy a monopoly. What was to stop anyone obtaining a piece of news and publishing it by walking down the street with a sandwich board? Did he not agree in any case that the press would derive considerable benefit from the 'wireless boom'? Murray answered none of these questions. He asked the manufacturers to get together themselves—without Post Office representatives being present—and decide what they wanted to do next. They should prepare 'a co-operative scheme, or at the most two such schemes, for consideration by the Post Office authorities'.[2]

The Post Office had proposed: it was now for the commercial interests to confer—and to agree. Once the problem had been passed over to them, it became in part at least a problem of business power. Godfrey Isaacs, the representative of the Marconi Company, told the meeting at the Post Office that his company owned 152 patents, that no efficient transmitter could operate without the use of some of them, and that there should be only one group which could use the patents. It was at this point that Murray remarked that this was as far as the meeting could go and asked the manufacturers to get together and form one or two corporations.[3]

[1] Letter of 15 May 1922; see also below, p. 130.
[2] The Post Office statement from which this phrase is taken referred to the formation of 'one or probably two groups'. *The Times* replaced the word 'probably' by the word 'possibly' (*The Times*, 19 May 1922). R. H. Coase draws attention to the difference in *British Broadcasting* (1950), ch. 1, fn. 48.
[3] A summary report of this meeting is in Post Office Archives, 22,310/25.

2. The Manufacturers Confer

LEFT to their own devices, the manufacturers arranged their first meeting on their own for 23 May. Godfrey Isaacs offered the use of Marconi House, but his colleagues preferred the neutral and yet in a sense hallowed ground of the Institution of Electrical Engineers.[1] They chose as chairman not Isaacs, as *The Times* erroneously reported,[2] but the President of the Institution, Frank (later Sir Frank) Gill, the chief engineer of the Western Electric Company. Gill, who was an excellent and respected mediator, remained chairman of what became known as the Manufacturers' Committee until the summer of 1922 when he went on a business trip to the United States. The choice of the Institution of Electrical Engineers as the rendez-vous in May 1922 had more long-term consequences. The close relations established with the Institution before the foundation of the BBC were strengthened still further after its foundation, and in April 1923 the offices and studios of the new organization were transferred to the west wing of the Institution building at No. 2 Savoy Hill. The name 'Savoy Hill' subsequently became a household word throughout the country, and it is common usage to refer to a whole period in the history of the BBC—before the opening of Broadcasting House in 1932—as 'the Savoy Hill days'.[3] What began with a concern for neutrality was to end in a wave of sentiment.

At the meeting of 23 May it was decided to appoint a committee of the so-called 'Big Six'—the Marconi Company, Metropolitan-Vickers, the Western Electric Company, the Radio Communication Company, the General Electric Company, and the British Thomson-Houston Company—'to consider and prepare a scheme for submission to the general meeting'.[4] Frank Phillips of Burndept Ltd. was added to the committee

[1] *H. A. Pease to P. F. Russell, Secretary of the Institution of Electrical Engineers, 18 May 1922.
[2] *The Times*, 24 May 1922.
[3] R. Appleyard, *The History of the Institution of Electrical Engineers, 1871–1931* (1939), pp. 257–61. See below, p. 211.
[4] *Minutes of the Meeting of 23 May 1922. These Minutes are handwritten.

as a representative of the smaller firms manufacturing radio apparatus. The addition of his name was in accordance with the wishes of the Post Office, which was anxious not to appear to be giving too free a hand to the big-business battalions.

The small committee became the centre of all the crucial negotiations, meeting frequently and referring to the bigger body only when decisions had been reached or when there was deadlock.[1] The members of the small committee were as indefatigable behind the scenes as they were round the council table, and they quickly got to know each other's strength and weakness. Godfrey Isaacs spoke with the full weight of the experience of the Marconi Company behind him and with the conviction, which he never conceded, that no other commercial concern could by itself run a successful radio station without infringing Marconi patents. Colonel Simpson was the other Marconi Company personality who was chiefly concerned: he had worked before the war with the Marconi Company in Russia. Archibald (later Sir Archibald) McKinstry represented Metropolitan-Vickers, which along with the Radio Communication Company, represented by Basil Binyon, and the Western Electric Company, represented by an American, H. M. Pease, constituted the nucleus of a possible 'second group'. H. (later Lord) Hirst represented the General Electric Company, and John Gray represented British Thomson-Houston. There were definite business links between the Marconi Company, G.E.C., and B.T.H. The Marconi Company and G.E.C. jointly owned a valve-manufacturing company, while B.T.H., linked with the American General Electric Company, had a common interest with the Marconi Company through the Radio Corporation of America and a patent-sharing agreement. Phillips had the almost impossible task of representing very small manufacturers in the presence of very big ones.

Once again it is difficult to avoid the impression that the main issues had already been formulated before the small committee met. Indeed, there is in existence a simple typewritten note (unsigned) dated 22 May, one day before even the big committee first met, on which the author—probably Gill—outlined the essential questions which confronted would-be broadcasters. There were two headings—'fundamental' and 'general policy'.

[1] The account which follows is based on BBC Archives.

Under the first there was only one question. 'Should all broadcasting stations be under one and the same management? or should there be more than one management?' Under the second, several questions were posed. 'Shall all patents on transmission be available?' 'What shall be the various holdings in the Broadcasting Company?' 'What name shall it use?' The other notes were briefer—'as to broadcasting news? Ditto speeches? As to sale of licences, first issue? Ditto, subsequent issue? Cessation of existing broadcasting stations not in the scheme? Are there to be two sets of licences, viz. any length and restricted length?'

Gill elaborated these points in a typewritten agenda for the first meeting of the small committee which was called for 25 May. The first item was 'patents' and the terms on which a 'Broadcasting Company' could use them. The second item was 'organization'. What should the new Company be called? What should be the relative holdings in it of large and of small firms? 'Who should be the directors? Who should the stations be purchased from?' There are two interesting additions in ink, which may or may not have been made before the meeting of the 25th. The name 'British Broadcasting Company' is set alongside the first of these questions, and against the heading 'Directors' there is a note 'representative of the public'. The third item was 'finance'. 'How shall it be provided?' Subheadings referred to action necessary 'as to pirates' (the first time this word was used in the context of broadcasting), 'as to approval by the Post Office of sets made by firms not in the Broadcasting Company', 'as to part of the yearly licence fee being allocated to the Broadcasting Company', and 'as to advertising'. Against the last of these references there is a note in ink, 'Leave alone for present.' Other headings are 'technical' —the appointment of a technical sub-committee; 'general policy'—'as to broadcasting news and speeches, sale of licences and cessation of existing broadcasting stations'; 'operation'— 'as to hours and testing during hours of non-operation'; 'drafting'—the appointment of a drafting sub-committee; and (written in ink without a formal heading)—'as to benefits of research being available at times'. The agenda for the meeting of 25 May thus began and ended with the question of 'know-how'. Who knew what, and how much? How much would each party be prepared to pass on?

Besides preparing this agenda, Gill prepared a paper which he read to the meeting. He noted that the small committee was not concerned with starting an 'ordinary business', employing 'the methods firms in competition would ordinarily employ'. 'The Government has imposed conditions which prevent us from selling broadcasting stations, and since there can be but a limited number of such stations erected, any direct profit from them is relatively unimportant.' The only hope of profit lay in extending the market for receiving sets. The best way of extending this market would be to provide 'a first-class broadcasting service'. In addition, the reputation of the radio manufacturing firms would rise if such a service were provided. 'There is also, I suppose, in each one's mind some idea of an advertising value in the broadcasting service.' As far as the Post Office was concerned, it was necessary that the manufacturers should present 'a united front'. Post Office aid was needed, and the manufacturers would have to convince the Post Office of 'the soundness of our views on certain points before we can get their aid'. All sectional business interests should be set on one side. 'If we believe that this broadcasting service has any real lasting place in the nation, let us be perfectly frank with each other, avoid mental reservations, free our minds from any prejudice, and with a single purpose honestly try and come to a solution which is best suited to the industry.'

The meeting not only agreed to follow Gill's agenda but went quite a long way towards meeting Gill's points. The name 'British Broadcasting Company' was accepted. It was decided that it should have a capital of £100,000 in cumulative ordinary shares, of which £60,000 was to be paid up. Dividends should be limited to 10 per cent. Shares were to be allotted only to 'genuine British manufacturers employing British labour'. 'As regards Directors, nothing was discussed except that it was desirable to include one to represent the general public.'

These provisions were all to be incorporated in the ultimate settlement. So too were many of the other suggestions made at this time—for example, that the Post Office should be asked to approve only wireless receiving sets made by members of the British Broadcasting Company, and that the Company should finance its current operations from two sources—a share of a 10s. Post Office licence fee (the size of share was not fixed) and a royalty on the sale of all receiving sets produced by member companies of the BBC. The minutes of the meeting begin and end, however, with pointers to the main difficulty of securing agreement between the manufacturers. The first item of the minutes reads: 'It was decided first to work out a plan on the basis of one Broadcasting Company for the whole country, and then if desired to work out another for two such Companies or more.' The last item reads: 'There was a long discussion on patents, by whom the stations should be constructed, how they should be named, and the distribution of the experience gained in the stations, but no results were reached.'

That the manufacturers were concerned about reaching conclusions quickly is shown by the fact that the small committee met again the next day, 26 May 1922. It was a tough meeting and there was a sharp difference of views. The main issue centred on who should construct the new transmitting stations. Isaacs argued that they should be of a uniform type, and that since the Marconi Company was the only company with the requisite technical knowledge it should be the sole constructor. McKinstry, Binyon, and Pease replied that the patents of all six firms should be firmly placed at the disposal of the new Broadcasting Company 'in order that the stations should have the greatest possible efficiency regardless of the patent situation'. The new Company should be free to place contracts with any of the six firms, and if possible each of the six firms should be linked with a broadcasting station. In the course of developing these arguments there were some tense exchanges. One of the members of the small committee said tartly that his firm would not 'go into this business on the basis of operating by leave of somebody else'. Isaacs replied bluntly that while the Marconi Company was willing to grant the new Broadcasting Company the right to use Marconi patents, it was not going to grant to any other company the right to build stations on the basis of their patents. Until this question was settled nothing else could be done. As at the previous meeting, 'the discussion was adjourned without a conclusion being reached'.

At the next meeting of the small committee on 1 June 1922, the first of three early June meetings, Gill began by pleading once again for a 'one group scheme', however great the technical difficulties might be. A 'one group scheme' would provide 'an efficient and stable programme', 'a minimum expense for broadcasting', 'no confusion', and 'readiness for national use'. The success of such a scheme would, of course, depend on the attitude of the Post Office, particularly on the official response to the manufacturers' suggestions of a double system of finance partly through a share of the licence, partly through royalties. To persuade the Post Office, unity of action was necessary. 'It may be difficult to persuade the Post Office to approve these conditions, and any division among the manufacturers may well jeopardize the whole method of financing the broadcasting.' At this point in the argument it is of interest to note how Gill's arguments for one group interlocked with the arguments used by the Post Office itself. The Post Office appreciated the technical advantage of one group managing broadcasting: Gill urged the manufacturers to act as one group to persuade the Post Office that such a group could operate broadcasting successfully only if certain conditions were fulfilled.

Gill's argument did not prevail, and after once more covering the ground of the previous discussion the meeting of 1 June was driven to discuss a two-group scheme. It was the kind of two-group scheme, however, which depended on co-operation or combination, not on competition. The financing of each of the two broadcasting companies was to be the same as the financing which had previously been suggested for the one, and there was to be a common treasurer for both. Moreover, the two companies were to make arrangements such as would 'prevent exploitation of one company against another by the artistes', and there was to be a Programme Liaison Committee. Manufacturers were to be free to join whichever company they wished, and the eight broadcasting stations projected by the Post Office were to be divided between the two companies on the basis of the number of manufacturers joining each group.

Discussion on the two-group scheme was resumed on the following day, 2 June. This time, however, there was talk not of combination but of conflict. Isaacs made it clear that if a two-group scheme were adopted and a second broadcasting company were formed, the second group would not be able to use the patents of the Marconi Company. 'I will facilitate the Broadcasting Company for the benefit of the general public', he explained, 'but not for the benefit of individuals.' When another member suggested that if two groups were formed each group should have the right to have a station in London, Isaacs replied, 'I oppose two stations anywhere as being totally unnecessary, undesirable and an inefficient arrangement.' Given this approach, the two-group scheme broke down as completely as the one-group scheme had done, and the small committee had no alternative but to report back to the large committee of manufacturers that it had failed to agree. Even then there were difficulties about exactly what should be reported to the larger committee. The facts of difference concealed differences of opinion and values. It was eventually agreed that there should be another meeting of the small committee on 7 June to discuss the outline of a draft statement to present to the bigger meeting.

The full resources of diplomacy were required both between 2 June and 7 June and at the meeting of 7 June itself. The general public might know little about broadcasting and some of the newspapers and some members of parliament might be chafing at the unwarrantable delay, but behind the scenes there was a dramatic confrontation of points of view and a debate about drafting which would have done justice to a committee of the League of Nations. The Marconi Company was accused of trying to perpetuate 'a monopoly of wireless working'; three of the other companies were accused of trying to benefit from its inventions without having contributed to them. 'We are not going to give you the opportunity of learning what we have learnt.' There seemed no room for compromise on matters of substance. When it was suggested that the Marconi Company might build six out of the eight stations, Isaacs retorted that he would not be prepared to license Marconi patents to another group even for one station.

Disagreement about how the division of opinion should be described in the statement made to the larger committee led eventually to a drafting compromise. Gill was to make a statement of what he believed had happened and then spokesmen of each side were to present their own versions. Gill was to introduce his own remarks with a statement that 'this disagreement is of necessity somewhat of a partisan matter and it is impossible for an impartial statement to deal adequately with the argument of each side'. In so far as this was true, it was a tribute to his chairmanship. As a representative of one of the firms wrote to him on 10 June, 'The meetings of the Special Committee must from all accounts have been most interesting and exhilarating, and I hear nothing but praise for your admirable chairmanship.'[1]

On 14 June the large meeting of manufacturers 'interested in Broadcasting' was summoned for the second time. It was brief. After Gill had spoken and the two sides had stated their respective points of view, McKinstry proposed and Isaacs seconded a motion that a deputation consisting of the chairman and three others should wait upon the Postmaster-General and explain the position clearly to him. Until then there had been 'an embargo on reporting to the Post Office'.[2] The meeting, Isaacs and McKinstry proposed, should adjourn until the deputation could report the result of their visit. Thus the scene shifted once again from Savoy Place to St. Martin's-le-Grand, the headquarters of the Post Office.

3. Negotiations Continue

IT was Sir Evelyn Murray who received the deputation of four at the Post Office on 16 June.[3] They explained to him not only the reasons why they differed, but the many points which they had in common. On 20 June Gill went alone to see Murray and there was a further exchange of views. The Post Office accepted the fact that there might have to be two broadcasting groups, although it was made clear that its ideal solution was still one single company covering and operating all stations. Murray refused to arbitrate between Isaacs and McKinstry, and promised that if two companies were formed each would be given a licence. Each company would have a station in London and between them they would divide the country on a geographical basis. If, on account of problems of patents or other difficulties,

[1] *A. P. M. Fleming to Gill, 10 June 1922.
[2] F. J. Brown to Murray, 12 June 1922. P.O. Archives, 22,310/25.
[3] Murray had been well briefed. A detailed memorandum by Brown set out proposals 'in the event of there being two broadcasting groups'. P.O. Archives, 22,310/25.

one of the companies could not provide a satisfactory service, its licence would be withdrawn.[1] Further discussion centred mainly on what the manufacturers had in common, and the arguments subsequently advanced both by the manufacturers and the Post Office went farther than the discussion within the small committee, or at least farther than the minutes of the small committee suggest.

Murray asked Gill what were the views of the manufacturers about protection against foreign competition. The question of protection had indeed been in the forefront of the manufacturers' minds and had been raised at the first manufacturers' conference of 23 May. At the small committee meeting on 7 June, when there had been such sharp differences of opinion about who should construct the new transmitting stations, Isaacs had been asked to produce a reasoned statement of the case for protection which could be used in discussions with other business interests and with the Post Office. Only their differences of opinion on other subjects had overshadowed their basic agreement on this. Isaacs maintained that broadcasting created 'a possibility of giving employment to many thousands of men, women and boys in this country'. Eighty per cent. of the cost of a receiving set would be taken up by the cost of labour, and all the new material except for a small quantity of copper would be obtainable in the country. The industry, however, was threatened from the outset by 'cheap installations being introduced into the country from both Germany and Austria' where there were seriously depreciated currencies, and it was necessary not only for British manufacturers to unite but for the Postmaster-General to decline to authorize any wireless receiving apparatus which was not of British manufacture.[2] Gill communicated these views to Brown on 14 June, two days before Murray received the deputation.

There was large-scale unemployment in 1922, but protection was a highly controversial political issue, and Murray told his visitors that the views they had expressed would have to go to other ministries and even to the Cabinet. He suggested, however, that if ministers were unwilling completely to prohibit the import of foreign-made wireless apparatus they might be willing

[1] This account is taken from P.O. Archives, 22,310/25.
[2] *Memorandum of 8 June 1922.

to prohibit the sale of such apparatus in Britain for a limited period—for instance, up to the end of 1923 or for two years after the beginning of regular broadcasting. Murray went on to suggest that the small committee might consider such a scheme.

On the means of financing broadcasting, Murray asked the deputation to consider whether the 10s. licence fee could be divided in the proportion of 5s. to the Post Office and 5s. to the manufacturers. In addition he suggested that the royalties charged on the sale of sets should be increased to a higher figure than that suggested by the manufacturers.

Both these points were to be incorporated in the final settlement. They were considered at a further meeting of the small committee on 21 June. The Post Office suggestion of protection for a limited period was accepted, although it was argued that 'if the manufacturers stood firm they would get what they had asked for'. A condition of membership of the new company was to be that only British-made apparatus should be used by member firms and that all the sets they produced should bear both the registered trade mark of the Broadcasting Company and a Post Office registration number. The Post Office would be called upon to approve the type of apparatus submitted by members of the Company.[1] The idea of a 10s. licence, 5s. of which should go to the broadcasting companies, was not accepted at this stage: 15s. was suggested, of which 5s. should be retained by the Post Office.[2] Income from licences would be insufficient, the committee argued, to carry on broadcasting efficiently. At the same time income from royalties would dwindle after a time, and there was a danger of obtaining too much from this source during the boom period. It was agreed that amounts collected during the radio boom should be employed for amortizing capital expenditure on stations and forming a reserve fund to meet expenses of improvement, maintenance, and extension. Licence fees should be used to

[1] *The first printed list of 'Conditions which broadcast receivers should fulfil to obtain Post Office Approval' was published by the BBC on 10 Oct. 1922 before the Company was officially founded. The items in the list were discussed by a small technical committee which included Simpson and Nash of the Marconi Company and Binyon. It dealt directly with Shaughnessy of the Post Office. This technical committee met for the first time on 30 Aug. 1922.

[2] Brown had originally thought of only 25 per cent. of the licence fee going to the BBC (letter to Murray) 12 June 1922. P.O. Archives, 22,310/25).

provide funds for the operational expenses of the broadcasting service.

All these points of agreement were still associated with the scheme for two separate broadcasting groups. Once again Gill tried to persuade the members of the small committee to agree at least on establishing certain common committees, for instance a technical committee to consider the allocation of wavelengths and a committee to standardize radio parts. Yet the small committee did not agree even about a possible division of the country on geographical lines. This time it was Isaacs who said that his company would 'make strenuous efforts to get stations to cover the whole of the country'. The meeting adjourned after Sir William Noble, taking the place of Hirst,[1] had warned it that he was sure that the Postmaster-General would never agree to two stations at any place other than London. 'It is a great pity to go to him without an agreement or a recommendation.'

Noble's intervention at the first meeting he attended is important on two counts. First, he knew the Post Office well. He had been engineer-in-chief at the Post Office before taking up a post with the General Electric Company. Second, he became chairman of the Manufacturers' Committee after Gill went to America early in August. There is an interesting letter from Murray to Noble just after he had taken Gill's place: 'I am interested and rather amused to hear that you have taken charge of the Broadcasting Committee . . . and I hope you will do all you can to get their Articles of Association &c. laid before the Post Office as quickly as possible. The Postmaster-General is rather perturbed at the length of time during which this has been dragging on.'[2]

Before Noble replaced Gill, agreement was reached to recommend not two groups but one. This agreement was reached not in the small committee itself but in talks between Isaacs and McKinstry. As late as 5 July, when Gill reported another long discussion with Murray,[3] the scheme for two broadcasting companies with identical rules was being worked out in detail. The assumption that there would be two groups was still accepted

---

[1] Hirst left England for several weeks on company business in July and Aug. 1922.

[2] *Murray to Noble, 11 Aug. 1922.

[3] *Gill to the members of the committee, 5 July 1922.

without question on 12 July when a further meeting of the small committee was held. This was an important meeting which followed the cancellation of an earlier meeting planned for 7 July. A long letter from Murray setting out the views of the government on the manufacturers' proposals was read and discussed.[1]

The government, Murray wrote, accepted the idea of two broadcasting groups, of protection to the radio industry in 'exceptional circumstances' for a period of two years, and of broadcasting revenue being derived from licences and royalties. The licence was to be fixed at 10s., however, and the profits of the companies were to be limited not to 10 per cent. but to 7½ per cent. The companies were to guarantee to maintain 'efficient services' for a reasonable period, say of five years. The licence for each transmitting station was to be terminable at any time by the Postmaster-General 'in the event of the Company failing to provide or to maintain efficient broadcasting services from that station'.

The small committee continued to press for a 15s. licence— 'if this sum is not allotted to the Broadcasting Companies the Committee are afraid the programmes must suffer'[2]—and agreed to recommend that the royalty fee on receiving sets should be based on 10 per cent. of the net wholesale price. It refused, however, to commit the manufacturers for a period of five years, and offered instead a guarantee of two years' 'effective broadcasting' from 1 January 1923.

During the week which followed this meeting Gill saw Murray again and learned definitively that while the Post Office would meet the wishes of the manufacturers on the period of two years and the amount of royalty to be levied, it would not budge on the issue of the amount of the licence. The most he could get from Murray was a promise that 'the Post Office is quite willing to take the question of funds into consideration, if they shall ever have to make any criticism of the broadcasting programme'.[3] Gill recommended, therefore, that 'we had better rest content with what we have achieved'. He thought that it was 'very important that the Broadcasting Companies should be formed quickly'.[4]

It was during this same week that private negotiations began

[1] *Murray to Gill, 12 July 1922.   [2] *Gill to Murray, 13 July 1922.
[3] *Gill to the members of the small committee.   [4] *Ibid.

between Isaacs and McKinstry which led to the abandonment
of the scheme for the two groups and the return to the idea of
one 'British Broadcasting Company'. Isaacs informed Gill and
some of the other members of the small committee on 17 July
that there was a 'possibility' that he and McKinstry would
come to an agreement 'as to a one Company scheme'.[1] Because
of this 'possibility' a meeting of the small committee fixed for
that week was postponed. Isaacs wrote again to Gill on 20 July
saying that he was meeting McKinstry in a few days' time,
'when considerable headway may be made'. It was perhaps
characteristic of his background, temperament, and certainly
of his public reputation, that he added, 'I am very much engaged this week with a Patent Action in the courts.'[2]

The negotiations between Isaacs and McKinstry, who together were formally recognized to be a sub-committee of the
small committee, are not documented. According to Binyon,
they had an element of bluff about them. He and McKinstry
on one occasion confronted Isaacs with a document purporting
on its cover to be the Articles of Association of a separate
broadcasting company: inside the cover, however, was some
quite unrelated matter about a cinema. Isaacs was impressed
by this degree of determination, and took his competitors
more seriously. The reasoning which lay behind the settlement
they arrived at is known. It was communicated to a meeting
of the small committee on 8 August, the first meeting at which
Noble took the chair.

Isaacs and McKinstry had agreed that there should be one
company on three conditions—first, that the chairman should
be 'neutral', that is to say he should not belong to any of the
constituting companies; second, that of the eight broadcasting
stations, six should be equipped by the Marconi Company and
the question of the equipment of the two remaining stations
should be left to the Board of the new Broadcasting Company
to decide; and third, that in the event of the tender for the remaining two stations being given to companies other than
Marconi, the Marconi Company would not undertake any
litigation in respect of patents. Indeed, the companies were to
waive their patent rights in respect of the eight stations.

[1] *Isaacs to Gill, 17 July 1922. Gill's reply on 19 July is missing.
[2] *Isaacs to Gill, 20 July 1922.

The reasoning behind this compromise was straightforward. First, both the Marconi Company and its competitors preferred one group to two groups. Isaacs made this clear publicly as well as privately.[1] Second, the manufacturers believed that the Post Office preferred one group and that they could safeguard their interests best by respecting this preference. Third, the most important of these interests was the sale of receiving sets. None of the companies was committed to the idea of competition in broadcasting, certainly not as a business objective. Broadcasting seemed likely to cost a great deal of money, and the profits which it would yield were to be deliberately limited.[2]

At the meeting of 8 August the manufacturers not only agreed with the compromise reached by Isaacs and McKinstry, but laid down the conditions of membership of the new Broadcasting Company. Each member was to undertake to sell only British-made sets, to pay to the Company 10 per cent. of the net wholesale selling price of all broadcast receiving apparatus, and to lay down a deposit of £100 to the Company. F. S. Gaylor was to act as solicitor and draw up the Memorandum and Articles of Association of the Company. George Pells of the Marconi Company was to act as temporary secretary. It was also agreed that Lord Derby should be approached to see if he would serve as independent chairman. Noble informed Murray of the most important of these decisions in a letter written two days later.[3] It was Brown who replied on behalf of the Postmaster-General. 'He is glad to learn', Brown ended his letter 'that it has been decided to form one Broadcasting Company only; and he hopes that in view of the time which has elapsed since 4th May when the proposals were publicly announced in the House of Commons, the Committee will use their best endeavours to avoid any further delay in arriving at a settlement.'[4]

The delay was being commented on very freely in the summer of 1922. Both Kellaway and the Assistant Postmaster-General answered questions on the subject in the House of Commons in May, June, and July. Some of the questioners queried the

---

[1] A statement of his was reported in some sections of the press on 15 Aug. 1922 and in *The Broadcaster*, Aug. 1922.

[2] Cf. the analysis in Coase, op. cit., pp. 12–15.

[3] *Noble to Murray, 10 Aug. 1922.

[4] *Brown to Noble, 11 Aug. 1922. A full meeting of manufacturers was held on 11 Aug.

rights of the Post Office to introduce 'what was a novel form of procedure and of monopoly'; others, speaking in the cause of free trade, pressed the Postmaster-General not to impose 'a protection system'.[1] Captain Wedgwood Benn challenged the Postmaster-General's interpretation of his powers under the Wireless Telegraphy Act of 1904. 'The powers of the Postmaster-General under this Act were being used in a very unexpected and improper way, and he was taking the first opportunity of seeking to limit these powers or to deprive him of them altogether.'[2] As rumours of what was happening behind the scenes reached parliament, there was an intermittent attempt at debate, largely on the part of only a handful of members. Free trade was the main theme, 'monopoly' the second.

Kellaway consistently answered the free-traders by affirming that it was 'inconceivable' to him that 'we should allow a new form of communication in this country to be exploited by foreign manufacturers'.[3] He answered the critics of 'monopoly' by pointing out that he was insisting that every *bona fide* manufacturer in the country could join the new broadcasting company. 'What you have to fear in this is not monopoly; it is more likely you will have cut-throat competition.'[4] On several occasions Kellaway described briefly what conclusions the Committee of Manufacturers had reached. But he did not seek to defend them. On 4 August, for example, he told the House, 'Frankly, I am disappointed at the progress they have made. If a Government Department had been as slow as this, the whole country would have rung with it.'[5]

The delay continued long after the small committee had agreed on the proposals of McKinstry and Isaacs.

The delay in the general introduction of wireless broadcasting [one of the big national newspapers complained early in September] is a sore blow to our pride in our business efficiency. The thing has been in the air for some six months since the *Daily News* first called attention to the example of America: the public has been ready to give wireless a warm welcome, but like people on the wrong wave-

[1] *Hansard*, vol. 156, col. 1226, 12 July 1922.
[2] Ibid., vol. 157, col. 923, 28 July 1922.
[3] Ibid., vol. 156, col. 1226, 12 July 1922.
[4] Ibid., vol. 157, col. 1951, 4 Aug. 1923.
[5] Ibid.

length, we can only hear vague rumours of more conferences. There is no clear note of policy.[1]

Despite Kellaway's criticism of the manufacturers, they were by no means entirely to blame for the delay. The problems which confronted them in July and August 1922 were difficult, and they were inevitably involved in two different sets of negotiations—first amongst themselves and second with the Post Office. It is too simple to say that the first set of negotiations raised the problem of business interest and the second set the problem of public interest, but what can be said is that neither 'business interest' nor 'public interest' was easy to define to everyone's satisfaction. The question of patents continued to hamper business agreement—in this case, thirteen patents held by the Marconi Company and related directly to the production of valve-receiving sets. Eventually a royalty of 12s. 6d. was agreed upon to be paid to the Marconi Company on each valve-holder. The Post Office refused to allow the Marconi Company to levy a lower royalty on members of the 'Big Six'. These discussions took a great deal of time.

Nor was the Post Office a force making for speed. It could and did exhort others, but it was slow to move itself. On 15 August 1922 Noble handed over to Murray the draft of the form of agreement between the BBC and its members: a few days later on 21 August he handed over the Memorandum and Articles of Association of the new body, asking 'for the early approval of the Postmaster-General'. It was not until 4 September that Brown replied on behalf of the Post Office, and he then raised a number of matters which it was clearly impossible to discuss very quickly.[2] When Noble asked Murray on 15 August whether BBC programmes could begin at once—and this was the only question in which the small radio-conscious public was really interested—Murray replied that they could not, 1 October was the earliest possible date. 'There were', he said, 'other preliminaries to settle, for example, the nature of the programmes [the Postmaster-General had undertaken to meet the press on the subject] and the conditions to be laid down for the approval of sets submitted by manufacturers who were members of the Broadcasting Company.'[3]

[1] *Daily News*, 9 Sept. 1922.   [2] *Brown to Noble, 4 Sept. 1922.
[3] *Noble to the members of the committee, 21 Aug. 1922.

It was the concern of the Post Office with matters like these—matters which involved its conception of the 'public interest'—which held back progress in the late summer and autumn of 1922. While some sections of the press fulminated against procrastination, others urged the Postmaster-General to take his time. 'We trust', reads a leader in the *Manchester Guardian*, 'that he will consider very carefully the power that may pass to this private corporation, which has already won for itself a two-year measure of protection.'[1] The State could not disclaim responsibility for the outcome of all the discussions: it had been involved in them and it would be called upon to superintend their consequences.

4. The Company is Formed

IT was not until 18 October 1922 that the BBC was formed. It was registered on 15 December 1922, but it did not receive its Licence from the Post Office until 18 January 1923.

Lord Gainford was the first Chairman. He was an ex-Postmaster-General (for a few months in 1916), and it was as one old Post Office man to another that Noble approached him after an informal meeting of members of the small committee on 18 August 1922. 'You may remember me as Assistant Engineer-in-Chief when you were Postmaster-General.'[2] 'Of course, I remember you at the Post Office', Gainford replied by return of post.[3] He told Noble, however, that 'the subject matter is rather outside my line of country, and all new to me'. At this date the BBC had not yet been formed, but Noble did not hesitate to acquaint Gainford with what he considered would be the main duties of the independent chairman. 'There will be no competition', he wrote, 'as it will be the only Broadcasting Company in this country. The Company will have no business to secure, as it will simply have to provide broadcasting pro-

---

[1] *Manchester Guardian*, 15 Aug. 1922.
[2] *Noble to Lord Gainford, 18 Aug. 1922.
[3] *Gainford to Noble, 19 Aug. 1922.

grammes.' The adverb 'simply' stands out in retrospect. 'As the six Directors represent six competitive firms,' Noble went on, 'the main function of the chairman will be to hold the balance evenly between the companies. The duties will not be arduous.'[1]

In retrospect this aspect of the office seems overstated. It was doubtless because of the memory of what had happened during the previous few months that Noble gave it such prominence. Gainford accepted formally in writing on 31 August, but for more than another month he was Chairman without a company. It was not until 5 October that Noble could tell him that 'all differences have been settled, and we shall be ready to register the Company at an early date'.[2] Nearly two months later, on 2 December, he was still writing that he hoped that at the meeting on the following Tuesday they would be able to reach a final settlement. 'It is very disappointing that the matter has dragged on so far, and the delay is certainly not doing the broadcasting business any good.'[3] The first Board meeting was held at Magnet House on 21 December 1922.

The reasons for the further delay were twofold—differences of opinion between the Postmaster-General and the Manufacturers' Committee and continued differences of opinion among the manufacturers themselves about patents.[4] On 7 September McKinstry was complaining that there were still disagreements about patent rights which were holding up his signature to the Memorandum and Articles of Association.[5] The dominating position of Marconi still influenced all discussions. Even after a 'Peace Treaty'[6] had been signed between the two biggest companies the question remained alive and continued alive in 1923. The former set of differences—between the Post Office and the manufacturers—chiefly concerned the position of the 'Big Six' in the British Broadcasting Company and the determination of the amount of income to be appropriated to reserve. The Postmaster-General was anxious, as Brown put it in a letter of 4 September, not to leave too much power to the guaranteeing companies. On the matter of reserves he felt that

[1] *Noble to Gainford, 22 Aug. 1922.
[2] *Noble to Gainford, 5 Oct. 1922.
[3] *Noble to Gainford, 2 Dec. 1922.
[4] For patent problems, see Sturmey, op. cit.
[5] *McKinstry to Noble, 7 Sept. 1922.
[6] *The term was used in a letter of 1 Nov. 1922.

the limitation on dividends would be useless if large reserves were accumulated.[1]

At further meetings with representatives of the manufacturers other issues were raised. Some of them, like the duration of the agreement, were old issues that had been raised and apparently settled. Some were new ones. They included patent rights in the manufacture of receiving sets, a subject which the manufacturers considered as 'substantially a domestic matter for arrangement among the members themselves'.[2] It was the question of separate and independent representation of smaller firms on the Board of the new Company, however, on which the Post Office insisted most—not without reason—and as late as the beginning of October the agreement was being held up on this point.[3] It was finally agreed that in addition to the six 're-presentative directors' of the 'Big Six', the companies that provided the original capital, there should be two additional BBC directors to be elected at the Annual General Meeting by constituent members of the Company other than the 'Big Six'. It was on the basis of this provision and the earlier agreement that any *bona fide* British manufacturer could become a member of the Company on taking up a £1 share that BBC representatives asserted vigorously that their Company was not a monopoly. As the formal evidence submitted to the Sykes Committee a few months later put it, 'The Broadcasting Company claim that there is no monopoly in the business resulting from broadcasting for any single British firm or group of firms, and if there is any monopoly it is one for British firms as a whole as distinguished from foreign firms.'[4]

At the meeting held at the Institution of Electrical Engineers on 18 October 1922, when the BBC was formed, there were present representatives of over 200 firms. This was only about half the number which had been invited, but it was an impressive enough figure.[5] Noble told the assembled manufacturers that there was now 'complete agreement with the Postmaster-

---

[1] *Brown to Noble, 4 Sept. 1922. The small committee considered this letter on the day that it arrived. Another meeting was held on 7 Sept.

[2] *F. Gaylor to Noble, 9 Sept. 1922.

[3] *Gaylor to Noble, 3 Oct. 1922.

[4] *Written evidence of Noble and McKinstry for the Sykes Committee, 8 May 1923.

[5] *Oral evidence of Noble to the Sykes Committee, 8 May 1923.

This Prospectus is sent only to bona-fide British Manufacturers of Wireless Apparatus who alone are eligible to apply for Shares.

The Subscription List will open on Monday, .the 5th February, 1923, and will close on or before Monday, the 12th February, 1923.

A copy of this Prospectus has been filed with the Registrar of Joint Stock Companies.

THE BRITISH BROADCASTING COMPANY, LIMITED.

(Incorporated under the Companies Acts 1908 to 1917.)

CAPITAL - - £100,000.

Divided into 100,000 Cumulative Ordinary Shares of £1 each.

ISSUE OF

99,993 Cumulative Ordinary Shares of £1 each at par payable in full on application.

The holders of the Cumulative Ordinary Shares are entitled to receive out of the profits of the Company a fixed Cumulative Dividend at the rate of $7\frac{1}{2}\%$ per annum on the capital for the time being paid up or credited as paid up thereon but are not entitled to any further or other participation in profits.

DIRECTORS.

THE RT. HON LORD GAINFORD, Headlam Hall, Gainford, Durham (*Chairman*).

GODFREY C. ISAACS, Marconi House, Strand, W.C.2 (Managing Director Marconi's Wireless Telegraph Co., Ltd.).

ARCHIBALD McKINSTRY, The Red Lodge, Southill Avenue, Harrow-on-the-Hill (Joint Managing Director of Metropolitan-Vickers Electrical Export Company, Limited).

MAJOR BASIL BINYON, "Hawthorndene," Hayes, Kent (Managing Director of Radio Communication Company, Limited).

JOHN GRAY, "Beaulieu," Park Farm Road, Bromley, Kent (Chairman of the Hotpoint Electric Appliance Company, Limited).

SIR WILLIAM NOBLE, Magnet House, Kingsway, W.C.2, (Director of The General Electric Company, Limited).

HENRY MARK PEASE, 18, Kensington Court Mansions, W.8. (Managing Director of Western Electric Company, Limited).

BANKERS.

BARCLAYS BANK LIMITED, Charing Cross Branch, W.C.2.

SOLICITORS.

STEADMAN, VAN PRAAGH & GAYLOR, 4, Old Burlington Street, W.1.

AUDITORS.

DELOITTE, PLENDER, GRIFFITHS & CO., 5, London Wall Buildings, E.C.

SECRETARY AND REGISTERED OFFICE.

MAJOR P. F. ANDERSON, F.I.S.A., 15, Savoy Street, W.C.2.

17. The Company's Prospectus

General', and the meeting welcomed with enthusiasm the creation of the new Company. Its Chairman was Lord Gainford
who was to be paid an annual honorarium, free of income tax,
of £500. Gainford's association with broadcasting was to
survive the passing of the Company itself, for he remained as
Vice-Chairman of the Governors of the British Broadcasting
Corporation in 1927. The first Directors of the Company, each
of whom was to be paid £200 a year free of income tax, were
Isaacs, McKinstry, Noble, Binyon, H. M. Pease, J. Gray, Sir
William Bull, and W. W. Burnham. The last two were independent Directors elected by the 'smaller firms',[1] Gray
represented British Thomson-Houston, and Pease was an
American citizen. He represented the Western Electric Company, but was no relative of Lord Gainford who shared the same
family name.

The first formal object of the new Company, which included
no one on its Board who was directly connected either with
entertainment or education, was 'to acquire from His Majesty's
Postmaster-General a Licence in such form and subject to such
terms and conditions as he may from time to time prescribe for
the creation, establishment and operation . . . of stations as a
public utility service to the public by means of wireless telephony and/or wireless telegraphy'. The stations were to provide
'news, information, concerts, lectures, educational matter,
speeches, weather reports, theatrical entertainment and any
other matter which for the time being may be permitted by or
be within the scope or orbit of the said Licence, and develop
and exploit the said service'.[2]

Obtaining the Post Office Licence in the form desired was
itself a difficult operation. In the discussions leading up to the
approval of the Memorandum and Articles of Association of the
Company it was the Post Office which had been the critic. In
the negotiations leading up to the granting of the Licence the
roles were reversed. Two issues were prominent at the time: a
third issue acquired prominence in the light of what happened
later. The two most difficult issues at the time were Post Office
licensing policy for the owners of receiving sets and the powers

---

[1] Bull was a director of Siemens, and Burnham was managing director of the
Burndept Company.
[2] Objects of the Company, clause 3.

of the new Broadcasting Company to transmit news programmes. The issue of the future was the extent to which the
BBC had been granted an exclusive right to provide the
country's broadcasting service.

All three issues involved outside parties. Licensing affected
the interests of the experimenters, the pioneer radio group and
the group which, as we have seen, pressed hardest in times of
difficulty for a broadcasting service. The broadcasting of news
affected not only the newspaper interest but the powerful
agencies which supplied news to the newspapers. The issue of
'exclusive right' affected all those interests, some strong, some
weak, many scattered, which were jealous of the BBC's powers
or wished to share in them. These interests were vocal from the
moment of the formation of the BBC and put forward their case
before the Sykes Committee during the following year.

Post Office licensing policy had been settled as far as licences
for BBC-marked sets were concerned in the negotiations of the
summer of 1922. The licence was to be fixed at 10s., half of
which was to be passed over to the BBC. The first broadcast
licences of this type were issued on 1 November 1922. But the
date chosen was itself confusing. It was seventeen days before
the BBC was formed and more than six weeks before the BBC
was registered. It is not surprising that there was confusion in
the wireless trade, some firms beginning to sell BBC-marked
sets, others maintaining cogently enough that they could not
be members of a Company which did not yet exist. Alongside
these new broadcast licences the Post Office continued to issue
experimenters' licences permitting experimenters to build their
own sets from separate components. In July 1922 the Postmaster-General explicitly stated that *bona fide* experimenters
could buy an experimenters' licence for 10s., and he refused
requests made to him by the manufacturers' representatives for
the amount of this licence fee to be raised. Noble had suggested
£2, of which only 5s. should go to the BBC—this, he argued,
would deter 'many of the amateurs who are not *bona fide* experimenters'. He also suggested higher fees for BBC receiving sets used
in places of public entertainment.[1] Neither of these suggestions
was acceptable to the Post Office,[2] and it was only after Gaylor

[1] *Noble to Brown, 28 Sept. 1922.
[2] *Brown to Noble, 2 Oct. 1922.

had criticized the omission from the draft Licence to the BBC of any reference to the BBC sharing the 10s. paid by experimenters for licences that a clause explicitly stating this was inserted.[1]

It was the manufacturers and not the Post Office who realized early in the autumn of 1922 that the experimenters' licence would probably be abused once the BBC had started regular broadcasts. Brown admitted, when pressed by the Sykes Committee, that the Post Office had made 'a series of miscalculations' in relation to this subject.[2] Yet the abuses became apparent very soon and led to a crisis in the relations between the Post Office and the BBC in 1923, which in its turn led to the appointment of the Sykes Committee.[3] The manufacturers were more prescient than the civil servants. Although Noble expressed willingness to be generous towards the experimenters in September 1922—in his words, at least '*pro tem.*'[4]—during the same month a representative of the Marconi Company, L. S. Agate, predicted almost exactly what did happen.[5]

The Post Office, of course, was especially sensitive to the pressure of the organized experimenters. On 21 September 1922 Brown met a deputation from the Wireless Society of London. It included Sir Henry Jackson, Campbell Swinton, Hope Jones, Scott-Taggart, and McMichael. Brown was told that 'the main object of the Wireless Society of London is to foster amateur effort, consequently their first and constant duty is to urge the granting of receiving licences with complete freedom. They hold that every Englishman is entitled to hear what is going on in the aether provided his listening apparatus does not annoy his neighbours.' The Wireless Society of London was undoubtedly a *bona fide* experimenters' association and it was affiliated to other societies throughout the country: it declared itself willing to accept an increase in the experimenters' fee from 10s. to 15s. No change was made by the Post Office, however, and the dead-

---

[1] *Gaylor to Noble, 21 Oct. 1922.
[2] *Oral evidence of Brown to the Sykes Committee, 3 May 1923.
[3] See below, pp. 145 ff.
[4] *Oral evidence of Noble and McKinstry to the Sykes Committee, 8 May 1923.
[5] *Memorandum of 27 Sept. 1922. The presence of a large number of so-called experimental sets, he wrote, would create difficulty not only for the salesmen of BBC sets but for the listeners to BBC programmes. Many of the people seeking to benefit from experimenters' licences were not *bona fide* experimenters.

lock of 1923 was implicit in the failure to act in 1922. Indeed the crisis had begun by the end of 1922.

The question of news broadcasts was even more complicated, and it too was to lead to further crises in 1923.[1] The Postmaster-General expressed the opinion from the beginning of the negotiations of 1922 that broadcasting should in no way alienate the press interest: the same view had been expressed in its most restrictive form by the Wireless Sub-Committee of the Imperial Communications Committee.[2] Even before that, international press conferences, notably the conference at Ottawa in 1920, had vigorously asserted the rights of the press in relation to radio—if not directly to broadcasting at least to wireless. Representatives of the British press made their position clear to the Post Office in the spring of 1922.

On 10 May Murray sent a memorandum to the Postmaster-General which made his own attitude clear. Among the conditions the Post Office should lay down in its talks with would-be broadcasting concerns was that no news should be broadcast which had not previously been published in the press. This condition had been laid down because 'the wireless companies should not, without very careful consideration, be allowed to enter into active competition with the news agencies, as considerable capital is invested in those undertakings and a large amount of Post Office revenue is derived from them'.[3] The Press Association had already represented to the Post Office that permission should not be given to broadcasting companies even to transmit news which had already been published. Broadcasting stations might forestall the local evening newspaper! Murray regarded this possibility as remote, but at least from this date onwards it was tacitly accepted by the Post Office and the government that the new Broadcasting Company would only be allowed to deal with news on terms negotiated with newspapers and press agency interests.

Once the negotiations for the formation of the Company had led to agreement between the various interests and the Post Office, talks began at the Post Office between the representatives of the new BBC, the news agencies, and the press. The Post

---

[1] See below, p. 142.   [2] See above, p. 97.
[3] Memorandum by Murray on 'Wireless Broadcasting', 10 May 1922, P.O. Archives, 22,310/25.

THE COMPANY IS FORMED

Office initiated the talks which started with a meeting on
26 October.[1] Murray was in the chair, and Noble, Isaacs,
Simpson, Binyon, Grey, Hirst, and Phillips represented the
BBC. The press representatives spoke for a very powerful coalition
of scattered but related interests, among them the agencies, the
great international news collecting bodies, the Newspaper
Proprietors' Association, which safeguarded the position of the
metropolitan newspapers, and the Newspaper Society, which
protected the provincial newspapers. Once again it was F. J.
Brown who acted as the main spokesman of the Post Office, the
guardian of the 'public interest'.

The interpretation of that interest was, as always, difficult
and controversial. On the one side were the representatives of a
great established institution, 'the Fourth Estate' of the realm,
which during and after the First World War had wielded unprecedented power. On the other side were commercial companies speaking in the name of 'experiment' and change. The
Post Office itself derived a very considerable income from the
established institution, and had no idea of the vast sums which
it would eventually derive from broadcasting. The outlook of its
representatives was conservative, and the last thing they wished
to do was to jeopardize their understanding with the press for
the sake of dubious gains in the future.

Lord Riddell stated at the conference that while the press
had 'no desire to take any steps which would interfere with
broadcasting', it had to ensure that the BBC did not 'lift' the
property of the newspapers and news agencies without payment.
Moreover, it had to be sure that the interests of newspapers
should not suffer through the broadcasting of news. An assertion
by Isaacs that the BBC had the same right to collect 'popular'
news—such as racing results—and to distribute it over the air
was strongly deprecated by the press representatives. 'If the
Company actually competed with the Agencies in regard to the
collection of racing results &c. it would be fatal to any idea of
co-operation.' Noble assured the press representatives that in
fact the BBC did not contemplate the collection of news, and a
small sub-committee was then appointed to try to work out the
details of an agreement. As had been the case during earlier discussions between representatives of manufacturing concerns,

[1] The following account is taken from BBC Archives.

the Post Office withdrew temporarily from the fray, and the meeting of the sub-committee on 6 November was held not in St. Martin's-le-Grand but at Marconi House.

As a result of the deliberations at this meeting a draft agreement was drawn up between the BBC and the news agencies. It was dated 11 November 1922. The news agencies agreed to supply to the British Broadcasting Company between the hours of 6 o'clock and 11 o'clock in the evening, 'solely for the purpose of distribution within the British Isles', a daily summary of the world's news. The summary would be long enough to 'constitute a broadcasted message of half-an-hour's duration, and approximating to between 1,200 and 2,400 words'. Thus began the compression of the world's news, scarce or plentiful, dramatic or dull, significant or insignificant, into a regular daily mould. Yet the drafters of the agreement were less concerned about the conditioning of the public than their own potentially conflicting claims. The BBC promised that it would make use of this news only in its broadcast programmes, and that BBC news bulletins would always begin with the acknowledgement 'Copyright News from Reuter, Press Association, Exchange Telegraph and Central News'. A clause stating that 'the selection of news for broadcasting purposes should not be such as to prejudice the interests of the newspapers' was amended to read 'the Parties to this Agreement enter into it in the full spirit and endeavour not to prejudice the newspapers'. In both versions the point was the same.

The financial arrangements were cautious. For the use of the news supplied, the BBC was to pay royalty on a sliding scale. The maximum royalty was 5d. per licence on the first 200,000 wireless receiving licences, and the minimum one farthing on all licences over half a million. The timing of the agreement was even more cautious. It was to remain in force for six months from 11 November 1922. Noble gave an assurance to Sir Roderick Jones that while the agreement was in force the BBC would not itself collect news from other sources or assist in establishing any other agency for collecting news. Brown acknowledged the receipt of the agreement on 16 November and on behalf of the Post Office gave the BBC a 'temporary and provisional permission to transmit summaries of news'.

The signing of the agreement by no means ruled off the question even for six months. Riddell continued to press Brown for the institution of a specific provision in the BBC's Licence that the BBC was not to be entitled to make use of exclusive news without payment 'whatever may be the technical legal rights of the newspapers or News Agencies to protect such news'. A further conference was held at the Post Office on 12 December when representatives of the press, including Riddell, Jones, and Sir James Owen of the Newspaper Society, explained their position to Noble. The meeting was cordial, and Noble gave a verbal undertaking that he would recommend to his Board that no news should be transmitted by the BBC before 7 o'clock in the evening. He added that his Company was anxious to avoid any dispute with the press, and the 7 o'clock rule would obviate all differences with the provincial press. This was an optimistic statement, which was to be the source of many further difficulties during the next few months. The Board of the BBC approved it, however, and the first BBC news bulletin was broadcast at 7 o'clock on the evening of 23 December. A second followed two hours later.

The Licence of the BBC, which was issued on 18 January 1923, included a clause stating that the BBC should not broadcast any news or information except that obtained and paid for from the news agencies. This clause had been added to the first draft of the Licence after the meeting of 12 December.[1] A Supplementary Indenture signed on the same day as the Licence dealt with the details of this arrangement and allowed for arbitration if disputes arose between the BBC and the agencies. The negotiations leading up to the preparation of this had held back the main Licence itself. The 7 o'clock rule was not formally written out either in the main Licence or the Supplementary Indenture. There was strong pressure from the press to have this rule formally inserted in 1924.[2]

By the middle of 1923 the representatives of the press were objecting to the BBC's request for a more generous news agreement both with the news agencies and with the press on the grounds that the BBC was a monopoly.[3] This objection was not

[1] *Gaylor drew the attention of Noble to this insertion in a letter of 15 Dec. 1922.
[2] See below, p. 263.
[3] *Oral evidence of Lord Riddell and Sir Roderick Jones to the Sykes Committee, 29 May 1923. See below, p. 173.

raised by the press in November and December 1922, yet the problem of monopoly in this context was not completely ignored. Noble wanted the BBC's 'exclusive right' to be protected in the Licence itself. In the discussions with the Post Office leading up to the granting of the Licence he pressed for a clause preventing the Postmaster-General for the duration of the Licence from granting another licence to any other broadcasting company, 'however improbable as a matter of business that may be'.[1] Woods assured him that the insertion of this clause was unnecessary since the BBC was already adequately protected.[2] Of even greater importance, the Post Office maintained, the insertion of such a clause would 'savour of monopoly which, from the point of view of the Department and for political reasons is extremely objectionable'.[3] It was even held that it was *ultra vires* for a department, by departmental action, to create a monopoly.

Haziness about the exact meaning of the word 'monopoly' led to some at least of the difficulties later in 1923. In the meantime the BBC believed that it had secured an exclusive right for the duration of the Licence. Noble and McKinstry told the Sykes Committee that the BBC existed as one organization because the Post Office had told the manufacturers that they must get together to form one broadcasting company.[4] The Licence recognized a marriage arranged by the Postmaster-General. When press representatives suggested that they were refusing to allow the BBC greater freedom to collect and distribute news because it was a monopoly, then the BBC expected the Post Office to come to its defence. The Post Office should make it abundantly clear that it was at its instigation that the arrangements of 1922 had been made. Unfortunately for the BBC, by the middle of 1923 there was a new Postmaster-General, and broadcasting had made such strides that the history of what had happened in 1922 seemed far less relevant than forecasts of what would happen in 1924, 1925, and the more distant future.

[1] *Notes of 29 Oct. 1922.
[2] *Oral evidence of Noble and McKinstry to the Sykes Committee, 8 May 1923.
[3] *Gaylor to Noble, 30 Nov. 1922, reporting discussions with Post Office representatives.
[4] *Oral evidence of Noble and McKinstry to the Sykes Committee, 8 May 1923.

5. The Appointment of J. C. W. Reith

THERE was not only a new Postmaster-General in May 1923 when the Sykes Committee began its work. There was a new and forceful representative of the BBC on the Sykes Committee itself, a man who changed twentieth-century British history by converting the controversial commercial Company into an established national institution. For more than fifteen years he continued to give that institution form and purpose. J. C. W. Reith was offered the position of General Manager of the BBC on 14 December 1922, a few weeks after BBC broadcasting had officially started. Less than a year later—on 14 November 1923—he became Managing Director. His rapid promotion was a recognition of the trust and respect he had won among the handful of people who knew his work from the inside. Yet his reputation outside was growing even faster. By the end of 1923 in most people's eyes he *was* the BBC. To many people, including his critics, he has remained the BBC ever since, although it is now more than twenty years since he completely severed his connexion with it.

So fixed and secure is his reputation that an effort is needed to recapture the mood of the brief period before it was established. In December 1922 Reith knew nothing of broadcasting, neither of its problems or of its opportunities. He did not even know the word until he read a public advertisement in the newspapers of 13 October 1922 giving details of four vacancies in the Company, which was described as still in process of formation. The four posts were those of General Manager, Director of Programmes, Chief Engineer, and Secretary. 'Only applicants having first-class qualifications', the advertisement went on, 'need apply.'

What first-class qualifications the directors had in mind was not made clear. Perhaps the nature of the qualifications was not clear to them. Only Eckersley and Burrows in their different ways had ideas about what was needed. In a letter written to Isaacs on 7 December Burrows 'respectfully submitted' his views on the situation, which he described as 'acute'. 'An adequate staff' was needed urgently 'to deal with the several matters arising out of broadcasting' and 'a definite policy' was needed 'as to what expenses may be incurred on this work'.

The opening of regular broadcast programmes has resulted in our being overwhelmed with correspondence, telephonic enquiries and personal visits, such as alone, to be dealt with adequately, would require a considerable staff. The staff of this department was at the outset a nucleus one in relation to the regular office work alone. It is hopelessly inadequate to perform the double duties and the result is at the moment there is the grave risk that both the Marconi Company's publicity and the broadcasting programmes may suffer. The fact has also to be faced that some organisation will be necessary in a day or two to deal with the Marconi Broadcasting stations at Newcastle and Cardiff.[1]

This letter was written in the strange transitional period after the BBC had begun to function but while it still depended entirely on the services of members of the individual commercial concerns. It shows how vague and untidy the picture was when Reith took up his post. Certainly Reith had no clear idea of the necessary qualifications. He was an engineer. He was a Scotsman. He was 'a son of the Manse'. He was thirty-four years old. He hated 'smooth-running soft jobs'. He was looking for an interesting opening where he could employ the talents which he knew he possessed. In March 1922 he had resigned his position as general manager of William Beardmore and Company, the Coatbridge engineering firm. In the spring and middle months of 1922 he was on the fringes of the political world.[2] He served for a time as a kind of A.D.C. to Sir William Bull, a Unionist politician who became one of the first two 'small-firm' directors of the BBC. In recommending Reith to Bull, J. R. Eccles, the headmaster of Reith's old school, Gresham's, Holt, wrote in enthusiastic language about his 'absolute integrity and high purpose'. 'I don't think', he added, 'that we can afford to lose men of character and earnestness of purpose like Reith, and, if you can do anything to give him scope for his undoubted powers, I think you will be doing something that you will never regret.'[3] The BBC was to provide him with ample scope for his

[1] Burrows to Isaacs, 5 Dec. 1922. Marconi Company Archives.
[2] See *Into the Wind* (1949), pp. 80–82.
[3] J. R. Eccles to Sir William Bull, 4 Oct. 1922. I am grateful to Sir George Bull for giving me permission to reproduce this extract from a private letter in his possession.

BROADCASTING.

CASE FOR G.P.O.

Ask - Mr Brown has just returned from Washington - JC.

1. ### Reasons for M.V. in Radio Field.

   a. Power applications of valves.
   b. Radio control of relays, switches, etc.
   c. Wired wireless control of relays.
   d. Possible wireless power.
   e. Probable developments in Ionic or Electrionic Engineering.
      (atomic sources of Energy).

2. ### Reasons for Broadcasting.

   a. Not a blatent advertising scheme.
   b. Build up a market for sets.
   c. Experience and Experiment. *(We are new in this field)*
   d. Research. (Lines.)
   e. Gain association in the public mind with "Radio" (Now "wireless "and "Marconi" are synonymous to many.
   f. Telephony experience in common with Radio Co.
   g. *Moscow soon.*
   i. *Public opinion may force concession soon .. Better to grant now at leisure*

3. ### Arguments in favour.

   a. #### Country.
      1. England at present behind in development of radio art, which is of great future importance. c.f. U.S.A. where large Engineering firms are directly interested.
      2. Possibility of foreign propaganda (indirectly)
      3. Let amateurs hear English music rather than Dutch only, *n French.*
      4. *unifying effect.*

   b. #### People.
      1. Broadcasting forms a most important social activity and should not be prevented, though it may be necessary to impose some limits.
      2. *Educational (stress) see Pittsburgh' instu. on broadcasting)*

   c. #### Government, P.O., and Services.
      1. Average amateur content to listen so long as there is variety , and therefore broadcasting on a large scale, tends to clear the air.
      2. Institution of one or two "responsible" station for many irresponsible amateur transmitting sets

Location of Station
Recving Station
? 10/ P.O. Licence

High Cost of big wave many sets - Weight of by broadcasting

18. Early 'Reasons for Broadcasting', 1922

19. Lord Gainford, Chairman of the British Broadcasting Company

20. J. C. W. Reith

21. P. P. Eckersley

undoubted powers, and his qualities of character made up a far more relevant first-class qualification than his experience as an engineer when he took up his post with the BBC.

Bull was a link in the chain, but it was to Noble that Reith addressed his letter of application. He posted the letter in the letter-box of the Cavendish Club, 'then did what should have been done before—looked up Sir William Noble in *Who's Who*'.[1] When he read that Noble was an Aberdonian, he hastily retrieved the first letter from the letter-box and rewrote it with a reference to his own Aberdonian ancestry. He drew attention also to his engineering training, his commercial experience, and his success in 'organising and administrative appointments of considerable responsibility'. His letter ended with the remark that 'the appointment is of the nature and degree which I came to Town hoping to obtain, and I should not apply did I not feel capable of discharging its responsibilities to your satisfaction'.[2]

There was no reply to this letter until 7 December, and unfortunately there are no surviving records of what was happening behind the scenes or of the considerations which Noble and his colleagues had in mind in appointing to the post. There is not even a surviving short list of the six people seriously considered for what was to be a strategic post in British twentieth-century history. One prominent journalist who enjoyed a distinguished later career is said to have been approached and to have turned down the offer on the grounds that the post was not big enough. Another person who is said to have been considered is Kellaway, who had not been returned to parliament at the general election of 1922. Instead, to the annoyance of some of the BBC Directors, he became a director of the Marconi Company. Whatever happened behind the scenes, however, Reith was summoned to an interview at Magnet House on 13 December. It was a brief interview, but long enough for Reith to be told that within a short space of time the newly appointed General Manager would know everybody worth knowing in the country.[3]

The following day Noble, who had been very cordial at the interview and at the end 'almost winked as if to say it was all right',[4] telephoned Reith to tell him that the Board was

---

[1] *Into the Wind*, p. 81.
[2] Reith to Noble, 13 Oct. 1922. This letter is in Lord Reith's possession.
[3] *Into the Wind*, p. 82.　　　　　　　　[4] Diary, 13 Dec. 1922.

unanimous in offering him the post. Reith had asked for a salary of £2,000: a majority on the Board was prepared to offer £1,750, but Isaacs insisted on seeing Reith before he would agree to this figure. An interview was duly arranged, and Isaacs, the dominating figure in the talks leading up to the incorporation of the BBC, met for the first time the man who was to be the dominating figure in the events which followed its foundation. All went off well. Reith was approved, and wrote formally to Noble on 20 December accepting the appointment. 'I note', he stated, 'that the General Manager will have the full control of the company and its staff, and will be responsible to the Directors.'[1] In the quiet of his own heart Reith knew that he 'had gotten what he had been waiting for'. 'I am profoundly thankful to God for His goodness in this matter', he wrote in his diary. 'It is all His doing.'

Before formally accepting, Reith met for the first time some of the men who were to work for him, including Burrows, who was appointed Director of Programmes, and C. A. Lewis, who was chosen as Burrows's deputy. Reith was still 'completely mystified as to what it was all about',[2] even after Burrows had shown him 'a sort of chart showing what staff was required'.[3] His first official BBC letter—to Noble—was entirely practical. 'I have had considerable talks with Mr. Burrows and Mr. Lewis, and have also had a meeting with Mr. Rowell, the secretary of the Institution of Electrical Engineers. There need not be any time lost when I am away in the matter of new offices.'[4] With that he went back briefly to Scotland. It was a Glasgow school-fellow, a chartered accountant, who finally enlightened him about the nature of the work.[5] Reith realized then, in his own words, that he had 'a great work to do'. He continued thereafter to see the problem of broadcasting in terms of high moral responsibility. C. A. Lewis saw the problem somewhat differently. 'We had been appointed guardians and attendants of the most voracious creature ever created by man—a microphone—which clamoured daily to be fed! At first it was satisfied with simple fare and a little of it, but as the days went by its appetite

---

[1] Reith to Noble, 20 Dec. 1922. This letter is in Lord Reith's possession.
[2] Diary, 14 Dec. 1922.   [3] Diary, 17 Dec. 1922.
[4] Reith to Noble, 20 Dec. 1922.
[5] *Into the Wind*, p. 83.

not only grew in the amount it wished to devour but also became fastidious in the extreme as to the quality of the repast set before it! A most terrible and insatiable monster!'[1]

Certainly the main theme in the first few months of the history of the BBC was incessant work. Reith revelled in it, but even he was so busy that the diary in which he regularly recorded both events and thoughts got several weeks behind. His work was remarkably varied. It included not only general supervision of staff and of programmes but high-level diplomatic negotiations with the Post Office, the press, and there presentatives of many different kinds of commercial enterprise.

He has vividly described his first day in his office and the general conditions in which he worked during this early period. Before taking up his post in London he briefly visited Newcastle *en route* where he saw 'transmitting station and studio place and landlords'. The first broadcast from Newcastle had been given a day or two earlier on Christmas Eve from a microphone mounted on a motor lorry in a stable yard. The first London office of the BBC was scarcely more pretentious. It was on the second floor of the General Electric Company's buildings in Kingsway, and consisted of a room and a small antechamber. When Reith arrived at Magnet House at 9 o'clock on the morning of Saturday, 30 December, the lift attendant asked him his business before allowing him to get into the lift.

'B.B.C.', I said deliberately. 'Nobody there yet, sir, but we're expecting them on Monday for the first time.' 'Who is them?' I asked. 'The new Company', he replied. So I told him that this was it, or part of it, one-quarter approximately. As he bore me upwards I detected a scornful curiosity in his veiled scrutiny. He was very polite. He conducted me to a door already labelled BBC, which he opened for me with some ceremony. I entered. The door shut, and I heard his footsteps echoing along the corridor. A wild thought came to me that I would hail him and bid him loose me again. But I had heard the clang of the iron gate. It was too late.[2]

Reith was left alone with his responsibilities. When Noble saw him just before his first Board meeting on 4 January 1923, he told Reith that 'we're leaving it all to you. You'll be reporting at our monthly meetings and we'll see how you're getting on.'[3]

[1] C. A. Lewis, *Broadcasting from Within* (1924), p. 26.
[2] J. C. W. Reith, article in *Picture Post*, 25 July 1942.
[3] *Into the Wind*, p. 88.

Reith's account is supplemented by some of the other accounts of these 'terrific early days', as Lewis described them. They cover the events of November 1922 when BBC broadcasting officially began. 14 November, the day chosen for the occasion, was the day of the general election, and the first programmes consisted in the main of election results. Birmingham and Manchester began their programmes a day later. Percy Edgar, in charge of programmes at Birmingham (and later Midland Regional Controller), has recalled the first news announcement made from the Birmingham station. 'Tonight and until further notice we will give in addition to musical items copyright news bulletins specially prepared for the British Broadcasting Company by the several English news agencies. It is my intention tonight to read these bulletins twice, first of all rapidly and then slowly, repeating on the second occasion, wherever necessary, details upon which listeners may wish to make notes.'[1] A. E. Thompson, first Engineer-in-Charge at the Birmingham station, introduced the first programme for children, which lasted for fifteen minutes, on 5 December. He called himself 'Uncle Tom' and was thus one of the first of the famous radio uncles.[2] London followed with its first children's programme on 23 December, which was also the day of the first London general news bulletin, the first orchestral concert, and the first broadcast talk by Captain E. B. Towse, V.C.

Early conditions in Manchester have been described by Kenneth Wright, then a young graduate of Sheffield University and an employee of the Metropolitan-Vickers Company, who later became Assistant Music Director of the BBC. 'I remember that when we broadcast the Grenadier Guards Band, the players were so crowded together that several had to sit on the piano. We had a unique contrivance for adjusting the height of the microphone to the singer's mouth. The singer stood on a pile of books. One night a tenor in taking a top note also took a step backwards, and there was a terrific crash as he slid under the piano. That ended the solo.'[3]

[1] *The Manager's Notebook. This interesting log book covers the period 15 Nov. 1922 to 3 Mar. 1923. Each day it had written in it details of the programmes and the hours of broadcasting. The Station Director's comments were added both on the quality of the performance and of technical transmission.

[2] A. E. Thompson, 'The Silver Jubilee of Broadcasting', in *Standard News*, June 1948.   [3] Leslie Baily, BBC Programme, *Scrapbook for 1922*.

These reminiscences have much in common. As Burrows put it, 'in three different parts of Britain there were functioning nightly three groups of men who had never met, who had no precedent to work upon, and not the faintest idea of what the future would bring forth in the matter of a balance sheet. They had, however, a common enthusiasm for their work [and] a desire to demonstrate to the public the extraordinary, but in the majority of cases unsuspected, possibilities of broad-casting.'[1]

Before Reith had been in London long, there was a rush of responsibilities, and the six telephones allotted to the Magnet House office were ringing almost continuously throughout the day. There was so little space that it became necessary 'to place one's hat on the top of one's walking stick against a wall in order to find room for it'.[2] The equally crowded Marconi House studio was fortunately near at hand, and since there was no clear-cut distinction between performing and administering there was much coming and going between the two places. As 5 o'clock, the programme hour, drew near there was many an 'enlivening sprint' between the office and the studio. One survivor of this hectic age has related how, during the evenings, he lived entirely on a diet of beer and meringues, presumably the only diet available which could both be obtained and consumed 'in an extremity of haste'.[3] Every member of staff worked an average of twelve hours a day and the strain became so great that Lewis told Reith one morning that he would break down if the state of affairs went on much longer. 'You might let me know when you're going to do it,' Reith replied, 'then we can arrange to take it in turns.'[4]

The excitement compensated for the effort, and gradually the BBC began to work not as a collection of individuals but as a single institution. Reith was at the centre of things but he was also at the head of the organization. He had to be versatile as well as determined, surveying alike people and programmes, sectional interests and public opinion. There was always more than one kind of problem to tackle. For example, two days after

---

[1] Burrows, op. cit., p. 68.
[2] Ibid., p. 79.
[3] 'The Old BBC' in the *BBC Year Book* (1930), p. 155.
[4] Lewis, op. cit., p. 31.

a new station had been opened in Cardiff on 13 February 1923, the press tried to place an embargo on the free publication of BBC programmes. A few weeks earlier on 13 January the Newspaper Proprietors' Association had given notice that the BBC would have to pay for the publication of BBC programmes in the newspapers at advertisement rates. The reason given was that 'the Broadcasting Company is a commercial institution with, it is understood, most favourable financial prospects'. If it wished to 'advertise' it should not do it for nothing. Reith had no intention of accepting this argument. He persuaded his Board to hold out, and won the battle when Gordon Selfridge offered him free space for programmes in his advertisement column in the *Pall Mall Gazette*. The circulation of the *Pall Mall Gazette* increased dramatically, and the Newspaper Proprietors' Association changed its mind and agreed to allow freedom of action to its members in their dealings with the BBC during the next six months. Nothing was ever heard of the matter again. Yet something positive emerged from the conflict. While the embargo was in progress, Reith hit upon the idea of a *Radio Times*. It was an idea which was to be put into practice with enormous success soon after the six months had elapsed.

Not all difficulties could be solved so satisfactorily. In the early months of 1923, almost before the ink was dry on the signature at the foot of the Licence, the BBC and the Post Office came into collision. The situation deteriorated sharply, and eventually in May 1923 the whole state of broadcasting was once more brought under review. Reith was to emerge from this ordeal triumphantly. The details belong to the next chapter. Yet a description of Reith's approach is a proper climax to this. 'I had nothing to do with the constitution of the B.B.C.', he has written, 'or with licence conditions; did not much like the former, thought the latter impossible of application. But it was my duty to bring the B.B.C. through these troubles; the establishment of broadcasting itself and of a policy in broadcasting depended on the survival of the B.B.C. despite all constitutional and licensing anomalies.'[1] The BBC had to survive before its place in national life could fairly be decided.

[1] *Into the Wind*, p. 90.

IV

ORDEAL AND EXPERIENCE
1923–1925

Difficulties were, of course, to be expected. What we did not expect, however, was that they would be deliberately created, and obstructions be put in our path from almost every conceivable quarter.

LORD GAINFORD
Speech to the BBC Shareholders, 21 September 1923

1. 'Frustrations, Difficulties, and Deadlock'

THE dispute between the BBC and the Post Office during the early months of 1923 was important not only in itself but because of its timing. In itself it raised basic issues relating to the financial future and the public status of broadcasting: because of its timing, it gave the numerous enemies of the BBC an excellent opportunity of attacking the Company before broadcasting had been established. As Reith put it with great restraint in 1924, 'we came in for an unenviable amount of public attention before we were quite ready for it'.[1] It was the extent of public attention as much as the sharpness of the dispute behind the scenes which accounted for the choice of means of ending the deadlock. In April 1923 the Postmaster-General announced the appointment of a departmental committee 'to consider the whole question of broadcasting—not merely the question of licences but the desirability of existing contracts'.[2] When Reith pressed the Postmaster-General to allow him to become a member of the committee, the Postmaster-General did not object. 'As the BBC was in the dock,' Reith wrote years afterwards, 'he might have declined; I was grateful to him for agreeing; and much relieved.'[3]

Although the Sykes Committee concerned itself with almost every aspect of broadcasting and laboriously covered all the ground which had been covered equally laboriously by fewer people less than a year before, the deadlock which led to the setting up of the committee was caused by only one specific issue—that of licences. As soon as regular broadcasting became a practical proposition in 1922, the number of requests to the Post Office for 10s. experimental licences increased sharply. From the Armistice of 1918 until the end of March 1922 only 7,690 licences were issued by the Post Office to what it was satisfied were *bona fide* experimenters: between 1 April and 1 November 1922 10,371 experimental licences were granted.

[1] J. C. W. Reith, *Broadcast Over Britain*, p. 67.
[2] *Hansard*, vol. 162, cols. 2442–6, 19 Apr. 1923.
[3] *Into the Wind*, p. 90.

The demand continued to increase—to such an extent that the Post Office became almost as alarmed as the BBC. 'I spoke to Mr. F. J. Brown about amateur licences', Noble wrote on 22 December 1922. 'They are greatly concerned about the big demand ... and they would very much appreciate any suggestions which we may have to make. .... I made the suggestion that except in very special cases they should refuse all amateur licences and advise the applicants to take out BBC licences. In the bulk of cases no doubt the applicants would take this recommendation lying down.'[1]

The BBC maintained that 'the bulk of the applications' came from people who were not *bona fide* experimenters. There was a large number of people, it was suggested, who built their own wireless sets not because they were interested in the science of wireless but because they could thereby avoid buying the more expensive British-made sets which bore the BBC mark. Kellaway had actually given them encouragement when he spoke in the House of Commons in July 1922 and stated that 'provision will be made under which amateurs who construct their own receiving sets ... will be allowed to use them'.[2] The implication was that if applicants were sufficiently skilled to make their own apparatus, they would necessarily have sufficient scientific knowledge to make proper use of experimental licences.

During the autumn of 1922, however, business firms, particularly those importing relatively cheap foreign radio components, began to place on the market ready-made parts which could be assembled by the most inexperienced person with the aid of a diagram and screwdriver. Such firms thereby avoided the necessity of paying royalty to the BBC on the purchase price of the apparatus—they might even evade paying royalty to the Marconi Company—and the purchasers of the parts, who went on to assemble them in home-made wireless sets, claimed that they were entitled to experimental licences in accordance with the Postmaster-General's promise. The BBC had promised to be 'liberal' in its approach to experimental licences,[3] but the liberality was being seriously abused. In the last few months of 1922 and the first few months of 1923 the market was flooded

[1] *Noble to Isaacs, 22 Dec. 1922.
[2] *Hansard*, vol. 157, col. 708, 27 July 1922.
[3] See above, p. 129.

with foreign-made parts, and the revenue of the BBC both from royalties and licences was far smaller than had been anticipated when the Big Six went into combination. The estimated 200,000 licence-holders were proving extremely difficult to recruit.

Naturally enough, the Board of Directors of the BBC was soon preoccupied with this question, which first appeared on its agenda at its meeting on 4 January 1923. A committee to investigate the question was then appointed: it included Noble, Isaacs, Binyon, and Reith. On 11 January 1923 it arranged a discussion at the General Post Office, at which Brown was the main Post Office spokesman on matters relating to official policy while Shaughnessy dealt with technical questions. The BBC case was carefully prepared before this meeting. It had two main headings. First, there were far too many experimental licences being issued: the figure for December 1922 was as high as that of the previous three months put together. Only one in five of these licences, it was suggested, was going to a *bona fide* applicant. Second, no attempt was being made by the Post Office to prosecute listeners without licences. Police action was necessary: it should be preceded by the publication of an official notice in the newspapers stating that the Postmaster-General was aware that many unlicensed sets were being used and that their owners would immediately be prosecuted.

On neither of these two points did the BBC get complete satisfaction, although the Post Office did not seek to minimize the problem. On the first, the Post Office representatives said that they had in mind the introduction of a third kind of licence, 'an intermediate licence' to be given to applicants who intended to construct their sets from component parts bought separately; on the second of the two points, the Post Office representatives said that they would arrange for inspectors to go into selected districts 'to fish out unlicensed people'.[1] A proposal by Binyon that the cost of experimental licences should be raised to £1 was not acceptable to the Post Office, despite the fact that the Radio Society of Great Britain, the most influential amateur association, was willing to accept the change. It would certainly have penalized the poor man with his home-made crystal set, the only set he could afford. Murray made the Post

[1] This account of the meeting is taken from the BBC Archives.

Office attitude abundantly clear in a letter written two weeks after the conference was held. If the cost of licences were increased, people who had bought their experimental licences before August 1922 would be penalized by what in effect was a new form of taxation. Moreover if 15s. out of a £1 experimental licence was to be handed over to the BBC, the Post Office 'would be inviting the criticism that it had drifted into the position of an agency for collecting the revenue of a private company through the Postmaster-General's licence'.[1]

This retort, based on absurd reasoning, at once raised bigger issues. So too did the accumulating complaints of the BBC, not only about loss of revenue but about interference by amateurs with regular broadcasting. 'BBC programmes are often rendered farcical', Noble complained, 'by interference caused by amateurs tuning up and causing disturbance and by the transmission of messages.' Among the stations which were said to be interfering was Writtle, which was broadcasting a programme from 7.30 to 8.30 on a wavelength of 440 metres. This was 'much too close to the BBC wavelengths'. The BBC, of course, could do something about this, and Writtle finally went off the air on 17 January 1923.

What the BBC could not do was to interfere with scattered experimenters, or to stop BBC programmes being broadcast from the platforms of theatres and music halls and being 'peddled' by private individuals. A case had arisen in December 1922 of 'two persons who described themselves as ex-Naval officers' applying to the Post Office for a licence to install a five-valve radio receiving set with a loud-speaker in a Ford van 'with the object of touring country towns and villages and giving "auditions" of the concerts broadcast by the BBC'. The object of the ex-Naval officers was plain enough—that of 'earning a living'. The BBC could do nothing about it, nor would the Post Office.[2]

So dissatisfied were Reith and his Directors with the attitude of the Post Office about licence questions in general that on 2 February 1923 Reith wrote formally to Murray asking the Postmaster-General—then Neville Chamberlain—to receive another BBC deputation. Three days later Reith and Noble met

[1] *Murray to Gainford, 31 Jan. 1923.
[2] *Brown to Noble, 1 Dec. 1922.

Chamberlain informally in Birmingham. 'He was entirely un-helpful', Reith wrote in his diary, and (this note was added later) 'scoffed at it being worth while from the Exchequer point of view to enforce licences'.[1] A second small BBC deputation visited the Post Office on 12 February, and suggested to the Post Office representatives that the issue of experimental licences should be suspended pending a new agreement about the whole licensing position. Reith followed up this suggestion on 20 February by pointing out that his Board had noted that slightly more experimental licences had been granted in January 1923 than in November and December 1922 put together. 'I am directed to say that they have received the figures in question with surprise and great anxiety.'[2]

The Post Office would not budge. Brown said that it was already scrutinizing the qualifications of applicants for experi-mental licences. In reply to a questioner in the House of Commons, who asked on 19 February whether he was aware that there was widespread irritation at delay in issuing experi-mental licences, Chamberlain said that the delay was caused by applications being received in very large numbers from persons who did not appear to be *bona fide* experimenters. He hoped, however, to 'make arrangements to obviate the delay'.[3] Murray made the same point even more strongly in a letter to Reith written a few days later. 'As you are aware, complaints have already been made as regards the delay which has occurred in the issue of licences, and any further delay would not only cause inconvenience to persons who require licences for genuine experimental purposes, but would no doubt have the effect of increasing the number of cases in which the obligation to obtain a licence is evaded, and thus accentuate the difficulties of which the Company complains.'[4]

In one sense Murray was right. The more scrupulously the Post Office investigated the qualifications of the would-be 'experimenters', the more tempted would people be to operate home-made sets without a licence. Indeed, only 80,000 BBC licences had been taken out by 1 March 1923. Yet what Murray

[1] Diary, 5 Feb. 1923; *Into the Wind*, p. 90. 'When Chancellor of the Exchequer with eight million licences in force,' Reith added, 'he thought differently.'
[2] *Reith to Murray, 20 Feb. 1923.
[3] *Hansard*, vol. 160, col. 661, 19 Feb. 1923.
[4] *Murray to Reith, 27 Feb. 1923.

left out was to the BBC the most important consideration. The Post Office was unwilling to enforce its own system. The people who evaded paying their licences altogether could rest secure in the knowledge that the Post Office would not sponsor a large-scale national drive against them, backed by the full resources of the police.

They could even feel self-righteous as well as secure, since some of the national newspapers violently attacked the licensing system as a whole and challenged the Postmaster-General's powers to enforce it. The BBC might call the evaders of licences 'eavesdroppers' or even 'pirates',[1] but they could also be depicted—all too easily—as heroes of free enterprise, little men confronted by big organized commercial interests which were seeking to invade the Englishman's 'sacred home'. This was the line taken by the *Daily Express* in March and April 1923 when it organized a lavish propaganda campaign to destroy the BBC.[2] The supporters of the BBC demanded 'sportsmanship' on the part of the listener,[3] but the opponents of the BBC claimed that the 'irregulars' were 'the best friends of the industry'.[4]

Both sides more or less agreed that there were far more 'irregulars' than disciplined troops, and neither side looked fairly or squarely at the economic side of the question. Were the 'irregulars' people who could not afford to buy BBC-mark sets? In a public speech Lord Gainford estimated that only one in four or five listening families held a BBC licence. To him and to his colleagues the whole financial basis of the BBC was being imperilled for lack of enforcement. Evasion was made easy and was becoming popular. Dog licences were so much more straightforward. 'If you keep an unlicensed dog, it may bite a policeman who will then ask you for your licence. A wireless set does not bite a policeman.' Furthermore 'it does not collide with steam rollers'.[5]

Eckersley, who joined the BBC as Chief Engineer in February 1923,[6] prepared a very interesting memorandum for Reith a few

---

[1] The BBC did its best to advertise the 'morality' of licence paying. In March 1923, for example, a chief official of the BBC described to the press how he had received £2. 5s. from an Admiral 'who discovered he was a transgressor and wished to make amends' (*Evening News*, 26 Mar. 1923).

[2] See below, p. 191.   [3] *Evening News*, 24 Mar. 1923.
[4] Ibid., 26 Mar. 1923.   [5] Ibid., 24 Mar. 1923.
[6] See below, pp. 158-60, 202.

weeks later on the technical aspect of the question. He emphasized how few *bona fide* experimenters there really were, and how difficult it still was for businesses to find employees who really knew a great deal about wireless. The people who wanted to make their own sets included large numbers of the ignorant, as well as of genuine experimenters. The difficulty was that stringent legislation to distinguish the first from the second would 'rob us of public support, however just our position from an ethical standpoint might be, and if public support fails, we fail also'.[1]

It was with this kind of consideration in mind that the BBC reverted to the idea, originally proposed by Post Office representatives, of a third kind of licence which would be issued to people who wished to build home-made sets. The Board discussed this suggestion at its meeting on 21 March 1923, and accepted it subject to certain important conditions. It was on the nature of the conditions that there was to be disagreement with the Post Office during the weeks that followed. The BBC made two proposals. The first was that applicants for 'constructors' licences' would have to agree to use component parts marked 'BBC' in the same way that ready-made complete sets were marked 'BBC'. This would guarantee British manufacture and protect the interests both of the manufacturers who had brought the BBC into being and of the very large number of manufacturers who had joined it later. It would incidentally raise the price of sets to the listeners! The second proposal was to fix the amount of the 'constructors' licence' fee at a higher figure than 10s.: £1 was suggested, of which the BBC should receive 15s.

During the negotiations which followed, the willingness of the BBC to compromise on their conditions was fully tested. The Company was disposed at first to weaken the first condition provided that a higher fee than 10s. was charged. When this compromise was not acceptable to the Post Office, the BBC tried the other alternative of standing by the first condition and expressing willingness to accept a lower fee. One or other of the conditions was thought to be essential. Not the least of the difficulties confronting the BBC was that each of the suggested compromises met with resistance from friendly or allied interests. The

[1] *Undated typewritten memorandum.

National Association of Radio Manufacturers of Great Britain, which was the trade association of the most important business concerns, stood firm against any idea of replacing the BBC mark on component parts by a simple marking that the goods were of British manufacture. The Radio Society of Great Britain was prepared to recommend a higher licence fee, but did not approve of a BBC mark on any component part. The most that it would do was to accept the suggestion that components should be marked 'British made'.

Reith had been drawn into discussions with both the N.A.R.M. and the R.S.G.B. earlier in 1923. He felt a little out of place with both bodies at the beginning, but he never failed to understand the implications of his business relationship with the first and the need to win the goodwill of the second. On 16 January he met the chairman of the N.A.R.M. and later in the day was asked to speak at a committee meeting of the R.S.G.B. and invited to join the Society.[1] A meeting was later arranged for 17 March at which the N.A.R.M. stated its case and Campbell-Swinton of the R.S.G.B. stated the case of the R.S.G.B. Although Reith described the outcome of the meeting as 'quite satisfactory',[2] the disagreement between the two points of view was plain, and the BBC was placed in the awkward position of not agreeing completely with either. In the immediate future BBC revenue depended not only on licence money but on royalties, and its fortunes remained linked with those of the radio manufacturing companies. In the more distant future, however, licence revenue would obviously gain in importance. The royalty system had serious flaws, particularly if it were enforced so rigidly that people with low incomes would desist from buying wireless sets altogether. Moreover, if broadcasting were to be treated as a genuine 'public utility service', it was important that the BBC should retain the approval of the most vocal section of organized 'radio opinion' —the Radio Society of Great Britain.

Reith and his colleagues were able to by-pass some of these problems by concentrating on the inadequacies of the Post Office. Indeed, a sense of common grievance dominated an important letter written by Reith to the new Postmaster-General, Sir W. Joynson-Hicks, on 5 April 1923. A few days

[1] Diary, 16 Jan. 1923.   [2] Ibid., 17 Mar. 1923.

before, Reith had met Joynson-Hicks in the street. The Post-master-General had then said that he had plans to revise the licence system, and was considering whether the 10s. licence might be restricted to crystal sets. 'He said he was going to Norwich the next day and asked me to write him there on the question.'[1] For this reason Reith's letter of 5 April 1923 has become known inside the BBC as the 'Norwich Letter'. It has something of the qualities of an encyclical, and deserves to be quoted almost in full.[2]

The manufacturers who came together by invitation of the Post Office [the letter began, immediately striking the right note] and eventually succeeded in laying the plans for the formation of our Broadcasting Company, are responsible for the popularity of wireless today. This has led to the formation of many new Companies and the entrance into wireless manufacture and wireless agency-work of many more. The original firms prepared the ground and supplied the capital. They launched out into large expenditures in new directions on the understanding that the Post Office regulations which were to afford them revenue and protection would be carried out.

This was the nature of the contract: it did not involve any infringement of the rights of experimenters.

The genuine experimenter was not to be handicapped, but the Experimental Licence was only to be issued to those with scientific knowledge, and not to such as developed a pseudo-interest in wireless consequent on the inception of Broadcast programmes.

The contract had not been honoured by the Post Office.

The enormous evasion of licence on the one hand, and the wide-spread use of non-BBC marked sets sold by new Companies, and of home-made sets, on the other was not foreseen. These factors represented a most serious loss to the Company. It was to be expected that the Post Office would take such steps as would to as great an extent as possible ensure the carrying out of the agreements under which they undertook to broadcast, and to manufacture. In this the manufacturers comprising the Company feel disappointed. It is obvious that the formulation and enforcement of new regulations are required. Reception is, in many localities, spoilt by the illegitimate use of reaction due to illicit dealing in and construction of sets. '4,000 firms' are said to be clamouring for a drastic revision of

[1] Ibid., 28 Mar. 1923.   [2] *Reith to Joynson-Hicks, 5 Apr. 1923.

the terms under which the BBC is constituted and revenue collected. It is doubtful if many of them had any interest in Wireless six months ago, and, apart from this, there is no monopoly, as is alleged, as membership in the BBC is open to any *bona fide* manufacturer. 574 have already applied. Some wholly unreasonable criticisms of the programmes are made by those with their own axe to grind. One newspaper offers to undertake broadcasting free, and states there should be neither licence fee nor tariff. The programmes are not as good as the BBC would like, but are improving in all stations. There is no desire on the Company's part to dwell on their difficulties, nor on the amount that has been accomplished. These facts are obvious to all but those whose judgments are dictated by prejudice and self-interest. The Company's voluminous correspondence is evidence of the acceptability of programmes. More rapid improvement is handicapped by antagonism of parties who consider their own interests would be prejudiced, and by the loss of adequate and expected revenue.

Having catalogued his grievances, Reith went on to make a number of suggestions. 'The BBC feel that the tendency will be towards higher licence fees of all kinds, and greater dependence on revenue from this source, but they maintain that for the period of the Agreement they are entitled to have as much protection as is practicable in the sale of BBC sets.' The first contribution the Post Office could make would be to reduce to a minimum the evasion of licences; the second would be to confine experimental licences 'to those qualified by real scientific knowledge'; and the third would be to introduce constructors' licences fixed at £1, with all component parts to be marked 'British Manufacture' but not necessarily BBC.

The suggestion that a third licence should be issued at ten shillings, to those who wish to make crystal sets only, meets with strong disapproval, as only opening the way for further infringement of regulations. The suggested estimate that 90% of those wishing to make sets have only crystal sets in mind is considered excessive: 50% is the highest the Company has heard, and they doubt even this. Many will not observe the terms at all in the first instance, and more will later add valves. It is not considered practicable to ensure the carrying out of the terms.

It was essential to introduce regulations, 'the simpler the better', which would be enforced. As things were,

every condition and regulation is being infringed and evaded, and from past experience the BBC feel they must ask the Post Office to give greater support to the Broadcasting enterprise. . . . They feel that they are entitled to expect that the Post Office will give them the promised protection (consequent upon which the Capital was guaranteed and the Company formed) for the definite period arranged by the preservation of the terms of the Broadcast Licence applicable to BBC sets only, and that it is this class of licence and sets which should predominate.

Already, apparently, the idea of a committee had been mooted. Reith in his conclusion, welcomed this. 'The suggestion of a Committee being appointed hereafter to investigate the whole matter of future arrangements meets with every approval; it is suggested that this should be arranged concurrently with the issue of the third licence.'

In this letter, which 'everyone thought was very good',[1] Reith had gone farther to make concessions than the National Association of Radio Manufacturers was willing to go. He did not go far enough, however, to satisfy the Postmaster-General, who threatened to issue 40,000 experimental licences at once unless the BBC accepted his proposal to introduce constructors' licences which would cost only 10s. The deadlock was near. A meeting of the Board of Directors of the BBC resolved on 12 April that 'any change in the conditions agreed between the Postmaster-General and the BBC other than the concession made by the Company in its proposal would constitute a serious breach of faith on the part of the Post Office'.[2] The same evening Reith reported orally to the Postmaster-General what had happened. Joynson-Hicks stated his case in a letter to Reith's directors written on the following day. 'I think it is right', the letter began, 'that before the negotiations which have been carried on between your General Manager and myself reach, as unfortunately appears to be likely, a complete deadlock, I should put before you my views for your final consideration.'[3] Set alongside Reith's Norwich letter, this letter of 13 April presents a completely different interpretation of the state of affairs.

It began with a tribute to Reith, who had conducted the negotiations 'with firmness and courtesy beyond praise'. Next came

[1] Diary, 6 Apr. 1923.
[2] *Minutes of Special Board Meeting, 12 Apr. 1923.
[3] *W. Joynson-Hicks to the Directors of the BBC, 13 Apr. 1923.

an acknowledgement of the fact that capital had been 'embarked' in the broadcasting scheme on the strength of agreements approved by his predecessors. From that point onwards, however, there was a keen challenge to the BBC, a challenge which was welcomed in the House of Commons by Ramsay MacDonald, the Leader of the Opposition, who claimed that Joynson-Hicks was 'more alive to the situation than his predecessor who effected the agreement'.[1] 'While holding myself fully bound by the conditions of the January Licence,' Joynson-Hicks told the directors of the BBC, 'I am equally compelled to consider myself the guardian of the public interest, based upon the enormous changes which have taken place in the development of broadcasting during the last four months.'

In no circumstances would he support constructors' licences of £1, which would cost twice the amount of a BBC licence.

The Home Constructor will represent the less wealthy portion of the population; and it would, in my view, be ridiculous to charge the ten shillings licence to the man who may purchase from your Company a hundred-pound receiving set, and the twenty-shillings licence to the man who desires to make at the lowest possible price a crystal set for his own use and experiment.

This sentence begged some questions, but it made its point: the second was more terse. It described as 'unacceptable' the idea that radio component parts should be marked BBC. Joynson-Hicks had obviously been talking to the small group of radio manufacturers who resented the radio-manufacturing 'monopoly' rights of the 'BBC': in Reith's view they were 'a little crowd of quite unimportant manufacturers and dealers who are in opposition to the N.A.R.M.'.[2]

Joynson-Hicks suggested that an agreement about constructors' licences would immediately stop evasion.

I have not felt myself, up to the present, bound to prosecute those who have evaded the licence duty, as there was no licence available for the Home Constructor. . . . I have, however, great hopes that on the settlement of the questions in dispute between us, a large proportion of these evasions will cease and that in a few months something like a quarter of a million licences will be issued, and this

---

[1] *Hansard*, vol. 162, col. 2447, 19 Apr. 1923.
[2] Diary, 13 Apr. 1923. See below, pp. 176-8.

would give you the sum of £62,500 towards the improvement of the broadcasting concerts which are now given.

The phrase 'improvement of the broadcasting concerts' suggests a very limited view of the possibilities of what Reith was beginning to recognize was potentially at least a vast national service. Yet there was worse to come.

If you decline to assent to these proposals [the Postmaster-General ended], and I admit that under the terms of the Licence you have that power, I am thrown back on my responsibilities to interpret your Agreement fairly as between yourself and the general public. From the public point of view the most important licence is that of the experimental constructor. No one could place a limit to the discoveries which a comparatively unimportant Experimenter or Home Constructor can produce, and having no other licence to fall back upon, I shall have no alternative but to grant experimental licences to those applicants who have filled up the necessary form stating that they desire to use wireless telegraphy for experimental purposes.

This threat endangered the whole position of the BBC. Moreover, given the financial limitations of broadcasting, Joynson-Hicks had paid no attention to the kind of arguments that had been advanced in the commercial talks of 1922. If he had had his way, he would have left broadcasting without adequate revenue so that it would have been compelled to depend on quite a different financial foundation.

It is scarcely surprising that the reply of the BBC was tougher and more astringent than any previous statement its spokesman had made.[1] The Company declared itself willing 'to consider sympathetically any modifications which do not violate the fundamental conditions of the Licence'. 'The Company is glad,' the statement went on, 'but is not surprised, that you intend that the Agreement shall be honoured. They would venture to point out that this Agreement has exceptional authority in that it was negotiated by one Postmaster-General, approved and signed by another, and its main purposes discussed and approved by the House of Commons.' Joynson-Hicks was firmly reminded that

the initiative which led to the formation of this Company came from the Post Office whose expert officials realised that control and co-ordination were necessary if, in this country, the confusion and chaos

[1] *The reply was dated 16 Apr. 1923.

which had accompanied broadcasting in the United States were to be avoided. The Post Office felt that this control and co-ordination could best be secured by the establishment of one broadcasting Authority. Experience has proved the wisdom of this decision. Even with one broadcasting Authority it is difficult to avoid confusion. How much greater would the confusion have been if the Post Office had taken a different line and approved of the existence of more than one broadcasting Authority?

Given this historical starting-point, all else was a matter of logic. One authority was possible only if it avoided 'any semblance of an onerous monopoly': membership of the BBC had been made open, therefore, to any *bona fide* British manufacturer on taking a £1 share. Abuse of business power had been further checked by a limitation on dividends. Protection was necessary not only in order that the British radio industry should develop but in order that due revenue could be provided for broadcasting purposes. 'Without such protection, the importer and merchant of foreign instruments would be making no contribution to the expense of the Company, whilst reaping the whole of the benefit of the expenses of his British competitor.' It was on the faith of the Agreement between the Company and the Post Office that capital had been subscribed. To substitute vague talk for concrete facts was not an advance in mutual understanding. The difficulties of the Post Office would not have become so acute if the Post Office had acted earlier in accordance with the spirit of the Agreement, by taking serious steps to avoid evasion.

While repeating its earlier proposals about constructors' licences, the BBC had itself taken the battle into still more contentious regions. Its clear statement of why there was one broadcasting authority was doubtless designed not only for Joynson-Hicks but for those sections of the press which in early April 1923 were reaching the climax of their first big campaign against 'monopoly in transmission'. On 5 April, the day that Reith wrote the Norwich letter, the *Daily Express*, the leader of the campaign, questioned the necessity for radio revenue at all. There were many commercial companies, it suggested, which were willing to broadcast for nothing. It was willing to do so itself. There should be competition in transmission so that there would be better programmes, but, especially important, there should be no manufacturers' monopoly in the production of radio sets.

This first attack was very general, rather like a shower of stones. It was followed on 6 April by a second leader called 'Our Air, We Believe' and by two columns of front-page news on the mobilization of forces against the BBC, particularly of business firms which for various reasons had been unwilling to join the BBC. They included the Electrical Importers' Trading Association, which dealt in foreign component parts. Clearly the *Daily Express* was paying no attention to the protectionist argument or to the view expressed by the BBC that uncertainty about licences was holding back the development of an efficient and well-organized British radio industry. The Post Office was a target also, and on 10 April the same newspaper questioned the legality of the collection of licence fees under the Wireless Telegraphy Act of 1904. Three days earlier it had published a cartoon which depicted an allegorical scene in a railway compartment. On one side sat a bearded old man in a top hat, smoking a pipe and issuing forth clouds of smoke containing the words 'Muddle, restrictions, licences'. Opposite him sat a listener holding his handkerchief to his face. The cartoon had the caption 'Mr. listener-in: "Excuse me, do you mind if we have a little air?" '.

On 14 April, the day after Joynson-Hicks wrote his final letter to the BBC, the *Daily Express* declared contentedly that a real bid was being made for freedom. 'An immense stride has been made towards the clarification of the wireless muddle, and the freedom of the air, for which the *Daily Express* has contended, is almost achieved.' On the same day, however, it printed a letter from F. J. Brown refusing an application for a *Daily Express* broadcasting licence—the application had been made on 6 April. 'I am directed by the Postmaster-General', Brown stated, 'to say that he would be unable to grant facilities in this respect to a particular newspaper which (owing to risk of interference) he would be unable to grant generally to other newspapers and organisations.'[1] From 11 April onwards the discussions between the Postmaster-General and the BBC were depicted in conspiratorial terms as a 'frantic effort [on the part

[1] This application was referred to several times during the Sykes Committee hearings. See below, p. 175.

of the BBC] to maintain a stranglehold on the whole industry of amateur wireless in Britain'.[1] The outcome, of course, was certain. A half-column on 19 April was headed 'Vain Fight for Monopoly': two days later the first leader began 'Freedom and Progress: End of Vain Dreams of Monopoly'.

Not only did Reith visit the Post Office frequently during this period, but he had talks with several representatives of the press 'to explain the facts of broadcasting'. On Isaacs's suggestion, he met the editor of the *Daily Mail*, with which the Marconi Company had always enjoyed good relations.[2] On 9 April he arranged a meeting with Lord Beaverbrook himself. 'I was not a bit afraid of him as I imagined he expected me to be', Reith wrote. 'He said I had impressed him very much. He said all he was out against was the manufacturers taking control of Broadcasting.'[3] Nonetheless, the Press attack continued. 'Fighting Freedom' was a heading in the *Daily Express* for the following day. Reith had said that 'freedom of the air would result in chaos': Isaacs had argued that it would mean imported materials and that the industry in this country would have to close its doors. All that the *Daily Express* would admit was that BBC programmes were improving. There was a simple explanation. 'The *Express* had stirred them up.'

It was in this atmosphere that the Post Office and the BBC stated their positions to the outside world. On 17 April the BBC made its first public statement on the controversy. Hitherto, the statement began, it had not been thought advisable to enter into public debate, 'in view of the delicate negotiations proceeding between them and the Postmaster-General'. Since the Postmaster-General had granted interviews, however, and stated his opinions unreservedly, 'the Board now consider it necessary that the public may have a fair opportunity of judging whether their claims are reasonable and just'. The statement went over what was by now very familiar ground to the people 'in the know' but was still unfamiliar outside. The initiative which had led to the formation of the BBC had come from the Post Office. 'They knew that, if the American chaos were to be avoided, one broadcasting authority was essential. Then came

[1] *Daily Express*, 17 Apr. 1923.
[2] See above, p. 77.
[3] Diary, 10 Apr. 1923.

the constitution of that authority. No monopoly was ever suggested, and there is no monopoly today, although the exploitation of the word is rife. Membership was, and is, open to every *bona fide* British manufacturer of wireless apparatus. Approximately 600 have already joined.'

Opposition to the so-called 'monopoly' came not from 'responsible bodies of considered opinion, but from importers and those who are prepared to reap where others have sown'. The Postmaster-General had yielded to pressure from people of this kind, and while the BBC was prepared to accept the idea of a constructors' licence—which itself was a change from the original provisions of the Licence—it was not prepared to accept the conditions which the Postmaster-General demanded. 'The constructors' licence is not a tightening-up of the conditions of the experimental licence, but is a relaxation to the terms of the Broadcast Licence.' To grant such licences in the way the Postmaster-General proposed would be to rob the British radio industry of its protection and to jeopardize good standards of broadcasting.

The protection promised to the Company is for a limited period, expiring at the end of next year. Having regard to the risks which the members were taking, this period is not excessive. The guaranteeing and the subsequent subscribing of capital to the Company by British manufacturers was on the strength of Mr. Neville Chamberlain's signature; likewise the subsequent large commitments in manufacture. The public can judge the seriousness of the situation which will arise if, by Departmental action, the Agreement in spirit or letter, be violated.[1]

Two days later on 19 April Joynson-Hicks stated his case in the House of Commons. He began by a *caveat*, in effect throwing doubt on whether what his predecessors had done was 'in accordance with public policy'. Was it right that the Post Office should collect 'what are in effect compulsory taxes' for the purpose of giving half of them to broadcasting companies? Sir William Bull, who was the only director of the BBC who was also a member of parliament, reminded Joynson-Hicks that it had been the Post Office which had suggested this arrangement. The Postmaster-General equivocated, saying that it had been

---

[1] *BBC, *Press Statement*, 17 Apr. 1923.

M

'the result of numerous negotiations between the Broadcasting Company and the then Postmaster-General'.

He also threw doubts on whether the BBC had in effect been given a monopoly Licence. 'I am not at all sure whether it is not open to myself to grant a Licence, if I so desire, to someone else.' He did not like the claim of the 'BBC' to be able to prevent any other radio manufacturer in Great Britain manufacturing broadcasting materials—this claim, in fact, was never made—and he could not 'possibly be a party' to the view that all component parts used by 'wireless constructors' should be marked 'BBC'. He admitted in answer to a question that any wireless manufacturer could join the BBC by paying £1, but this, he said, made no difference to his attitude. 'I am not going to be a party to compelling any British manufacturer to join any particular combine.' Nor would he wait any longer in issuing experimental licences. Since January he had held his hand 'because of the opposition—I can quite understand the legitimate opposition—of the British Broadcasting Company': he proposed in the new circumstances to ask experts on his staff to examine the 33,000 applications for experimental licences which had been held over since January. After they had decided which were 'honestly experimental', licences would be issued forthwith.

Finally, since the BBC had stated that there were 200,000 infringers of regulations working without licences, he proposed to institute 'the strongest Committee I can get in order to consider the whole question of broadcasting—not merely the question of licences, but the desirability of existing contracts and the questions that have arisen on contracts'. The committee would include three or four members of parliament, two or three members of his expert staff, and representatives of the Radio Society of Great Britain, 'the great scientific body dealing with wireless', and the BBC. He hoped that this committee would give him helpful advice which would enable him 'to solve one of the most difficult problems' that had ever come before him. 'I can assure the House', he ended, 'that I have devoted days, and almost nights, to try to find a solution, fair on the one side, and without inflicting, what I do not want to inflict, a real monopoly against the would-be manufacturers in this country.'[1]

[1] *Hansard*, vol. 162, cols. 2442–6, 19 Apr. 1923.

It was almost half-past eleven when the Postmaster-General ended his speech, and this was consequently almost the last word in the House of Commons. The committee was duly appointed on 24 April with Major-General Sir Frederick Sykes as chairman. The BBC was not willing, however, to allow the Postmaster-General to have the last word in the country before the committee met. Its attitude was in no sense defensive. A statement issued on 20 April appealed to every 'fair-minded person' not to be taken in by the Postmaster-General's *'ex parte* speech'.

The Agreement in question entered into between the Broadcasting Company and Mr. Neville Chamberlain is neither a combine in the sense in which the word is usually understood, nor is it in any sense a monopoly. The Post Office wished broadcasting to be undertaken by manufacturers in general. There has never been any thought or attempt to protect one British manufacturer against another, and nothing in the Agreement justifies the suggestion. The whole object of the introduction of the BBC mark was to make broadcasting possible, and to protect all British manufacturers equally against dumping of foreign sets manufactured by labour paid at a rate of about one-fifteenth part of what British labour is paid, with which British manufacturers could not compete. . . . It is regrettable that the public should not have before them a statement to enable them to appreciate the reasons which induced Mr. Neville Chamberlain to enter into the agreement with the Broadcasting Company, and what were really the objects and benefits of the Agreement. There would have been no broadcasting without that Agreement. Under it broadcasting has made amazing progress, and if it were capable of being destroyed, the broadcasting wireless industry and broadcasting must be destroyed with it.[1]

This was a public statement dealing with general principles. Behind the scenes Reith, with the help of Eckersley, continued to press the Post Office on specific questions. Who were the expert members of the Post Office staff who were to decide which experimental licences should be granted? What qualifications were considered necessary?[2] Above all, why were so few broadcasting licences being issued? Less than 100,000 broadcasting licences had been issued by the end of March 1923. It was not merely the finances of the BBC which suffered. How

---

[1] *BBC, *Press Statement*, 20 Apr. 1923.
[2] *Reith to the Postmaster-General, 25 Apr. 1923; 25 May 1923.

could the future of broadcasting be secure if this position continued?

2. The Sykes Committee

THE Sykes Committee included ten members. Apart from Sykes himself, there were three other members of parliament— Major the Hon. J. J. Astor, Sir Henry Norman, and Charles Trevelyan; two Post Office officials, F. J. Brown and Sir Henry Bunbury, the Comptroller and Accountant General; one representative of the Press, Viscount Burnham, the chairman of the Newspaper Proprietors' Association; one representative of the Radio Society of Great Britain, Dr. W. H. Eccles, its president; one representative of the BBC, Reith; and, for good measure, Field Marshal Sir William Robertson. The committee held thirty-four meetings, examined thirty-two witnesses, and reported to parliament in August 1923.

On the main issue of contention it recommended that rather than three licences there should be only one: one single broadcasting licence, costing 10s., should be substituted for the existing experimental and broadcasting licences. Of the 10s., 7s. 6d., not 5s. as hitherto, should go to the BBC. Since broadcasting was likely to develop rapidly, however, the 75 per cent. should be subject to a sliding scale with a decrease in the proportion paid by the Post Office on each licence as the number of licences increased.

The committee paid a warm tribute to the 'enterprise and ability' of the BBC, and advocated substantially greater freedom in its conditions of broadcasting. At the same time it did not endorse the existing system of finance by royalties. It recommended the complete discontinuance of royalty payments on wireless sets, and reliance only on licences for broadcasting revenue. Other means of raising revenue, for example, by advertising, were firmly rejected. Radio advertising had been strongly opposed by the newspapers on the grounds that it would interfere with their own interests, but in reaching its con-

clusions the committee was swayed by a different argument—
that advertising 'would lower the standard'.

Concern for the 'great potentialities' of broadcasting was
expressed in various sections of the Report, and it was suggested that public control could best be achieved by the setting
up of a Broadcasting Board to whom all complaints and proposals relating to broadcasting could be addressed. It should be
so composed that it would 'inspire confidence in the public
mind'. Within this framework the BBC would continue to
function. It should be open not only to radio manufacturers but
to all British wireless dealers and retailers, and it should no
longer be specially protected against foreign competition.
Although protection 'was an object of the existing scheme, it
must be left to be dealt with by Parliament as part of the fiscal
policy of the country'.

Behind the statement of these bald facts there is a story of
many trials of strength, keen disagreements, and sharp con-
frontations of principle. Because of this hidden story, the typewritten minutes of the Sykes Committee, which run into many
volumes, are more illuminating than the compact and extremely
well-arranged final White Paper, which consists of less than
fifty pages.[1] On financial grounds it was decided not to print
the full minutes of evidence: the cost would have been 'in the
neighbourhood of £400'.[2] As a result much interesting material
is buried away. There is no complete set of the minutes even in
the BBC archives: they survive only in the Post Office where
the idea of the committee was born.

Appropriately enough, the Post Office evidence was given
first. R. W. Woods dealt with the legal position, E. H. Shaughnessy answered questions on organization and engineering, and
Brown, who, like Reith, was in a strategic position as both a
member of the committee and a witness before it, concerned
himself with policy. Woods, who was questioned first, made it
clear that the Post Office had decided as a matter of high policy
not to prosecute wireless licence offenders.[3] It was difficult, he
said, to find out who the offenders were, but once offences had
been discovered, he would only prosecute if he were given a

[1] Cd. 1951 (1923), *The Broadcasting Committee Report.*
[2] *F. W. Phillips to Reith, 20 July 1923.
[3] *Oral evidence of R. W. Woods before the Sykes Committee.

definite directive from his superiors. The written order of the Postmaster-General was necessary. When asked bluntly whether it was not a breach of the Agreement with the radio manufacturers that no adequate steps had been taken to deal with evasion, he replied that 'the Postmaster-General does not undertake to prosecute everybody who commits a breach of the law'.

Reith took the opportunity to restate the view of the BBC that it was 'one of the fundamental essentials of the Agreement' that there should be no evasion: Noble added later that the only satisfactory way of preventing evasion was to prosecute people who did not possess wireless licences in exactly the same manner as people who did not possess dog licences were prosecuted. When a member of the committee pointed out the practical difficulties in detecting the absence of wireless licences—'a dog runs about the street and wireless apparatus sits in an attic'—Noble replied tartly that 'there may be a difference of behaviour in the two animals; it does not get away from the principle'.[1] He might have added that while dogs did not have licences tied about their collars, most owners of wireless sets had prominent outdoor aerials. Although it might have been difficult to prosecute all offenders, the psychological and moral effect of prosecuting a few known offenders would have been very great.

Woods was called upon to deal with two other matters, which were to be discussed time and time again in the course of the committee's inquiry—the first was 'monopoly' and the second 'censorship'. Dr. Eccles asked him whether the BBC's Licence gave it a monopoly of broadcasting. 'In my opinion', Woods replied, 'neither in fact nor in law is there a monopoly granted by this Licence.' The 'essence of every monopoly' was an 'exclusive grant'. This exclusive grant was not conferred in the Licence. Once again Reith took up the challenge without delay. He asked Woods whether in view of the fact that the BBC 'combine'—if he could call it such—had come into existence as a direct consequence of Post Office policy, it would not be 'an extraordinary action' on the part of the Post Office to licence another transmitting company. In 1922 twenty-four firms had been told by the Post Office that they could not all broadcast but must form one authority or two. What had happened in the

[1] *Oral evidence of Sir William Noble and A. M. McKinstry before the Sykes Committee, 10 May 1923.

intervening year to change Post Office policy? Sykes suggested
that Reith might put this question to Brown since the Post Office
solicitor was qualified to deal only with the strictly legal aspect
of the question. There was agreement that the committee, of
course, had a completely free hand to make quite new recommendations relating to the period after the original BBC Licence
had expired.

On 'censorship' the most vigorous questioner was Charles
Trevelyan. Throughout the whole of the committee's hearings
he asked difficult and searching questions, which led him
eventually to sign a minority reservation stating that broadcasting should pass out of private hands altogether and be
treated as a 'public service'. He asked Woods whether 'for
public reasons' the government of the day could intervene to
prevent the broadcasting of something that was considered
'undesirable'. At this stage Woods was probably unaware of the
importance which was ultimately to be attached to this particular question. 'I rather doubt', he replied, 'whether the Government could intervene to prevent a concert, lecture, educational
matter, speech, weather report, theatrical entertainment and
any other such matter. They could intervene to prevent news,
because it would have to be approved by the Postmaster-
General. I do not think the Postmaster-General could prevent
the Broadcasting Company from disseminating concerts.' 'Or
speeches?', asked Bunbury. 'Or speeches', Woods replied.

Burnham, speaking for the press, noted that the committee
had reached the nub of this question at this early stage. To what
extent could the 'mere fiat' of the Postmaster-General interfere
with the liberty of the broadcaster? Once again Woods gave
what may be described in retrospect as an extremely 'broadminded' reply. The BBC was subject to common law in respect
of matter which was contrary to public morals and so on, but
there was nothing to prevent it broadcasting political speeches
or religious matter if it wished to do so. He admitted later in his
evidence that the Postmaster-General could intervene to maintain standards if the BBC was broadcasting programmes 'of the
most trivial possible character'. By clause 5 of the Licence the
BBC was required to provide 'a programme of broadcast
matter to the reasonable satisfaction of the Postmaster-General'.
Trevelyan suggested very pertinently to Woods that if the

Postmaster-General could intervene to prevent the broadcast of trivial matter, he could surely intervene to prevent matter being broadcast which he did not think was in 'the public interest'. Woods, however, did not budge on this point. The Licence was not intended to give the Postmaster-General power to censor things of which he disapproved on political or religious grounds. The specific reference to satisfying the Postmaster-General was introduced to protect the public. There were no precedents when the BBC was founded, and it was considered right that the Postmaster-General should have the power of ensuring that the public got 'a fair return for their money'. 'I do not think that it amounts to anything more than that.'

The answer was too simple to suffice. On each side of this issue there were steep precipices which it was far more easy to tumble down than to explore inch by inch. The Post Office had probably not been aware of the existence of the precipices in 1922. In concentrating on the single issue of the relationship between the 'newspaper interest' and the BBC, it had by-passed the bigger and more general issues of 'controversy' and 'censorship'. Brown dotted the 'i's' and crossed the 't's' of Woods's statement.[1] It had not entered 'our mind' in 1922—he qualified this remark at once by adding 'at all events we did not regard it as a practical proposition'—to control news and views. 'But certainly we did want to be able to exercise some sort of control over the nature of the programmes as a whole. If the ether was to be occupied we hoped that it would be worthily occupied. We tried to word the Licence in such a way as to give us some right of objecting.' In other words, the initial concern of the Post Office had been with what we would now call 'standards' of broadcasting. When Trevelyan pressed him, Brown went farther, however, than Woods had done. He conceded the fact that since the BBC had a monopoly of distribution of news as compared with newspapers where there was a variety of distributors, the Post Office must continue to concern itself with the question of relations between the BBC and the press. By insisting that the BBC should secure its news from news agencies this would give 'some sort of assurance that the news was of the general type of uncoloured news'.

Trevelyan, as a Labour politician, was afraid of a private

[1] *Oral evidence of F. J. Brown before the Sykes Committee, 3 May 1923.

broadcasting corporation being biased, not of its being too 'uncoloured' and 'uncontroversial', and he probably got little satisfaction out of Brown's reply to a further question as to whether the Post Office would have a 'policy' towards the BBC's reporting of a general election. 'I think you might say', Brown remarked, 'that we have no definite policy with regard to that now: I think it would depend very largely upon the views of the Minister-in-Charge.' The BBC, he went on, could be 'as partisan as it pleases about political or economic or other questions'. This was not to be the Post Office line a few months later, and Brown added immediately afterwards that if the BBC were really to be as partisan as it pleased 'I am quite sure that the Licence would never be renewed'. Whether or not this could be called 'intimidation', 'that is the kind of line we should take'.

Clearly the Post Office, whatever it thought about the extent of its own powers, had an extremely powerful weapon in its hands in all its dealings with the BBC. Brown explained that no one in the Post Office listened to radio programmes every day or officially 'knew' or 'watched' what the BBC was doing. None-theless, it had already exercised a measure of control at least once, after a Labour member of parliament had objected to a broadcast talk relating to a London building strike and had asked a question on the subject in the House of Commons. 'I think it is undesirable', the Postmaster-General had told the questioner in the House of Commons, 'that the Broadcasting service should be used for the dissemination of speeches on con-troversial matters and I have had the attention of the BBC called to the incident to which the Honourable Member refers.'[1] This statement went much farther than either Woods or Brown was prepared to go in their evidence before the Sykes Committee, but both the question and the answer had been noted by the members of the committee, who asked Woods specifically about it. Burnham referred to the Postmaster-General's statement as implying 'a censorship far more severe than was exercised during the War by the Censor's Department'. 'Whether it is good or bad, it implies a censorship in fact. That is what we have got to face.' 'Not a legal censorship,' Trevelyan added, 'only a censorship on the understanding that the Postmaster-General had said

[1] *Hansard*, vol. 163, col. 300, 24 Apr. 1923.

that it was "undesirable" to broadcast a speech of that kind.'
'Not censorship,' Burnham went on, 'an influence'; and after
Trevelyan had agreed, he added the further words 'and possibly
intimidation'. It was this reference to 'intimidation' which
Brown took up when he referred to the Postmaster-General's
ultimate authority not to renew the BBC's Licence. Woods
translated this threat into the most gentle of language. The
Postmaster-General's intimation of the undesirability of the
BBC broadcasting a talk of this kind was not intimidation
because the BBC had a fixed Licence for only two years. It
remained to be seen not whether the Postmaster-General would
renew the Licence but whether the BBC itself would wish
to ask for its renewal.

The question of 'controversy' in broadcasting was to arise on
many occasions throughout the history of the BBC, and in later
phases the terms of reference of the Postmaster-General and the
BBC were very clearly set out. It is important to note that in
this early phase, at the time when the Sykes Committee met, the
main sanction of the Postmaster-General was the threat that if
the BBC behaved in a 'partisan' manner its Licence would not
be renewed. The BBC and its General Manager knew that they
had to 'behave well', however nicely the Postmaster-General
might refer to his own powers. 'You might misbehave once,'
Sir William Noble told the Sykes Committee, 'but the Post
Office under this Licence could come down on us very severely
and take our Licence away.'[1] Whatever the Postmaster-General
said, foolishness would be followed by withdrawal of the Licence,
and the power of the Postmaster-General had actually already
been deployed. Reith called the Postmaster-General's intervention during the building case an 'instruction': the Postmaster-General preferred to call it 'conveying an opinion'.
What it was called was immaterial: it placed Reith under an
obligation.

Reith and the Company accepted the obligation. 'The
Broadcasting Company', Reith stated while Woods was giving
his evidence, 'have never, I think, broadcast anything controversial, and, of course, they are taking very great care not to.
Whether or not they are prevented from doing it, they obviously

---

[1] *Oral evidence of Noble and McKinstry before the Sykes Committee, 8 May
1923.

would not do it.' McKinstry was even more cautious. 'The Broadcasting Company', he said in evidence, 'wish to keep away from controversial matter and has endeavoured to do so; we do not wish to have the Broadcasting Stations used for propaganda which will excite one section of the population and would be very distasteful to another.'[1] This was a very narrow view of broadcasting as a social medium, and Trevelyan wisely pointed out that 'if you are going to exclude anything which anybody thinks is doubtful you are going to make yourselves very dull'.

He also pointed out, however, why it was difficult for the Board of the BBC to take a broader view in 1923. Not only was the Postmaster-General watching their behaviour, but some sections of the public did not feel that it was 'safe' to trust controversial statements put out by a private company. The press encouraged public fears of BBC bias. If all parties were allowed to put their case over the air, McKinstry told the committee, 'we could certainly have no objection to having the case handled in that way, but then you would run straight into the newspaper interests'. Could any broadcasting company have taken a different view in the interim conditions of 1922 and 1923? 'If you depart very far from the present position,' McKinstry went on, 'you run into some other interest which is very strongly opposed to the line of action you may take.'

In point of fact, the experience of the BBC in 1922 and 1923 went a little farther than McKinstry and Reith allowed. Despite the fear of Post Office intervention, anxiety concerning the attitude of the press and the public, and a highly developed sense of 'editorial control', there were occasional controversial broadcasts—including debates on tariff reform, the topical bone of contention between the Liberal and Conservative parties, and the ideology of Communism, with one of the speakers a Communist. Reith himself modified the statement he had made before the Sykes Committee. 'Great discretion has to be exercised in such matters,' he wrote, 'but if on any controversial matter the opposing views were stated with equal emphasis and lucidity then at least there can be no charge of bias.'[2] Of course, bias would be just as likely to be imputed by sections of the general public as by the Postmaster-General. After the general

[1] Ibid.   [2] *Radio Times*, 30 Nov. 1923.

election of 1923, 'I had three personal letters complaining that there had lately been an undue preponderance of extracts from the speeches of one party. Incidentally I also had two others asking why that same party had received so little attention.'[1]

Burnham was sharp and incisive in his questioning of Woods and Brown on the issue of censorship, yet the press which he represented was always at least as anxious as the Postmaster-General to limit the powers of the BBC to broadcast controversial and colourful material. Much of the time of the Sykes Committee was taken up by the examination of press witnesses. Sir Roderick Jones for the news agencies not only reiterated the view that the BBC should in no circumstances be allowed to collect news, but argued also that the BBC should not be able to arrange news. 'News values must always be to some extent a matter of opinion. But it is better to have trained, expert and dispassionate opinion rather than the reverse, and this is secured by the agreement of the News Agencies, endorsed by the newspapers and the Post Office, to work together as far as broadcasting is concerned.'[2] Sir James Owen, representing the Newspaper Society, suggested that not only should the times of broadcast news bulletins be severely controlled, but the content should be watched also. 'The public interest requires that it [broadcasting] should be given its due facilities to demonstrate its utility provided that such facilities do not with official assistance and support destroy or injure other undertakings at present serving the public interest.'[3] Lord Riddell, representing the Newspaper Proprietors' Association, was more specific.

The Broadcasting Company, it is known, would like to disseminate the cream of the news amongst their subscribers. Attempts have been made to secure permission to broadcast the Boat Race, the King's speech, and other outstanding incidents occurring before the authorized time for broadcasting news. This would probably have a most prejudicial effect on the newspapers. In particular, the broadcasting of racing and football results and similar matter would certainly seriously interfere with the sale of newspapers—for example, a publican with a broadcaster would be able to supply the requirements

[1] *Radio Times*, 7 Dec. 1923.
[2] Written evidence submitted by Sir Roderick Jones to the Sykes Committee, 5 June 1923.
[3] *Oral evidence of Sir James Owen before the Sykes Committee, 5 June 1923.

of his customers, who would be eagerly waiting in the bar for the results.[1]

If the Post Office was frightened of the BBC dabbling in controversy, the press was frightened of it dabbling in 'surprise'. Once it did that, all other news would become 'stale'. 'If the edge is taken off the news by dissemination through the broadcaster of all the important items immediately they occur, it is highly probable that the interest in newspapers will be seriously diminished and the circulation adversely affected.' There was no recognition on the part of the press representatives in 1923 that newspapers and broadcasts could be anything other than competitive. The dream (or nightmare) of one single mass communication system with the press as one constituent agency and wireless a second was completely alien to everyone who took part in the debate.

It is necessary to add that the press representatives before the Sykes Committee claimed that this fear of an extension of the scope and influence of broadcasting was bound up with their opposition to the BBC as a monopoly. 'Is it fair?' Owen asked, 'is it consonant with public policy that a monopoly set up by the Government, or at least guaranteed by Government, protected by Government, should compete, unfairly compete, with businesses which are established, or which may be established?' If a monopoly were necessary on technical grounds, then the monopoly should be 'circumscribed' so that it would not injure existing interests. It should not, for example, be employed to spread 'certain social, political and religious ideas which suited the Company and which could not be answered'. Broadcasting news of outside events might be 'the thin end of a wedge': 'before we knew where we were, knowing the enterprise of the BBC [this was an interesting side tribute to a 'monopoly'] we might find that you had driven a coach-and-four through the agreement'.[2] Lord Riddell also attacked the broadcasting of outside functions. When Reith asked him if his objection would apply, for instance, to the broadcasting of parliamentary debates, he added that it would. 'You are trying to take the bread out of our mouths.' He refused to admit that he and his colleagues were following 'the mad policy of trying to push back

[1] *Oral evidence of Lord Riddell before the Sykes Committee, 29 May 1923.
[2] *Oral evidence of Sir James Owen before the Sykes Committee, 5 June 1923.

the waves'; 'we recognise that this is a great invention, with great possibilities, but in dealing with new things you have got to consider existing things'. Like Owen, he objected to 'monopoly', but he was pertinently reminded that the news agencies which he represented were themselves, as a 'combine', seeking to perpetuate their monopoly of news collection. 'You call it a monopoly,' he replied, 'I call it a privilege.'[1] This was language that Reith, at least, could understand.

Whether or not the press was seeking to stand in the way of 'progress', as more than one member of the committee suggested, on two points—one technical, one organizational—the representatives of the press showed how little they understood the shape of things to come. Owen, Riddell, and Jones were asked by Reith and others whether their objection to 'outside broadcasts' applied only to news items relating to them—the term 'running commentary' had not been invented—or whether they were thinking of actual broadcasts of the voices of people involved. In the case of a public speech by the Prince of Wales, for example, were they objecting to a report at the time or immediately afterwards of what he had said or to a broadcast of the Prince's voice? Owen said that he was not thinking of the actual voice being broadcast, and speaking on the spur of the moment—he had not thought of the matter before—he would say that there would be no objection to broadcasts of the actual voice. Riddell, when asked the same question, replied, 'Oh! I see; well we have not gone into that.' What they had not gone into was to be the staple of most outside broadcasts in the future. Jones had to be told plainly that what Reith had in mind was 'putting the microphone in front of the speaker', and he then stated simply, 'That is not our sphere; it is a matter for the Broadcasting Company. . . . An occasional speech here and there is not a matter to worry about. But no more!'

On the organizational point, also, none of the press witnesses could see beyond the present structure of the BBC as a combine of commercial firms to the possibility, however vague, of some kind of public corporation. This term had never yet been used in this context, but some of the members of the Sykes Committee were contemplating at a very early stage in the proceedings the idea of a 'Broadcasting Board' to organize broad-

[1] *Oral evidence of Lord Riddell before the Sykes Committee, 29 May 1923.

casting in the 'public interest'. When Bunbury asked Owen
whether the BBC should still be circumscribed in its news policy
if it were controlled not by the manufacturing interest but by
'a body representing the people who receive the news', Owen
said that he did not follow the question. Only after further
elucidation did he say that the Newspaper Society would object
to 'a monopoly under any guise whatsoever'. Riddell's response
to similar questions was almost the same. This time, however,
it was Sykes himself who asked him whether he agreed that if
the public instead of the manufacturing interests were to control
broadcasting, then the public should be entitled to get what it
wanted—news, outside broadcasts, and so on, at any time.
Riddell replied:

I am sorry that I did not quite follow your question. You say you
can conceive that the time may come when broadcasting will be
controlled not by the manufacturers but by the public. Well, I
gather the fact that you gentlemen are sitting here today indicates
that the public already indirectly controls broadcasting, if a government can be said to represent the public, as I suppose it ought to
do. The Government obviously control the whole business, and if
they grant a Licence they do so because they think that it is the best
way to make use of their power.

It is not altogether fanciful to discern in these vague and
tentative answers and in the often equally vague and tentative
questions that elicited them the birth of the idea of a broadcasting system free from the direct control both of the manufacturers and of the Post Office. Reith, at least, must have been
aware of the trend that the discussion was taking, and, since he
was the chief prompter, he had good grounds for welcoming it.
Trevelyan was thinking of the Post Office itself taking over.
The Post Office did not wish to do this if only because 'a Minister
might well shrink from the prospect of having to defend in
Parliament the various items in Government concerts'.[1] Only
Herbert Morrison and the London Labour Party, among the
witnesses before the committee, pressed for a full shift of responsibility and demanded that broadcasting 'instead of being in
the hands of a partially controlled but otherwise irresponsible
private monopoly, should be publicly owned and controlled'.[2]

[1] Cd. 1951 (1923), para. 25.
[2] *Memorandum of evidence submitted by the Executive Committee of the
London Labour Party. See also *The Wireless Weekly*, 30 May 1923.

The majority of the committee came to the conclusion that 'a Broadcasting Board should be established by statute to assist the Postmaster-General in the administration of broadcasting and to advise him on important questions concerning the service'.[1]

This was as far as the Sykes Committee went; the Crawford Committee of 1925, the second committee appointed to determine the future of broadcasting, was to go farther and in its Report of 1926 to recommend the establishment of a public corporation. In retrospect Reith saw a direct link between the two committees.

The trade had put me in office, [he wrote in his autobiography] expected me to look out for them; there was a moral responsibility to them. But I had discerned something of the inestimable benefit which courageous and broad-visioned development of this new medium would yield. There lay one's commission; and there need be no conflict of loyalties. Whatever was in the interests of broadcasting must eventually be in the interests of the wireless trade. Would the trade see it? Could they, my own directors especially, be persuaded of it? If we could get through the first year or two there need be no further issue between service and trade.[2]

The path was not always so well defined, even for Reith: 'the Committee', he wrote in his diary on 10 June, 'is a dreadful struggle, and I have to watch everything that is said and read every word of evidence afterwards'.[3] The final Report, unlike the Report of the Crawford Committee, did not commit itself to one single solution for the future organization of broadcasting. 'Subject to existing rights,' it stated, 'the Government should keep its hands free to grant additional licences, and should consider various alternatives for the question in the future, either by the Company or by other authorities, of local or relay stations in addition to large stations.'[4]

In 1923 by far the larger part of the radio industry supported the BBC and accepted Reith as an able and dedicated spokesman. A smaller section of the industry, however, joined with the press in challenging the BBC's monopoly. Majority opinion in the trade was represented by the National Association of

[1] Cd. 1951 (1923), paras. 22-23.
[3] Diary, 10 June 1923.
[2] *Into the Wind*, pp. 90-91.
[4] Cd. 1951 (1923), para. 76.

Radio Manufacturers of Great Britain; minority opinion, to which Reith believed that the Postmaster-General was paying far too much attention,[1] was represented by a number of smaller bodies, some of them of doubtful membership and standing. Majority opinion, expressed before the Sykes Committee by F. Phillips on 15 May, stood by the Agreement between the Post Office and the BBC as the foundation of national broadcasting policy. 'The interests of manufacturers lie in the provision of efficient and ever improving quality of broadcasting. We are anxious to ensure that sufficient revenue is available for the BBC to adopt any new developments in the art.'[2] The BBC was not a monopoly, the N.A.R.M. argued, since any *bona fide* British radio manufacturer could join both it and the N.A.R.M. So successful had the BBC become that even after its Licence expired it should not disappear. 'In our opinion the position should be very carefully reviewed to see that all the advantages accruing from the elaborate and expensive organization of the BBC should not be lost under the succeeding arrangement.'

Minority opinion, represented by the British Radio Manufacturers' and Traders' Association and the Electrical Importers' and Traders' Association, challenged all these statements. The Agreement had been in the interest only of the big firms, who had tried to corner the market in 1922. The BBC was in effect a monopoly. 'A small group of large firms in uniting ostensibly to acquire a licence to transmit have, in fact, acquired practically the complete control of the conditions of manufacture of listening apparatus.'[3] The BBC could inspect the books of small firms and disclose their trade secrets to the 'Big Six'. In addition it could keep out some of the smaller firms by insisting on a £50 deposit from each member. More seriously, the whole royalty system penalized certain kinds of business enterprise.

The E.I.T.A., founded in 1919 with the Electrical Wholesalers' Federation as one of its affiliates, was closely associated with the B.R.M.T.A. with which it had a joint meeting in November 1922. It stood by the principles of free trade, and laid down as part of its policy that its members should

---

[1] Ibid., 13 Apr. 1923. Representatives of the Electrical Importers' and Traders' Association had an interview with Joynson-Hicks on 19 Mar. 1923.

[2] *Evidence of F. Phillips before the Sykes Committee, 15 May 1923.

[3] *Memorandum of evidence submitted by the British Radio Manufacturers' and Traders' Association.

'encourage the handling of British goods, but resist in the strongest possible manner any system of prohibition which hampers trade and tends to deliver it into the hands of any particular group of manufacturers (or privileged licence holders) to the detriment of traders generally'.[1] The effect of the existing broadcasting arrangements, the E.I.T.A. argued, was 'to attempt an import embargo by the indirect method of departmental administration. . . . The public loses the benefit of improved service which they might derive from use of imported parts available from abroad from time to time.'[2]

Both these 'rebel' organizations urged that revenue for broadcasting should be collected entirely from licences, and they tried to associate their campaign with other campaigns against the BBC, including that in the press. Another 'rebel' manifesto published late in 1922 had a nineteenth-century ring about it.

Chaos . . . public doubts . . . veiled threats . . . inclusive rights claimed . . . all these point to and cry aloud the absolute necessity for manufacturers and traders to co-operate together in establishing a STRONG ASSOCIATION with UNITY OF PURPOSE and METHOD and the FORCE of combined WILL and POWER to achieve it. *Unorganised* each of us has only the weakness of isolation; *organised* each can possess the strength of all. Public opinion must be influenced; Government Departments brought to a realisation of the fact that their duty is to serve the industry as a whole and not any one section of it.[3]

Whatever the justification for language of this kind—and it came from a small section of the radio industry—majority opinion was stirred by genuine and growing grievances of its own just before the Sykes Committee met and while it was holding its first meetings. P. F. Anderson, the first Secretary of the BBC, wrote on 1 May to F. W. Phillips of the G.P.O., who was also secretary of the Sykes Committee, that 'owing to the agitation and the statements which have been made to the Press', the member firms of the BBC found themselves 'with large stocks left on their hands and a most serious falling off in sales. Many

[1] *Memorandum submitted by the Electrical Importers' and Traders' Association, 29 May 1923.
[2] *Objections to the present British Broadcasting Company submitted to the Postmaster-General, 19 Mar. 1923.
[3] *The Wireless Manufacturers' and Traders' Association, *Manifesto* of Oct. 1922.

report that they have not sold a single BBC set since the agitation commenced.' Their large commitments, he added, 'were
incurred on the strength of the BBC Agreement with the Post
Office'.[1] A few weeks later Reith himself wrote to Sykes heading
the page 'a personal letter only'. Radio manufacturers everywhere, he stated, were complaining to the BBC of 'the very
serious position in which our manufacturing members are
placed. It is no exaggeration to say that the wireless trade is
practically at a standstill, with the exception of the dealers in
imported parts.'[2]

Reith believed in late May 1923 that the Sykes Committee
should immediately concern itself with three questions only—
the evasion of licences, the terms of issue of constructors'
licences, and the contents and interpretation of the initial
Agreement between the Post Office and the BBC. Such matters
as relations with the press or the development of public control,
important though they were, could be dealt with separately and
later.[3] The chairman refused, however, to support the idea
of an interim report dealing with the specific points at issue and
the committee continued its deliberations into August 1923.
Noble and McKinstry had appeared as witnesses for the BBC
on 8 and 10 May, and Reith himself had given evidence on
14 June. So much time elapsed, however, and so many other
witnesses had been heard that the Board of the BBC decided to
demand a further opportunity of presenting the essentials of its
case. On 23 July Gainford, with the full approval of the Board,
wrote to Sykes asking him to receive a new deputation. He
reminded Sykes, who acceded to his request, that 'the contentious points of the Constitution and so on [which the Committee had been considering] were not by any means all of the
manufacturers' seeking. Much that is troublesome arose from
the Postmaster-General's own views, and the entire scheme was
opposed by him. Conditions today are very different from those
eight months ago. This we believe should be made very clear.'
In these circumstances, Gainford went on, 'the BBC had done
extraordinarily good work in spite of serious difficulties and
obstructions. I believe we are technically as far advanced after
six months as America is after two and a half years. We have

[1] *Anderson to Phillips, 1 May 1923.
[2] *Reith to Sykes, 25 May 1923.   [3] *Ibid.

acted without regard to revenue and in spite of the apparent lack of any steps by the Post Office to carry out their own regulations, solely in the public interest.'[1]

This was the burden of the BBC's evidence to the Sykes Committee, as it was presented not only by Gainford but by Noble, McKinstry, and Reith. During the course of the evidence, however, additional reasons were advanced for single and unified control of British broadcasting. The original reason, as has been suggested, was technical—the desire to avoid 'chaos' of the American kind—and it was the Post Office, not the manufacturers, who had insisted on a single or (at worst) a dual broadcasting authority to ensure that there would be no chaos. 'It was the desire of the Post Office that we should have one company and one company only,' Noble told the committee, 'and we fell in with the view.'[2] When Trevelyan asked Noble whether the desire to avoid chaos might still have been appeased if a few broadcasting concerns had been established, and not just one or two, he did not receive a very clear answer.

Perhaps the reason was that the question of chaos had been related to other questions from the very start of the negotiations. The Post Office witnesses produced an additional technical reason for having preferred in 1922 to press for one broadcasting company rather than two or several. A large number of radio firms and other interested parties of widely differing size and status had asked for permission to broadcast. How could the Post Office select a few of them as suitable? 'The solution of the problem', Shaughnessy told the committee, 'seemed to be to make all these firms get together to form one Company for the purpose of doing the broadcasting.'[3] There was difficulty in selecting, no matter what kind of outside body was applying for permission to broadcast. That the Post Office was particularly worried about the question was shown by its refusal to consider granting a special transmitting licence for the *Daily Express*. The Postmaster-General, Brown told the Sykes Committee, 'did not want to give facilities to one particular newspaper or organisation which he could not give to other newspapers and

---

[1] *Lord Gainford to Sykes, 23 July 1923; Diary, 31 July 1923.

[2] *Oral evidence of Noble and McKinstry before the Sykes Committee, 8 May 1923.

[3] *Oral evidence of E. A. Shaughnessy before the Sykes Committee, 14 June 1923.

organisations and he asked the *Daily Express* how they would propose to meet that difficulty'.[1]

In the case of applications from radio firms there was an even greater difficulty. The Post Office was aware that only a small number of firms held key patents, and that one firm, the Marconi Company, was in a particularly powerful patent position. Murray and Brown were so afraid of reinforcing the 'monopoly' of the few firms holding key patents that they did not realize that as a result of encouraging all the established radio firms (big and small) to form one single broadcasting 'combine' they might later be accused of creating a 'broadcasting monopoly'. 'It was contrary . . . to the policy of the British Government', Brown later wrote, 'to grant a monopoly of broadcasting to one, or even two or three manufacturing firms, as this would place them in a superior position to their competitors for pushing the sale of their goods.'[2] The corollary of this was that it was in line with public policy to create a single broadcasting authority in which the interests of the smaller firms were adequately protected by the Post Office. Noble gave his support to this interpretation of public policy. Encouraged by the Post Office, the manufacturers who joined the BBC had pooled their patents on 'a basis of absolute equality'. 'The best of anything held by my Company is at the disposal of the British Broadcasting Company. No one else could erect a station in this country without getting permission from those holding patents, but as all patents are held by members of the BBC, I do not think that anyone else could erect a station in this country.'[3] The arrangement was economical: as Brown argued later, it had avoided duplication and saved money.[4] Moreover, it adequately protected the interests of small firms which otherwise might not have shared in the broadcasting venture at all. Gainford had only consented to become Chairman of the BBC, Noble told the committee, on condition that no unfair advantage was given to any of its member firms. 'If that was ever likely to take place, he would

[1] *Oral evidence of F. J. Brown before the Sykes Committee, 2 May 1923.

[2] F. J. Brown, 'The Story of Broadcasting in England', in *Radio Broadcast*, June 1925.

[3] *Oral evidence of Noble and McKinstry before the Sykes Committee, 8 May 1923.

[4] F. J. Brown, 'Broadcasting in Britain', in *The London Quarterly Review*, Jan. 1926.

cease to be Chairman.'[1] Noble emphasized in addition that the limitation on dividends, agreed to by the Post Office and the BBC, was not usually a feature of monopolies.

When Reith gave evidence, he provided an additional reason for maintaining broadcasting under one single control. 'There is a very great advantage', he said, 'in having a uniform policy of what can or cannot be done in broadcasting.' Definite continuous control over the individual stations was applied from the centre. Programmes were submitted in advance, and there were periodic conferences between himself and the Station Directors. No alternative system could ensure such a sense of unified direction in British broadcasting.[2] For Reith this argument was more telling than any of the technical arguments cited by engineers. He was already dominated by what he described in his book *Broadcast Over Britain* as a 'high conception of the inherent possibilities of the service'.[3] This conception was to lead him eventually to the view, boldly expressed, that given a proper sense of responsibility and a will to lead, 'the brute force of monopoly' was a necessity in British broadcasting.[4]

By contrast, much of the language of 1923 was far less down-to-earth. Instead of pointing to the advantages of unified control, some of the BBC representatives—excluding Reith—got caught in the recurring conundrum 'when is a monopoly not a monopoly?' Noble and McKinstry, who admitted that they did not like the word 'monopoly', denied that this was because 'everybody in business wishes to enjoy a monopoly but prefers to have it described by some other name'.[5] They were so anxious to rebut the charge that the 'Big Six' had a monopolistic control over the making and selling of radio apparatus that they did not dwell on the same points as Reith. In the long run their relative lack of interest in constitutional questions appertaining to broadcasting enabled Reith to develop his own views about public control in an atmosphere of genuine independence.

That was the future logic of the relationship. It rested in 1923,

---

[1] *Oral evidence of Noble and McKinstry before the Sykes Committee, 8 May 1923.

[2] *Oral evidence of Reith before the Sykes Committee, 14 June 1923.

[3] *Broadcast Over Britain* (1924), p. 32.

[4] *Into the Wind* (1949), p. 99.

[5] *Oral evidence of Noble and McKinstry before the Sykes Committee, 10 May 1923.

however, on reciprocal loyalties. Reith stood out in the Sykes Committee for continued protection of the British radio industry even though he was the only member of the committee to do so. Not only did he sign a reservation asking for the Postmaster-General to honour his undertakings relating to protection in 1923, but he resisted considerable pressure from Brown and even tried hard to win over other members to his point of view. Before joining the committee he circulated a letter to all BBC member firms asking for their views on this issue, and spent many hours interviewing some of their representatives.[1] After the draft Report had been completed he laboriously went over its details—including his own reservation—with Isaacs, Kellaway, Hirst, McKinstry, and Sir Philip Nash. Isaacs in particular was greatly impressed by Reith's conduct. Although he was disposed to take 'an unyielding line' on any of the committee's conclusions of which he disapproved,[2] he praised Reith's contribution in private and in public. 'Nash said afterwards that I must have done something very special to make Godfrey Isaacs have such confidence in me.'[3] The Board agreed unanimously with the views of their most forthright member, and a resolution was carried at the Board meeting of 3 September thanking Reith for all he had done. 'Mr. Reith', it read, 'was nominated by the Board as representing the Company with the express purpose of defending its interests and explaining its views. In the opinion of the Board Mr. Reith acted with fairness, moderation and great skill, and it is their opinion that their interests could not have been in better hands whatever the result of the enquiry may be.'[4]

3. The Results of the Inquiry

THE last meeting of the Sykes Committee was held on 17 August and the Report was handed in to the Postmaster-

---

[1] Diary, 27 Apr. 1923.   [2] Ibid. 1 July 1923.
[3] Ibid., 23 July 1923.
[4] *Board Minutes: Sir William Bull to Reith, 3 Sept. 1923.

General on 23 August. Publication was delayed, however, until October. There were good reasons for the delay, for while it lasted, intricate negotiations were continuing between the Postmaster-General and Reith.

A new Postmaster-General, Sir Laming Worthington-Evans, had taken office on 4 June 1923 while the committee was sitting. Reith noted at the time, quite correctly as events proved, that 'he will be very friendly and helpful to us'.[1] A few days before the Report was presented to the Post Office, Reith asked that it should not be published until the views of his Board had been secured. 'Publication prior to an agreement with this Company might not only be prejudicial to a settlement satisfactory to both parties, but might result in a great deal of damage being done to the wireless industry.'[2] Brown replied on behalf of the Postmaster-General on 22 August stating that while the Postmaster-General could not agree to postpone the publication of the Report, he would be glad to allow the Board to consider it during the period when preliminary arrangements for publication were being made. It would be very helpful, he added, if the Board of the BBC could announce that it accepted the committee's recommendations as they stood provided that the government for its part also accepted them.[3]

This was an optimistic expectation. When the Board of the BBC considered the Draft Report at its August meeting, it paid less attention to the praise the committee had showered on the BBC than to the proposal that protection, 'the cardinal principle on which the broadcasting service was established', should be abandoned. What inducement would there be under the revised scheme, it asked, for members of the BBC to remain members, or still less, for new members to join the Company?[4] The Report could certainly not be accepted as it stood, although the Company would be willing to submit a new scheme which would incorporate certain features of the Sykes Committee Report while at the same time safeguarding the interests of the manufacturers. Once again the Postmaster-General was reminded of the part that his predecessors had played in initiating

---

[1] Diary, 4 June 1923.
[2] *Reith to Sir L. Worthington-Evans, 17 Aug. 1923.
[3] *Brown to Reith, 22 Aug. 1923.
[4] *Reith to Postmaster-General, 24 Aug. 1923.

the earlier Agreement and of the need to maintain 'unified control' in broadcasting to avoid 'the trouble which arose in America'.

On 28 August Reith visited the Postmaster-General at his country home and had a long and useful talk with him, 'two hours' talk before lunch and two hours afterwards'. 'It was quite surprisingly successful', he wrote in his diary. 'He thinks the Report is most complimentary to us and he listens quite often.'[1] In thanking Reith for his services the Postmaster-General had already attributed to him something of the 'comprehensiveness' with which the Report dealt with the major issues of broadcast-ing,[2] and now Reith was successful in persuading him to delay publication of the Report a little longer.[3] This left time for the BBC to submit the details of the new scheme it had promised a few days earlier.

Not much time—but a great deal of effort—was needed. On 30 August Reith wrote to Brown suggesting an arrangement which would last until June 1925. During that period no new broadcasting undertaking would be licensed by the Post Office; experimental licences to amateurs would be issued 'with the utmost discretion', and there would be only one other licence— a standard broadcasting licence at 10s. which would be issued to people buying BBC-marked sets or assembling sets of their own. The assemblers of sets or 'home constructors' would have to use headphones, amplifiers, loudspeakers, and valves marked BBC. Of this licence, 7s. 6d. should pass direct to the BBC. Member-ship of the Company should be given to all manufacturers or dealers in wireless apparatus who signed an undertaking to use British labour and materials only. The royalty system should go at once, as the Sykes Committee had suggested, but an attempt should be made by the government to protect the British radio industry under the Key Industries Act.[4]

Very difficult and complex negotiations followed not only between Reith and the Postmaster-General, whom he saw again on 31 August and still found 'very friendly indeed', but between Reith and the members of the Board of Directors of the

[1] Diary, 28 Aug. 1923.
[2] *The Postmaster-General to Reith, 28 Aug. 1923.
[3] *Reith to the Directors of the BBC, 21 Aug. 1923.
[4] *Reith to Brown, 30 Aug. 1923.

BBC. In the meantime the publication of the Report of the Sykes Committee continued to be delayed through the month of September. Alternative schemes were canvassed, including the scheme proposed by Reith, but discussions of principle were inextricably bound up with discussions of tactics. The Directors of the BBC felt that they had a choice—either to follow a 'stand fast policy' and 'make a claim on the Post Office for breach of agreement' or to 'adopt a policy of compromise'.[1] Most of them favoured the latter course subject to the Postmaster-General promising to enforce vigorously and effectively any new agreement which was reached. They did not agree at first, however, about what the nature of the compromise should be, and it was not until 5 September that Reith, who took the initiative throughout, could communicate their view to the Post Office.[2]

For his part, the Postmaster-General not only had to take the advice of his officials, but had to refer the more important matters to the Cabinet. He quickly made it known that his colleagues did not believe that new and special forms of protection for the radio trade were practicable, and on 7 September he threatened to continue the existing unsatisfactory arrangements unless the BBC accepted the principle of a constructors' licence costing 15s.[3] He was willing, however, to re-examine all old demands and to press for a compromise settlement on the other basic points. He was even willing to follow Reith's line of reasoning when it contradicted that of his officials. It was recognized at the time that had his predecessor been as willing to reach agreement, the dispute would never have reached the deadlock which had led to the Sykes Committee being appointed.[4]

There was a press leakage of what was happening behind the scenes on 26 September,[5] and by the time that the Report was published on 1 October the Postmaster-General was able to announce that he had reached a new agreement with the BBC.[6]

---

[1] *Pease to Reith, 10 Sept. 1923.
[2] *Reith to the Postmaster-General, 5 Sept. 1923.
[3] *Murray to Reith, 7 Sept. 1923.
[4] *The Times*, 20 Oct. 1923.   [5] *Evening Standard*, 26 Sept. 1923.
[6] *An Extraordinary Meeting of the Board of the BBC discussed the Agreement on 26 Sept. and appointed a committee of the Directors to sign and seal it after consultation with Reith and the Company's solicitors.

All the major recommendations of the Sykes Committee were accepted, but the Company's trade interests were legally protected against foreign competition until 31 December 1924, the date when the original Licence was due to expire. A useful distinction was drawn between the 'short run' and the 'long run', always a fruitful source of compromise. After December 1924 the Sykes Committee's proposal for a uniform 10s. licence was to come into force and there was to be no legal prohibition of the employment of apparatus of foreign manufacture. Between October 1923 and December 1924, however, the experimental licence and the general BBC receiving licence were to remain as before except that 7s. 6d. instead of 5s. should go to the BBC. Royalties on BBC sets were to be maintained during this period, although on a reduced scale. A new constructors' licence was also to be introduced at a fee of 15s. A condition of this licence was that the principal parts should be British made, and the additional cost of 5s. was intended to compensate the BBC for the loss of royalties. For those home constructors who had already assembled their sets before October 1923—often from foreign materials—but had not yet paid any licence fees, there was to be an interim licence of 15s. Such constructors were not to be penalized for breaking the law before 1 October 1923, but they would be able to secure interim licences only if they applied for them before 15 October. After that, the Post Office made it quite clear, it would enforce the new regulations.[1]

This rearrangement of licences settled the immediate crisis which had confronted the BBC earlier in the year. With the announcement of the new plan, the number of licences issued increased in ten days from 180,000 to 414,000, of which 200,000 were interim licences—a measure of the extent of 'evasion' about which the BBC had rightly complained—and 27,000 were new constructors' licences.[2]

The other main recommendations of the Sykes Committee were accepted both by the Postmaster-General and the BBC, and came into effect soon afterwards. The period of the amended Licence was extended for another two years—that is to say,

---

[1] The details are set out in Cd. 1976 (1923), *Copy of Supplementary Agreement between the Postmaster-General and the British Broadcasting Company Ltd., providing for the modification of the Licence of the 18th of January.*

[2] *The Times,* 18 and 19 Oct. 1923.

until the end of 1926. An advisory board was set up to assist the Postmaster-General in dealing with broadcasting problems. Membership of the BBC was broadened so as to include wireless dealers, and the requirement of a £50 deposit was abolished. In fact, only 77 dealers had joined the BBC by the end of 1925, although the total number of member firms rose from 564 in May 1923 to 1,716 at the end of 1925. Many of the new entrants were very small firms holding the minimum number of shares.

The Postmaster-General went out of his way to praise the eventual compromise. 'The continuation of the present situation', he said in his official statement on the day of the publication of the Report, 'would be bad for all parties, the broadcasting company because it is losing a revenue upon which it had counted, and the Post Office because, as the Department entrusted with the administration of the law regarding the licensing of wireless apparatus, it is unable to enforce the law as it stands.' He had been right, he believed, to accept a continued measure of protection for an interim period 'having regard to the unemployment which at present exists, and which would be accentuated by the importation on any considerable scale of wireless receiving apparatus from abroad'. During the period up to 31 December 1924 he would not license 'any other person to carry on broadcasting in Great Britain'. This policy had not been explicit before (and Worthington-Evans's predecessor did not seem to regard it as even implicit), but it was added that the BBC's monopoly of broadcasting was subject to the Company supplying 'a satisfactory broadcast service'. There was a further condition—that the BBC should 'erect additional stations where the Postmaster-General may himself consider them to be necessary within a reasonable time after being required by the Postmaster-General to do so'. Between 31 December 1924 and 23 December 1926, the extended period of the Licence, the Postmaster-General reserved to himself the right to license additional broadcasting authorities, but he declared that he would not give them a share of revenue from receiving licences unless the BBC had first refused to provide adequate broadcasting facilities.

There was one point in the original Agreement which was clarified in the Supplementary Agreement. The original Agreement had included an obscure clause relating to the prohibition of advertising:[1] in the new Agreement the clause was rewritten so that it forbade direct advertising while specifically allowing the BBC to broadcast sponsored programmes and commercial information approved for broadcasting by the Postmaster-General.[2] During the Sykes Committee hearings Lord Riddell had criticized the BBC for having broadcast a concert earlier in 1923 which had been 'sponsored' by Harrods: he even questioned its legality. On this occasion it was Brown who came to the aid of the BBC and asked Riddell whether it would not be 'rather a tall order' for the Postmaster-General to refuse to allow the BBC 'to accept a concert of a character markedly superior to that which they could themselves provide out of their present comparatively limited resources, merely because the giver announced in the newspapers beforehand that he was giving this concert'.[3] The new Agreement specifically permitted concerts of this kind, and several such programmes—eight in all—were given in 1925. Among the sponsors were the *Evening Standard*, the *News of the World*, the *Daily Herald*, the *Weekly Dispatch*, *Answers*, and *Titbits*. The *Daily Graphic* sponsored a concert in 1925, and a further one (the only sponsored concert of the year) in 1926. The practice then lapsed. The BBC did not choose to take advantage of the permission to broadcast to its audiences commercial information in code. It rested content with Stock Exchange prices.

Parliament was not sitting when the Report of the Sykes Committee was published, but the Report received a qualified—if far from unanimous—welcome from what was still a small minority interested in broadcasting. Reith himself had proved sensitive, as he always was to be, to the need for 'mobilising the sympathy of listeners in', and he had kept in close touch with his Station Directors during the period between the final preparation of the Report and its publication.[4] He also met several members of parliament during this period, and made good use of a Publicity Officer, W. C. Smith, whom he had appointed in February. Reith never had any doubts that the best of causes needed the best of publicity.

[1] Cd. 1822 (1923), clause 4.
[2] Cd. 1976 (1923), clause 2.
[3] *Oral evidence of Lord Riddell to the Sykes Committee, 29 May 1923.
[4] *Reith to all Station Directors, 28 Aug. 1923.

The press reaction to the Report was generally favourable although some newspapers almost ignored it. Reith's reservation was printed in full in several of the newspapers which devoted much space to the problem. Some of them were critical of the 'radio trade interest', but the BBC itself got more praise than blame. 'The Company has admittedly done excellent work in developing the system in the face of serious technical difficulties,' the *Glasgow Herald* commented, 'and it is but right that its efforts should receive both acknowledgement and encouragement.'[1] The settlement was generally felt not to be a 'final one',[2] but as the *Westminster Gazette* put it, whatever else the Postmaster-General had done, he had left the future of broadcasting very much in the keeping of the public interested in it. 'This is all to the good; and if the new arrangement is admittedly a compromise between what the Broadcasting Committee recommends and the privileges granted by the Licence ... a serious attempt has been made to remove the practical difficulties which led to the deadlock earlier this year.'[3]

The Times was more critical. Not only did it regret the absence of 'finality', but it agreed that all the difficult problems instead of being solved had been merely postponed. It discerned 'a vast difference' between the recommendations of the Sykes Committee and the decisions of Worthington-Evans. At the same time it welcomed the continued protection given to the radio industry, regretting only that the position after the end of 1924 had been left very 'vague'. British manufacturers would have been placed in a very awkward position had the Postmaster-General chosen October 1923 to end protection. The seasonal summer slump in the sale of radio sets had left them with large stocks on which heavy losses would have been certain had the market been flooded with cheap products from the Continent. The Postmaster-General had been right to pay attention to the legitimate needs of the trade as he had also been right to help the BBC in its 'present difficulties'.[4]

This comment in *The Times*—not a leader, but a column signed by 'a correspondent'—did not appear until nearly three

---

[1] *Glasgow Herald*, 2 Oct. 1923.
[2] *Morning Post*, 2 Oct. 1923; *Daily News*, 3 Oct. 1923.
[3] *Westminster Gazette*, 3 Oct. 1923.
[4] *The Times*, 20 Oct. 1923.

weeks after the Report was published. The delay—and the placing of the comment—suggests how dangerous it is to assume that because control of broadcasting is now a topic of recognized public importance it was felt be a major topic of importance in 1923. Paradoxically it was the enemies of the BBC who publicly magnified the importance of the topic at that time. The *Daily Express* had forecast in August 1923 that the end of the BBC monopoly was in sight and that the Company would now lose its 'right to levy tribute on listeners' buying sets.[1] On 2 October it had to admit implicitly, not explicitly, that it had been wrong. It described the Postmaster-General's 'settlement' as a 'bad compromise'. All he had done was to secure the worst of both worlds, and he would no more be able to enforce the new system than the old.[2] Further leaders referred to 'the wireless muddle' and roused popular indignation against 'spies'. On 10 October an article with the heading 'Secrets of the BBC' claimed to describe 'how the Postmaster-General was forced to surrender'.[3] A few days later the *Express* included a cartoon showing the Postmaster-General inspecting troops.[4] The caption read 'The P.M.G. over the top today. Wireless pirates beware'. In the foreground Worthington-Evans stands in a military uniform with cocked hat bearing pillar-box and feathers and carrying a telescope instead of a sword. All his medals are marked BBC. His troops are postmen with telescopes instead of rifles sloped over their shoulders, and they carry magnifying glasses in their right hands. In the far background there is a tree 'occupied' and surrounded by wireless 'pirates' singing, 'and it's a glorious thing to be a pirate king'.

It should be added that Worthington-Evans, who had been Secretary of State for War from 1921 to 1922, scarcely saw the problem of enforcement in this vivid form. In his press release announcing the Agreement he had expressed the hope that the 'listening public' would require no pressure to make them obey the law. 'He is confident that they will not only be willing, but anxious to put themselves right as regards the law, and at the same time to contribute their quota towards the cost of a service which is affording them so much enjoyment.'[5]

[1] *Daily Express*, 24 Aug. 1923.   [2] Ibid., 3 Oct. 1923.
[3] Ibid., 10 Oct. 1923.   [4] Ibid., 16 Oct. 1923.
[5] *Press Release, 1 Oct. 1923.

Worthington-Evans proved more right than the *Daily Express*. There were continued difficulties about licences in 1924 and 1925, but they never reached the dimensions of the difficulties of the first few months of 1923. By 31 December 1923, 595,496 wireless licences had been issued: by the end of 1924 the figure had risen to 1,129,578. And by the end of 1924, 'pirates' were generally thought to be more of a menace to the proper development of broadcasting than Post Office 'spies'. At the same time the BBC still found it necessary to apply pressure on the Post Office and on the listeners, reminding the Post Office that it expected proper enforcement and reminding listeners that 'it is unsporting and unfair to let other people pay for a service which is, for what is given, the cheapest possible form of entertainment'.[1] Routine warnings were coupled with occasional dramatic news stories—of the Post Office swooping down on a whole village,[2] of great ingenuity being shown by Post Office engineers in an attempt to secure an arrest,[3] or occasionally of daring gestures of defiance of both Post Office and BBC by bold individualists[4]—but most listeners automatically took out their annual licences in the same way that they would buy their licences for dogs or motor-cars. They would occasionally be as annoyed by evasions as was the BBC itself. A letter from a 'perfect listener' in London still survives in the BBC archives.

I have just had the pleasure of renewing my wireless licence, [he wrote] and I regard the payment of ten shillings as the finest ten shillings worth I have ever expended—I get infinite enjoyment out of my set and I am deeply indebted to the BBC for the way in which they have organised and developed a great public service. . . . There is one other point over which perhaps you have no control, and that is with regard to those 'scroungers' who would steal a penny from a blind man's tin, that is the people who possess wireless sets and yet pay no licence. . . . Something must be done, for surely the BBC will need more money in the near future if the radio service is to be further developed. Those who pay will get tired of subsidising a service for dishonest listeners.[5]

The BBC had little control over this situation, but Reith

[1] Message from Reith read out by Station Directors on 14 Nov. 1924.
[2] *F. W. Phillips to Reith, 9 Feb. 1926.
[3] *Manchester Evening News*, 8 Nov. 1926.
[4] *Evening News*, 27 Oct. 1924.
[5] *Reith to Brown, 4 June 1925.

complained frequently that the Post Office, which had control, did not adequately employ it. In fact, in cases of deliberate defiance of the law, it still proved remarkably difficult for the Post Office to uncover the necessary evidence to lead to a successful prosecution. The powers of the Post Office to prosecute were derived from the Wireless Telegraphy Act of 1904 which did not specifically mention wireless telephony, let alone wireless receiving sets. The need for new legislation was being examined by the Post Office while the Sykes Committee was sitting, and the members of the committee were asked to comment on the draft of a Bill amending the 1904 Act to cover the issue and withdrawal of wireless licences and the use of wireless in aircraft, visual and sound signalling, and the use of ether waves for non-telegraphic purposes.[1] The committee stated in its report that it had been glad to have the opportunity of studying the Bill, but that the main proposals it embodied did not appear to affect materially the various other aspects of broadcasting they had been asked to consider.

It was not until February 1925 that Sir William Mitchell-Thomson, the fifth Postmaster-General with whom the BBC had had to deal, introduced a Bill to remove any doubt as to the right of the Postmaster-General to collect licence fees.[2] The press described the Bill as an attempt to consolidate the Postmaster-General's position as 'policeman of the ether', but it ran into considerable opposition inside and outside the House of Commons. The Radio Society of Great Britain objected to the way that it proposed to deal with experimenters and owners of crystal sets;[3] the press attacked its 'inquisitorial' aspect—its clauses relating to the right of search and the size of the penalties it proposed;[4] and several members of parliament who were known critics of the BBC joined forces with the outside opposition in what was described as a 'storm of public disapproval'.[5] The BBC had not been consulted about the drafting

---

[1] Working Paper No. 6 of the Sykes Committee was called 'The Wireless Telegraphy and Signalling Bill'. It served as an introduction to the draft of the Bill. See also Cd. 1951 (1923), paras. 52–53.

[2] *Hansard*, vol. 180, col. 187, 11 Feb. 1925.

[3] *The Times*, 18 Feb. 1925.

[4] There is an excellent leader in the *Daily Telegraph*, 'Regulating Wireless', 18 Feb. 1925.

[5] *Evening Standard*, 25 May 1925.

of the Bill or the arrangements for conducting its passage through the House of Commons,[1] and it was strongly opposed by the Labour Party, led on this issue by Thomas Johnston who demanded a greater measure of public control.[2] Reith himself had considerable sympathy with Johnston's view that if the Postmaster-General were to be granted such 'arbitrary powers' the BBC would have to become a newly constituted public institution.[3]

The opposition to the Wireless Bill was tough enough for the Bill to be withdrawn in May 1925, and there was a further trickle of opposition when in the following month the Post-master-General introduced a very short Wireless Telegraphy (Explanation) Bill to replace the bigger and more comprehensive measure. 'The Government are very wise in dropping their Wireless Bill,' one newspaper had commented on the withdrawal of the first suggested measure, 'it had no chance whatever of passing. It contained more absurd provisions than any government measure proposed to be put before Parliament in modern times.'[4] The criticism recalls a trenchant criticism made by Eckersley within the BBC when he was asked his opinion of the draft of the Bill drawn up in 1923: 'if the Government authority is deemed advisable, let the authority be maintained in matters of real urgency, not manifested in petty repressions.'[5]

The short Wireless Telegraphy (Explanation) Bill was passed without amendment in July 1925. Its only object was to legalize the doubtful question of broadcast licences, and once it became the law the Post Office immediately issued a statement saying that there was now a definite and incontrovertible legal obligation on everyone who owned either a valve set or a crystal set to take out a licence. The position of the BBC was finally consolidated, and it began to be possible realistically from this date to contemplate finance by licences rather than by any other means.

A year before the bill passed the licence position had improved so much that the BBC took the initiative in May 1924 in suggesting that the issue of the special 15s. constructors'

---

[1] *Memorandum by Gladstone Murray, 23 Apr. 1925.
[2] *Into the Wind*, p. 97. Johnston was founder and editor of *Forward*.
[3] Diary, 6 Mar. 1925.
[4] *Evening Standard*, 26 May 1925.
[5] *Eckersley to Reith, 30 May 1923.

licences should be suspended from the first of July instead of the first of December 1924, as the Agreement of October 1923 had stipulated.[1] The Post Office agreed,[2] and in consequence from 1 July 1924 until the end of December, the formal end of protection, a uniform 10s. licence was in operation. In making this concession, which cost the BBC a considerable sum both in licence revenue and income from royalties, Reith asked for certain assurances. First, the Post Office should provide 'definite and consistent support' in the matter of enforcement. Second, the Postmaster-General should not reduce the licence fee below 10s.: there was evidence that Mitchell-Thomson and some of the Post Office officials wished to reduce the amount as a *douceur* to soften the passage of a new Wireless Telegraphy Bill.[3] Reith took the opportunity to state a few home truths about BBC finance. 'In some quarters it may be felt', Reith wrote, 'that our income is more than we require. The Board do not feel that this could ever be the case. There will always be the necessity for funds for improving and extending the service.' He continued to state this case in 1925 and 1926. The financial 'crisis' might be over, but the financial needs of the BBC still demanded sympathetic attention. Finally, Reith asked the Postmaster-General to give the BBC more substantial security of tenure. He asked him to promise not to issue a new broadcasting Licence between the end of 1924 and the expiry of the BBC's Licence. The Post Office's replies on the second and third of Reith's requests were somewhat ambiguous,[4] but agreement was reached with the BBC, and the new uniform licensing system came into operation.

Protection survived only a little longer, although Reith carried on a tough fight on this issue to the last. In March 1924 he had approached Brown to ask what the prospects would be for further protection after the end of the year: he was told then and again later in the year that there was 'no chance for any further protection on imports'.[5] In May the Board of the BBC decided that it would be practically useless to raise objections to the lapse from protection, but in November—with

[1] *Reith to Brown, 30 May 1924.
[2] *Brown to Reith, 17 June 1924.
[3] *Into the Wind*, p. 97. See below, p. 229.
[4] *Brown to Reith, 13 and 17 June 1924.
[5] *Reith to Brown, 13 Mar. 1924. Note by Reith on his conversation with Brown, 24 Mar. 1924. Brown to Reith, 15 July 1924.

a new Conservative government in power—they made a final attempt.[1] In the same month a questionnaire was sent out to the member firms of the BBC asking them for their views. Of 545 firms replying, 529 declared themselves in favour of protection. They ranged from big firms employing 300 people or more—one employed 1,000—to one-man firms, some of which were either on the brink of failure or had already failed. The answers give a revealing picture of the state of the radio industry which broadcasting had brought into being.[2] It was a curiously competitive industry, despite its continued pressure for protection. There was little need of capital or knowledge, and consequently people entered and left the industry with remarkable ease. The big firms—including the 'Big Six'—were devoting only a relatively small part of their energies to the manufacture of wireless sets, and neither by aggressive advertising nor by exploitation of their patent rights did they try to keep small men out.

It is reasonable to argue that the economic history of the industry is as relevant to an understanding of the disappearance of protection as the history of the Sykes Committee and its proposals.[3] Despite all Reith's labours to please his directors and the weight of business opinion, protection disappeared, as had been planned, at the end of 1924. With its disappearance, the BBC was strengthened rather than weakened. The cord which bound it to the trade still held, but it had been loosened, if not cut. As the trade prospered—particularly a number of the most adaptable small men—it could easily stand on its own feet. The 'Big Six', whose manufacturing business in wireless sets prospered least, were probably less concerned than they had been in 1922 with the economics of broadcasting from which they were deriving no substantial business benefits. Reith drew the lesson from experience that the BBC could establish its independence. It was no longer engaged in an ordeal for survival: it was gradually acquiring a more mature and confident personality of its own.

All this is to anticipate. When the Sykes Committee reported

---

[1] *Board Minutes: 8 May 1924, 13 Nov. 1924.
[2] The answers are filed in the BBC Archives.
[3] An interesting account of some of the details of the history is given in Sturmey, op. cit., ch. viii.

in October 1923, there was not as much confidence as there was at the end of 1924. Lord Gainford in his address to the first shareholders' meeting, held on 9 October, was still dwelling on the trials as much as the triumphs of broadcasting. 'The establishment of any new industry, in which revolutionary conceptions are involved,' he told his hearers, 'has always been a difficult and trying experience. I do not think it possible that in any other instance have so many complications and troubles been encountered as have fallen to our lot since last we met.'[1] The emphasis was right in the circumstances. The miracle was, as Gainford also said, that the BBC had become a real 'going concern'.

4. 'Getting on with the Job'

By 'going concern' Gainford meant that the BBC was providing a 'regular service' day in, day out, of a standard which could be relied upon not only by the Postmaster-General, but, more important, by the listeners. The detailed account of high-level negotiations is at most only one aspect of the history of the BBC: while the complicated negotiations of 1923 were continuing, work had to be carried on, the work of engineers and of planners of programmes, work which determined the ordinary listener's approach to the new organization. Field Marshal Sir William Robertson, a member of the Sykes Committee, stated this bluntly in his own forthright way. Just before the Sykes Committee Report was presented to the Postmaster-General he wrote to Reith, 'I hope all will now settle down as regards the wretched Committee (Committees are never *any* good to any one, I know them well) and that you will be allowed to get on with your job.'[2]

Reith's first job—in trying to make the BBC a going concern—was to find the right people to whom he could delegate

[1] *Address to the Shareholders, 9 Oct. 1923.
[2] *Field Marshal Sir William Robertson to Reith, 22 Aug. 1923.

authority. It was their task in their turn to produce the people who would provide the programmes. In his autobiography Reith has written little about this aspect of his life in 1923, explaining that his is a personal story, not a history of broadcasting. 'There may be little reference to other members of the staff', he adds. 'Not that I forget or under-rate their contribution. Indeed no. Just because I shall try to keep off the things about which others can write; deal with those which, more or less alone, I had to handle. Less with the play and the players than with setting and serving of the stage.'[1] By contrast this history of broadcasting must be directly concerned with providing the details Reith deliberately left out.

First, Reith found himself a good secretary, Miss F. I. Shields, a graduate of Newnham. She was recommended to him by Miss Stevenson, Lloyd George's secretary, now the Dowager Countess Lloyd George. Next, he brought in P. P. Eckersley as Chief Engineer, a key appointment, which was one more link between the old times and the new. One day later he decided that he must have a 'publicity man', and he invited W. C. Smith, a journalist and formerly a missionary, to come down from Glasgow for the day to see him. Smith did not go back.[2] All these recruits, like Reith himself, were young. So too was the Marconi Company team of A. R. Burrows, C. A. Lewis, and L. Stanton Jefferies. Broadcasting was a young man's game whether it was developed from Writtle or from London.

Nonetheless, Reith felt that he needed an older man to serve him as Deputy Manager, a man of experience and judgement who would ensure that the organization would run smoothly and wisely. He told Gainford of his needs on 10 May and started looking around for the right man. It was F. J. Brown of the Post Office who suggested a naval officer with a magnificent record, Rear-Admiral C. D. (later Vice-Admiral Sir Charles) Carpendale.[3] The Rear-Admiral had five 'ones' to his credit, and had been a captain at the age of thirty-four. On 14 June Reith interviewed Carpendale: 'he was amazed', Reith wrote in his diary, 'at the dissecting he got'. It lasted two hours, and it 'covered everything'. None of the difficulties of the task was minimized, Reith emphasizing that he expected something

[1] *Into the Wind*, p. 88.   [2] Diary, 1 Feb. 1923.
[3] Ibid.; 14 June 1923.

more from his subordinates than 'efficiency in its general sense'.[1]
Reith liked Carpendale 'and thought that he would do'. On 5
July at their second meeting Reith offered him the post, adding
'I believe he will be a great help.'[2] Carpendale was. He started
work on 13 July as Assistant General Manager and was immediately sent to one of the outlying stations where there had
recently been administrative difficulties.[3] Carpendale did not
leave the BBC until 31 March 1938. Only a few months later
Reith followed him. In 1925 C. A. Lewis said that Carpendale's
chief service to the BBC had been that 'he came fresh to everything, and was able to throw a new light on all problems': he
also played a most active part in international radio circles.[4]
By 1938, like Reith, he had become a fixture. When he retired,
Reith himself wrote, 'It is difficult to think of the BBC without
him; I doubt if I can.'[5]

With this little group of people to advise him—and he only
needed a little group—Reith created a central organization. It
was not an easy task, and it required patience as well as work.
Until Carpendale arrived, Reith confessed that he was 'dread-
fully dissatisfied with the organisation of the B.B.C.'.[6] Changes
were then made, including the replacement of the first Secretary of the BBC, P. F. Anderson, by G. V. Rice. Fortunately
for Reith the Board of Directors always gave him full backing,
confiding in him and at the same time allowing him complete
independence to carry out his ideas. Board meetings took place
once a month, and Reith carefully prepared General Manager's
Reports which provided the framework of the agenda. Very
soon he not only knew more about broadcasting than any of the
members of the Board, but he was taking all the most important
decisions relating to policy. It was scarcely surprising, therefore,
that at the Board meeting of 9 October it was recommended
that Reith should become Managing Director. The promotion
had been mooted even earlier in the year, in April, but had
proved impracticable on constitutional grounds.[7] It was finally
carried out in November.[8] The minute referred to Reith's

---

[1] Carpendale to Reith, 19 June 1923. This letter is in Lord Reith's possession.
[2] Diary, 5 July 1923.   [3] Ibid., 13 July 1923.
[4] See below, p. 316.   [5] 'How he started', Ariel, Mar. 1938.
[6] Diary, 10 June 1923.
[7] *F. W. Gaylor to P. F. Anderson, 25 Apr. 1923.
[8] *Minutes of the Board Meeting, 14 Nov. 1923.

'consummate ability and tact', and Godfrey Isaacs, by far the toughest of the members of the Board, made a special telephone call to Reith congratulating him and telling him that he could not find adequate words to express his admiration.[1] Reith was surprised, for Isaacs was usually 'so undemonstrative'. A year later Isaacs retired from the Board on the grounds of ill health, and was succeeded by F. W. Kellaway, who had been Postmaster-General when the 1922 negotiations had started and had afterwards been thought of as a possible General Manager of the BBC. This was the only change in the Board during its effective existence. The staff of the BBC grew: the Board remained a fixed point in a moving world.

In December 1922 the staff of the BBC numbered four. By the autumn of 1924 it had risen to 371.[2] Less than a year later it was 552.[3] Of the 552 only 179 were engineers. Given the range of broadcasting activities, these figures were modest, and it was the deliberate policy of the BBC to keep 'station staffs as low as possible'.[4]

Broadly speaking, the early staff was divided between three departments—Engineering, Programmes, and Administration. The Programme Department was responsible for the content of broadcasting, the Engineering Department for seeing that the matter was broadcast in the most faithful and effective manner possible, and the Administrative Department for making sure that everything was efficiently organized and properly paid for.

Each of the departments had its sub-divisions, although it took time before the sub-divisions were institutionalized. On the programme side there was an early division of responsibilities for music. In May 1923 Percy Pitt, formerly Director of Music of the British National Opera Company, was made Musical Controller with L. Stanton Jefferies, who had been appointed by the Marconi Company, as Director of Music. Almost from the start the Music Department started building up a library, which in time became one of the biggest libraries in the world. Bundles of orchestral scores were dispatched round the provinces in large hampers, which looked so much like laundry

[1] Diary, 3 Oct. 1923.
[2] Article by Reith on 'Broadcasting', Sept. 1924.
[3] *Memorandum of Information on the Scope and Conduct of the Service* (1925), p. 14.
[4] *Reith to the Postmaster-General, 25 June 1925. At the end of Sept. 1925 the staff numbered 630.

baskets that on at least one occasion, it is said, the two were confused on the eve of a concert.[1] Artists were also dispatched round the provinces. This work had to be carefully planned, and it represented the first and in some ways the most difficult experiment in programme planning.

The first plays broadcast by the BBC were handled by outside producers, and there was little recognition of the special problems of 'radio drama'.[2] In July 1924, however, a Dramatic Department was started in London and several months later the London Radio Repertory Players were recruited. Dramatic effects remained somewhat primitive. When the first Dramatic Director, R. E. Jeffrey, was appointed, he wished to signal his début by introducing greater realism into radio sounds. He began with the sound of a gun, and to the dismay of the staff spent his first few hours firing a shot-gun over the banisters into the well of the staircase. He did not succeed: the noise sounded like flat champagne.[3] A few months later Jeffrey was allowed to spend £50 'for experimental purposes in connection with the production of sound effects',[4] and in November 1924 A. Whitman joined Jeffrey's staff as an 'effects man'. It was not until 1927 that the 'dramatic control panel' was brought into regular use, and radio drama began to develop rapidly in its own right.

Education became a separate department at about the same time as drama. The need for a close link between broadcasting and education had been stressed at a conference in February 1924, and the Education Department secured as its Director J. C. Stobart, a member of the Inspectorate of the Board of Education. Reith took the greatest possible pains with this appointment. He first met Stobart in Trevelyan's room at the Board of Education in April 1924, when Trevelyan, as President of the Board, and some of his senior administrators were listening to Sir Walford Davies's first schools educational programme.[5] He signed him on only after very careful thought. It was from the Education Department that many later departments were carved out—notably talks and religion.[6]

---

[1] B.B.C. Yearbook (1930), 'The Old B.B.C.', p. 164.
[2] See below, pp. 280 ff.
[3] B.B.C. Yearbook (1930), 'The Old B.B.C.', p. 169.
[4] *Minutes of the Control Board, 14 Oct. 1924.
[5] Diary, 4 Apr. 1924.
[6] See below, pp. 270 ff.

On the other two sides of BBC work—the engineering and the administrative—sub-divisions were also drawn early in the history of the organization. When Eckersley became Chief Engineer, the BBC had no engineering staff of its own. The few stations then working were superintended by engineers temporarily seconded from the large radio firms which had provided the substantial core of the capital of the BBC. Engineering during the next few years had three aspects, although the three could never be completely separated—the maintenance of a ,high technical standard of broadcasting by the existing stations; the 'spreading of the broadcasting service' into new areas of the country hitherto uncovered; and third, but not least, research. Research indeed was still so essential in relation to the first two that it could never be treated as a 'frill'. Sometimes there were complaints that there was not enough of it, and certainly the BBC had a heavy responsibility in that few of the radio firms in existence had either the ability or the desire to undertake engineering research into the special problems and needs of the expanding broadcasting service. Innovation between 1922 and 1925—apart from limited development in the valve industry—was 'largely a matter of detail'.[1]

It was Eckersley's ambition—although he was a technical expert—to use his unique skill to 'enable the listener to forget about the technique of the service'.[2] Already in 1924 he joked that by the end of the year his department would be fully organized and would run itself automatically. All he would have to do was to sit back in a comfortable padded chair and watch the wheels go round.[3] It did not work out like that, partly because of Eckersley himself. He and most of the engineers who worked with him were so interested in the technical side of radio that they created a dynamic of their own inside the BBC. 'Our enthusiasm', Eckersley has written, 'was maintained by a competition with ourselves: we were on trial against the measure of our ambitions and so we never became complacent.'[4]

In the Administrative Department of the BBC the work was almost as many-sided as it was in the Programme Department. The general office and filing system were at first under the control of Miss Banks and the cashier's work under the control

[1] Sturmey, op. cit., pp. 155-6.   [2] Eckersley, op. cit., p. 64.
[3] Lewis, op. cit., p. 153.   [4] Eckersley, op. cit., p. 80.

of Miss Mallinson, but when W. H. B. Harley arrived on 19 February 1923 as BBC accountant there were no books of account to examine. On the direct initiative of Reith a book-keeping system was designed on the spot—a conventional manual system appropriate to a limited liability company—with ledger, cash book, journal, salaries and wages books, and day books. Practically all payments in 1923 and 1924 were made direct from Head Office. The stations sent lists of artists and their fees and expenses. For several years all the cheques were made out by hand. As the number of stations multiplied so too did the sub-divisions of the accounts and the number of appropriate forms —purchase authorization forms, petty cash forms, and pro-grammes as broadcast.

A quite separate section of the office was concerned from the start with the registration of members, tariffs, and commercial questions: it was managed at first by R. M. Page. Publicity was separately handled after the appointment of W. C. Smith: from the start he was directly responsible to Carpendale and Reith, not to Anderson. What was called 'publicity' soon became such a comprehensive and basic concern in 1924 that there was need of a major reorganization. This took place when Major Glad-stone Murray, a colourful Canadian Rhodes scholar and former R.F.C. pilot, joined the BBC from the Radio Communication Company in 1924.[1] He was recommended by Basil Binyon, and he had a large number of friends both in journalism and the House of Commons. He watched BBC interests skilfully and energetically both in the wings and before the footlights.

One single aspect of publicity—the publishing of the *Radio Times*—became a major business in itself in 1924.[2] Another and different aspect—that of dealing with listeners' letters—was thought to be particularly important by Reith. In 1924 the BBC was receiving approximately 2,000 letters a day. Most of them were about programmes. Before May 1924 there was no routine arrangement for answering listeners' letters and many of them just accumulated. From 19 May 1924 onwards, however, they were all answered with care by a programme correspondence section started by R. Wade. At a time when there was no concern for statistical listener research

[1] See below, p. 296.
[2] See below, pp. 296-308.

—the BBC was quite deliberately slow in developing this even when facilities were available[1]—the scrutiny of letters was thought of as perhaps the 'main link between the Company and the listening public'. At its best it is an imperfect link, but it was conceived of in strictly personal terms in 1924 and 1925. Reith hated what has later come to be called 'the dictatorship of percentages', and used the listeners' letters as much to acquaint himself with minority opinions as with the views of the majority. 'With us', he once wrote, ' "minorities" are very important sections of the community, and a "limited appeal" may still involve many hundreds of thousands.'[2] In discussing the programme correspondence section as a whole, he claimed that 'if there has been any fault in this matter it may be that of over-punctilious attention to correspondence'.[3] In the absence of a special research department dealing systematically with listeners' views and attitudes, the BBC was probably right to err on the side of over-punctiliousness. If it did not always get what it most needed to have—statements of listeners' wants—it got what was less important, but was always required—better public relations. 'It all tends towards the establishment of some degree of confidence and intimacy between the broadcasting organisation and the public, and we know this to be of the highest importance.'[4]

With the growth of 'organisation' some of the 'old hands' in the BBC began as early as 1924 to contrast the complicated broadcasting structure of the present with the impromptu activities of the recent past. C. A. Lewis, for instance, in his *Broadcasting from Within* wrote of the 'great days' which were clearly over. 'Already', he added, 'I look back on them with a certain wistfulness and regret. There is something very attractive about unorganised methods, particularly when they are handled by intelligent people.' He went on to describe the earlier phase as one of 'democracy', 'a democracy of young pioneers, doomed like all the pioneering of youth to come up against the rigidity of age, discipline and experience'.[5] Lewis was a romantic. Other romantics—and Lewis himself on other occasions—still looked to the future rather than to the past for

---

[1] B. Paulu, *British Broadcasting* (Minneapolis, 1956), pp. 342-3.
[2] *Broadcast Over Britain*, p. 151.   [3] Ibid., p. 119.
[4] Ibid., p. 120.   [5] Lewis, op. cit., pp. 36-37.

most of the romance. 'Broadcasting', Burrows wrote, 'is really only in the position of the prehistoric fisherman who put out a few hundred yards from the shore in his frail coracle or dug-out. He could see the greater scene, but its extent was hidden by a horizon set by the fisherman's limited knowledge of materials and their uses.'[1]

Nearly forty years later we can see that 'the democracy of young pioneers' was not yet ended, that the contrast between what came later and what existed then was to be far greater than the contrast between 1924 and 1922. There was, after all, no complete overnight transformation from the impromptu to the formal. In 1923 and 1924 most people on the staff of the BBC had to display two qualities seldom associated with 'big' organizations—versatility and unremitting voluntary enthusiasm. 'We all seem to combine a number of jobs in the B.B.C.,' C. A. Lewis admitted, 'chiefly because up to the present, we have been working at such pressure that it was usually easier to do a thing oneself than farm it out to others who would not be so conversant with the work.'[2]

Reith himself liked to be versatile—trying his hand at announcing as well as administering, writing a weekly article for the *Radio Times* (and not usually liking it), supervising a hundred details that somehow seemed relevant to his conception of what broadcasting was and what it might become. He pulled the various departments together, insisting, for example, that Eckersley, as soon as he was appointed, should see Smith. 'Some of the technical publications were asking for articles on our future plans: publicity was essential.'[3] Above all, Reith knew how hard others worked because he worked so hard himself, and he left Lord Gainford in no doubt about where credit should be attributed for the fact that broadcasting had been made into a 'regular service'. In his speech to the first shareholders' meeting in September 1923 Gainford told his audience bluntly that 'I do not suppose that any of you can have much idea of the amount of work this [the arrangement of a regular service] has involved in the general administration, the perfecting of engineering arrangements, and in the compiling and transmission of

[1] Burrows, op. cit., p. 177.
[2] Lewis, op. cit., pp. 158–9.
[3] *The Power Behind the Microphone*, p. 62.

programmes.'[1] The shareholders of the BBC seldom met. They were too busy making or selling radio sets. Only at their third ordinary general meeting in July 1926 was there any criticism of the BBC, and what was being complained of then was not the record of the previous year but the fact that the Company was to be changed into a public Corporation.

Undoubtedly, the fact that Reith worked so hard and took such a keen personal interest both in the organization and the people working in it—'right down to the office boy'[2]—saved it from becoming remote and unwieldy. 'One can tell something of the personality of a manager from his office boy', was one of Reith's phrases.[3] At the same time Reith recognized the necessity of concentrating authority in a few hands. However much the constitution of the BBC changed with the years, two 'cardinal principles' were maintained throughout—first, that only five or six individuals were directly responsible to the Managing Director; second, that these people, along with Reith, were in 'control'.[4] A newcomer to the BBC in 1924 or 1925 could not fail to note the existence of a 'core' or 'stratum' of authority within the organization. There was as yet no clear-cut or even gossipy distinction between 'them' and 'us', but there was an immediately apparent and definable leadership and direction. The BBC was not just a collection of individuals: it had a genuine corporate existence.

The small group of people directly responsible to Reith were bound to him by genuine loyalty. 'I can't tell you how much I have enjoyed and appreciated all your trust and confidence in me during the last four months', Carpendale wrote to him in November 1923; 'it has done so much to ease the difficulties of taking a brand new type of job (after thirty years at sea) and amidst new surroundings.'[5] A few weeks later C. A. Lewis, enjoying a brief holiday, did not hesitate to express his 'esteem and affection', and added that there had never been any one like Reith on 'the constructive initiation side'.[6]

---

[1] *Gainford's speech at the First Extraordinary Meeting of Shareholders, 9 Oct. 1923.

[2] *Carpendale to Reith, 19 June 1923. This letter is in Lord Reith's possession.

[3] *Broadcast Over Britain*, p. 49.

[4] *Into the Wind*, p. 298.

[5] Carpendale to Reith, 14 Nov. 1923. This letter is in Lord Reith's possession.

[6] Lewis to Reith, 9 Apr. 1924. This letter is in Lord Reith's possession.

These were private tributes. In public Reith did not approve of Lewis writing flattering personal vignettes: he had a marked distaste for public displays of his personality. When Lewis wrote the first draft of his book, *Broadcasting from Within*, he included 'penetrating sketches' of Reith and Carpendale. They would have been most illuminating, he felt, to all his readers. But Reith and Carpendale 'sternly refused' to allow him to publish them. Lewis was left to speak in the most general terms, 'to convey to the public the enormous respect and admiration in which all the staff held their chief'.[1]

In order that the disadvantages of a functional division of staff should be avoided as numbers grew, there was need not only of forceful personal leadership but ultimately of some kind of central unifying apparatus. This was provided by the Control Committee, later called the Control Board. The very title of this piece of apparatus is significant. The first meeting of the Control Committee was held on 14 January 1924. It consisted of Carpendale—his title was changed from that of Assistant General Manager to Controller when Reith became Managing Director—Rice, Eckersley, and Burrows. The Control Committee met regularly and Reith intended from the start that it should be a 'real management committee'.

The Control Committee dealt with broadcasting policy: programmes were submitted to a Programme Committee, later called the Programme Board, four weeks ahead of broadcasting. Unlike the Control Board, the Programme Board included specialists in particular kinds of broadcasting—for example, the Directors of Music and Education. The Programme Board was instituted in May 1924. It met weekly and was in close touch with the Station Directors of the provincial stations as well as with the people at the centre. It dealt with everything from the idea of installing a cinema organ[2] to hiring Richard Strauss as a conductor (at a very high fee).[3] At one of its early meetings 'a suggestion was put up to hold a competition on a number of questions, one to be asked each night for a month, and the results of each question to be read out three days later than the question'. This suggestion was 'very carefully considered' but

---

[1] *Broadcasting from Within*, p. 147.
[2] *Programme Board, Minutes, 26 Jan. 1925.
[3] Ibid., 5 July 1924.

was 'not accepted'.[1] Quiz competitions were not to become staple fare of the new listening public, although at a later meeting attention was drawn to 'the popularity of competitions of all kinds'.[2] Not all the points raised within the Programme Board have contemporary undertones. In September 1925 'Mr. Eckersley was to be asked to see if something could be done with regard to complaints that the studio clock could be heard ticking through some of the performances.'[3]

The first main concern of the Programme Board—indeed, the chief reason given for its coming into existence—was the inauguration of 'simultaneous broadcasting', the transmission of the same programme by all stations in the country.[4] During this early period of the BBC's existence, when simultaneous broadcasting was developed in face of great technical difficulties, there was no regional organization of the BBC. Care was taken, however, to allow the Station Directors a considerable measure of independence. 'It is not our intention to dispense with the local station', Gainford told the first shareholders' meeting. 'We intend that local individuality shall be preserved, being of paramount importance.'[5] The opening of the first two provincial stations, Manchester and Birmingham, has already been described.[6] In July 1923 the Manchester studio was moved from Trafford Park to the heart of the city. Once again there were complaints that something of the 'family spirit' of 2ZY had gone with the abandonment of the small canvas-lined room in the research department of Metropolitan-Vickers,[7] but there was no lack of civic and regional pride after the move. Kenneth Wright ('Uncle Humpty Dumpty'), who set the pace before July 1923, moved to London, but his successor, Dan Godfrey junior, used the more conveniently placed central studio to attract artists who did not want to bother to go to Trafford Park. In particular, he set especially high standards of musical broadcasting.

In Birmingham the move from the outskirts to the centre came a little later, in August 1923. Percy Edgar was in charge there, and he too initiated distinctive Birmingham features. The first of the Children's Hours was made the central point of a

[1] *Programme Board Minutes, 13 Oct. 1924.   [2] Ibid., 9 Feb. 1925.
[3] Ibid., 29 Sept. 1925.   [4] See below, pp. 216 ff.
[5] *Gainford's speech, 9 Oct. 1923.   [6] See above, pp. 85 ff.
[7] *Evening Chronicle*, 18 Nov. 1930; *Manchester Evening News*, 13 Nov. 1947.

'Radio Circle', consisting of child listeners throughout the Midlands. The members of the circle were encouraged not only to take a keen interest in the programme but to do useful work for afflicted children throughout the area. The studio in Birmingham was one of the first in the country to develop more elaborate methods of programme control. The musical soloists, for example, were kept informed of the strength or weakness of their voices by a system of coloured signalling lamps operated from the control room.[1] Birmingham was also the first provincial station to employ a full-time announcer.[2]

Of the other provincial stations, Newcastle had been visited by Reith before he officially took up his duties in London.[3] The stable-yard he inspected was 'for one night only', and permanent but cramped premises were acquired soon afterwards in the central area of the city. A succession of early Station Directors—Tom Payne, Bertram Fryer, and Lynch Odhams—experimented with their own distinctive types of programmes, which included a farmers' corner and broadcasts of plays by the Newcastle Repertory Theatre. Burrows, who was almost as fond of brass bands as he was of tubular bells, regretted that the Newcastle studio was not big enough to house one of the well-known northern brass bands.

Bertram Fryer left Newcastle for Bournemouth, where the station was opened on 17 October 1923. Newcastle listeners, some of whom had resented the disappearance of their first Station Director, were glad to be able to hear Fryer speaking from Bournemouth just as clearly as they had done from Newcastle itself.[4] This they could do only if they bought valve sets, and it was said that many listeners converted their crystal sets into valve sets when he moved. Bournemouth was, in fact, the eighth of the main provincial stations specified in the first Licence. Cardiff had been opened on 13 February 1923, Glasgow on 6 March, and Aberdeen on 10 October.

Naturally enough, Reith took a special interest in the third of these, 2BD, which had R. E. Jeffrey as its first Station Director. Noble, who was also an Aberdonian, shared his interest and made the first speech at the formal opening. Lord Aberdeen ventured to say that the effect of broadcasting in northern

---

[1] Burrows, op. cit., p. 150.
[2] Ibid., p. 153.
[3] See above, p. 139.
[4] Lewis, op. cit., pp. 163-4.

P

Scotland would be 'to impart to country life some of the advantages and attractions of the cities'.[1] Comments of this kind were common at the formal station openings when local celebrities sought to prophesy what would be the consequence of the development of the new medium. Viscount Burnham, the press lord, speaking at Bournemouth, showed that he had learned much from the deliberations of the Sykes Committee of which he had been a distinguished member. 'The newspapers had nothing to fear from broadcasting of news. On the contrary insofar as it increased public *curiosity* and stimulated public interest it rendered splendid service to the community.'[2]

There was considerable mobility from station to station in these early days of broadcasting, for Reith knew what was going on everywhere and did not hesitate to deploy people where he thought that they would be most useful. Jeffrey, for instance, was on the staff at Glasgow before moving to Aberdeen, and in the middle of 1924 moved from Aberdeen to London to become 'Drama Director'. Major Corbett Smith, the first Station Director at Cardiff, moved to London in the same year to develop features broadcasting. Reith himself was behind the most important of these moves. He believed that Station Directors should be men of an 'exceptional range of qualifications . . . diversity of gifts, but the same spirit'. He admitted, however, that at first the choice of Station Directors had to be 'a matter of trial and error' and that many mistakes were made.[3]

His emphasis on the 'vocation' of broadcasting did not relate only to the Station Directors. He wrote to all the Station Directors in June 1924 asking them to consider the staffing problem in terms of 'the rapid extension of the Company's activities' and 'the growing status which it is attaining'. He asked them in particular not to hesitate to give full and frank reports on their junior staff. 'In our work there is demanded a wider range of qualifications than in any other business. Our people should be of social, educational and business standing. In addition to this there are peculiar qualities demanded of them, and the one which is most conspicuously lacking is, I think, imagina-

---

[1] *Aberdeen Press and Journal*, 11 Oct. 1923.
[2] *Bournemouth Daily Echo*, 18 Oct. 1923.
[3] *Broadcast Over Britain*, pp. 34–35.

tion.'[1] It was in letters of this kind as well as in regular and intensive interviewing that Reith demonstrated how interested he was not only in every office boy in London but in every junior programme assistant in the provinces. A few months later in December 1924 a further letter asked for information under definite headings to be submitted by the Station Directors on extensive lines.[2]

The most important of the stations was London, and the first London Station Director was one of the great 'veterans' of early broadcasting, Rex F. Palmer. A science graduate and Flying Officer during the First World War, Palmer joined the BBC very early in its career—about two months after it was formed. He has remained closely associated with it throughout the many phases of its subsequent history.

Some of the early programmes from London will be described later.[3] In 1923 and 1924 there was a remarkable change both in the organization behind the programmes and in the studio arrangements while they were being broadcast. The change began with a striking improvement in the conditions of working. In April 1923 new offices at 2 Savoy Hill were opened. They overlooked the Savoy Hotel and the river. Small though they were in retrospect, they marked a great advance on the cramped accommodation at Magnet House. On 1 May 1923 a new studio at Savoy Hill was also completed. A second studio was opened in the autumn of that year. From now on offices, studios, and equipment were in the same building. This was the beginning of the 'Savoy Hill era' of the BBC which lasted until 1931. It was to be an era of almost constant development and change, not least in the accommodation.

It is an era which has already acquired a romance of its own. 'Next to the House of Commons,' one of the first radio critics has reminisced, 'Savoy Hill was quite the most pleasant Club in London. There were coal fires, and visitors were welcomed by a most distinguished looking gentleman who would conduct them to a cosy private room and offer whisky-and-soda. And you could always be certain of running into great men like H. G. Wells, Bernard Shaw, G. K. Chesterton or Hilaire Belloc.'[4]

---

[1] *Reith to the Station Directors, 24 June 1924.
[2] *Reith to the Station Directors, 10 Dec. 1924. [3] See below, pp. 250 ff.
[4] Gale Pedrick, BBC programme, *These Radio Times*, 18 Dec. 1953.

The romance lingers, and it has been evoked—and is still evoked—in a large number of BBC programmes about the 'golden days' of radio, by records of the music of the Savoy Havana Band and Savoy Orpheans.

There was, of course, another side to the picture. John Snagge has clearly stated it. 'As the work gradually expanded, we absorbed neighbouring offices, adding one floor and then another, converting offices into studios, and all the time adapting a building which was completely unsuited to the growing needs of broadcasting.'[1]

Both early studios would today be regarded as period pieces. Number Three on the third floor was pleasantly decorated in blue and gold. Its dimensions were 38 feet by 18 feet, and it was very heavily draped. On the walls and ceiling were wooden fences holding six layers of fabric spaced about an inch apart to damp reverberation. For the same reason there was a thick, heavy carpet on the floor. Not unnaturally artists complained that they had to force their tone. Apart from acoustic deficiencies, the studio had other limitations. The drapery collected an enormous amount of dust, and there was extremely bad ventilation. Exhaust fans were fitted on the roof, but since they made a humming sound they could not be used during transmissions. 'After a brass band of twenty-five players had occupied the studio for an hour, the need for reform in planning the structure required no further argument.'[2]

Studio Number One on the first floor, immediately above the Institution Council Chamber, was a larger room of about 45 feet by 30 feet. Large orchestras and a chorus could now be more reasonably housed, but the Company had to enter into an agreement not to play music during the meetings of the Council of the Institution. There was give-and-take about this, as there was in all the dealings between the BBC and the Institution. Certainly there was as much take as give. The BBC was anxious to rent all the accommodation the Institution could provide. The first, second, and third floors of the west wing were fully occupied and part of the basement was converted into an engineers' workshop. Even this was inadequate. At last the northwest corner site, not the property of the Institution, was acquired.

---

[1] John Glyn-Jones, BBC programme, *Over Ten Million*, 24 Feb. 1946.
[2] R. Appleyard, op. cit., p. 258.

The site had been derelict since 1917, when it was bombed in an air raid. Extensions to the new block continued eastward until by 1927 they too were inadequate.

The bustle of building and conversion was perhaps the most obvious visible token of growth. Almost equally conspicuous, however, was the flurry of work. The BBC grew in an atmosphere of incessant work. 'We worked like lunatics', Burrows later wrote, 'in a pandemonium such as I hope may never fall to any one else's experience.'[1]

Palmer's early collaborators in the crowded London studio included Dan Godfrey junior, who moved from Manchester to become the London Station Musical Director, and K. A. Wright, who had made the same journey a little earlier. Lindsay Wellington and Stanford Robinson joined the staff later, and there were only two announcers, J. S. Dodgson and J. G. Broadbent. Stuart Hibberd became an announcer in 1924. He has described how the things which impressed him most as a new-comer at Savoy Hill were the general atmosphere of friendliness, 'the way I was at once made to feel at home—one of the family as it were', and the 'all-pervading pioneering spirit, which seemed to proclaim from the housetops, "Here's a wonderfully worthwhile job. Nothing matters but broadcasting—unless it is still better and more extensive broadcasting."'[2]

5. More Extensive Broadcasting

'MORE extensive broadcasting' was the dream of everyone connected with the BBC: very soon it became the demand of the public. It is one of the essential characteristics of the 'mass media' that they never stop growing until they have obtained what is usually called 'universal coverage'. Throughout 1923 and 1924 continuous lines of wireless aerials became a familiar feature of the urban landscape. The building of eight main broadcasting stations was only the first stage in the story of

[1] *Over Ten Million.*
[2] S. Hibberd, *This—Is London* (1950), p. 3.

development. By the end of 1924 'simultaneous broadcasting' had linked the stations together, 'relay stations' had been opened in crowded industrial areas, and experimental work had begun with a new high-powered long-wave transmitter at Chelmsford.

Reith regarded this extension of broadcasting facilities as a justification of the national claims of broadcasting as a public service: Eckersley saw it as a technical challenge. From the moment of taking up his post he decided that the main basis of his policy should be that 'every one should be able to hear one programme clearly on a cheap set'.[1] Yet the extension was neither universally nor unreservedly approved, and there were many difficulties—both technical and social—to overcome. The Services, in particular, were determined to resist 'too much broadcasting', and the Post Office was careful to safeguard both their interests and the claims of government departments and international wireless agencies. Eckersley prepared a memorandum in May 1923 on 'The BBC as an Aid to the State', but an attempt in that month to secure direct BBC representation on the Wireless Sub-Committee of the Imperial Communications Committee failed.

The amateurs also were restive, not only about licences but about wavelengths and power. Many of them resented the BBC's increasing 'dominion of the air'. Alan Archibald Campbell Swinton, giving evidence before the Sykes Committee on behalf of the Radio Society of Great Britain, demanded more 'blank hours' on Sundays 'for the use of students of wireless' and urged that each broadcasting station should close down each evening for a period of not less than half an hour. 'Experimental receiving stations', he complained, 'within a few miles of a broadcasting station are jammed so badly that practice in picking up other stations, in learning the morse code, and in testing apparatus, is impossible during the hours usually available to the experimenter.'[2]

During the Sykes Committee hearings, the Wireless Telegraph Board, representing the Army, Navy, and Air Force, was at pains to support the amateurs' point of view. Broadcasting, it was argued, was not in the best interests of imperial defence: in

---

[1] *The Power Behind the Microphone*, p. 63.
[2] *Prepared evidence submitted to the Sykes Committee by A. A. C. Swinton, 7 June 1923.

particular, it inhibited the work of 'genuine experimenters' who were making a real contribution to national security. No attempt was made by the Services to understand broadcasting as a medium of entertainment or education, and it is scarcely surprising that the BBC's marginal comment on one item in the Wireless Telegraph Board's evidence was couched in the form of a question. 'Is it not true that the advent of Broadcasting has brought wireless into public notice in a hitherto undreamed-of manner?'[1] Reith put an even more basic question to Brown in a letter of October 1923: 'Is the hobby of a few to interfere with the pleasure of thousands?'[2]

Restriction was the theme of much of the other evidence presented to the Sykes Committee, the arguments used displaying a remarkable variety of fears and prejudices. Sir Roderick Jones, for example, demanded that the electrical power used by broadcasting stations should be severely limited so that British news broadcasts should not be heard on the Continent. If it was capable of being 'intercepted' on the Continent, he went on, the legitimate sale of news in foreign countries would be interfered with 'to the serious detriment of News Agencies and newspapers'.[3] Fortunately the Post Office, while safeguarding other people's interests, did not forget the interests of the BBC. Shaughnessy was at pains to defend the amateur, but he admitted that at important places such as Bristol and Sheffield the wireless signals from London and Birmingham were so weak that they 'rendered broadcast reception unworthy of attempt'. The solution in his opinion, as in the opinion of the BBC engineers, was 'an increased number of broadcasting stations'.[4]

Eckersley has written a full account of his own approach to what he calls 'spreading the service'.[5] The main BBC stations, which were provided for in the original Licence, had a normal service area for crystal users of no more than twenty-five miles in radius. In many parts of the country reception was appalling.

---

[1] *Prepared evidence submitted to the Sykes Committee, 12 June 1923.
[2] *Reith to Brown, 22 Oct. 1923.
[3] *Prepared evidence submitted by Sir Roderick Jones to the Sykes Committee, 29 May 1923.
[4] *Prepared evidence submitted by E. H. Shaughnessy to the Sykes Committee, 31 May 1923.
[5] *The Power Behind the Microphone*, ch. iv.

In Sheffield, for example, which had rightly been singled out by Shaughnessy, wireless reception sounded like an 'insurrection in hell'. It was scarcely better in important cities like Leeds, Edinburgh, and Plymouth, which were outside the effective range of the main stations. The BBC had to satisfy the disgruntled inhabitants of those places if it were to justify its claims to be a 'public service'. Merely to increase the power of the main stations was inadequate, even had the Post Office been willing to accept this policy. It would have drowned the amateurs of Manchester and Birmingham without satisfying the inhabitants of Sheffield or Plymouth. The Board of the BBC decided, therefore, in the autumn and winter of 1923, to build a number of low-power transmitters. Once this decision had been taken, economic as well as technical considerations became relevant. Given a large number of low-power transmitters, who would pay for a large number of separate local programmes?

The answer seemed to be the rapid development of 'simultaneous broadcasting', that is the use of telephone wires to interconnect different stations 'so that the output from one microphone would operate many stations simultaneously'. The advantages of 'simultaneous broadcasting' were recognized even before the question of increasing the number of low-power stations was raised. National programmes could be broadcast, particularly if outstanding public events and artists who were reluctant to embark on provincial tours could be heard all over the country from a London studio. At the same time interesting provincial programmes could be shared by more than one station.

The first experimental simultaneous broadcast took place in May 1923, but there were several technical obstacles to progress. One was the inadequacy of the national trunk-line telephone system for the transmission of speech of high quality: another was the difficulty in satisfactorily transmitting musical programmes. Fortunately there was close co-operation between Eckersley and his staff, the Post Office engineers, and the engineers of the Western Electric Company, and all the difficulties were successfully overcome by the spring of 1924. The first complete 'simultaneous broadcast news bulletin' was broadcast on 29 August 1923. At once the press talked of a 'new wireless era': 'the vast possibilities opened by this unexpected development,'the *Glasgow Herald* remarked, '[and] the rapidity with which all the technical difficulties have been overcome have surprised even the investigators themselves . . . the public will benefit by each successive advance which is made'.[1] The foundation of the first Programme Board, as we have seen, was a by-product of this technical development.[2] It was known at first as the Simultaneous Broadcasts Programme Board, and it was its chief task at its weekly meetings to review a skeleton draft of simultaneous broadcast programmes. In August 1923, the month of the first simultaneous news broadcasts, it was decided that two complete programmes each week should be simultaneously broadcast from London for all BBC stations. The details of the programmes were to be worked out by the headquarters staff of the BBC subject to approval by the Control Board.

Although there were many complaints from the provinces about the poor quality of some of the early simultaneous broadcasts, C. A. Lewis promised Station Directors that 'the saving of expenditure by closing provincial stations for a few hours twice a week' would be such as 'to enable artistes of world-wide reputation to broadcast from London'.[3] The complaints continued, but they provided a necessary stimulus to the producers of programmes. By the end of 1924 there were signs that technical progress had been followed by a necessary further advance in the technique of broadcasting itself.

The building of low-power 'relay stations' began with Sheffield, and a station, using a power of only 100 watts, was opened there on 16 November 1923. This project taught the BBC many lessons. It was originally intended to link Sheffield with Manchester by telephone wire so that the Manchester programme could be relayed by Sheffield. There were technical difficulties in doing this in 1923, but a more awkward obstacle was the opposition of people in Sheffield to taking their programmes from Manchester. 'Why should we have to listen to Manchester programmes?' they asked. 'Why, if we have a local station, should we not have a local programme of our own?' Birmingham was no more acceptable to the inhabitants of Sheffield than Manchester, and finally the BBC had to link

[1] *Glasgow Herald*, 31 Aug. 1923.   [2] See above, p. 207.
[3] *Memorandum of Lewis to Reith, 22 Aug. 1923.

Sheffield with neither city but directly with London. 'It appears', Reith wrote, 'that no city counted sufficiently important to have a relay station could listen to the programmes of any station other than London without loss of dignity.'[1]

Once Sheffield had acquired its relay station, a large number of other places asked for local transmitters also. The extent of the demand brought to the surface once more the major limiting factor in British wireless development—the shortage of wavelengths. In October 1923 the government accepted a proposal of the Sykes Committee that the wave band available to the BBC should be extended, but the extension to cover additional wavelengths from 300 to 350 metres, from 425 to 439 metres, and from 461 to 500 metres, thereby giving the BBC control of the 300- to 500-metre band, was inadequate to meet all the claims of the great centres of population.[2] Indeed, in allowing the extension of wave band, the Wireless Sub-Committee of the Imperial Communications Committee specifically asked the BBC to make every effort to explore any technical improvement which might have the effect of reducing the many calls for separate wavelengths.

Because of wavelength limitations, only one new main station was constructed by the BBC—that at Belfast. It was officially opened by the Governor of Northern Ireland on 24 October 1924, and even in this one case there was a dispute with the Post Office about the most suitable wavelength.[3]

The extension of the broadcasting service was achieved through the building of more relay stations on the Sheffield pattern, each working on a power of 200 watts. The stations were constructed in various parts of the country. The selection of sites depended not only on population, distance from existing stations, and—in the light of the experience of Sheffield—'civic importance', but on technical considerations such as geographical 'shielding' or 'jamming' by other stations. Plymouth was opened on 28 March 1924, Edinburgh on 1 May, Liverpool on 11 June, Leeds/Bradford (a precarious combination) on 8 July, Hull on 15 August, Nottingham on 16

---

[1] *Broadcast Over Britain*, p. 62.
[2] *Brown to Reith, 19 Oct. 1923.
[3] The BBC asked for 485 or 435 metres, but the Post Office pressed hard for a wavelength below 400 metres. It was only after negotiation that 435 metres was agreed upon.

September, Dundee on 12 November, Stoke-on-Trent on 21 November, and Swansea on 12 December. It seemed absurd to Reith that Swansea should relay London rather than Cardiff, and Dundee and Edinburgh should listen to London rather than to Glasgow or Aberdeen, but the experience of Sheffield was copied and all the new relay stations became 'London's babies'.[1] There were some local programmes in the afternoons and on one evening a week, but on economic grounds they had to be kept to the minimum.

The programmes of the relay stations could be picked up in their localities and for a normal radius of about five miles by the cheapest crystal sets. This gave a fillip both to the sale of licences by the Post Office and the sale of receivers by the industry. The bold engineering feat of opening one new relay station each month produced immediate economic returns and the number of licence-holders doubled between December 1923 and December 1924. The engineers had thus contributed manfully to the solvency of the BBC. Of course, there were freaks of transmission which the engineers could hardly have allowed for. Plymouth, for instance, could be heard on its first night on a single-valve receiver in Sunderland. Liverpool 'had the audacity to trespass on the territory of Manchester, and actually usurped the position of Manchester in Blackpool'.[2] The radio 'craze', as the popular newspapers called it, was enlivened by the urge to demonstrate just what your crystal set would do. The gentle art of tickling the crystal with the cat's whisker was supplemented by the far from gentle art of triumphing technically and morally over your next-door neighbour.

Home construction was a fascinating hobby, but even when the crystal-set craze gave way to the valve-set craze the radio game still remained complicated. Its rules were set out in the numerous radio magazines which enjoyed exceptional popularity in 1923 and 1924. *Amateur Wireless* had a circulation of 100,000 in the autumn of 1924, *Modern Wireless* 100,000, *The Popular Wireless Weekly* 125,000, *Wireless* 150,000, and *The Wireless Constructor* 250,000. The jargon was as bewildering to the uninitiated as it was immensely satisfying to the people 'in the know'. Practical work was far more exciting than reading. There

---

[1] *Broadcast Over Britain*, p. 63; Burrows, *The Story of Broadcasting*, ch. xviii.
[2] Ibid., p. 165.

was still an art in delicately handling your apparatus, even if it was more expensive than a crystal set. 'Distant listening', usually the object of buying a valve set, involved long periods of waiting for station identification signals and careful tuning, and when the programme started you were always liable to be upset by your neighbours' efforts to pick up the station also. Eckersley had to concern himself with the anti-social effects of 'oscillation' and to enlist the services of the Post Office motor vans not to detect but to intimidate regular offenders.[1]

22. Loudspeaker

With the provision of nine main stations and ten relay stations, between 60 and 70 per cent. of the total population of England, Scotland, and Wales could receive on simple and cheap apparatus at least the programme from the nearest centre. And by August 1924 this programme included a considerable amount of material from London. Reith and Eckersley were not satisfied, however, and wished to provide 'universal coverage'. There were still many small towns where reception was extremely poor, and there were large areas of the countryside where, even given large resources, it would have been impossible to provide sufficient relay stations to allow for regular listening. The countryside seemed to provide a challenge to broadcasting. Some social commentators argued that the country population *needed* broadcast programmes even more than the town and city population. Radio could serve as the ideal device to carry diversion and contentment to the village and thereby help to equalize the amenities of the two halves of Britain.

It was largely to meet the needs of countrymen that the BBC planned the building of a single high-power long-wave station. The alternative of increasing the power of the nine main stations was still impracticable, and there were limits to the efficiency of land-line interconnexion. The choice of long-wave to augment medium-wave transmission was Eckersley's. He thought correctly that long waves would travel farther than medium waves

[1] Eckersley, op. cit., pp. 73 ff.

under a 'push-off' of the same power. Unfortunately, there were relatively few available long-wave channels, and both the Post Office and the Services were concerned about the effects of long-wave broadcasting on other wireless services. For different reasons some sections of the radio industry were also unhappy about the new development. They argued that the public would be unwilling to convert their wireless sets by adding an extra switch and considerably increasing the cost of listening. Technical objections were advanced as well—that the longer the wave, the greater would be the interference; that proper modulation of long waves was impossible; and that there would be serious likelihood of jamming by wireless telegraph stations. Yet the doubts of the Post Office and the Services were overcome, and the fears of the wireless trade were quickly shown to be quite unfounded. In retrospect the success of the BBC's high-power long-wave station was a crucial event in the history of British broadcasting. It invigorated the British radio industry at the critical season of the year—autumn—and it provided complete protection against American-made sets which did not cater for long-wave reception. It marked a considerable victory over Services' objections and, not least, it gave listeners who could already hear one programme the chance of listening to an alternative.

The idea of a high-power transmitter was first raised at the Board meeting of December 1923. Reith submitted a memorandum suggesting that there should be two stations in London, one of which should employ a high-powered transmitter of 20 kilowatts. A strong committee was appointed, which included Gill, Burnham, Binyon, Gray, and Round of the Marconi Company, and Eckersley. This committee reported to the Board in January 1924 that a high-powered station 'would solve once and for all the questions of jamming, that it would be possible by this means to get crystal reception up to nearly 100 miles, and that it would enable the larger towns of England to be served by relay stations working off the main stations'.[1] The best wavelength would be somewhere between 1,400 and 2,000 metres and the question of the site depended not only on geographical conditions—high ground, geological suitability

[1] *Minutes of the Meeting of the Committee to consider proposals for the erection of a high-power Broadcast station near London, 28 Dec. 1923.

for mast foundations and wireless 'earth' and access to water,
electricity, railways, and suitable land-line facilities—but also
on the approval of the Post Office and the Services. Before com-
mitting the Board to the choice of a site and a wavelength, it
would be better to carry out experiments. The Board agreed,
and decided to apply to the Post Office for a temporary licence
to carry out experiments at the Marconi Works in Chelmsford.

  The object of the experiments was to establish three points—
the range of crystal-set reception, the extent of interference of a
high-powered station with existing broadcasting stations, and
the possible danger to other wireless interests. Experimental
transmissions of speech and music began on 9 July 1924, and
from 21 July to 9 August the London programmes were relayed
from Chelmsford after 7 o'clock in the evening. Two BBC
engineers co-operated with Ditcham and the Marconi Company
engineers in this venture. Reports received from various parts
of the country suggested that the experiments had been highly
successful, and the Board decided at its meeting in August 1924
to ask the Post Office for permission to open a permanent high-
power station.[1]

  The Postmaster-General called a meeting of the Wireless
Telegraph Board on 26 September 1924, making it clear that
the opinions of the Services as represented on the Board and on
the Wireless Sub-Committee of the Imperial Communications
Committee would be decisive. 'An objection from the I.C.C.
would be upheld by the Imperial Defence Committee', Reith
was told, 'in spite of any agitation, Parliamentary and otherwise,
which the B.B.C. might raise.'[2] At first the Services were
obstructive. They objected to any station south of a line from
Gloucester to King's Lynn, and complained that their wireless
activities were already being disturbed by interference from
Chelmsford. Twenty-five kilowatts should be the maximum
power allowed to the BBC, and any new station should be
contained within the 350-500 metre wavelength band. After
further discussions, however, the Services' representatives withdrew some of their objections and the BBC modified its own
scheme to win their support. It was agreed that a long-wave

  [1] *Minutes of the Board Meeting, 7 Aug. 1924.
  [2] *Minutes of the Committee appointed by the Board at their Meetings on
7 Aug. 1923, 30 Sept. 1924.

station working on 1,500 metres, with a power not exceeding 25 kilowatts, should be built north of a line drawn from the Severn to the Wash, including as little sea space within its service area as possible. Pending the building of this new station, which the BBC naturally hoped (for reasons of coverage) would be only just north of the dividing line, Chelmsford would continue to broadcast London programmes after 7 o'clock. The Services agreed to this reluctantly, and on 24 November 1924 F. J. Brown, who had been chairman at a critical meeting between the BBC and the Service representatives on 26 September, asked Keith whether the Post Office could assume 'that there would be no avoidable delay in regard to the transfer'.[1]

It was unnecessary for the Post Office to dwell on the need for speed. At its August meeting the Board of the BBC had decided to go ahead as quickly as possible, and to supervise the building of the station itself rather than to put out the tenders to the 'Big Six' companies. Masts and aerials would be supplied by the Radio Communication Company, transmitting apparatus by the Marconi Company, and the amplifiers and apparatus associated with land-lines by the Western Electric Company. BBC engineers were to be sent off to the Northampton district to examine possible sites, and a public announcement about the new station would be made to coincide with the opening of the All-British Wireless Exhibition in September.[2]

Half a dozen sites were carefully examined by the engineers, who included Captain Round and Harold (later Sir Harold) Bishop, the present Director of Engineering of the BBC. A site at Borough Hill, three-quarters of a mile from Daventry in Northamptonshire, was considered 'pre-eminently suitable'. It consisted of a flat plateau of over fifty acres at an average height above sea level of 650 feet. The Board agreed that this was an excellent site; the freehold cost of the original site was £2,670 and work on the station began almost at once. It was completed in the early summer of 1925, and the new Daventry station was opened on 27 July by Sir William Mitchell-Thomson, the Postmaster-General. The Prime Minister, Stanley Baldwin, sent his apologies for not being able to be present. 'It is not too much to say', he told Reith, 'that broadcasting is

[1] *Brown to Reith, 24 Nov. 1924.
[2] *Managing Director's Report for the Board Meeting of 16 Oct. 1924.

already contributing appreciably to the happiness and knowledge of the present generation. . . . I look upon Daventry as another milestone along the road to the social betterment of our people'.[1]

The Daventry station (5XX) was not only the biggest broadcasting station in the world but the first long-wave station. It had a 25-kilowatt transmitter, an excellent land-line link up with London, from which the programmes continued to be provided, and a T-type aerial held up by two triangular steel masts each 500 feet high and set 800 feet apart. It was a new building for a new age, dominated by many of the architectural and engineering features which were to be treated as symbols by the young new poets of the 1930s. As it was, Alfred Noyes wrote a poem for the opening, which stressed the strange and compelling contrast between ancient and modern on Dane Tree Hill, a site of historic importance, one of the oldest military encampments of the Midlands and a place mentioned in Shakespeare's *Henry VI*.

> Daventry calling . . . Daventry calling . . .
> Daventry calling . . . Dark and still.
> The tree of memory stands like a sentry
> Over the graves on the silent hill.

There was still a powerful sense of mystery about wireless. Leslie Baily, later of *Scrapbook* fame but then a young wireless correspondent of the *Yorkshire Evening News*, was present at the official opening. 'Here, outside in the night air,' he wrote, 'all was quiet. Silence—and yet one felt the mystery of these invisible waves, the miracle of the hidden voices, sweeping out through the night.'[2]

The Postmaster-General chose the occasion of the opening of the Daventry station to pay a warm tribute to the BBC. It had now provided effective wireless coverage even by crystal sets for 85 per cent. of the population. Those with one-valve sets would be able to pick up Daventry within a radius of 150 to 200 miles: many people would now have the choice of two programmes. 'This is of importance because it makes possible continued development upon the footing that the broadcasting service should aim at being not only popular but also educational.'

[1] Baldwin to Reith, 21 July 1925. This letter is in Lord Reith's possession.
[2] Leslie Baily, BBC programme, *The Story of Scrapbook*, Nov. 1957.

23. BBC Head Office Staff, November 1924

24. Arthur Burrows

25. C. A. Lewis

The BBC had always recognized the importance of educational standards. Although in its inception it had been organized 'upon a trade basis', its directors had boldly and wisely insisted upon the ideal that they should function largely as 'a public service operating upon a democratic policy'. This was a remarkable achievement. Whatever the future of broadcasting might be, the community, he concluded, should be thankful that its 'infant steps had been wisely guided'.[1]

[1] Report of the Proceedings, 27 July 1925. See also the souvenir brochure of the BBC, *5XX, 1he High Power Station of the British Broadcasting Company*.

The BBC had always recognized the importance of educational standards. Although in its inception it had been organized 'upon a trade basis', its directors had boldly and wisely insisted upon the ideal that they should function largely as 'a public service operating upon a democratic policy'. This was a remarkable achievement. Whatever the future of broadcasting might be, the community', he concluded, should be thankful that its 'infant steps had been wisely guided.'[1]

[1] Report of the Proceedings, 27 July 1925. See also the souvenir brochure of the BBC, 5XX, The High Power Station of the British Broadcasting Company.

V

POLICY, PROGRAMMES, PUBLICITY, AND PERSONALITIES
1923-1925

Early days are crucial ones in either individual existence or corporate organisation.

J. C. W. REITH
Broadcast Over Britain (1925), p. 24

1. Broadcasting as a Public Service

THE Postmaster-General's eloquent tribute would have been more convincing had he not been attempting for some time to reduce the licence fee on receiving sets.[1] Some disgruntled members of parliament were pressing him to do this: others were asking for differential licence fees for the owners of crystal sets and valve receivers.[2] There was a substantial body of opinion, however, which argued the other way, and complained that the Post Office was retaining a disproportionately large share of the licence fee from each listener for the costs of administering the licence system.[3]

Reith recognized that if broadcasting were to be treated as a public service it needed financial as well as oratorical support. In the summer of 1925 he stated that the work of the BBC could not be carried on for less than £600,000 a year on the revenue account alone. The figure of £700,000 would be far safer. 'Public appetite is insatiable and our activities must be extended and the standard of programmes continually improved at all costs.'[4] In fact, during the whole period from the advent of broadcasting to the end of March 1925 the BBC had received less than £500,000 from the Post Office in respect of licence fees.[5] And the method of payment, which was changed four times between 1922 and 1926, was always most unsatisfactory. Monthly instalments were paid to the BBC in arrears on the basis of the number of paid licences in force at the beginning of the fiscal year in April. In a period of rapid expansion of licences and facilities financial provision always lagged behind. Unless the BBC had collected sizeable sums from the *Radio Times* and from tariffs—it continued to receive these in arrears after the final ending of the tariff system in 1924—there would have been inadequate funds to develop the service. The capital cost of

[1] Diary, 13 Mar. 1925; *Into the Wind*, p. 97. See also above, p. 195.
[2] See, for example, *Hansard*, vol. 181, col. 2069, 17 Mar. 1925; vol. 186, col. 1072, 14 July 1925.
[3] Ibid., vol. 181, col. 1130, 10 Mar. 1925; col. 2477, 19 Mar. 1925; col. 428, 25 Mar. 1925.
[4] *Report of the Second Annual General Meeting, 16 July 1925.
[5] Ibid. See Appendix II for detailed figures.

improving the main stations in 1924 and 1925, along with the building of the Belfast station, the Daventry station, and the relay stations, was in the neighbourhood of £200,000, a sum greatly in excess of the subscribed capital of the Company. This figure had to be met out of revenue at a time when the cost of providing 'superior' programmes was taxing the BBC to the utmost.

By the middle of 1925 Reith was convinced that he would need far more money, not less; not a fixed dole but a realistic allocation which could be reviewed annually. The very most that the Post Office would grant him in January 1926 was a fixed share of licence revenue. The sum of £500,000 was to be paid to the BBC in ten equal 'monthly' instalments of £50,000.[1] This arrangement lasted until 31 March 1926. It provided no guarantee that the BBC would ever benefit from the greatly increased number of licence-holders, yet, as Reith saw, the future of the BBC depended almost entirely on receipts from licences. The 'trade basis' of broadcasting had lost its significance long before the Company gave way to the Corporation.

The radio industry recognized this also, or at least sufficiently large sections of the industry to make effective Reith's stress on 'public service' rather than commercial exploitation. The economic position of the industry was complex. The 'giant' electrical firms, which were concerned with broadcasting only as one of their activities, had enjoyed mixed fortunes since 1922. For example, while the profits of the General Electric Company rose steadily from £751,486 in 1923 to £1,076,809 in 1926, the Marconiphone Company, which purchased the set-making branch of the Marconi Company in December 1923, suffered losses until 1926. Broadcasting was at best a somewhat dubious financial venture for the firms which had taken the initiative in 1922. At the same time there were very large profits still to be made by small 'assemblers', firms with little capital and equipment. Many of them had survived the abolition of protection with no difficulty, and it was still easy to enter what was a competitive but thriving trade with an annual turnover estimated at upwards of £10 million.[2] There were 1,600 manu-

---

[1] *Hansard*, vol. 191, col. 2133, 18 Feb. 1926.
[2] Crawford Committee, paper 47, W. W. Burnham, 'A Trade View on the Broadcasting Service', p. 2.

facturing concerns associated with the British Broadcasting Company in its last year and many of them were prosperous. Their interest in 'controlling' broadcasting was at best intermittent, something of a seasonal preoccupation with the chief anxieties being expressed about BBC programmes in the difficult selling months during the summer. In the same year that the British Broadcasting Company died—1926—a new trade association was born, the Radio Manufacturers' Association. In September 1926 it united, in one compact body, the National Association of Radio Manufacturers, which had been founded in 1923,[1] and the British Radio Manufacturers' and Traders' Association, which had been critical of the BBC.[2]

Competition within the radio industry tended to centre on prices and obvious advertisable features rather than on prices in relation to quality,[3] and here there was a divergence of interest between sections of the 'trade' and the BBC. As far as the consumer was concerned—and he was often an ignorant consumer—the important point was that the price of receiving sets was falling. Crystal sets had always been cheap—you could buy one complete for 7s. 6d., headphones for 2s., and aerials for 1s. 8d.—but the price of valve sets began to fall also. A two-valve set cost £17. 10s. in 1923: by the end of 1925 you could buy one for £5. 5s.

At the first All-British Wireless Exhibition and Convention at the Horticultural Hall at Westminster in October 1922 it was regarded as a matter of pride that there were on display 'handsome cabinets in which the "works" were completely hidden so that wireless receivers need not turn the drawing room into a mixture of electrical laboratory and ship's deck'. By the time of the Exhibition of October 1925 such an advertisement sounded completely unsophisticated. You could buy wireless sets with the cabinets designed in the style of 'any period', imitating ambitious ornamental furniture and designs which would specially 'appeal to the ladies'.[4] An *avant-garde* design of 1926 was the so-called Rose-Bowl Model Hornless Loud Speaker. It

[1] See above, pp. 176–7.
[2] Some of the details are set out usefully in S. G. Sturmey, *The Economic Development of Radio*, pp. 160–1.
[3] Ibid., p. 263.
[4] These details are taken from the catalogues of the various radio exhibitions, the *Radio Times*, and the daily press.

looked like an ordinary rose bowl and was guaranteed to perform equally well whether empty or filled with water and flowers.[1]

26. 'Improved Styles'
'Cabinet-work in any period, batteries all enclosed. *All* British and most continental stations on head-phones and most on the cunningly incorporated loudspeaker.'

Given this social and economic background and the limita-tion of BBC dividends to $7\frac{1}{2}$ per cent., it is scarcely surprising that a divorce between broadcasting and the radio industry was not difficult to achieve.

This is not, of course, to say that there were not other com-mercial interests which were drawn towards the possibilities of broadcasting. Had there been no limitation of dividends, broadcasting could have been a very lucrative business and con-siderable windfall gains might have been made out of it. Ecker-sley has pointed out, for instance, how a relay station, which cost no more than a few thousand pounds, would have been a gold mine had it been sponsored commercially and allowed to

[1] M. Gorham, *Broadcasting and Television since 1900* (1952), p. 39.

collect licence fees for its listening area. 'For a capital of two thousand pounds and an expenditure of about fifteen hundred pounds per annum, it was possible, in some districts, to secure twenty thousand new licences in the first year, mounting to fifty thousand in the next, representing an increased licence revenue, after saturation-point had been reached, of twenty-five thousand pounds per annum.'[1] This figure, of course, completely ignored possible advertising revenue. Had broadcasting been developed in this way, the content of programmes would probably have been quite different, and there would have been a tendency to concentrate broadcasting facilities in the big towns where the biggest profits would have accrued. This would have been a completely different policy from that followed by the BBC. Both to Reith and to Eckersley the opening up of the rural areas was a matter of the highest priority.

There is one interesting letter from Reith which brings out clearly the danger to the BBC of alternative broadcasting schemes in May 1925. The Post Office had complained about Reith giving too much publicity to high-power stations. This publicity, said Murray, irked the Services and brought in protests from other interested parties. Reith replied, defending the action of the publicity department of the BBC:

As you no doubt know, there are cross currents at work in the press and various interests are already making preliminary dispositions for attacking the public service character of British broadcasting, which it is our endeavour to consolidate, and, which we trust, with your support, will be perpetuated after the end of the present Licence. We have had to take special measures to ascertain in advance the probable lines of attack calculated to serve the purpose of those who are working for commercialised broadcasting in Great Britain. About a week ago we got wind of a projected attack based on the ground that under the present system we had already reached the limits of our expansion. The deduction to be drawn was that the British people would never be supplied with adequate alternative services unless the principle of competitive commercialism were admitted. We had definite reason to believe that an attempt would be made to prejudice public opinion through the medium of several leading newspapers. If this attack had developed it would have spread over a large proportion of the press of the country, and would

[1] *The Power Behind the Microphone*, p. 76.

certainly have embarrassed both your Department and ourselves, particularly at a time when the Wireless Bill is down for a second reading. What our publicity people did, therefore, was to turn the flank of this attack before it developed. When asked definitely whether we had any plans for future expansion, to reply in the negative would have been merely to play into the hands of our enemies. We refrained from saying anything until continued silence would have been much more damaging in the long run than a general indication of possibilities.[1]

Reith's concern for public service was always coupled with a concern for the right kind of publicity. His book *Broadcast Over Britain* is the best evidence of this. Written reluctantly and quickly,[2] it remains an impressive social document, the best statement of the public service character of broadcasting before the sittings of the Crawford Committee in 1925. Reith used the occasion it provided to set out his own ideals and objectives for the attention of 'the great audience'.

Since it was published as early as the autumn of 1924, it 'lays bare the heart and mind and policy of the BBC'[3] at the turning point of its history, when it was still a company but there were signs that it might become a corporation. The strength of Reith's opinion and the skill with which he presented his case help to account for the change in the status of the BBC at the end of 1926. His personal contribution was—and remains —unique. In 1924 and 1925 Reith was managing the BBC as if it were a public corporation while it was in fact still a public company. Opponents of commercial broadcasting thought of this state of affairs as what Reith called 'an accident of management'.[4] In a sense, so it was, but, as *Broadcast Over Britain* shows, there was nothing casual or accidental about the policy. Reith and his colleagues had been moved by a 'high conception of the inherent possibilities of the service'.[5] What 'incalculable harm' might have been done, Reith asked, if those in charge of the BBC had been without principles? What would have happened had the controllers of the BBC been 'content with

---

[1] *Reith to Phillips, 25 May 1925.
[2] Diary, 28 Feb. 1924; 15 May 1924; 11 June 1924. It was on the last of these dates that the contract was signed.
[3] Review in the *Yorkshire Observer*, 2 Dec. 1924.
[4] Diary, 6 Mar. 1925; *Into the Wind*, p. 98.
[5] *Broadcast Over Britain*, p. 32.

mediocrity, with providing a service which was just sufficiently good to avoid complaint'?[1] 'The responsibility weighs heavily with us; let there be no misunderstanding on that score. It is realised to the full; it is apt to become an obsession. It is a burden such as few have been called upon to carry. Whether we are fit or not, is for reasoned judgement only, but at any rate it is relevant and advisable that our recognition of the responsibility should be known. Pronouncement may be reserved till the proofs of the effort are established.'[2]

For Reith, the public service aspect of broadcasting had four facets. First, and not least important, the BBC was not out to make money for the sake of making money. Although it had been brought into existence by a combination of manufacturing interests, such 'elements of commercialism' as had been evident in the early days of the Company had one by one disappeared. Protection had gone, restrictive licensing had gone. Profits were still limited, and there were no hopes of a distribution of capital gains.

It is interesting to note that Reith gave prior attention to this facet of broadcasting as a public service—its lack of dependence on the profit motive. It is even more interesting to note that at this relatively early stage in the history of broadcasting he had come to the conclusion, somewhat negatively expressed, that 'it would be fatuous to deny a strong element of rationality' in the contention that 'a service fraught with such potentialities should be under the direct care of either the State, or a Board composed of representatives of the public, with no other interests at stake'.[3] He had already begun to fall back on an historical explanation of the existing constitution—the fact that in 1922 broadcasting could not have started without commercial companies providing the initial impetus. He was already very close to the position which he took up later before the Crawford Committee and which he has summed up in *Into the Wind*. 'Though the B.B.C. had been administered as a public service and manufacturing policy had been adapted to public requirements . . . and though any action flagrantly contrary to the public interest could have been detected, it would have been impossible to detect abstinence from its positive pursuit. No one denied the anomaly of the existing constitution. The B.B.C. should be a

[1] Ibid., p. 25.   [2] Ibid., p. 34.   [3] Ibid., pp. 57 ff.

public service not only in performance but in constitution.' The quotation is, however, incomplete without the last few words, which were emphasized—'but certainly not as a department of State'.[1]

The second facet of broadcasting as a public service was its national coverage. Because profit was not the criterion, broadcasting could and should serve everybody in the community who wished to 'listen'. The willingness of the BBC to broadcast to 'the greatest possible number of homes'—Reith did not add 'the greatest possible number of programmes'—was 'a radical departure from the original scheme'.[2] Eckersley made this point also, without sharing all Reith's philosophical explanations. He has argued convincingly that unless broadcasting had been treated as a public service in its early days there would have been confusion. Without some central authority 'to decide the claims for relay stations in relation to a national plan there would have been chaos'.[3] The account already given of how the service of broadcasting was extended strongly supports the important conclusion that it is fortunate that the central authority was the BBC and not the Post Office. The caution of the Post Office, its special concern for Services' interests, and the excessive formality of some at least of its methods would have been an obstacle to development. The BBC regarded itself as a 'public service', but this did not mean that it pushed aside the claims of enterprise or allowed bureaucratic rules to stifle the processes of growth. The rapid development of its plan may properly be compared with the planlessness of early railway development during the nineteenth century. How much waste would have been avoided had the design of physical communications been given as much attention as the shaping of social communications by the makers of the BBC?

The third facet of broadcasting as a public service was closely related to the second—'unified control' was substituted for sectional pressure. Reith had made this point when appearing before the Sykes Committee.[4] In his diary he describes how on an Italian holiday in December 1923 he was 'expatiating on the advantages of unified control for broadcasting'.[5] He reiterated

---

[1] *Into the Wind*, p. 102.   [2] *Broadcast Over Britain*, p. 61.
[3] *The Power Behind the Microphone*, p. 79.
[4] See above, p. 182.   [5] Diary, 20 Dec. 1923.

the point in *Broadcast Over Britain*: 'in a concern where expansion is so rapid and the problems so unique, unity of control is essential'.[1] Whereas the charge of 'monopoly' had been contested by the representatives of the BBC when they appeared before the Sykes Committee, Reith now openly and unashamedly admitted its existence. He went farther and argued that 'on diverse technical grounds one cannot conceive any other system'.[2] He deliberately chose to associate broadcasting with other experiments in public ownership. 'In these days, when efforts are being made towards the nationalisation of the public services and of certain essential industries of the country, the progress of broadcasting has been cited as the most outstanding example of the potentiality of a combination of private enterprise and of public control.'[3]

In referring to broadcasting in this context, Reith was anticipating the conclusions of historians and students of public administration who have traced in detail the pattern of events during the inter-war years. Professor W. A. Robson, for example, took the BBC as a case history in his study of public enterprise, arguing that bodies like the BBC 'form the most significant development in the field of political institutions which has taken place in Great Britain during the present century'.[4] An American scholar, Lincoln Gordon, one of the contributors to Professor Robson's volume, dwelt at length on the BBC in a book of his own,[5] calling it one of the prototypes of 'a new and unique administrative form', christened 'the public corporation'.[6] It recognized explicitly that *Broadcast Over Britain* 'contained the seeds of B.B.C. programme policy as it exists today in almost every aspect'; although for Gordon 'today' was 1938.[7]

Reith did not write in 1924 with quite as much relish on the

---

[1] *Broadcast Over Britain*, p. 64.
[2] Ibid., p. 70.   [3] Ibid., pp. 71–72.
[4] W. A. Robson (ed.), *Public Enterprise, Developments in Social Ownership and Control in Great Britain*, p. 9 and ch. iv, *passim*.
[5] L. Gordon, *The Public Corporation in Great Britain* (1938).
[6] Hugh Dalton in his *Practical Socialism for Britain* (1935), p. 94, ascribed the popularization of the phrase 'Public Corporation' to the Labour member of parliament and minister, William Graham. It was adopted by Herbert Morrison in *Socialization and Transport* (1933).
[7] Gordon, op. cit., p. 162; see also T. H. O'Brien, *British Experiments in Public Ownership and Control* (1937).

subject of 'monopoly' as he did in his autobiography, which was published in 1949, but he was clearly beginning to think in the same way. In retrospect he wrote in 1949 of 'the brute force of monopoly', claiming that this force of monopoly reinforced the three other 'fundamentals' of broadcasting—public service, a sense of moral obligation, and assured finance. In retrospect it seemed that without monopoly even public service would have lost its weight. 'Almost everything might have been different. The B.B.C. might have had to play for safety; prosecute the obviously popular lines; count its clients; study and meet their reactions; curry favour; subordinate itself to the vote. *Might* have had to; probably would not; but its road would have been far harder.'[1] It was Reith's genius that he made other people approach the question of monopoly in this way and thereby won substantial and influential support from surprisingly influential people during the years 1924 and 1925. He is sure that Isaacs, the toughest of the bargainers of 1922, would have been converted had he still been alive. By the time that the Crawford Committee met, both the radio industry and the Post Office had been won over to his point of view. The 'brute force of monopoly' was in Reith's keeping, but this was because a number of important people and large sections of the interested public felt that it was right that this should be so. The adjective 'interested' must, of course, be introduced. It was only a tiny minority of the population who were interested in the 'control' of radio. More than thirty years later the 'interests' opposed to public broadcasting had realized the need to mobilize 'opinion'.

The fourth facet of public service was the maintenance of high standards, the provision of the best and the rejection of the hurtful. Reith had no sympathy with the view that it is the task of the broadcaster to give the customer what he wants. 'It is occasionally indicated to us that we are apparently setting out to give the public what we think they need—and not what they want—but few know what they want and very few what they need. . . . In any case it is better to over-estimate the mentality of the public than to under-estimate it.'[2] Arguments on this subject continue: they are the stock-in-trade of the opponents of public broadcasting, and they are often based not on the retail trade from which they derive but dubious views of 'cultural democracy'.

[1] *Into the Wind*, p. 100.   [2] *Broadcast Over Britain*, p. 34.

'A mass medium', the American broadcasting director Stanton has written, 'can only achieve its great audience by practising . . . cultural democracy . . . by giving the majority of the people what they want.' The words have echoed round the world and have been repeated in a thousand variants. Yet Reith's thought and allied thoughts have echoed round the world also, and the debate is not yet over. 'It is right', Gilbert Seldes has written, 'to let people have the chance to get what they want. To talk of *giving* them what they want is nonsense unless we know the capacity of the giver to satisfy wants and—the essential question—how people come to want what they want.'[1] Reith would have agreed with Seldes that, before you talk of giving, you have to know a great deal about the giver. He would have agreed also that you must not use the word 'mass' in relation to listeners without remembering that the mass is composed of individual people. He was very proud of the fact that listeners could describe the BBC as a 'friendly thing'.[2] There is no reference to 'mass media' or 'mass communication' in *Broadcast Over Britain* or any of Reith's later writings: there is rather an emphasis on the 'public' or the series of 'publics', which together constitute 'the great audience'. The 'publics' are treated with respect not as nameless aggregates with statistically measurable preferences, 'targets' for the programme sponsor, but as living audiences capable of growth and development. In other words, Reith's theory of public service began with a conception of the public. Without such a conception the conception of public service itself becomes bleak and arid.

To state the case in these terms is by no means to share all Reith's own preferences or philosophies, to accept in detail his ideas about the planning of programmes, or to suggest that the state of the public and of the BBC was the same in the 1920s as it is in the 1960s. It is to recognize, however, that there was a purpose there, and that the purpose animated and directed early broadcasting. Without it there might well have been pandering and confusion, a distortion of values and an indifference to standards. Neither commercial pressure nor 'art for art's sake' could have provided an equally effective stimulus.

---

[1] See G. Seldes, *The Great Audience* (New York, 1951), pp. 217 ff. This is a cogent analysis which deserves careful study.
[2] *Broadcast Over Britain*, p. 64.

As it was, since 'the policy of the Company was to bring the best of everything into the greatest number of homes', it followed naturally that genuine differences of opinion would be expressed about what constituted 'the best'. The debate about the nature of 'the best' had begun long before 1926; it ceases only when there is no recognition that 'the best' is relevant. Reith did not shun this debate: he recognized that his opinions and attitudes would be accountable. He remarked in the last section of his book that while there were 'ideals and principles' which in a great measure controlled BBC policy, idealism was always a dangerous confession. It was difficult to define what was meant by it, and those who professed it were always liable to charges of inconsistency and opportunism.[1] Nonetheless, so long as he was in control his were the decisions and his was the responsibility. 'We are here to carry on the service until such time as, for any reason or combination of reasons, control is vested or entrusted elsewhere.'[2] 'Idealism' without firmness is a disastrous policy: Reith was in no danger of pursuing it.

Nor was he in danger of relying exclusively on his own tastes or even on his own principles. He tried to reinforce his conception of public service not only by developing the Programme Board and the programme correspondence section but by employing outside programme advisers and critics and by creating a network of advisory committees which drew upon the services of experts in various fields. The first programme critics were chosen from the listening public in May 1925. Sometimes their reports 'were too flattering and not much use': on other occasions they were so tough that they were thought 'offensive'. They were considered sufficiently useful, however, to provide the basis for programme planning by Station Directors. The advisory committees were both local and national, and through them Reith hoped—sometimes rather too optimistically—both to tap opinion and to mobilize support.

The first of the national advisory committees was concerned with religion, which for Reith was the most important subject of all. He wrote to Archbishop Temple years later in 1930 that he had been 'more anxious about the general religious policy of the BBC in matters great and small than about anything else'.[3] In

[1] *Broadcast Over Britain*, p. 212.   [2] Ibid., p. 214.
[3] BBC Archives.

27. Wireless Receiving Sets, 1926

28. The Daventry Transmitter

his *Broadcast Over Britain* he wrote a chapter on religion called 'Beyond the Horizon', in which he stated at the outset that the BBC had developed 'a definite, though restrained, association with religion in general, and with the Christian religion in particular'.[1] The association dates back to the very beginning of broadcasting, a religious address being broadcast by the Rector of Whitechapel, the Rev. J. A. Mayo, the first 'radio Padre', on Christmas Eve, 1922. In 1923 the association was greatly strengthened. Reith met Davidson, the Archbishop of Canterbury, for the first time on 16 March 1923. 'He is very much interested in the possibilities of wireless', Reith wrote in his diary,[2] and he was delighted when Davidson and his wife accepted an invitation to dinner to listen to wireless the following week. It was a fascinating meeting, not least because of Reith's sense of having quickly won the support of a major figure in what would now be called the Establishment. For all his interest in the possibilities of wireless, Davidson was hardly knowledgeable about it. His wife inquired whether when listening to wireless it was necessary to leave a window open, and Davidson himself was 'entirely amazed', 'thunderstruck indeed', with what he heard.

The delightful informality of early wireless is shown by the fact that since there was no piano solo being played that evening and the Archbishop particularly wanted to hear one, Reith rang up Stanton Jefferies and got him to play Schubert's 'Marche Militaire'.[3] The following day Davidson summoned a meeting of ecclesiastical leaders in his room in the House of Lords—the beginning of the Religious Advisory Committee. He asked the people he invited whether they thought there 'ought to be a religious element' in broadcasting; 'if so, what? and by whom arranged?' He paid tribute to 'the officers of the Broadcasting Company, whose aim is obviously a high one and who are anxious to have wise advice'.[4] The Committee met formally for the first time on 18 May 1923 under the chairmanship of Dr. Garbett, then Bishop of Southwark, and it included representatives of the Church of England, the Free Churches, and the Roman Catholics. Its first title was modest—'The Sunday

---

[1] *Broadcast Over Britain*, p. 191.   [2] Diary, 16 Mar. 1923.
[3] *Into the Wind*, p. 93; Diary, 19 Mar. 1923.
[4] G. K. A. Bell, *Randall Davidson* (1935), vol. ii, p. 1211.

Committee'—and although it soon established itself as an important body in relation to the development of religious broadcasting, it did not take as much initiative as Reith wished.[1] Its activities were supplemented by local Religious Advisory Committees at the various provincial stations.

A Central Educational Advisory Committee was appointed in August 1924.[2] It followed a meeting on 18 July at King's College, London, when delegates from various bodies connected with adult education expressed an interest in the work of the BBC and 'were obviously desirous of rendering assistance by advice and propaganda'.[3] To the Central Advisory Committee were nominated representatives of various educational associations from all parts of the country. In addition to this central committee, each station had its own Local Educational Advisory Committee, and Stobart made it an important part of his duties to visit these committees and meet local education officers. Their attitude to broadcasting varied widely from area to area, some officials proving 'utterly apathetic', others keenly enthusiastic. Reith himself attached the utmost importance to this work.

One of its offshoots was the Advisory Committee on Spoken English, which was formed in April 1926. This was a most distinguished body which included the Poet Laureate, Robert Bridges, George Bernard Shaw, Logan Pearsall-Smith, and later Rudyard Kipling. It met about three times a year and discussed a list of 'debatable words'. A. Lloyd James, first a lecturer in and then Professor of Phonetics at London University, was secretary, and he was the person to whom Reith turned for advice even before the Advisory Committee met. Some of the debatable words related to broadcasting itself. They included the verb 'to broadcast', which the BBC decided should be conjugated like the verb 'to cast', so that its past tense was 'broadcast' and not 'broadcasted'. 'Listener-in' also caused some trouble. For many months it was used only in inverted commas, and then the BBC decided that it did not like it either with or without the inverted commas and that it should be replaced by

---

[1] For religious programmes, see below, pp. 272–5.

[2] The following account is taken from miscellaneous papers in miscellaneous BBC Archives, including notes made by Mr. B. E. (now Sir Basil) Nicolls and Miss Edwin (now Mrs. Partridge), who was in charge of BBC Archives from 1931 to 1939.

[3] BBC Archives.

the word 'listener'. In *Broadcast Over Britain* Reith defined proper usage. It was an objectionable habit to refer to the listener as the listener-in. 'This is a relic of the days when he actually did listen in to messages not primarily intended for him; now he is the one addressed, and he accordingly listens. Only the unlicensed listen in.'[1] The last word to cause trouble during this period was

29. Unrecognized Heroes. The Announcer who
said 'broadcasted'.

Daventry. Should it be called 'Daintry'—its historical pronunciation—or 'Daventry', its phonetic pronunciation? Lloyd James gave a firm ruling: 'The B.B.C. has, I think, sufficient authority to decide which pronunciation it will adopt. Let it be *Daventry*.'[2]

The influence of the BBC both on education and the pronunciation of 'standard English' has been noted by almost all the people who have described its work. In music too there was a parallel influence, which illustrates in concrete terms Reith's view that the 'great audience' was not to be fed on the basis of today's statistics but treated more seriously as a large number of

[1] *Broadcast Over Britain*, p. 162.
[2] *Lloyd James to Reith, 21 July 1925.

people, some of whom at least were capable of developing new tastes. 'Music for all' was to be provided, for music was 'the common property and common enjoyment of mankind'.[1] Getting everyone interested in music, however, was far more difficult than providing music for all: 'for years the man in the street has been content to be pleased with music which is easily and quickly assimilated, and therefore not always of the best'. Had the BBC allowed itself to be alarmed by complaints received against the playing of 'good music', had it been granted access to the computations of a precocious 'Tam' or 'Trendex' system, not only would broadcasting have failed to appeal to existing music lovers but 'disastrous havoc would easily have been wrought in the growing musical taste'.[2] All this was obvious enough in 1925. Indeed, for a few enlightened people it was obvious enough even earlier. Percy Scholes, for example, wrote in October 1923 that as a result of the influence of broadcasting, 'in five years' time the general musical public of these islands will be treble or quadruple its present size'.[3]

The first Musical Advisory Committee was formed in July 1925. Its first meeting was described by Reith as 'quite successful', although he rightly added that 'such committees are awfully difficult to handle'.[4] Its chairman was Sir Hugh Allen of the Royal College of Music, and it included Professor Tovey, Sir Walford Davies, J. B. (later Sir John) McEwen of the Royal Academy of Music, Sir Landon Ronald, Dr. Whittaker, and Colonel J. A. C. Somerville, the Commandant of the Royal Military School of Music, Kneller Hall. In the very last months of the 'old BBC', an Advisory Committee on Opera was also formed, which included Allen, McEwen, and Ronald along with other new members, notably Professor Granville Bantock. In his chairman's remarks Allen stated that the co-operation of the BBC might be 'the one remaining opportunity of establishing opera on a sound basis in this country'. He paid tribute to what the BBC had already done.[5] Listeners had formed 'the habit of hearing' and when they visited London they were anxious to have the chance of seeing also.

Two other central advisory committees were concerned,

---

[1] *Broadcast Over Britain*, p. 173.   [2] Ibid., pp. 174–5.
[3] See above, p. 204.   [4] Diary, 8 July 1925.
[5] *Advisory Committee on Opera, Minutes, 13 Dec. 1926; see below, pp. 275–6.

although only for a brief spell, with women's programmes and the Children's Hour. The former met for the first time on 18 January 1924 and the latter on 24 March. Hand-written minutes were kept, but, perhaps because it was more difficult in relation to both these 'fields' to define objectives or to draw on genuinely 'expert' opinions, both committees soon lapsed. The Children's Hour Committee was incapable of making any 'good suggestions'. Clearly many of its members had never heard the programmes, and talked vaguely of introducing more 'riddles' or more 'historical episodes'. The Women's Advisory Committee was a little more precise. It suggested, for example, that women listeners would like to be given 'simple summer drink and salad recipes'. To make such suggestions it hardly seemed necessary, however, to call together Margaret Bondfield, Lilian Braithwaite, Lady Denman, Mrs. Cambridge, and Dr. Chesser. In September 1925 the members were politely informed that as only one women's talk was then being given in the afternoon and as the title 'Women's Hour' no longer existed, the need for an advisory committee to meet regularly had disappeared, 'except when special cases of policy arose'. Members were invited to 'maintain their interest in the broadcast programmes and to make any suggestions that occurred to them from time to time'.

The provincial advisory committees were patterned on those at the centre, but there was rather more informality about their work, less reliance on experts and more stress on participation. Most of the early Minute Books of the Manchester committees still survive.[1] They evoke a rather cosy atmosphere. People who already knew each other—if only on other committees—were getting together for a new purpose, probably a purpose which was considered at the time to be far less important than the purposes of most of the other committees. The Women's Advisory Committee actually suggested speakers and virtually sponsored them when they appeared before the microphone. It also suggested subjects—'Women in Public Life', 'Openings for Girls with a University Education', 'Women in Other Lands', but also 'The Road to Angkor', 'My Acquaintance with Royalty

---

[1] *Manchester Advisory Committee Minute Books. In all cases the information relating to the early history of advisory committees is gleaned from surviving Minutes.

in Central Africa', and, a little surprisingly, 'The Life of Dean Fawcett'. At the Religious Advisory Committee it was carefully explained by its Archdeacon chairman that the Manchester Chapter would *never* agree to the broadcasting of actual even-song services. It was also agreed that there should be no broadcasts from Manchester relating to Christian Science, Theosophy, or Spiritualism.

The Sales Managers' Advisory Committee was concerned with more practical preoccupations. It first met on 9 January 1924 and A. R. Burrows from London was in the chair. At later meetings one of the main topics on the agenda was the quality of the simultaneous broadcasts. These broadcasts were freely criticized, hostile comments in the wireless press were noted,[1] and London was reminded 'that it should not be assumed that what appealed to a Londoner would necessarily appeal to a labourer in Northern England'. Praise from Manchester was welcome because it was rare. The meeting of 3 July 1925 must have warmed the hearts of members of the BBC staff in London. 'In the opinion of this meeting,' a unanimously carried resolution stated, 'the programmes this summer have reached a very high standard.' Several members added that 'it was a pity that, owing to the fine weather, so few people were listening-in to them'.

Comments from the provinces suggest that in certain communities at least broadcasting was a genuine local preoccupation, that there were reasons why the 'civic pride' which had so surprised Reith in the case of Sheffield was strong.[2] In general, however, the advisory committee structure had weaknesses. It rested on the conception of broadcasting as a 'public service' with all that 'service' implies, but it did not reach deep enough or perhaps sufficiently democratically into the subsoil of the community to ensure that people felt—without thinking —that the BBC was theirs. Raymond Williams has written sensitively both of the strength and limitations of the idea of service itself, and has remarked wisely that it is no substitute for the idea of active mutual responsibility. This alternative idea, in its turn, is the prerequisite of what he calls a 'common culture'.[3]

[1] For example, an article in *The Wireless Trader*, 14 Jan. 1925.
[2] See above, pp. 217–18.
[3] R. Williams, *Culture and Society, 1780–1950* (1958), pp. 295 ff.

It would have been extremely difficult in the circumstances of the 1920s—with a divided community, divided by age and by social class—to have gone further than the BBC actually did, but there was a further point and the BBC did not reach it. Since the 1920s the difficulties in doing so have become even greater. The temptation to exploit large numbers of people has grown as it has become abundantly clear that effective technical means lie at the disposal of would-be exploiters and that the profits of exploitation are huge. Moreover, the moral issues have been blurred by a great deal of loose thinking and equally loose writing. Much of the recent writing on the BBC falls into this category.

In the circumstances of the period from 1922 to 1926 the one 'public' attempt to express the conception of public service through public representation failed completely. As a result of the recommendations of the Sykes Committee a Broadcasting Board was set up by the Postmaster-General.[1] It consisted of Sykes as chairman, Reith as BBC representative, and Brown as the voice of the Post Office. All its other members were spokesmen of particular interests. Lord Riddell, for example, spoke for the newspaper press, Guy Burney for the wireless trade, A. A. Campbell-Swinton for the Radio Society of Great Britain, and Fred Bramley for the T.U.C. Representation of interests at this high level is always perilous, and the Broadcasting Board was no exception. The Post Office did not allow it much scope, despite the fact that Brown was a member and F. W. Phillips was its secretary, while Reith clearly regarded its concern with broadcasting as at the same time superfluous and inadequate. The Board met only six times, and all the six meetings took place between 9 April and 8 July 1924. The Postmaster-General apologized for not attending the opening meeting: he did not choose to apologize for not attending further meetings. He had supported the idea of such a Board on the grounds that he could refer to it difficult questions of policy. In fact, he only referred to it a very limited number of questions —facilities for broadcasting news, whether there should be broadcasting of commercial information and prices, the provision of additional stations, and the extent to which there should be controversial broadcasting. The Board backed Reith

[1] See above, p. 165.

on most of these issues, all its members agreeing that the inhabitants of large towns at least should have the chance of listening to the radio, and most of its members recommending greater power for the BBC to discuss 'controversial' topics. This substantial measure of agreement did not inhibit Reith from concluding that successive meetings of the Board were 'a complete waste of time',[1] 'a ghastly waste of time',[2] and 'fatuous as usual'.[3] All that has survived from the Board's deliberations is a collection of working papers—eighteen in all—which were prepared by the Post Office.

On 19 August 1925, after a long spell when the Board had not met at all, the Postmaster-General wrote to Sykes to say that since he had appointed a new committee to examine the future of broadcasting—under the chairmanship of the Earl of Crawford and Balcarres—it might be necessary to review the existing arrangements.[4] This was not to imply that they had not been running smoothly: indeed, in his considered opinion, they had been running so smoothly that 'there has recently been no occasion to consult the Board'. Sykes replied somewhat tartly that it had been his impression and that of his colleagues on the Board that the Board would be the body entrusted with the task of advising the Post Office as to the future of broadcasting after the expiration of the BBC's licence at the end of 1926. When the Postmaster-General told Sykes that it was important that the Crawford Committee 'should be in no way dependent on previous enquiries' and that its members should start with 'an entirely open mind', several of the members of the Board were undoubtedly extremely disappointed.[5] After the publication of the Crawford Committee's Report in the summer of 1926 and the Postmaster-General's decision to accept its main recommendations, the Broadcasting Board's days were numbered. It is certainly significant that the Postmaster-General made no attempt to consult the Board about the Crawford proposals. A final lunch party was arranged by Sykes in November 1926, and the members of the Board decided to hand in their resignations forthwith. They were thanked by the Postmaster-General, who told them that 'under the new broadcast-

[1] Diary, 9 Apr. 1924.   [2] Ibid., 14 May 1924.
[3] Ibid., 18 June 1924.   [4] See below, pp. 330 ff.
[5] *The Postmaster-General to Sykes, 7 Sept. 1925.

ing arrangements' the conduct of the 'service' would be 'entirely in the hands of the corporation', and the control of the Post Office would in the main be limited 'to harmonizing the requirements of the various wireless services'.[1]

This was not the end of the story of advisory committees. There were to be many new turns and twists of experience during the 1920s and 1930s. The account in this volume must end with a prelude, not with an epilogue. Just before the demise of the Company in December 1926, Sir Arthur Stanley, chairman of the Wireless League, wrote to Reith that in view of the fact that the new Corporation would have at its disposal a larger income than the Company, 'we feel that the principal obstacle to the provision of better programmes has now been removed, and are of the opinion that the time is opportune for the formation of an Advisory Committee to assist with regard to the interpretation of public opinion on the subject of programmes'.[2] Other people also felt that the time was opportune, and a new Wireless Organizations Advisory Committee was set up in January 1927.

The work of this committee, active between 1927 and 1929, does not fall within the scope of this volume, but its formation does. One of its chief sponsors was the Wireless League, a new organization which had been founded in March 1925 on the initiative of the *Daily Express*. Beaverbrook did not consult or inform Reith before the League was founded, but he assured him that it was meant to be friendly—'he had made up his mind that there must be monopoly in Broadcasting'.[3] Certainly the League's first chairman, Sir Arthur Stanley, Lord Derby's brother, consulted Reith from the start about the best form its help could take.[4] They frequently lunched together to discuss plans of co-operation. The cordiality of this co-operation did not appeal to all the members of the Wireless League, and there was a breakaway by a number of them (the New Wireless League Ltd.) in August 1925.

The main body of the League was exceptionally loyal to the BBC: it stated that its first objective was 'to perpetuate, consolidate and extend the public service character of British broadcast-

---

[1] *The Postmaster-General to Sykes, 15 Nov. 1926.
[2] *Sir Arthur Stanley to Reith, 18 Dec. 1926.
[3] Diary, 23 Mar. 1925.
[4] Ibid., 17 Apr. 1925.

ing, and with that object to support centralised executive control'. Its second objective was 'to exercise unceasing influence to protect British broadcasting from any lowering of its standards and ideals'; and its third was 'to bring to notice of the broadcasting authorities such criticisms as may seem to be constructive, and generally to act as a link between the listening public and the authorities'. These objectives were so clearly defined that they obviated the need for separate BBC listeners' organizations, some of which had been started on a local basis—the Radio Guild at Cardiff, for example—as early as 1925. In December 1926, when the first overtures were made which led to the setting up of the Wireless Organizations Advisory Committee, the League had 20,000 members. The Radio Association had about 300 members, and the other bodies which were associated with the new committee were the well-established Radio Society of Great Britain and the Wireless Association, which had been founded as recently as April 1926 with Lord Drogheda as its chairman.[1] Within the new structure the League was the closest of all the bodies to the BBC. Indeed, Gladstone Murray wrote to Stanley that 'your direct contact with us is so close and continuous that it is worth a dozen committees'.[2]

2. The Content of Programmes

IN his letter of December 1926 Stanley specifically mentioned 'better programmes'. What kind of programmes were being broadcast by the BBC in 1924 and 1925? General talk of 'principles' and 'service' is best tested by actual evidence about programme content. In particular, how far was broadcasting influenced by Reith's belief that to use 'so great a scientific invention for the purpose of "entertainment" alone' would be 'a prostitution of its powers and an insult to the character and intelligence of the people'?[3]

[1] *Radio Times*, 26 Apr. 1926.
[2] *Gladstone Murray to Stanley, 4 Jan. 1927.
[3] *Broadcast Over Britain*, p. 17.

In practice it was difficult, even if desirable, to draw a sharp dividing line between 'entertainment' and 'education'. Reith himself recognized this. The word 'entertainment' is loosely used: in a sense, the object of all programmes is to entertain. Yet he felt that 'entertainment', pure and simple, quickly grows tame; dissatisfaction and boredom result. It would be a sad reflection on human intelligence, he stated, if entertainment, in the accepted sense of the word, was thought to be the only means for 'occupying hours agreeably'.[1] As examples of 'pure entertainment' Reith chose jazz bands and 'sketches by humorists'. 'To entertain means to occupy agreeably. Would it be urged that this is only to be effected by the broadcasting of jazz bands and popular music, or of sketches by humorists?'[2]

Jazz bands, popular music, and 'sketches by humorists' figured regularly in BBC programmes from 1922 to 1926—in what was considered to be their proper place. There was very little 'serious' jazz, however; much of the popular music was that which appealed to the older generation; and there was no separate 'revue and vaudeville' section in the BBC until 1930. Most of the leading personalities who made BBC policy during the early years were entirely ignorant of what would now be called 'show business'. And their attempt to penetrate that world was made exceptionally difficult by the agents and managers who controlled it. Clauses were inserted in artists' contracts by which they were barred from broadcasting while the contracts were in force; even artists who were not under contract were intimidated by threats not to sign them on again if they broadcast for the BBC. 'Live broadcasts' from theatres and music halls were either barred completely or arranged in a small number of cases by complicated and controversial private agreements. A small number of them had been permitted before April 1923—in February, for example, *Cinderella* was relayed from the London Hippodrome—but the permission stopped with the formation in May 1923 of a Committee of theatre managers, concert givers, copyright owners, music publishers, composers, artists, and stage hands to protect this coalition of interests against the BBC.[3]

It was not until June 1925 that a strictly limited agreement

[1] Ibid., p. 147.   [2] Ibid., p. 18.
[3] *Board Minutes, 13 June 1923.

was reached between some of the entertainment 'interests' and the BBC. Walter Payne, president of the Society of West End Theatre Managers, signed it, but the Variety Artistes' Federation stayed aloof. The agreement provided for the setting up of a joint committee with two representatives from the BBC and two from the entertainment associations to 'remove those elements of friction hitherto encountered in securing from the stage items suitable for broadcasting' and 'to ensure effective cooperation and harmonious interchange of opinions'. Brief stage broadcasts were to be permitted, but as far as possible only on Friday and Saturday nights. No cabaret performances were to be broadcast during theatre hours. Most variety managers continued to refuse to have anything to do with the BBC unless heavy compensation were paid for the use of their artists, and guerrilla warfare gave way to vigorous campaigns against the BBC in 1926 and 1927. Only one performance from a music hall was broadcast in the days of the Company—the Variety Artistes' Benevolent Fund Concert from the Alhambra in May 1926. The BBC regarded this as merely a gesture on the part of the music hall magnates to show how broadminded they really were.

These difficulties would have been avoided only if broadcasting had been directly sponsored and promoted by the entertainment industry. But the industry was aloof, and the very people in the BBC who knew least about 'entertainment' were most far-sighted in anticipating the power and nature of the impact that broadcasting would have on the entertainment industry. They quickly saw that broadcasting was capable of creating new reputations, greatly augmenting artists' incomes, and attracting people to the theatres to see broadcasting 'stars'. In retrospect the attitude of the entertainment industry to broadcasting—like the attitude of the press or of some of the stage stars themselves—was at best timid and at worst obscurantist. One great artist of variety entertainment, who was soon acknowledged to be a 'leading light' of radio, insisted, for example, on having a clause put into his first radio contract that the BBC should indemnify him if his theatre audiences fell after he had 'broadcasted'.

The theatrical managers for their part were slow to appreciate the enormous potential influence of mass entertainment:

their horizons were limited by footlights or auditorium. They were, of course, living in a decade of decline, when many of them were burdened by an intractable box-office problem. What they did not realize was that without radio their industry might decline more sharply and with little prospect of recovery. The music hall had lost its pre-1914 vitality and much of its power to attract; radio was to come to its rescue during the 1930s, and might have rescued it earlier had it been given the chance. The concert world was in the doldrums: until the BBC took them over, for example, the Promenade Concerts were given up as lost. The 'movies' were wrecking the chances of the small theatre and of the small entertainer: some of the displanted artists made their way straight into radio. Many of them proved more successful as radio performers than most of the more established and less adaptable stage 'stars'.

If 'entertainment' was difficult to define, so too was 'education'. Reith himself included under this heading several activities which would hardly be grouped under the same heading today. He thought of education as 'a systematic and sustained endeavour to re-create, to build up knowledge, experience and character, perhaps even in the face of obstacles'.[1] Not only did it encompass both school and adult education, but it took account of talks from London of all kinds and a fair share of wireless 'features'. Stobart was both Director of Education and the member of the BBC staff in charge of talks. Before he arrived, in the summer of 1924, the first radio talks from London had been arranged by Burrows or his subordinates. As the work increased under Stobart's direction, the number of sub-departments grew with it. J. G. Broadbent worked with him from November 1924. Miss Mary Somerville impressed Reith at their first meeting (while she was still an undergraduate) as 'a very clever and self-confident young lady'.[2] Reith advised her to go back to Oxford and take a 'decent degree' before joining the company. She did so, and became a member of Stobart's department in July 1925, with schools work as her special responsibility. B. E. (later Sir Basil) Nicolls arrived a few months later from the Manchester Station. Mrs. Fitzgerald was in charge of Women's Hour programmes and C. E. Hodges of Children's

[1] *Broadcast Over Britain*, p. 18.   [2] Diary, 11 Apr. 1924.

Hour. When Nicolls left just before Christmas to become London Station Director and Broadbent moved to Bournemouth, Lance Sieveking came in—in April 1926—with special responsibilities for topical talks and news. He was associated in this work with G. H. G. Strutt. In September 1926 Miss Hilda Matheson joined Stobart in over-all charge of the Talks and Education Department, and in January 1927 under the new régime she took over talks when the responsibility for arranging them was removed from Stobart. She too had greatly impressed Reith from the moment of his first seeing her.[1] Both her appointment and Miss Somerville's were evidence of the willingness of the BBC to take women on to its staff on terms of complete equality.

The first talk broadcast was on 23 December 1922. The second talk on 27 January 1923 had the somewhat unexpected title of 'How to catch a Tiger'. The first regular series of talks was written by Edward Lewis, C. A. Lewis's father, using the pseudonym 'Philemon': they were later published in book form in two volumes of the Broadcast Library—*From my Window* and *As I see It*. Another popular series, which began in 1924, was given by A. Bonnet Laird (Captain Johnston) under the title of 'My Part of the Country'. Even more popular was Sir Walford Davies's series on 'Music and the Ordinary Listener'. This began on 5 January 1926 and, along with M. Stephan's wireless lessons in French, they made education in its own right both interesting and entertaining.

Many of the so-called topical talks could scarcely be called educational: they had far more in common with later running commentaries and outside broadcasts. For example, Mrs. Cawson, a mother of four, was asked to give a 'topical talk' on landing at Dover after swimming the Channel. In a completely different category were the talks given by the 'critics'. John Strachey was the BBC's first literary critic: he first broadcast on 3 September 1923. Percy Scholes took over Music on 16 June, G. A. Atkinson Films on 11 July, and Archibald Haddon Drama on 27 July. Haddon left at the end of 1924, having already established something of a radio reputation. His talks were printed in book form with the title *Hullo Playgoers*, the book being dedicated to 'Listeners unknown and unseen'. When he

[1] Diary, 26 Mar. 1926.

30. 'How to catch a Tiger.'

left the BBC he was presented with a cheque in a little ceremony in front of the microphone. He was succeeded in January 1925 by James Agate, who was to establish the most formidable of all reputations as a theatre critic during the inter-war years. In 1925 Strachey was succeeded as book critic by Desmond MacCarthy.

In complete contrast to these talks by men who were either very well known or quickly became well known were the talks from the provincial stations—including the relay stations. Several distinguished men made their broadcasting début in this unobtrusive way from studios which were locked for most of the day and only came into their own in the evenings. Many people who were far from being distinguished then or since also made their début. Reith warned Station Directors in March 1924 of the dangers of complete freedom of the air. 'In some stations I see periodically men down to speak whose status, either professionally or socially, and whose qualifications to speak, seem doubtful. It should be an honour in every sense of the word for a man to speak from any broadcasting station, and only those who have a claim to be heard above their fellows on any particular subject in the locality should be put on the programme.'[1]

Two sets of speakers had a special claim to be heard. The representatives of wireless societies were felt to be in a privileged position, and regular talks were given in 1923 by the spokesman of the Radio Society of Great Britain. The Radio Association, the Wireless Association, and the Wireless League were later added to the list of approved bodies arranging their own talks both nationally and locally. In June 1926, however, it was decided to cut down these talks to one a quarter for each society. Government departments were not only felt to be in a privileged position: by the Licence they were actually granted direct access to the microphone. The Ministry of Health was the first government department to take advantage of the opportunity. It was followed soon afterwards by the Ministry of Agriculture, the Board of Trade, and the Ministry of Education. Some of these talks were extremely dull, and were widely and rightly criticized in the press. So, indeed, was the talks policy as a whole, which was often attacked in the newspapers, particularly in 1925. The label 'adult education' was used more sparingly

[1] *Memorandum from Reith to the Station Directors, 3 Mar. 1924.

after this date, and it was conceded that 'not all the speakers had the gift of projecting their personality via the microphone'.

Stobart did his best to help by planning and publishing a syllabus of BBC talks and a small booklet *Suggestions to Speakers* which reminded performers that 'the most experienced speaker will realise that, if he has not broadcast before, he is about to undertake something which is quite different from any other form of speaking'. This simple advice was wholesome, yet once he had entered the studio the wireless speaker could scarcely have been in any doubt about the truthfulness of the proposition. Little attempt was made to rehearse him, but he would be given ominous warnings not to rustle his papers, not to sneeze, not to shuffle his feet on the floor, and so on. Sometimes there were forbidding notices, like 'If you cough, you will deafen thousands.' Long before he entered the studio the speaker's talk would have been carefully scrutinized, and, if it contained anything dangerous, controversial, or in what was thought to be bad taste, it might go up to Stobart himself for approval. Moreover it might well have been cut. 'Experience has shown that the utmost the public can absorb with interest is fifteen hundred words, which takes about fifteen minutes to deliver. It is only in very special circumstances that any talk is allowed to exceed this.'[1]

It says much for Stobart's enthusiasm and Reith's backing that the BBC did not waver in its desire to make broadcasting something more than a vehicle of light entertainment. By 1926 there was definitely an audience for talks of all kinds, but there was equally definitely an organized resistance.

In October 1924 Stobart had noted that the evening talks had 'gone far better' than had been anticipated, but he was bound to add that 'there are a few listeners who resent anything but Music Hall [items]'. In July 1925 he stated frankly in his quarterly report that 'when all is said and done, this department must remain a target for criticism, inasmuch as it has to perform the least popular function of the BBC'. He had tried, he said, to bring 'men of the moment' to the microphone to record their impressions of cricket, football, tennis, and boxing, but only too often their displays had been 'little short of lamentable'. Stobart knew where *he* stood in relation to the criticism.

[1] *Stobart's Quarterly Report, 15 Aug. to 10 Oct. 1924.

The ultimate success of broadcasting does not, in my opinion, depend upon the provision of a constant series of thrills and stunts. Appetite grows by what it feeds on. We can easily create an appetite for sensation, but in the long run broadcasting will only be accepted as an integral feature in the life of millions in as far as it can provide a steady supply of enjoyment, entertainment and interest. I think we should be well advised not to risk the substance for the shadow.

Summing up his experience in March 1927, he claimed that he had been 'sowing hopefully' and 'reaping a little now and then'. There were, he was glad to say, some people who preferred talks to any other item of the programme. This encouraged him. 'Wireless must fulfil its destiny, and those who have the handling of it cannot shrink from using it to the full extent of their resources for Education, as for all other public uses.'[1]

Approximately one-quarter of the total BBC daily transmissions took the form of speech, but this figure included, of course, women's programmes, news bulletins, weather reports, and the Children's Hour. What were beginning to be called 'feature' programmes played a small part, although Corbett Smith as Artistic Director was particularly concerned with them between leaving Cardiff and his departure from the BBC in April 1925. Difficulties in execution and lack of expert advice about content held back progress in such programmes, although there were interesting experiments in 1925 in the combination of descriptive narrative, dialogues, sound effects, and music. A series of dramatized episodes in the history of famous British regiments certainly pointed the way 'to the possible development of the whole vast field—or jungle—of such programmes'.[2]

The first regular daily weather forecast was broadcast as early as 26 March 1923. By then the most regular 'speech and music' programme of any length was the Children's Hour. It usually lasted for forty-five minutes, and it played a somewhat disproportionately large part in the early life of the broadcasting stations.

The first officers of the BBC both in London and the provinces had to reconcile themselves to becoming 'uncles' and 'aunts', with all that this meant, not only in the eyes of the children but

[1] *All these references are taken from Stobart's reports.
[2] Val Gielgud, British Radio Drama, 1922–1956 (1957), p. 22.

31. Weather Forecasting

to some extent at least in the eyes of the public as a whole.
Uncle Arthur, Uncle Caractacus, Uncle Leslie, Uncle Jeff,
Uncle Rex, Uncle Humpty Dumpty, Uncle Jack Frost, and
Aunts Sophie and Phyllis became household names in the course
of 1923. Burrows, who greatly enjoyed playing the part of one
of the first radio Uncles, Uncle Arthur, wrote in 1924 that 'there
is no section of our programme work upon which more time
and thought is spent than that termed the Children's Hour'.[1]
C. A. Lewis, who perhaps enjoyed playing Uncle Caractacus
rather less, was at least jolly enough to write, 'I wonder if there
is any one in the world who has such a jolly mailbag as a broadcasting uncle.'[2] Reith himself stressed the social value of the
Children's Hour as a 'happy alternative to the squalor of
streets and back yards': he scarcely mentioned 'uncles' and
'aunts' at all.[3] Perhaps it was the fact that the Children's Hour
was one of the earliest of programmes and in its origins one of
the most informal which made many people cling to its fantasy
world as long as they could: perhaps it was on more serious
grounds that the young listeners of today would be the great
wireless audience of the future or that character-building could
be effected by radio that the BBC devoted so much attention to
this programme.

In April 1923 attempts were made to control more tightly
the discipline of broadcasting, and Mrs. Ella Fitzgerald was
appointed Central Organizer of Children's Hour programmes.
A few months later in December 1923 Miss E. Elliott (Auntie
Geraldine) was chosen as her assistant. It was decided then to
make Children's Hour programmes less 'haphazard', to give
the various uncles and aunts set periods each week to appear,
and to introduce more prepared material. Yet as late as
February 1925, after various adjustments of organization had
been tried—some in vain—it was still felt that there was need for
further 'rationalization' of the programme. The 'rationalization'
included the elimination of much of the back-chat and the
appointment of a new full-time official, Mrs. Fitzgerald having
moved over exclusively to Women's Hour programmes. In

[1] *The Story of Broadcasting*, p. 121.
[2] *Broadcasting from Within*, p. 101.
[3] *Broadcast Over Britain*, p. 185. Yet see ibid., p. 53, where he described broadcasters casting their 'reticence' aside and, as 'one of their little relaxations', emerg-
ing 'from their obscurity in the guise of uncles to countless children'.

April 1925, therefore, C. E. Hodges (Uncle Peter) was appointed on a part-time basis to be in entire charge of the running of the programmes. From 1 January 1926 he became a full-time official, reporting direct to J. C. Stobart. Early in 1926 the words 'uncle' and 'aunt' disappeared from the pages of the *Radio Times*, and in May of that year Station Directors were asked to aim at greater dignity in the programmes without loss of brightness. A few months later in November the words 'uncle' and 'aunt' were dropped completely from the programme.

By this time, however, the Children's Hour had attracted the enthusiastic support of so many children—and some of their parents—that there was strong opposition to the changes. There had to be a relaxation of the ruling in 1927. The strength of the opposition demonstrates that whether or not disproportionate amounts of energy had been devoted to the Children's Hour, the BBC had succeeded remarkably well in mobilizing its child audience. It had succeeded in making them feel that the world of Children's Hour was a world in which they could freely participate. The announcement of birthdays on the radio doubtless contributed to this, but the participation was fuller. The radio circles of child listeners which had started in London and the provinces in 1923 were among the most effective of listeners' pressure groups, and children were encouraged to write to the *Radio Times* with both news and views. Moreover the organizers of Children's Hour took the children into their confidence. In an interesting article in the *Radio Times* in October 1926 the children were asked how *they* would like to pick a programme to suit children of all preferences—easy-going children who liked everything that 'rolled in out of the ether', children who studied programmes and had carefully formed tastes, children who did not study programmes but listened on 'a hit-and-miss principle' at any odd time that was convenient, children whom it was impossible to please—who knew what they wanted and did not care what other children wanted—and children who talked patronizingly of Children's Hour as something silly and 'fit only for kids'. Of course, there were good children too who liked a great deal of the programmes, understood something of the difficulties, put up with things that they did not like very much for the sake of others who did, and took a definite share in trying to make the programmes better. 'They realise that the programmes are *theirs*, not ours.'[1]

Sometimes the Children's Hour programmes were not only very good, but introduced genuinely new radio forms and developed new radio techniques. The first play written specially for radio was a play by Burrows for Children's Hour; the first orchestral piece broadcast by a BBC ensemble was Roger Quilter's 'Children's Overture'; the first stories told over the air were stories for children. The first zoo noises were broadcast for children on 16 November 1924, and the Grand Howl by George, Uncle Jeff's (Stanton Jefferies's) dog, was as much talked about by child listeners as the famous woodland song of the nightingale, first broadcast in May 1924, was among adults. Miss Beatrice Harrison, the 'cellist, who introduced the nightingale to the public, received 50,000 letters from grateful listeners: Stanton Jefferies received a regular fan mail each week.

There was one point about Children's Hour which always had to be stressed to children: it had never to be 'like school'. The school broadcasts which had started experimentally with the music talk by Sir Walford Davies on 4 April 1924 were well established by the end of 1926, although they sometimes (but not always) met with far more criticism from teachers than the Children's Hour did from children. 'They are not related to the ordinary school work', wrote one hostile critic, 'and they lack the human touch, the personality and appeal of the teacher.'[2] The criticisms were less strong during the last days of the Company. In June 1926, with the aid of a grant from the Carnegie Trust, a year's experiment in school broadcasting was begun in the Kent schools by the BBC and the Kent local education authority working in co-operation.[3] A few months earlier the *Teachers' World* had expressed the hope that the BBC would persist in its efforts to serve the schools, and that teachers would co-operate in the friendliest way with its officials.[4] Both Children's Hour and school listening programmes were to remain essential but distinct parts of the Corporation's work.

The news bulletins and outside broadcasts, which later accounted for such a substantial amount of radio time, gained

[1] *Radio Times*, 15 Oct. 1926.   [2] *Teachers' World*, 24 Dec. 1924.
[3] *The Times*, 30 Oct. 1926.   [4] *Teachers' World*, 14 Mar. 1925.

little in importance between 1923 and 1926 since the early restrictions imposed by the press were only tardily and incompletely relaxed. The Sykes Committee had recommended that there should be a gradual extension of the broadcasting of news, 'under proper safeguards', and that more latitude should be granted to the BBC to broadcast news of special events 'without regard to the hour'. Before this suggestion was considered by the newly-founded Broadcasting Board there was an important conference of BBC and press representatives on 11 February 1924. Reuters, the Newspaper Proprietors' Association, the Newspaper Society, the Press Association, Exchange Telegraph, and Central News were all represented. Reith asked for press approval for the BBC to broadcast day-time public ceremonies, speeches by prominent people before 7 o'clock in the evening, 'descriptions' of the Boat Race, the Derby, and the Cup Final 'by a reporter into a microphone on the scene', 'speeches at important dinners and other functions after seven o'clock', and 'narratives by experts from the studio in the late evening'.

The press representatives insisted that the 7 o'clock rule was 'part and parcel of the terms and understandings under which the BBC obtained its broadcasting monopoly powers', but the Post Office representatives showed some willingness to back up Reith in his efforts to secure greater freedom. After a further meeting on 12 March and long and complicated negotiations, a draft of agreement was eventually signed by the BBC and press representatives on 16 September 1924. It recognized that the BBC was at liberty to broadcast 'ceremonies', speeches, and official functions provided that such broadcasts were limited to a preliminary announcement and a microphone record of the occasion without any further description or comment. News bulletins, however, were still not to be broadcast before 7 o'clock in the evening, and 'addresses, narratives and papers by experts on matters of topical and public interest' could only be broadcast on condition that they did not interfere with newspaper reports. The Agreement was to continue until 31 December 1926, and the press representatives promised that during that period the press would not allow greater facilities to be given to any other broadcasting concern 'should one be instituted'.

Discussions about further 'freedoms' continued after the Agreement had been signed. At a meeting on 20 February 1925 the BBC specifically raised four proposals for broadcasts: a 'running story of the first half of the England *versus* Scotland Rugby Match'; a 'coded narrative of the Boat Race from a wirelessly equipped launch' (the key to the code, together with a plan of the course, having been published exclusively in the early editions of the newspapers on the day of the race); a 'coded narrative of the Football Association Cup Final'; and 'the broadcasting from Epsom on Derby Day, in addition to various "impressions" such as a fortune teller at work, a tipster, a bookmaker taking odds, a welsher and a three-card trickster [*sic*], of the actual microphone record of the noises of the race'. The press representatives rejected all four ideas. They would not support the idea of broadcasting even the first half of the football matches, and they insisted that at Epsom only the sound of the horses' hoofs and the shouts of the crowd could be regarded as acceptable 'natural noises'. Disagreement between BBC and press was so complete that Reith referred the matter to the Post Office for arbitration under a clause in the Agreement of September 1924.

A most interesting meeting took place at the Post Office on Friday, 13 March 1925. It was not clear from the start for whom the omens were favourable. Riddell, Reith, H. C. Robbins, the joint General Manager of the Press Association, and W. L. Murray of Reuters were present with two other press officials in attendance, and Sir William Mitchell-Thomson, the Postmaster-General, was accompanied by Viscount Wolmer, the Assistant Postmaster-General, Sir Evelyn Murray, R. W. Woods, and R. A. Dalzell, who took F. J. Brown's place after Brown's retirement that month. Riddell began by describing the deputation as 'appealing to Caesar', but the Postmaster-General was loath to take on this role. He was mainly concerned with whether the press would accept any decision he might make as decisive. At this point Riddell in his turn was loath to give a definite answer. He complained of having been dragged to St. Martin's-le-Grand by Mr. Reith.

The two parties went on to state their case. Reith said that he regarded as pre-eminently reasonable the proposals which had been put forward on 20 February. They marked a general attempt to co-operate with the press, not to seek to undermine its interests. The goodwill of the press was important to the

BBC and he had no wish to forfeit it. Riddell exchanged compliments, describing wireless as a 'wonderful invention', but he would not budge on any of the four proposals. Even if the BBC were to succeed in convincing the Postmaster-General that they were reasonable proposals, it should hesitate before putting them into practice, knowing that they would be bound to alienate the press.

The Postmaster-General not surprisingly reserved his decision. He reminded both sides that there would have to be another major inquiry into broadcasting before the end of 1926. 'Even at the time the last Broadcasting Agreement was entered into neither Mr. Reith nor the Government, I think, foresaw what a giant this baby was to grow into, and I do not know what size it will be in December 1926.' He said that he regretted that in the meantime Riddell would not be prepared to accept the idea of experiments, for instance in broadcasting the first half of a rugby match. Riddell replied that it was not the right time to experiment. Reith's work with the BBC during the previous two years had been a 'bit of wizardry': it would be best to let the wizardry stop at that point for the moment. The interview concluded with references to the old issues that had been brought up so many times before—the interests of the evening newspapers, the fact that the BBC was a commercial company, the future of broadcasting after 1926, and, not least, the powers of the Post Office. Riddell described Mitchell-Thomson as 'the pontifical head of broadcasting' and admitted that it was his 'manifest duty to have regard to the interests of the public'.

It was not until January 1927—in the first month of the new Corporation—that the BBC was given freedom to arrange early news bulletins, running commentaries, and eye-witness accounts. The public had to be satisfied in the meantime with broadcasts from railway trains, pit shafts, the Surrey woods, and Derby Day without the race. The first report on a boxing match, that between Johnny Curley and Henry Corbett, was on the air in March 1926, and there were vociferous demands in August 1925 for a better service of football results on the grounds that football deserved at least as much attention as cricket.[1] The interest of the public in more 'live' news was recognized by the

[1] *Programme Board Minutes, 25 Aug. 1925.

Crawford Committee which considered once again all the relevant evidence relating to news and outside broadcasts, and concluded in its final report that concessions would have to be made by the press to meet the growing needs of broadcasting. During

32. What do *you* think of it?

the General Strike the Press Agreement had to be waived and five news bulletins were broadcast each day.[1] After the strike—indeed, largely as a result of it—a BBC News Section was formed for the first time under the aegis of Stobart and the Education Department. It dealt chiefly with topical talks and special news items from government offices, and it was staffed by Sieveking and Strutt.

[1] See below, pp. 368 ff.

An important and illuminating paper drafted by Strutt in September 1926 emphasized the importance of BBC editorial control of the news service. News should be 'what those in control of the BBC think listeners *should* hear (a responsibility greater than any that has arisen since Adam's fateful choice)'. The BBC need not compete with the press. If it chose above all else to guarantee accuracy, it need not pander to sensationalism. Nor would its development of a proper news service destroy the demand for newspapers. 'It would be interesting to know if evening papers have ever noted that those coming away from a Cup Tie or a Derby seem just as keen on reading an account of what they have just seen as anyone else.'[1] Strutt's memorandum was the basis of further talks between Reith and Riddell which led ultimately to the new Agreement being signed in January 1927. It falls outside the scope of this volume. Throughout the whole period when the BBC was a company, therefore, it was subject to such severe restrictions on the broadcasting of news and outside events that the ordinary listener had only the remotest idea of what the shape of future broadcasting would be.

Hemmed in on one side by restrictions imposed by the press, Reith was hemmed in on the other side by restrictions imposed by the Post Office. He has gained the reputation in some quarters of being unwilling to allow controversy on the air. In fact, he had no choice. The Derby and political speeches were alike taboo. Confronted by both kinds of restrictions, his instincts were to suggest experiments, ways of testing the logic of prohibition. Year after year he tried to gain permission to broadcast the King's speech at the Opening of Parliament. He tried 'every conceivable source' to achieve this—from winning the support of individual members of parliament to appealing to the Prime Minister, from approaching the Cabinet to putting out feelers with the Royal Household. Sometimes he was given the most cursory of replies: on other occasions, notably the first time he tried in February 1923, he was given polite answers. 'I am afraid the decision thus reached is final. . . . You have at least the consolation of knowing that if anybody could have succeeded you would.'

[1] *Memorandum by Strutt, sent to Reith, Gladstone Murray, Stobart, and R. H. Eckersley, 29 Sept. 1926.

At Budget time he tried to persuade the Post Office to allow the BBC to put the Chancellor of the Exchequer on the air with the chance of a radio reply from his opponents. Reith won the backing of Snowden, Keynes, and many members of parliament for this idea, which is now taken for granted.[1] In March 1926 the Post Office turned it down flat, giving no reasons. Reith was goaded to write in pencil in the margin of the reply, 'Isn't it absurd? What can we do by way of agitation?' When Reith planned a talk by William Graham, M.P., on 'Budgets', in which Graham was to trace the history of budgets through the ages and discuss the general problem of fiscal control which lay behind the budgets, the Post Office wrote tartly to him objecting that the manuscript had not been submitted for approval. Since it might 'conceivably be of a controversial character', it was essential that it should be checked there.[2] When Snowden gave a talk on 25 November 1925 which included a reference to the Treaty of Versailles, the Post Office objected that the Foreign Office had not been given time to study it.

Political broadcasts and debates were always highly suspect. A request to the Postmaster-General to allow three speeches to be broadcast by party leaders during the general election of 1923 was turned down, again without reasons being given. At the general election of 1924, however, three uncensored political speeches were broadcast by the party leaders—MacDonald on 13 October, Baldwin on 16 October, and Asquith on 17 October. Reith had argued most strongly in letters to the Post Office that these speeches should be broadcast 'in the national interest', going so far as to state that 'the utility of broadcasting as a medium of enlightenment is prejudiced owing to the ban upon such matters':[3] Vernon Hartshorn, the Postmaster-General in the first Labour government, responded to this appeal, thereby setting a most important precedent. The ban persisted, however, once the election was over. In March 1925, for instance, the Post Office refused permission for the BBC to broadcast part of a debate on the King's speech from the Oxford Union. Reith had expected that permission might be granted to broadcast this debate since the Broadcasting Board, which advised the Post-

[1] They wrote interesting articles on the subject in the *Radio Times*, 26 Feb. 1926.
[2] *Phillips to Reith, 27 Mar. 1926.
[3] *Reith to Brown, 3 Oct. 1924.

master-General, had declared in June 1924 in favour of greater freedom to broadcast controversial matter under safeguards. He wrote to the Secretary of the Post Office regretting the decision, 'since we feel sure it would have evoked considerable interest'. Speeches would have been delivered in support of each of the three main political parties. Once again the Postmaster-General gave no reason: 'as the speeches to be made would be of an essentially political character, he regrets that he is unable to agree to the debate, or any portion of it being broadcast'.[1]

By the time Reith asked for permission later in the year for the BBC to stage its own debates—for instance, on unemployment and free trade—the Post Office had at last found a reason. 'The question of the broadcasting of speeches or pronouncements on political and other controversial questions will no doubt be one of the aspects of the subject to be considered by the Committee which the Government propose to appoint to undertake a general enquiry into broadcasting towards the end of the year; and in the meantime the Postmaster-General does not consider it advisable to make a fundamental alteration of the present policy on the lines you suggest.'[2]

These negative decisions frustrated Reith's desire to make broadcasting 'educational' in the broadest sense. He believed that a debate on unemployment would be 'of the greatest interest' and would express the 'public service character of broadcasting'.[3] There had been a debate on Communism in February 1923 with a real live Communist, J. T. W. Newbold, as one of the speakers: it had produced not revolution but interesting discussion.[4] The BBC would guarantee completely impartial handling of the most controversial people and the most controversial issues. Many of the most interesting public figures were controversial. 'We find that restrictions are depriving us of the assistance in our programmes of many eminent men,' the Control Board complained in March 1924, 'men who have achieved a national position by the strong line they have taken in various movements.'[5]

It is sometimes argued that the BBC helped to stifle the free

[1] *Dalzell to Reith, 26 Mar. 1925.
[2] *Dalzell to Reith, 28 May 1925.
[3] *Reith to Sir Evelyn Murray, 16 May 1926.
[4] See above, p. 171: *Daily News*, 23 Feb. 1923, has a good report of the debate.
[5] *Control Board Minutes, 18 Mar. 1924.

discussion of public issues during the inter-war years and joined with other national agencies in imposing a blanket of silence. The record of the years 1922 to 1926 demonstrates that this statement is quite untrue in relation to this period. Reith wanted to use the BBC more than other people were prepared to use it —in fostering both industrial and political argument. 'It has been said', he wrote, 'that the industries of the country suffer from the ignorance which prevails concerning them. If that be so, then there are means at hand whereby the ignorance may be dispelled.'[1] What was said about industry was also said about foreign affairs. Reith arranged a monthly survey by the British Institute of International Affairs and a very large number of talks on the League of Nations and the politics of peace—Lord Robert Cecil on 'The Price of Peace' for example, J. R. Clynes on 'World Peace', Vernon Bartlett on 'The Work of the League of Nations' (18 January 1923), and Lord Balfour on 'The Change in the Method of Conducting Foreign Affairs implied by the Establishment of the League of Nations'. In addition Sir Halford Mackinder and other speakers lectured on the Commonwealth.

Many of these and others speeches instantly raised objections from people who said that the BBC was biased, but Reith rightly insisted, as the records bear out, that the accusations of bias came from both sides. The fear of public controversy in Britain is not something that can be attributed to the BBC. It was there when the BBC was in its infancy, and the officers of the BBC, while they knew that they were always under the keen eye of the Post Office, did their best to press for greater freedom. When complaints poured in, for example against political references in a speech by Winston Churchill at the Annual Dinner of the Engineers' Club in October 1925—an occasion which was itself non-political and where Churchill had promised not to deliver a political speech—Reith replied, 'there is always a great public demand to hear public men, and Churchill is perhaps a better draw than any other Minister or ex-Minister. The occasion on which he spoke at the Engineers' Club was a non-party one, and I think that our staff were well-advised in not switching off Churchill in the middle of his speech.'[2]

[1] *Broadcast Over Britain*, p. 153.
[2] *Reith to Gainford, 27 Oct. 1925.

Not all the opposition to controversial political broadcasting could be attributed to party feeling. Some members of parliament, like some leaders of the entertainment industry, did not see the potentialities of radio as a medium. Ramsay MacDonald, for example, at first showed no eagerness to meet Reith or to talk over broadcasting possibilities with him. He was quicker to take offence in the early days of radio than to exploit opportunities. 'As you know,' he once wrote in 1924, 'so far as I am personally concerned I am absolutely indifferent to all this talk, whether it is done by hostile or friendly people. I prefer to be left alone.'[1] This Garbo pose was not shared by Baldwin, who was the quickest of the national political leaders to realize the value of broadcasting. Reith tells the revealing story of how when he and Baldwin met in March 1925 they talked of power in the modern community. Baldwin said that he had been very conscious of it the week before when, being late for an official ceremony, he had been driven down the wrong side of Piccadilly. There was nothing, he remarked, in Reith's office to equal that. Reith told him in reply that he could pick up the private telephone in his study, give two simple orders—'S.B.' which would connect him with the control room and 'All Transmitters' which would link him with other stations—and he could then talk to several million people. Baldwin agreed that this implied greater power than his car exploit.[2]

Baldwin always took trouble with the BBC and it was trouble which was abundantly worth-while to him. In the first election speeches of 1924, for example, while MacDonald took no special pains and made what Reith described as a 'hopeless speech' which might 'do him harm', Baldwin arrived at the studio well in advance 'to see what he had to do when he broadcast': he had dinner with Reith and gave an excellent twenty minutes' talk which Reith felt at once would 'win the election for him'.[3] Baldwin, of course, was quite exceptional in his own party. Birkenhead gave one scintillating broadcast at the opening of the new Savoy Hill studio, but Neville Chamberlain was always far more cautious. Reith asked permission from the Post Office in January 1925 for a speech to be broadcast by Chamberlain

[1] BBC Archives.
[2] Diary, 27 Mar. 1925; *Into the Wind*, p. 98.
[3] Diary, 15 and 16 Oct. 1924.

—then Minister of Health—on housing. It was being delivered at a non-political dinner in Plymouth, and Reith thought that it might give Chamberlain the chance to talk to large numbers of people about a topic with which everyone was keenly concerned. The Postmaster-General said flatly that he had consulted Chamberlain and neither of them thought it desirable that the speech should be broadcast.[1]

Religion was almost as controversial during the 1920s as politics, and in religious matters Reith, as we have seen, had strong Christian feelings and beliefs of his own.[2] It was he who took the initiative. In *Broadcast Over Britain* he explained his attitude quite clearly.

Christianity happens to be the stated and official religion of the country. . . . This is a fact which those who have criticised our right to broadcast the Christian religion would do well to bear in mind. It may be given as an actual justification, if justification be required. To be quite candid, however, this was not in mind when, at the beginning of our operations, a ruling on the subject was given, to which conformity has been maintained ever since. . . . Perhaps we simply decided that the Christian religion was, or should be, non-controversial. The decision was made to do what we believed to be right, and because we believed it to be right.

Reith's whole conception of moral standards derived from Christian principles, and when Christianity was attacked he believed that the attack was misplaced. It should have been directed, he thought, not against Christianity as such but 'against the patent limitations and deficiencies of its presentation and practice'.[3] He had no sympathy with those who objected to religious programmes from a position of indifference or apathy. He went much farther than this. Not only he but the Religious Advisory Committee as a whole was unwilling to give freedom of the air to those who wished to attack or question the religion of large numbers of people.

In the long run, it was because Reith believed that the final truths of religion were beyond controversy that his own position was controversial. He assumed that if the Christianity which was broadcast was unassociated with any particular creed or deno-

---

[1] BBC Archives.   [2] See above, p. 240.
[3] *Broadcast Over Britain*, p. 192.

mination, all would be able to profit from it. This was an assumption which not everyone shared, nor did everyone agree with him that 'the secularising of Sunday is one of the most significant and unfortunate trends of modern life'. There was always considerable opposition to his view that the Sabbath should be treated differently from the other six days of the week and that the programmes which were broadcast on Sunday had to be framed 'with the day itself in mind'.[1] The fact that the growth of the BBC coincided in time with a period of declining social and moral influence of the churches necessarily made Reith's position a difficult one: he [himself] would have added, of course, that it made it a strategic one. The BBC was capable of influencing large numbers of people who were already outside the effective range of the churches. Its success would be measured not by the degree to which it reflected the secularist tendencies of the age but by the vigour with which it resisted them.

Many of the difficulties—and achievements—were in the future. There was no daily radio service, for example, until January 1928.[2] Until the end of 1923 there was not even a weekly Sunday service although Reith urged the Religious Advisory Committee to press for one. All that the BBC did was to include a religious address in the middle of an orchestral concert. The addresses were given by popular preachers like the Rev. P. B. Clayton of Toc H, Prebendary Carlile, the Rev. G. Studdart Kennedy, Father H. Vaughan, Gipsy Smith, and the Rev. John Mayo. The Rev. H. R. L. Sheppard, Vicar of St. Martin-in-the-Fields, was one of the first religious broadcasters, and the Religious Advisory Committee suggested in May 1923 that complete services from St. Martin-in-the-Fields might be broadcast. Sheppard, who was a member of the committee, asked for a formal letter making the request so that his parishioners would not feel that he was 'trying to fix up any sort of a "stunt" with the Broadcasting Company'. The committee duly sent the letter and his parishioners gave their blessing. An experimental service was broadcast from St. Martin's on 6 January 1924. Letters of congratulation showered on the BBC, and a series of undenominational services were arranged at St. Martin's on Sundays at 8 o'clock in the evening from 23 April onwards. The

[1] Ibid., p. 193.
[2] The account following is taken largely from BBC Archives.

first service from a church other than St. Martin's was from the Baptist Metropolitan (Spurgeon's) Tabernacle on 24 August 1924.

Studio services gradually took shape around the original feature of the religious address. Hymns and later an anthem were added, and by the end of 1924 the services lasted for half an hour. Organ music was introduced because 'the practice of singing hymns with a piano was reminiscent of a village hall'.[1] It was only on 7 December 1924 that the first Bible reading was introduced into the service. In June 1925 it was agreed that such services should never be broadcast during regular church hours.

A supplementary feature of the Sunday evening programmes —the Week's Good Cause—was first broadcast on 24 January 1926, immediately after the Sunday evening service. The first Epilogue was broadcast on Sunday, 26 September 1926. Reith had suggested as early as 1924 that broadcasting on Sunday evenings should end with a suitable item of a definitely religious character, but it was not until 1926 that the right kind of arrangements could be made. The item consisted at first of a few verses from the Bible chosen by Palmer, Stobart, or Stuart Hibberd. Eventually to verses from the Bible were added a hymn or a psalm. Rex Palmer's singing of 'Abide With Me' and 'Nearer, My God, to Thee' was greatly appreciated, and later the Wireless Singers took part in the 'service'. It was B. E. Nicolls, then the London Station Director, who chose the title 'Epilogue'. The first evensong was broadcast from Westminster Abbey on Thursday, 7 October 1926.

Many people contributed to the success of these programmes, but there were some ecclesiastical bodies which did not. Broadcasts were made from York Minster and Worcester, Durham, and Lincoln Cathedrals in 1925 and 1926, but the Dean and Chapter of St. Paul's Cathedral would not co-operate. It would be too simple to dismiss their intransigence as another variant of the intransigence displayed by the entertainment industry and the newspaper magnates, but it was certainly a blind intransigence which prevented them from realizing the full possibilities of the medium. Fear that the size of church congregations would fall was as conservative a reason as could possibly be given, and Reith was driven to remind the timorous—no doubt

[1] *Programme Board Minutes, 5 July 1924.

to their annoyance—that 'attendance at church while excellent and desirable is not necessarily a criterion of any religious or spiritual virtue'.[1]

In relation to programmes, it is necessary to put the whole question of religion into proper perspective. The time occupied by religious broadcasting was only 1 per cent. of the total broadcasting hours each week. It was only after 1926, when broadcasting hours were extended, that the question of the organization of Sunday programmes became a really topical matter in the newspapers and periodicals.

Music accounted for by far the biggest single slice of broadcasting time. In November 1923, for example, London was broadcasting on an average each day 3 hours and 25 minutes of music to 2 hours and 5 minutes of everything else. In 1926 the figures were 4 hours and 40 minutes of music to 2 hours and 20 minutes of everything else. The Daventry and provincial station figures were very similar. Of course, music is a composite term and includes everything from dance music to symphony. A detailed breakdown of the programmes reveals an attempt to cater for all tastes, including the tastes of recognized and even of exotic minorities.

In certain branches of entertainment, notably opera, the BBC played the part of a patron. The first outside opera broadcast was in January 1923—*The Magic Flute* relayed from Covent Garden by permission of the British National Opera Company. Unlike most 'musical interests', the B.N.O.C. helped the BBC from the start. When it got into serious financial difficulties later in 1923 and in 1924, the BBC responded by helping it. The secretary of the B.N.O.C. went so far as to tell Reith that 'it was the broadcasting of our operas which did much to establish your Company on a firm basis'.[2] Singers from the B.N.O.C. toured the provinces and broadcast for the BBC from the studio, but it was not until April 1925 that the first studio opera, *Carmen*, was broadcast. There were also broadcasts by the Carl Rosa Opera Company, and in 1926 a series of broadcasts were made from Covent Garden during the International Grand Opera Season.

It has already been noted how Sir Hugh Allen prophesied in

[1] *Broadcast Over Britain*, p. 200.   [2] BBC Archives.

1926 that the future of British opera might be in the hands of the BBC.[1] Certainly the opera programmes were very enthusiastically received whatever their technical deficiencies. *The Magic Flute* in January 1923 created a greater interest not only in opera but in broadcasting itself than almost any other radio performance of the period. It was technically superior to earlier musical performances because a new type of electromagnetic microphone, developed by Round, was used for the first time, and listeners were quick to notice the difference. 'It was the first time in this country', wrote a critic in the *Daily Express*, 'that Grand Opera has come under the ever-growing magic of wireless, and no theatrical manager could have wished for a more wonderfully successful first night. From North, South, East and West came messages of delight over the old-fashioned telephone.'[2] 'This first experiment in bringing Covent Garden direct to one's hearth was triumphantly successful', was the comment of the *Daily News*; 'it was fitting that the first opera to be broadcast by wireless should be this enchanting work of genius by Mozart, with its melodies of liquid silver bubbling up like fountains, its airy grace, its brilliant fun.'[3]

Outside concerts were at least as popular as outside opera, but the BBC ran into more difficulties in successfully planning them. Concert givers were loath to co-operate with the BBC, and Reith decided in November 1923 that it would be necessary for the BBC 'to go out into their own field and show them what we can do if we like'.[4] Even then it was only after every effort of persuasion that the Trustees of the Central Hall, Westminster, agreed to the BBC broadcasting six subscription concerts of its own from their premises. They objected at first that 'they were not too sure about this "new-fangled medium"'.[5] The Central Hall held 2,700 people, and six fortnightly symphony concerts were broadcast from there, beginning in February 1924. These concerts were followed a year later by four monthly symphony concerts from Covent Garden. Queen's Hall, however, long remained closed to the BBC. Its managing director, William Boosey, maintained that broadcasting would ruin the concert world and that people would never pay for concerts when they

---

[1] See above, p. 244.   [2] *Daily Express*, 9 Jan. 1923.
[3] *Daily News*, 9 Jan. 1923.   [4] *Board Minutes, 13 Dec. 1923.
[5] *Letter from G. Morris, Esq., F.A.L.P.A., to the BBC, 22 Feb. 1960.

could sit comfortably at home. He not only banned the use of the hall to the BBC, but refused to allow artists under his control to accept broadcasting engagements. It was not until 1927 that a limited agreement was signed with him. In the provinces local stations co-operated with local interests, including orchestras, like the Hallé and the City of Birmingham, but their initiative was necessarily limited.

All the main stations had their own orchestras, consisting of about eighteen players, including a piano. Belfast was granted special dispensation to include a harpist. London gradually created quite an elaborate organization. On 23 December 1922 a combination of eight BBC players broadcast from the Marconi House studio, each with a microphone in front of him. After the move to Savoy Hill it was possible to increase the size of the ensemble from eight to eighteen. It was also possible to increase the repertoire. Schubert's Unfinished Symphony had figured four times in the 2LO programmes in the pre-Savoy Hill days. As an early historian of the BBC put it in 1930, 'played by such a small orchestra there can be little doubt that it lived up to its name'.[1]

Percy Pitt, who became Music Adviser on 1 May 1923, had ambitious ideas about the future. He broadcast a symphony concert with an augmented BBC orchestra on 21 June and a complete Wagner programme—with an orchestra of forty—on 26 November. In these two concerts the present practice was adopted of placing the different musical instruments at suitable distances from one common microphone. When Dan Godfrey was transferred from the Manchester station to London in May 1924 he became the first full-time conductor of the '2LO Wireless Orchestra', a title which had first appeared in programme notes in January of that year.

In an attempt to avoid the employment of deputies, full-time contracts began to be prepared and signed early in 1924, and in August 1924 all the 'full-time' BBC instrumentalists were signed on regular contracts providing for at least six performances each week. In January 1926 regular contracts were drafted for 'part-time' players. Percy Pitt became full-time Director of Music in November 1924 and the orchestra acquired a secretary in July 1925. In 1926 it amalgamated with the Covent Garden

[1] B.B.C. Year Book (1930), 'The Old B.B.C.', p. 156.

Orchestra, giving its first performance on 30 September with Sir Hamilton Harty. Later concerts in its series were conducted by Elgar, Richard Strauss, and Siegfried Wagner.

Chamber music and light music continued to be provided by small combinations, many of them local. The London Wireless Trio, for example, provided continuity in the early afternoon programmes. It was converted into a quartet, and after the opening of the Daventry station was known as the Daventry Quartet. It used to play every morning. A BBC Military Band was collected by Dan Godfrey in London: it first broadcast in July 1924 and supplemented the frequent military band performances which had been given since January 1923 by the Bands of the Irish Guards, the Grenadiers, and the Royal Air Force. Choral singing also was 'institutionalized'. At the end of 1923 and early in 1924 there was a small outside choir which used to sing at Savoy Hill. It was used offstage at Covent Garden to augment the stage chorus. This group was succeeded in 1924 by the London Select Choir, which performed in one of the most rousing if hardly the most inspiring of early BBC musical successes, a specially written 'musical' called *The Dogs of Devon*. This was first broadcast on 28 January 1924. Four other request performances of it were given between then and the end of 1926. The London Select Choir was succeeded in September 1924 by a permanent chorus conducted by Stanford Robinson, who was transferred from the Music Department of the BBC to the London station to take it over. Besides these developments within the BBC, there was a close association with certain 'outside' light musical combinations. Two of the best-known of them enlivened Sunday programmes for many years—De Groot and the Piccadilly Orchestra, which first broadcast on 27 April 1924, and Albert Sandler and the Orchestra from the Grand Hotel, Eastbourne, which first broadcast on 28 July 1925.

From October 1923 onwards, dance music was supplied several times a week from the Savoy Hotel by the Savoy Orpheans and Havana Bands. The first dance music programme was broadcast before the opening of Savoy Hill, however, on 23 March 1923, when a 2LO dance combination—consisting of nine members of the Wireless Orchestra with a saxophone added—entertained British listeners with some of the popular tunes of the day, several of them American. One of the earliest regular dance bands to broadcast was that of Sidney Firman. His London Radio Dance Band played twice a week for most of 1926. Firman's band was replaced in 1928 by Jack Payne's BBC Dance Orchestra, which had previously played on many occasions from the Hotel Cecil. In his first few months with the BBC Firman had provided a certain amount of music for what would now be called variety shows, but in November 1926 this task was handed over to a full-time quartet in charge of Sidney Holt.

Jack Hylton and Carroll Gibbons were among the other broadcasters of dance music during these early days. There were some striking moments—in 1926, for example, Hylton took part in a famous radio debate with Sir Landon Ronald on the respective merits of jazz and classical music, and in the same year George Gershwin himself played *Rhapsody in Blue* from the Savoy some time before it was recognized as a popular classic. Gershwin was in London for the Astaires' production of *Lady Be Good*, and in Carroll Gibbons's opinion wireless listeners heard a performance of better quality than the Whiteman version. 'I shall never forget the moment', he has said, 'when Bill Debroy Somers took up his baton and the augmented Savoy Orpheans began to play the new theme which would soon become familiar all over the world.'[1]

The growing range of BBC musical activities and the organization of special BBC groups to provide them was something of a distinctive feature in British broadcasting. There was certainly no reliance on gramophone record programmes, which were such a useful, low-cost staple of local American broadcasting. Yet gramophone record programmes were broadcast in Britain in 1922, and they figured prominently both in programmes from Writtle and 2ZY, Manchester: in November of that year Binyon protested against their use by 2ZY on the grounds that they were not being broadcast by 2LO or 5IT and that Manchester was losing prestige by using them.[2] The BBC began to include them in mid-day programmes from 23 August to 1 November 1923, and it introduced a weekly programme of new records—the Week's Concert of New Gramophone Records —on 27 March 1924. One large gramophone company supplied

---

[1] Gale Pedrick, BBC programme, *These Radio Times*, 25 Apr. 1952.
[2] Binyon to McKinstry, 25 Nov. 1923, A.E.I. (Manchester) Ltd. Archives.

its records to the BBC free of charge, but copyright fees were regularly paid by the BBC to the copyright owners. There were many discussions about the propriety of using records, and on one occasion early in 1925 the Control Board decided to recommend that broadcasting of all gramophone records should cease within two months and suitable outside broadcasts be substituted for them.[1] There was talk of a pianola instead: indeed, a pianola was actually installed in the studio, and announcers were given instructions to use it for 'fill-ups' instead of records. The gramophone record triumphed, however, without the assistance of 'disc jockeys'. In 1925 the first electric gramophone records made in America reached London: they were described as 'a revelation' with the depth and quality of their tone. The most notable of all the disc jockeys, Christopher Stone, did not make his début with his morning recital of new records until July 1927: even then it was a début by accident, since he appeared as a deputy for his brother-in-law Compton Mackenzie, the founder and editor of the magazine, *The Gramophone*.

Music and the drama are often linked together. Radio drama had made only limited progress by the end of 1926, although there was talk even at this stage of the emergence of a new art form.[2] The first transmission of drama by the BBC was on 16 February 1923, when the quarrel scene from *Julius Caesar* was broadcast from Marconi House with Robert Atkins as Cassius and Basil Gill as Brutus. This transmission, which also included scenes from *Henry VIII* and *Much Ado About Nothing*, remained exceptional for several weeks. It might have done so for longer had not the theatres changed their attitude to broadcasting. They had been prepared to allow excerpts of West End productions to be broadcast until April 1923. They then clamped down, and the BBC was left to fend for itself. C. A. Lewis, who was extremely interested in drama, immediately obtained the services of Miss Cathleen Nesbitt, the well-known actress, and she adapted (chiefly by cutting) and produced several of Shakespeare's plays for radio. *Twelfth Night*, for example, was broad-

---

[1] *Control Board Minutes, 29 Jan. 1925.
[2] C. A. Lewis, *Broadcasting from Within*, p. 119.

33. Melchior singing from Chelmsford, 1920

34. An audition at 2LO

35. Studio No. 1, Savoy Hill

36. The
Manchester
Radio Trio

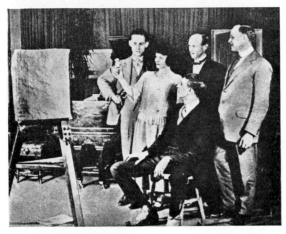

37. 'Aunt Sophie'
and the London
Uncles

38. 'Uncle Jeff'
and his orchestra

39. The Chorus of 'Radio Radiance', one of the first revues

40. General Booth broadcasting with the Salvation Army from Trafalgar Square

cast on 28 May, and *Romeo and Juliet* and *A Midsummer Night's Dream* in July. Lewis Casson also produced several early plays in 1924. He and his wife Sybil Thorndike were regular broadcasters, sometimes in the most unlikely plays like the *Medea* and Maurice Maeterlinck's *The Death of Tintageles*. In all these early theatrical ventures broadcasting copied the stage. Indeed, as late as 1926, long plays were prefaced by four or five minutes of conventional stage 'overture' and music was always played between the acts.[1]

Lewis was imaginative and forceful, but drama was only one, if the most cherished, of his occupations. With R. E. Jeffrey's arrival from Aberdeen in July 1924,[2] efforts were made to discover new plays and new ways of handling old ones. Earlier in the year, in January, Jeffrey had produced the first play actually written for broadcasting—*Danger*, by Richard Hughes: it was set in a coal mine. It was followed soon afterwards by the first of the many radio plays written by L. du Garde Peach, a comedy called *Light and Shade*.

Jeffrey had firm ideas about what could and could not be done on the air. He believed, for example, that radio plays should not normally last more than forty minutes, that they should be concerned with 'some situation, emotion or experience which will be appreciated, or rather, applicable to the average mind' and that they should adopt 'broad methods of building and sustaining the required picture'.[3] Clever dialogue was not necessary: 'dramatic action is seen in complete detail by all those who listen with close attention'.[4] He believed also that the best radio plays had genuine advantages over stage productions: they would grip the listener more and appeal more profoundly to his 'mentality, imagination and emotion'. Jeffrey wrote several articles in the *Radio Times* on this subject, took great interest in a competition to find the best radio play, and won the good will of many famous actors and actresses who appeared in early BBC performances. He was less successful, however, in a short period of collaboration with the actor Donald Calthrop,

---

[1] Val Gielgud, *British Radio Drama, 1922–1956* (1957), p. 20.
[2] See above, p. 210.
[3] For Jeffrey's views, see three articles in the *Radio Times*—'Wireless Drama' (6 June 1924), 'The Need for a Radio Drama' (17 July 1925), and 'Seeing with the Mind's Eye' (5 Nov. 1926).
[4] 'Seeing with the Mind's Eye.'

who worked as a part-time BBC producer for a brief spell between October 1925 and January 1926.

One hundred and forty-one 'plays' were broadcast between August 1924 and September 1925. Of these 55 per cent. were said to be comedy, 35 per cent. popular drama, and 10 per cent. plays of a 'classical or high-class nature'. Some of the plays would be called 'features' today—'One Hundred Years of Railways' or 'Pictures from the Past', for instance—but there were several straight plays which introduced Lady Forbes Robertson, Mrs. Kendall, Lady Tree, Henry Ainley, Gladys Cooper, Sybil Thorndike, Lewis Casson, Arthur Wontner, Cathleen Nesbitt and others to the 'unseen audience'. About 900 would-be actors and actresses had been given microphone auditions during this period. Jeffrey's closest collaborator was Howard Rose, with whom he produced many plays which were 'the embryos of practically all the later and well-known offspring of the Drama Department'.[1] Rose produced the radio adaptation of *Westward Ho!* in April 1925, a few months before he joined the full-time staff of the BBC. On Armistice Day 1925 he was responsible for the first full-length play specially written for radio—*The White Château* by Reginald Berkeley. There was to be unprecedented progress in radio drama in 1927 and 1928, but *The White Château* was the limit of achievement in the days of the Company. There was some truth in the charge made in 1926 that 'the BBC has not yet discovered a modern play-writer who has the correct technique for a broadcast play'.[2] Jeffrey himself, in the opinion of his successor, was unwilling or unable to go far enough in his experiments because of the restricted facilities available at this time.[3]

Reith himself, to whom Val Gielgud has dedicated his study of radio drama, wrote in an intelligent way about the possibilities. He commended Jeffrey's work and advised Station Directors to read a book on the subject published by Gordon Lea of Newcastle in 1926. 'It seems to me', he remarked, 'that in many of our productions there is too much striving for theatre effect and too little attempt at discovering the actual radio effect when the play is received in distant homes.'[4] Jeffrey made the

---

[1] Gielgud, op. cit., p. 21.   [2] *The Observer*, 23 May 1926.
[3] Gielgud, op. cit., p. 26.
[4] *Memorandum from Reith to Station Directors, 20 Dec. 1926.

same point about the kind of audience in relation to the actor and actress. 'The audience is a need of the artist. They react to his moods. The effect is cumulative and reciprocal . . . broadcast artists must develop finer shades of expressiveness, finer sensibilities and realize to the full the innate power which everyone worthy of the name of artist feels when working at his art.'[1]

3. The Broadcasters

JEFFREY directed attention to the special artistic qualifications necessary for successful broadcasters. His concern went much deeper than Burrows's preoccupation with 'a wireless voice' in 1922.[2] Already by the end of 1926 there was an identifiable group of broadcasters who had made their mark, men and women who were thought of as 'stars' of their profession. They were people of widely different talents, but they all had one point in common—their ability to project their personalities to an unseen and (equally important) to a scattered audience. This audience was far more heterogeneous than that which gathered in the theatres. 'There is in the nightly audience', wrote Reith, 'every order of social class, every grade of educational and intellectual attainment, every variety of like and dislike, taste and distaste, on every conceivable subject. To the same audience, every night, a different programme has to be transmitted. A theatre has the same performance and a different audience night after night.'[3]

Successful broadcasters not only had to know how to 'reach' such an audience: they had to triumph over the technical weaknesses of the medium. Not the least of these weaknesses was the poor quality of many people's receiving sets. It was through the haze of 'atmospherics' and the roar of distortion and interference that the first broadcasters made themselves known to their public. Some of them were so supremely successful that if

---

[1] *Undated note by Jeffrey.   [2] See above, p. 80.
[3] *Broadcast Over Britain*, p. 123.

for any reason they ceased to broadcast, their listeners regarded
the event as the breaking not of a public but of a personal link.
This was said of 'Dick Sheppard' when he retired in October
1926. Listeners might never have seen his face, 'but the tones of
his voice have become as familiar as if they had been sitting in
the Church or in his vicarage study'.[1] It was said of many other
people, too.

Almost every branch of broadcasting had pushed into prominence its own 'personality'. Sheppard was greatly loved, but
by no means alone. 'This was the age of personalities in radio.'[2]
Listeners had not become hardened to 'routine' listening, and
they opened their hearts to a number of successful broadcasters
whom they had long ceased to regard as distant strangers. These
included clergymen, popular educators, singers, like Dale Smith,
talkers, story-tellers, and comedians. The variety of professions
and performances was as striking as the variety of individual
talents with which the successful broadcasters were endowed.
'They all made themselves of the family circle. There never was
such audacity, such successful audacity.'[3]

One of the first stars was Sir Walford Davies. He first met
Reith on 1 March 1924 and expressed himself as 'much
interested in our [broadcasting] work'.[4] He soon proved himself
to be the greatest popular evangelist of the gospel of music:
equally important, he proved himself to be one of the first great
broadcasters, knowledgeable but never opinionated, persuasive
and confidential. 'He used the piano with consummate skill',
Stuart Hibberd has written of him, 'and had that sense of intimacy—of having a little chat with one listener or one family
alone—which broadly speaking is the pre-requisite of all successful broadcasting.'[5] He was far more widely known than any
of the individual pieces of music he introduced or played. Sir
Oliver Lodge, one of the great pioneers of radio, whose scientific
contribution to wireless invention has already been described,[6]
also proved to be one of the great popularizers of early broad-

[1] *Radio Times*, 3 Oct. 1926.

[2] M. Gorham, *Broadcasting and Television Since 1900* (1952), p. 48.

[3] J. W. Robertson Scott, 'A Salute to the Microphone', in *Radio Times*, 24 Sept.
1926.

[4] Diary, 1 Mar. 1924.

[5] S. Hibberd, *This—is London* (1950), p. 27.

[6] See above, pp. 26–27, 35–36

casting. He has been called 'the wisest and friendliest of all broadcasters'. He broadcast on difficult subjects—'Worlds and Atoms', for example—when he was already in the last phase of his long and active life. He knew how to speak simply and directly, and no one has ever been more successful than he in establishing confidence between 'expert' and 'layman'. Like Davies, he persuaded rather than lectured, shared secrets rather than imparted information. He paused frequently, and seemed to be searching for the perfect word. And he projected his personality as well as his ideas. 'He had a little trick of clearing his throat immediately after he had been announced and before he began to speak. So regularly was this sound produced that we used to call it his "signature tune".'[1]

Both Davies and Lodge were well-established public figures before broadcasting was born. Some of the other 'talkers' or 'lecturers', as they were sometimes known, were 'creations of radio'. Dr. C. W. Saleeby, for example, talked of health and Mrs. Marion Cran of gardens. Mrs. Cran proved almost as popular with her radio audience as did the later universal favourite, Mr. Middleton. One of the most striking first 'creations of radio', however, was a civil servant, Leslie Harrison Lambert, known to his audience as A. J. Alan. More clearly than anyone else Alan realized that radio offered completely new possibilities of communication. He realized also that radio could make a broadcaster into 'a mystery man', a topic of universal conversation. Alan first broadcast in January 1924. He had been listening to Sir William Bull complaining over the air of the decay of story-telling. The next day Alan called on Rex Palmer, said that he had some ideas for radio stories, and asked for an audition. Palmer was so impressed by his visitor that he signed him on at once. His very first broadcast—'My Adventure in Jermyn Street'—was a wireless 'hit'. Again, Alan was a remarkable character. He always used to carry with him to the studio candle and matches in case the lighting failed during his broadcast. When he broadcast, he used to sit on a high stool close to the microphone: his script, which sounded quite informal, was in fact pasted on to sheets of cardboard in a pile on his knees. Thereby he avoided all sounds of rustling of paper. At intervals in the script there would be notes reading

[1] Hibberd, op. cit., p. 26.

'cough here', 'pause', 'sigh', and so on. What seemed so informal was extremely carefully contrived. Alan would never smoke or drink for at least a week before broadcasting, and everything that he said—and the way that he said it—was meticulously rehearsed: moreover, he carefully maintained the 'mystery' of his reputation by broadcasting only a few times each year.

More regular successful broadcasters were quick to realize that radio could disseminate quips and catchwords which would soon enjoy a national currency, that 'character playing' could be projected as effectively as 'character'. The first radio 'character', in the comic sense of the term, was Helena Millais, 'our Lizzie', a forerunner of Mrs. Buggins. Miss Millais made her wireless début remarkably early on 21 November 1922. ''Ullo me ducks,' were her opening words to her listeners, ''ere I am again with me old string bag.' One of the songs she sang was 'Ours is a nice 'ouse, ours is'. Mrs. Buggins herself, Mabel Constanduros, first appeared on the air in 1925. She had written 'Buggins' sketches to amuse her mother and sisters, and when she asked to have an audition at the BBC in 1925 she performed a 'Buggins' sketch. One day Kenneth Wright told her that the BBC was going to make her into a 'star'. 'What does that mean?' she asked, and she was carefully told that in future she would get five guineas for a performance instead of two.[1]

The most famous comedian of the early days, however, was John Henry, a henpecked Yorkshireman with a dry sense of humour and a sheaf of refreshingly original material. Henry soon established himself as radio's first 'natural' artist of humorous entertainment. He remains interesting not only on account of the particular form of his art—his tales of his exploits with his friend Joe Murgatroyd or his 'tiffs' with his wife Blossom, and his comic voice which was an oral substitute for a red nose—but on account of the way in which he rose to fame. It was radio which made him. Other stage comedians, far better known to the public in 1922, were either debarred from broadcasting by their contracts or too set in their ways to appreciate the possibilities of broadcasting. Some of them, indeed, felt lonely and isolated away from the glamour of the footlights. Wireless offered a means of advancement to 'local' comedians who were conscious of the pressure of the cinema on their liveli-

---

[1] Gale Pedrick, BBC programme, *These Radio Times*, 20 Oct. 1951.

hood and were engaged mainly in appealing to small intimate audiences in provincial after-dinner shows or summer holiday audiences on the pier at seaside resorts. Rex Palmer booked John Henry for the BBC and was the first person to realize that he had discovered a 'natural' broadcaster. And Henry was given very effective publicity. One of his early shows in 1924, for example, was done from an aeroplane. Sir Alan Cobham piloted Henry and 'Blossom' high over London, and 'Blossom' was probably right in claiming that she was the first woman ever to broadcast from an aeroplane.[1] Henry was surprised by his own success. Phrases like 'John Henry, come here' were known all over the country. People recognized him wherever he went. Even roses were named after him.

Henry's art was unique, but in many respects his career was not untypical. Far from ruining the variety theatre, radio gave new opportunities to people who might not otherwise have found them. Willie Rouse, another early radio comedian, better known as 'Wireless Willie', introduced to radio Bertha Wilmot, who broadcast her first quarter of an hour of radio entertainment in 1924. She did much to make music-hall songs nationally popular. Entertainers like Wish Wynne and Norman Long— 'A Song, a Smile and a Piano'—soon became known throughout the whole country: they first broadcast in November 1922.

Tommy Handley, the greatest of all radio comedians, broadcast for the first time in the relay of the Royal Command Variety Show of 1924, but at the time when he was given his first nervous audition at Savoy Hill, he had shown no signs of 'star' quality in his work. His constant repetition of his sketch 'The Disorderly Room', which first went the theatre round in 1921, was beginning to do him harm with managers and the public. The audition proved to be a turning-point in his career. As Ted Kavanagh has written, 'up to this point there had been nothing really outstanding in Tommy's career. It had followed the usual line; the rather mischievous schoolboy with a penchant for dressing up, the youth with a voice and certain gifts of comic invention becoming stage-struck. It had all happened a hundred times before.'[2] What was to happen to him later— and to British comedy—had never happened before. 'Itma' was

[1] Gale Pedrick, BBC programme, *These Radio Times*, 15 Jan. 1952.
[2] T. Kavanagh, *Tommy Handley* (1949), pp. 69–70.

years ahead, but Tommy Handley soon made himself a radio personality.

'Itma' was to be a triumph of collective as well as of individual broadcasting, of Tommy Handley's team as well as of Tommy himself. Although 'collective broadcasting' was in its infancy in 1926, a few ensembles had already established themselves. They were of the 'concert party' type rather than shows especially designed to meet the needs of radio. The Co-optimists broadcast in 1921 before the birth of the BBC. They were paid 10s. for a five-minute broadcast, and their listeners were in a room a few streets away in the Strand.[1] The Roosters Concert Party, which had made a great name for itself during the First World War, broadcast on many occasions from Savoy Hill under the direction of Percy Merriman, the first occasion being in October 1923. The name 'Roosters' was derived from Captain Roose, the Camp Commandant at Salonica, who had given Bobby Warren, the concert party's producer, a 100-drachma note to back the show.[2] The concert party was as successful in its appeal to the radio audience as it was in the theatres. Burrows suggested in April 1924 that more shows of this kind would be popular. To 'offset the Summer slump' in wireless sales he proposed 'the broadcasting of famous seaside concert parties by means of a microphone placed in the auditorium on the sands or in the concert hall'.[3]

The first revue put on by the BBC itself was 'The 7.30 Revue' from Manchester in March 1925. One of the first revues arranged in London was 'Radio Radiance'. One of its authors was Peter Cheyney and one of its performers was Tommy Handley. Jean Allistone, a very successful young singer who performed in it, became Mrs. Tommy Handley: indeed, this was one of the first studio romances. The effects for the programme were very difficult to contrive, and one of the artists connected with the production has recalled how it was quite easy in retiring from the microphone to fall backwards over a bucket, or to catch coat tails in a 'Heath Robinson' contraption.[4]

[1] Leslie Baily, BBC programme, *Scrapbook for 1921*.
[2] Gale Pedrick, BBC programme, *These Radio Times*, 6 Oct. 1951.
[3] *Burrows to Eckersley, 10 Apr. 1924.
[4] Gale Pedrick, BBC programme, *These Radio Times*, 3 Nov. 1951.

Comedians and concert parties were warned in these early days of the charges of 'vulgarity' creeping into the programmes. As early as January 1923 Burrows wrote to Stanton Jefferies telling him that complaints had been made about 'vulgarity by a humorist'.[1] In January 1925 precise instructions were given to 'all entertainers and concert parties' not to include advertisements in their programmes, not to dwell on either 'drink or prohibition', not to make clerical impersonations, not to make political allusions, and not to introduce 'vulgar or doubtful matter'.[2] A card was handed to new artists—'No gags on Scotsmen, Welshmen, Clergymen, Drink, or Medical matters. Do not sneeze at the microphone.'[3]

So far most of what has been said about the broadcasters has left on one side the work of established 'stars' or public personalities who did occasional broadcasts despite all the inhibitions of contracts or the fettering of inclinations. The first artists who made their national name on the radio, Helena Millais, for example, were paid very small sums of money for their appearances—one guinea was not exceptional. There were 'big names', however, who commanded big salaries. Sir Harry Lauder, who first appeared in December 1925 and proved an excellent broadcaster, was paid considerable sums, while the fee of around £1,000 paid to Chaliapin for a broadcast in November 1925 was considered exceptionally large for a very long time afterwards.

Some of the most expensive early programmes were sponsored by sections of the press. An *Evening Standard* concert of March 1925, for example, included among its artists Ysaÿe, Dinh Gilly, and Tetrazzini. Among other interesting 'big names' who figure at least once in the early broadcast programmes are Tom Mix, the film-star cowboy, Douglas Fairbanks and Mary Pickford, Noël Coward, who sang his own songs at the piano, Bransby Williams, and George Bernard Shaw, who in November 1924 read his play, *O'Flaherty V.C.* G. H. Elliott, 'the Chocolate-Coloured Coon', was one of the best-known established music-hall stars who successfully won the support of the radio audience. He began with an act which people liked to see: he ended with

[1] *Burrows to Jefferies, 13 Jan. 1923.
[2] BBC Archives.
[3] Gale Pedrick, BBC programme, *These Radio Times*, 15 Jan. 1952.

a broadcast which people wanted to hear. One of his first radio songs was 'Listen in, Virginia', which is quoted at the beginning of this volume.

Singers and actors either turned naturally to the new 'medium' or refused to have anything to do with it. 'Talkers' and 'lecturers' were in a somewhat different position. BBC policy towards them changed during this period of history. There were some good speakers during the 'early days', but the initiative for talks often came from them, curiosity about radio and the local 'prestige' of a performance serving as powerful motives.[1] The speakers were often unpaid, even the guinea seeming to the BBC to be too much. In March 1924 Reith wrote to the Station Directors telling them 'that nowadays the initiative should come almost invariably from us, that is, we should not wait for people to send in manuscripts or suggested talks'. The interest of a talk was greatly enhanced if the listener knew that he was listening to an 'authority'.[2] In July 1924 a definite distinction was drawn by the BBC between fees payable to those who offered to broadcast (class A) and those who had to be persuaded to broadcast (class B). In the case of class A broadcasters, no fees at all were to be paid 'where the talk was given for the purpose of publicity' and fees of three to five guineas were maxima. In the case of class B, 'the fee should range up to ten guineas,—this latter fee being paid only occasionally for specially distinguished speakers'.[3]

The broadcast of outstanding distinction in 1924 was that by King George V, when he opened the British Empire Exhibition on 23 April 1924. This was to be the first broadcast of many which King George gave. It has often and rightly been argued that the practice of royal broadcasting lent a new dimension to constitutional monarchy. It was estimated that George V's speech in 1924 was heard by at least ten million people. The *Daily Mail* claimed a large share of the credit for the publicity of this broadcast, and made special arrangements for massed crowds to hear the King's speech in some of the big national centres of population such as Manchester, Leeds, and Glasgow. In order that members might hear the broadcast an official

[1] *Notes by Ralph Wade.
[2] *Reith to the Station Directors, 3 Mar. 1924.
[3] *Control Board Minutes, 22 July 1924.

government inquiry at Cambridge suspended its sittings; at Gateshead the Police Court proceedings were adjourned. 'Of all the wonders of yesterday,' a *Daily Mail* leader read, 'by the general consent of the public, the most wonderful was the broadcasting of the King's speech and of the whole audible pageant at Wembley.'[1] The 'audible pageant' included the combined bands of the Brigade of Guards. Harold Bishop was responsible for the arrangements behind the scenes, and he and his engineers were confronted with extremely difficult and complex problems. Their success was a sign of the great progress being made in the technique of outside broadcasting. Reith himself also played an important part well away from the public gaze. 'Thursday was a triumph,' wrote Archibald Fleming to Reith's mother, 'and his triumph, although he kept, as he always keeps, in the background. It is something to have made history as he has done.'[2]

For years it was thought that there had been no recording of this historic speech, but after a BBC *Scrapbook* programme in 1955 had discussed this subject, a listener, Mrs. Dorothy Jones, wrote to the BBC that a recording of the speech had been made privately by her husband in his laboratory at Croydon. A copy of the recording is now in the BBC Library. Among other royal broadcasters who made their début in 1925 were the Duke of York (later King George VI), Prince Henry (later the Duke of Gloucester), and Princess Mary (later the Princess Royal).

The section of the regular BBC staff which was in closest contact with the 'broadcasters'—indeed they were often outstanding broadcasters themselves—were the announcers. It is hardly surprising in consequence that some excellent pen portraits of the early broadcasting personalities have been produced by Stuart Hibberd, who joined the BBC on 14 November 1924 and kept a day-by-day diary which, as he hoped, provides most useful data for the historian.[3] When Hibberd first arrived at Savoy Hill, J. S. Dodgson was senior announcer.[4] He was the first of the full-timers, although earlier in 1923 W. Savary, R. Keene, and G. C. Beadle had all served for a time as announcers. The month of Hibberd's arrival coincided with an important

[1] *Daily Mail*, 24 Apr. 1924.
[2] Sir Archibald Fleming to Mrs. Reith, Apr. 1924. This letter is in Lord Reith's possession.
[3] S. Hibberd, *This—is London*, Preface.
[4] See above, p. 213.

change of BBC policy. Hitherto both local and national announcers were quite well known by name to the radio public: their names, indeed, were given in the first pages of the *Radio Times*. On 16 November 1924 it was decided that a strict anonymity rule should be followed. The exceptions to this rule were so rare that they stand out in retrospect. In December 1926, for example, the *Radio Times*, bidding farewell to the Company, included both names and photographs.[1]

Anonymity and greater formality went together. In March 1924, with Burrows objecting, it had been decided to insist on 'a standard form of announcing' in the provinces as well as in London. In November Reith urged Station Directors to think of announcers as 'men of culture, experience and knowledge': 'they should devote their whole energies to the preparation and study of the material which they are to speak on the microphones, to the end that the greatest effect may be secured for their programmes'. In July 1925 the idea of 'a school for announcers' was canvassed. 'Highly individualized announcing in the American style' was explicitly rejected, and it was argued that announcers were better placed than any other BBC employees 'to build up in the public mind a sense of the BBC's collective personality'. This was an important idea. 'The training and equipment of an efficient body of announcers', wrote Walter Fuller, was a means of presenting to the general public 'not only the daily programmes in an attractive way', but 'the BBC itself, its policy and ideals, as a great public service institution for entertainment, education and inspiration.'[2]

We would now speak of the announcers helping to create 'the public image' of the BBC. In several respects this was to be an image drawn from upper-class or upper middle-class life. Speech was to be correct, although not stilted. Lloyd James began a series of talks to announcers on good English in June 1925. 'We are daily establishing in the minds of the public', he told them, 'the idea of what correct speech should be, and this is an important responsibility.'[3] And dress was to be at least as correct as speech. The first announcers did not wear evening dress. In the autumn

---

[1] *Radio Times*, 17 Dec. 1926.
[2] *W. J. Fuller, *Memorandum on Programme Presentation and the Organisation of a special Department*, July 1925.
[3] Diary, 10 June 1925; BBC Archives.

of 1925, however, it was decided that they should be required to wear dinner jackets. An initial dress allowance was paid by the BBC as if to underline the importance of the change, which duly took place on 4 January 1926. Stuart Hibberd has defended the change. 'After all, announcing is a serious, if a new profession,

41. 'Good Evening, Everybody. XXX calling!
We will now have a Fugue.'

and the wearing of evening dress is an act of courtesy to the artists, many of whom will almost certainly be similarly dressed if they are taking part in a programme from 8.0 p.m. onwards.'[1] The customs of the inter-war years, which seemed so much more informal to the people of the 1920s than the customs of the period before 1914, in their turn now seem extremely formal to us. Yet the formality, like the insistence on anonymity, was a way of creating the 'image'. The image itself has dated with the vast changes in twentieth-century society, and even at the

[1] Hibberd, op. cit., p. 16.

time, when only a small section of the population wore evening dress, it lent itself to caricature.

Reith himself always went behind appearances. He always
emphasized the 'moral' qualities of the good broadcaster, stressing them as much as the artistic. Some of the most interesting
and eloquent passages in *Broadcast Over Britain* relate to this
subject. Showmanship, Reith held, was vulgar and bombastic
unless it was accompanied by discretion: showmanship always
had to be the 'spontaneous product of knowledge and culture,
imagination and restraint'.

The Broadcasters [he went on] are mostly young men. From the
nature of things in the beginning this was, I think, to be expected;
in view of the arduous and diverse nature of their labours it is
probably fortunate. They are rather shadowy personalities to the
average man; they are aloof and mysterious. You will probably not
find them at garden parties or social functions; their names may not
figure among the distinguished ones present, even if they do go; most
likely they are much too busy to spend time in this way. . . . [Yet]
they are personages of much importance in the land, although this
so far may not be recognized. It matters little or nothing to them
whether it be recognized or not. In many ways I believe it is desirable
that they should continue in their comparative obscurity. . . . The
desire for notoriety and recognition sterilizes the seeds from which
greatness might spring. A place in the stars is of more importance
than a place in the sun.[1]

There was to be a contrast at the core of broadcasting between the regular members of the BBC staff, who were not to
seek the limelight, and the broadcasters from outside who were
often to have thrust upon them notoriety if not fame. This contrast was accentuated from November 1924 onwards, when the
Board decided under 'any other business' that no member of the
BBC's staff should be permitted to publish books in future, and
that no member should publish articles except with the consent
of the Managing Director.[2] Definite instructions about 'personal publicity' were issued later in the same month to all members of the staff.[3] These were important decisions in the history
of the 'institutionalization' of the BBC: behind them both was
Reith's concern for the good name of the Company, which, as we

---

[1] *Broadcast Over Britain*, pp. 51–52.
[2] *Board Minutes, 13 Nov. 1924.   [3] Diary, 24 Nov. 1924.

have already seen, he was increasingly anxious should become an instrument of public service. Eckersley remained an exception to the rules. He was an extremely popular broadcaster and what he had to say about the technical side of radio was important enough to deserve to be said well. He continued to stimulate great public interest in how the BBC 'worked'.

It should be added, of course, that the early staff of the BBC, like the broadcasters from outside, was an extraordinarily varied collection of people. Eric Maschwitz has referred to them as 'a mixed Bohemian flock' with Reith as a strange but kindly shepherd. 'He had under his aegis a bevy of ex-soldiers, ex-actors, ex-adventurers, which a Carton de Wiart, a C. B. Cochran, even a Dartmoor Prison Governor might have found some difficulty in controlling.'[1] Maurice Gorham has described them somewhat less colourfully as 'a mixture of enthusiasts who believed in the possibilities of radio, pioneers who loved any new enterprise, ready-made specialists like musicians, actors and journalists, and a proportion of people who just wanted a job and found it hard to get one in the conditions that followed the First World War. Some of them were geniuses, some were unable to grow with their jobs, some were misfits.'[2] Reith watched them all carefully: he believed that public service and personal indiscretion never went well together. Some of the staff were shunted away, others left for very different kinds of organizations. Ex-BBC staff are now widely scattered, sometimes in the most unlikely places.

4. Facing the Nation

REITH's concern for the right kind of publicity was as profound as his distaste for the wrong. Two major events of importance stand out in the planning of his strategy—first, the launching of the *Radio Times* in September 1923, and second, the appoint-

---

[1] Maschwitz, op. cit., p. 50.   [2] Gorham, op. cit., p. 43.

ment in December 1924 of Major Gladstone Murray as Director of Publicity. The *Radio Times* was designed to be something more than a mere Bradshaw of Broadcasting: it too was to shape the public 'image' of the BBC. The appointment of Gladstone Murray was something more than a routine measure: he was given extensive powers, including authority to co-ordinate branches of the BBC—among them control of the editorial side of all publications and responsibility for all public relations—which had hitherto been considered separate and distinct. W. C. Smith left the BBC to take up a publicity post with the Liberal Party soon after his arrival. Gladstone Murray himself stayed with the BBC until 1936 when he was appointed general manager of the newly-founded Canadian Radio Commission. He was a genial, gregarious, and energetic man with great organizing ability and the capacity to canvass the BBC's case in the most unlikely—as well as the most likely—places. He was on close terms with the press, with a number of members of parliament, with 'key people' in government and administration. The confidential memoranda which he submitted to Reith at this time on a large number of subjects were models of acuteness, lucidity, and forceful argument. Like most members of the BBC's executive staff, however, he was often overworked, and there was no busier member of the staff both during the General Strike and in the discussions on the Crawford Committee.

Gladstone Murray was one of the keenest advocates of a powerful *Radio Times* which he considered to be 'the logical development of our general conception of the service'.[1] The idea of the *Radio Times* was born in Reith's mind much earlier in February 1923 during the short and ineffective boycott of BBC programmes by the leading newspapers.[2] Once born, it grew, and there is an entry in the Minutes of the Board of Directors for May 1923 which reads: 'it was resolved that the General Manager make the appointment of an individual to deal with propaganda publicity and the production of a magazine'.[3] Reith was already convinced that it would be extremely valuable to possess a medium of more detailed and familiar communication between the broadcasters and their audience than was

[1] *Memorandum of 23 Jan. 1926.
[3] *Board Minutes, 10 May 1923.
[2] See above, p. 142.

possible or desirable by wireless itself. He conceived of the *Radio Times* as 'the connecting link of the service'.[1]

In fact, it was to become something more than that. There were few more spectacular successes in the journalism of the inter-war years. A quarter of a million copies of the first issue were printed and quickly sold out. Reith knew that the initial print was far too small, and circulation soon leapt to 600,000. At the end of December 1925 circulation was over 800,000 and a year later had risen to nearly 850,000. By the end of 1928 it had passed the million mark. Profits from the *Radio Times* helped to carry the BBC through its financially lean years.[2]

Considering its great success as a business proposition, it is remarkable that Reith found it difficult in the spring and summer of 1923 to find a publisher willing to sign a contract to publish the *Radio Times* on the terms offered—a share of profits and the guarantee of a minimum annual sum to the BBC. Only the firm of George Newnes would take the risk. By a coincidence the chairman of the firm was Lord Riddell, one of Reith's toughest and most voluble sparring partners in the prolonged discussions about the scope of broadcasting and relations between the BBC and the press.[3] The first agreement made with George Newnes Limited was that profits should be divided on the basis of a scale, at the bottom of the scale two-thirds to Newnes and one-third to the BBC, at the top of the scale on a fifty-fifty basis. Editorial control was in the hands of the publishers, the first editor being Leonard Crocombe, the editor of *Titbits*. The only function of the BBC was to supply to Crocombe programmes and information about programmes through one of its officials, first Burrows and soon afterwards Herbert Parker.

All kinds of opposition to the new venture had to be overcome with a combination of tact and firmness. The radio industry had to be promised that there would be some censorship of advertisements—particularly the advertisement of radio component parts.[4] The wireless press had to be reassured that it was not intended that the *Radio Times* should drive out of business the *Wireless World*, *The Popular Wireless Weekly*, *Modern Wireless*, or

---

[1] *Broadcast Over Britain*, p. 82.   [2] See above, p. 229.
[3] See above, p. 131; *Into the Wind*, pp. 93–94, 114, 128–9, 157, 165, 184.
[4] *Board Minutes, 12 Sept. 1923 and 14 Nov. 1923. W. W. Burnham to Reith, 30 Aug. 1923.

similar periodicals. Although elaborate technical articles were not to be included in the new journal,[1] the opposition of the wireless press grew the more the new journal prospered. The provincial stations did not need to be appeased, but they had to be encouraged. A message from Reith to all Station Directors, dated 27 October 1923, asked for a 'regular supply of photographs, anecdotes, talks, and any other material to make the magazine of the greatest value'.[2]

Crocombe has described the whirl of excitement during the seven days before the publication of the first number of the *Radio Times* on 28 September 1923.[3] There was only a week to think it out, gather it together, and see it through the press. It was at the time a very creditable first number and it remains a worthy historical document. The opening feature was a causerie by the Director of Programmes, 'What's in the Air?'. There was an article on 'The Miracle of Broadcasting' by Sir Ernest Rutherford: this was based on his address as president of the British Association, which had been transmitted simultaneously by six of the main BBC stations a week before. There were 500 words on musical programmes. Uncle Rex (Rex Palmer) had a page to himself called 'The Children's Corner'. The Assistant Chief Engineer gave good but cautiously worded advice on how to choose a wireless set. Peter Eckersley wrote on the problems and opportunities of simultaneous broadcasting. There was an article on Reith 'By One Who Knows Him', and a special message from Lord Gainford, in which he told his readers that he and his colleagues anticipated 'a closer intimacy between our lecturers and artists and their vast unseen audiences by publishing week by week little sketches of the personalities of those who charm, entertain or instruct us through the medium of the mysterious air'. Finally, one of the vast unseen audience, 'P. J.' of Birmingham—it is not known how he was selected— was given the chance to grumble. 'Do they [note the "they"] really think the majority of their "listeners" are really interested in such lectures as the Decrease of Malaria in Great Britain,

[1] *Reith to Brown, 24 Sept. 1923.
[2] *Memorandum from Reith to all Station Directors, 27 Oct. 1923.
[3] L. Crocombe, 'Ten Years Ago: How the First Number of the *Radio Times* was Planned, Put Together and Sent to Press All in Seven Days' in the *Radio Times*, 29 Sept. 1933. See also his article 'How "Radio Times" Began' in the *Radio Times*, 25 Sept. 1953.

How to Become a Veterinary Surgeon—etc? Why is it apparently not thought advisable to repeat the "Request Nights" which are now so popular? Would it not be sufficient to have only one thoroughly classical night a week?'

'Frankly', P. J. concluded, 'it seems to me that the BBC are mainly catering for the "listeners" who own expensive sets and

THE
RADIO TIMES

THE OFFICIAL ORGAN OF THE B.B.C.

Vol. 1. No. 1. [Registered at the G.P.O. as a Newspaper.] EVERY FRIDAY. Two Pence.

OFFICIAL
PROGRAMMES
OF
THE BRITISH
BROADCASTING
COMPANY.

42. The first number of the *Radio Times*

pretend to appreciate and understand only highbrow music and educational "sob stuff". Surely like a theatre manager, they must put up programmes which will appeal to the majority, and we must remember that it is the latter who provide the main bulk of their income.' Thus was the anti-BBC case expressed in the first number of its official journal. The letter inspired a brief reply: 'The B.B.C. is untiring in its efforts to judge the requirements of the majority. Every "listener" is invited to express his opinions freely and the comments are carefully collated.'

The influence of Crocombe can be traced throughout the whole number. There was one article on 'Writers and Wireless' which reflected, if not his own experience, that of many people he knew. Wireless writers, the article reads, were almost universally chosen by editors because they knew nothing about wireless. There was only one way to deal with them—to tire them out with technicalities. Very soon they would be flying the white flag. Crocombe was not only an experienced journalist, but a figure of some importance in the whole story of the development of 'mass communication'. He was editor of *Tit-bits* from 1918 to 1945, and in 1913 he was the editor of the first paper specially published for film fans. He included articles on Writtle in *Titbits* and after pressing Eckersley to allow him to broadcast a programme of his own finally gave a talk from 2LO in March 1923. He wrote in 1933 that in order to maintain his record of moving with the times in mass communication he was awaiting the offer in the near future of the editorship of the *Inter-Planetary News*. Coming from this background, Crocombe nonetheless had a very high opinion of Reith. Long after he had severed his connexion with the *Radio Times* in 1926 he wrote that 'The General Manager (as he then was) proved a tower of strength and an inspiration; always did he appreciate the difficulties one was up against in those experimental days.'[1] He persuaded Reith to write a weekly article, which Reith often complained was 'an awful plague'.[2]

Crocombe's views on the right way to run the *Radio Times* by no means coincided with those of all members of the BBC's staff, nor were the interests of the BBC and of George Newnes Limited always identical. Throughout the whole of 1924 and most of 1925 there were sharp divergencies of opinion. Stobart in particular always expressed the view that the educational matter in the *Radio Times* was completely inadequate. Instead of matters improving, in his opinion they usually got worse. In February 1925, for example, space for reprinting talks was cut down for a second time and they were printed in the smallest possible type. 'This week I was told on the telephone that no space could be found for M. Stephan.'[3] In September 1925 he complained again about the 'continual inadequacy of our official publication'. 'When I first undertook this job', he went on, 'I saw clearly that Wireless Education ought to be reinforced by some sort of printed record. The Managing Director agreed with this in principle. . . . This promise has not been fulfilled.

---

[1] Crocombe, 'Ten Years Ago'.   [2] Diary, 22 Nov. 1923.
[3] *Memorandum by Stobart, 11 Feb. 1925.

... Publicity matter relating to education, when contributed by us, is quite inadequately treated; in fact there has been, instead of the advance promised, a distinct decline in the utility of the *Radio Times* from our point of view.' Less and less did the *Radio Times* represent 'the true aims and methods of our company'. 'I imagine it will always be bought for the sake of the programmes. Can it possibly be argued that anybody buys it for anything else?'[1]

Stobart had allies, and there were suggestions from many quarters in 1924 that the *Radio Times* might be supplemented by additional BBC journals of a more 'highbrow' character. Stobart himself suggested an educational journal to be called 'The Radio Academy'. Eckersley pleaded for a journal where he could include serious technical articles.[2] The Music Department pressed for 'Radio Music', and a dummy of this was actually made up during the summer of 1924. 'No concert organisation would *think* of putting such music [as the B.B.C. chose to transmit] before its audience without explanation', wrote Percy Pitt. 'The present method is like taking a schoolboy to the National Gallery and expecting him to appreciate Velasquez and El Greco. . . . The B.B.C. has led the way in practical organisation of wireless facilities and in quality of programmes, and it should also lead the world in securing attention to its programmes.'[3] All suggestions for further magazines were turned down in 1924, including a suggestion that stations might be allowed to produce station magazines which would include both details of programmes and journalistic features. The reason given was that they might imperil the circulation of the *Radio Times*. Herbert Parker, who succeeded Burrows as liaison officer with Newnes Limited, supported Crocombe's view.

Whilst it is agreed that in every possible way the editorial pages should assist the educational and musical programmes, it should be remembered that if the *Radio Times* is definitely to establish itself as a weekly paper of interest to a large body of the community, apart from the monopoly information its programme pages contain, its appeal must be of a wider nature than a mere anticipation of programme matter will allow. A preponderance of educational matter

---

[1] *Stobart to Gladstone Murray, 21 Sept. 1925.
[2] *Memorandum by Carpendale to Reith, 29 Oct. 1924.
[3] *Undated memorandum from the Music Department.

would considerably weaken the general interest of the ordinary reader. . . . At present the *Radio Times* meets a known demand on the part of the public. To take away much that it now possesses with a view to developing a new paper, which the public have so far not demanded, would be damaging the existing sound property for the purpose of experimenting with one possessed of purely hypothetical chances of success.[1]

When Gladstone Murray took over the job of Director of Publicity in December 1924, he stepped right into the middle of this controversy which was, of course, far from academic. He quickly noted that there seemed to be unanimity on only one point—'dissatisfaction with the obvious limitations of the present *Radio Times*'. The first idea which he himself contributed to the debate was that of an eighty-page *Radio Times* which would serve as 'a great national weekly magazine of the style of production of *The Saturday Evening Post*'.[2] Newnes dismissed this idea as impracticable, and Gladstone Murray set about looking for possible alternative publishers. These negotiations were abortive, and Newnes, which had found the magazine far more profitable than had been anticipated, saw no reason for revolutionary changes. Murray himself quickly came to the conclusion that Newnes's existing publishing and distributive organization was 'so good that we should try to retain it',[3] but he continued to express himself dissatisfied with format, content, and policy. Reith agreed with him, once again stressing the general social and moral value of the *Radio Times*. 'With a more efficient journal really worthy of our service,' he informed Sir Evelyn Murray in April 1925, 'we should have a much stronger link with our listeners, and one which might well be the determining factor in enabling us during 1926 to withstand the attacks of those interests which are already preparing their plans to bring unified control to an end and to commercialise the basis of British Broadcasting.'[4]

At this point the differences between Newnes and the BBC still centred mainly on the basic question of editorial control. They were sharply focused in August 1925 when the London Station

---

[1] *Memorandum by Parker, 15 Sept. 1924.
[2] *Gladstone Murray to Reith, 18 Mar. 1925.
[3] *Gladstone Murray to Reith, 11 June 1925.
[4] *Reith to Sir Evelyn Murray, 20 Apr. 1925.

Executive complained that articles in the *Radio Times* about a radio performer were giving publicity to someone for whom at that stage the BBC did not wish to provide publicity. 'We have constantly to be watching their [artists'] welfare from a publicity point of view, and there are certain people whom we wish to help to become big names on the radio; others to whom it is not policy from a programme standpoint to give publicity at present. . . . The public look on the *Radio Times* as our official paper, and it is a little difficult to tell artists who might query the chance of publicity, that such "puffs" have been given to others by mistake.'[1] From his editor's desk Crocombe rightly challenged this approach, and he was an experienced and responsible editor. Programme publicity should not determine editorial policy. 'We want their co-operation, we want helpful ideas, we want constructive criticisms . . . but the *Radio Times* would fail as a popular journal and as your official organ if it were edited, as the Programme Department seems to think is possible, by a very scattered committee representing various interests.'[2]

While this domestic debate was continuing, the *Radio Times* was subject to more than one challenge from outside. The press, particularly the wireless press, objected strongly to *Radio Times* advertisements, viewing with a jealous eye the appeal of the new mass magazine to prospective advertisers. They had objected to the advertisement of the *Radio Times* itself over the wireless, and the Newspaper Proprietors' Association even expressed alarm that the advertising of the *Radio Times* was merely the prelude 'to larger spheres of advertising, perhaps subtle but none the less effective and competitive'.[3]

This attack on BBC policy reached its height during the hearings of the Crawford Committee.[4] While the wireless press complained that BBC advertising threatened their interests, some sections of the radio industry complained that there was not enough advertising by the BBC. In addition they objected to the cost of the advertisements, claiming that as members of the BBC they were entitled to differential rebates and to low advertising rates in general. Reith notes correctly that the one

[1] *Memorandum from the London Station Executive, 26 Aug. 1925.
[2] *Crocombe to Gladstone Murray, 31 Aug. 1925.
[3] *Memorandum from Gladstone Murray to Reith, 16 Dec. 1924.
[4] See below, pp. 339–43.

occasion between 1922 and 1926 when there was the shadow of
a radio trade versus BBC issue was early in 1926 when some of
the BBC Directors, who represented radio interests, objected to
a proposal he made to raise advertising rates in the *Radio Times*.
They thought that the rates were quite high enough and that
part of the profits accruing from the *Radio Times* should be used
to advertise broadcasting in other journals. Even after the matter had apparently been disposed of at one Board meeting, it
was brought up again at the next.[1] When Reith pointed out that
the manufacturers' suggestions implied that the BBC should
subsidize the trade's advertising and do some of it for them and
that this would be unfair to the BBC, 'nothing more was said'.
'This aberration', Reith comments, 'enhances their credit.'[2]

What with complaints from outside and pressure from inside,
the *Radio Times* was, in Lord Riddell's words, far too often 'dug
up by the roots for examination, refreshment, pruning and
reparation'.[3] To add to the troubles, its circulation fluctuated
more than might be thought likely for a paper of its kind.
Phenomenal business success though it was, its circulation
tended to decline in middle and late summer just at the time
when the BBC was most anxious that it should be sustained.
On one occasion in September 1925 Reith was driven to complain that the paper was 'in a bad way, and something needs
to be done to recover the circulation'.[4] Sales had fallen from
near the 750,000 mark in December 1924 to 610,000 in August
1925. Nor were fluctuations in circulation the only kind of
fluctuation. The number of pages available for the three in-
gredients of the *Radio Times*—editorial comment, programmes,
and advertisements—varied considerably from year to year.
The first few numbers in September 1923 had seven pages of
comment, twelve pages of advertising, and thirteen pages of
programmes. In September 1925 when the number of BBC
stations had greatly increased and the size of the paper had gone
up to fifty pages, ten were devoted to editorial items and nineteen and two-thirds to programmes. Throughout the whole of
1926 there was a 'fight for space'—interminable discussions

[1] Diary, 11 Mar. 1926.
[2] *Into the Wind*, p. 105; Board minutes, 11 Feb., 11 Mar. 1926.
[3] *Riddell to Gladstone Murray, 3 Sept. 1925.
[4] *Reith to Gladstone Murray, 9 Sept. 1925.

about what should be the relative proportions of the three in-
gredients. There were also considerable changes in layout. The
day-to-day grouping of the programmes was abandoned for
station-by-station grouping, and at the end of the year two
editions were produced.

There were far more important changes in the autumn and
winter of 1925–6. A measure of editorial control was secured for
the first time in October 1925 when an 'educational section' of
two pages was taken over directly by the BBC. Even in the
other parts of the paper, wrote Gladstone Murray, who was
appointed BBC joint editor, care would be taken 'to exclude
matter conflicting with the policy or general outlook of our departments'.[1] But this taste of greater power merely served to
quicken appetites. D. C. Thomson, who for a brief time
was called 'Station News Editor' under the new arrangements, stated at once that the chief lesson of the change
was that the *Radio Times* would never be an official organ in
the true sense until 'entire editorial control' rested with the
BBC.[2] P. Darnell, who became sub-editor and liaison officer
between Newnes and the Programme Department—Herbert
Parker had left the BBC in March 1925—was given a full and
precise list of duties, which included 'assembling and putting
together all the material for the news and views pages'. It was
he who put to the Station Directors the case for a greater measure of editorial control, and promised them that under a new
arrangement they would be allocated space to discuss their own
programmes and the ideas that lay behind them. He found the
Station Directors appreciative of the value of the *Radio Times*
as 'a shop window in which they could display the merits of their
goods', but they almost all felt that as a window it was not 'sufficiently attractive'. They felt also that they themselves did not
always know what was happening at the centre. Darnell's
memorandum on his meetings with the Station Directors impressed Reith. 'Have read it all', Reith scribbled in pencil on
the margin. 'Information to Station Directors is highly important and is still deficient.'[3]

---

[1] *Gladstone Murray to Stobart, 23 Sept. 1925; Memorandum to Carpendale,
P. P. Eckersley, Lewis, Stobart, R. H. Eckersley, Palmer, and Fuller, 6 Oct. 1925.
The first number under the new arrangement was published on 9 Oct. 1925.

[2] *D. C. Thomson to Gladstone Murray, 9 Oct. 1925.

[3] *Memorandum by P. Darnell (undated).

Full editorial control was taken over in February 1926.[1] Walter Fuller, who had previously been Managing Editor of the *Weekly Westminster* and had worked at the London Station in 1925, was appointed Editor. He remained in the post until his sudden death in September 1927, when he was replaced by Eric Maschwitz, who had joined him as Managing Editor to tidy up business matters in December 1926. Maschwitz recalls Fuller as 'a vague genius', whose desk was always piled with papers. Once he lost the entire corrected proofs of the *Radio Times* in a tube-train on the way to the printing works.[2] Yet Fuller was the symbol of the transformation. Under his editorship the work of producing the *Radio Times* was delegated to various sub-editors. Thomson was in charge of music, Darnell in charge of news, and Munn (and later H. G. Hodder and N. D. Slatter) in charge of programmes. Hodder, who had previous experience with *The Morning Post*, became Programme Editor in August 1926. Something of the informality was going out of the *Radio Times* as it was already going out of radio, and members of the staff of the Organizer of Programmes had ceased to be part-time sub-editors as they were in the early stages. Work, however, remained hard, there were still administrative difficulties, and circulation did not increase 'with the alacrity anticipated'. What could not be denied was that the new *Radio Times* for the first time was felt to have become a 'conscious auxiliary to the programme service'.[3]

It is interesting to compare the last numbers of the *Radio Times* published under the Company's dispensation with the first numbers which had appeared in 1923. Broadcasting had arrived. There was a friendly informal competition for 'the champion radio village' in July 1926. Stoke Davy in Rutland claimed eleven radios for twelve houses, Wilcote in Oxfordshire a set for every house. A popular radio advertisement for a firm manufacturing valves showed a picture of a contented listener and his wife sitting beside their fireside. Its caption read 'LIFE IS WONDERFUL NOW! The hours and money and temper I wasted on wireless would make *any* man's wife sore with broadcasting. The only piece of humour in the whole affair was the reception

---

[1] The first issue under the new arrangement was 19 Feb. 1926.
[2] E. Maschwitz, *No Chip on My Shoulder* (1957), p. 51.
[3] *Memorandum by Gladstone Murray, 6 Jan. 1927.

I was forced to call "music". *NOW* everything has changed. Our evenings are an endless pleasure.'[1] The advertisement was allegorical. This was how many people felt.

The first article in the *Radio Times* was usually mildly propagandist in character. It might have a title like 'The Healing Power of Radio', 'Salute to the Microphone', or 'Radio in the Changing Home', and it would often be written by a well-known author. The programmes were annotated with useful notes. This innovation was warmly appreciated, particularly by listeners to serious music. Correspondents were still given the opportunity freely to criticize programmes, and if the criticisms were often repetitive or similar, this was because there were the same recurring divisions of opinion from one year to another. In addition to the *Radio Times*, the BBC published a *Radio Supplement* which dealt with the foreign programmes that BBC listeners were now encouraged to hear. This supplement was first published in July 1925; and in June 1926 it changed its name to *World Radio*. In 1926 the Christmas Supplement of the *Radio Times* itself had a modern Christmas-number cover by McKnight Kauffer instead of 'the kiddies-round-the-loudspeaker' type of cover which had been designed in previous years. Newnes opposed the new cover and prophesied that the Christmas number would not sell. In fact it sold better than any previous Christmas number had done.

Not only was there a change in editorial control in February 1926. The business arrangement was changed also. The agreement made with Newnes in September 1923 was superseded by a new agreement signed on 27 January 1926. The profit-sharing basis of the partnership was abandoned, and the BBC promised instead to pay to the publishers a commission on net receipts from sales and advertisements. The revised arrangement greatly benefited the BBC, which, as we have seen, was able to put aside for general expenditure substantial sums raised as profits from the *Radio Times*.

At the end of 1926 Gladstone Murray was in charge of a number of 'information' departments each with direction and staff of its own. They included not only the *Radio Times* and *World Radio* but press, publications management, intelligence, 'lectures, photographs, and visitors', and 'district liaison'. The

[1] *Radio Times*, 2 Oct. 1925, p. 89.

tendency to increased departmentalization can be well illustrated from one of these departments alone, that concerned
with publications management. It had a committee, which met
for the first time on 6 October 1926, and it was concerned with
quite a wide range of activities. Its chairman was R. Gambier
Parry (later Brigadier Sir Richard Gambier Parry) who had
joined the BBC on 5 January 1926, and two of its four members
were to have influential careers in the new Corporation.
One was B. E. Nicolls, who had passed through almost every
branch of administration, beginning in Manchester; the
other was C. G. Graves, who did not join the BBC until July
1926. Both were to become 'knights of broadcasting'. But not all
the projects of the Publications Committee were successfully
executed. At the second meeting there was a discussion about
producing a book to be called *Four Years of Broadcasting*; it
would describe the life and times of the Company while the experience was still fresh and the people were still on the spot. This
book never appeared. Had it done so, much of the research for
this present volume would have been greatly simplified.

5. Facing the World

No book would have been complete—even in 1926—unless it
had sketched in the development of wireless in other parts of
the world. In 1922 it was the United States which had led the
way in the broadcasting 'boom': in 1925 and 1926 the number
of broadcasting stations in Europe rapidly increased. 'Chaos in
America' had provided a warning to the British in 1922: the fear
of 'chaos in Europe' in 1925 and 1926 encouraged Britain to take
a lead in organizing the international control of broadcasting.
Technical questions were basic, but other issues also made for
international discussion and agreement. One was the vexed
question of copyright, which was not settled by the courts in
the period covered in this volume; another was the recognition
that although broadcasting systems were national, part of the

radio audience was international. There were possibilities of sharing 'the ether' in the interests of the listener.

Broadcast messages were exchanged between the BBC and the United States in November 1923—with Marconi, Reith, and Georges Carpentier participating. A year later in November 1924 the BBC relayed to all its listeners a programme from the Brussels radio station. In September 1925 the presidential address to the League of Nations Assembly was broadcast from Geneva. The international implications of broadcasting were being talked about as they had never been talked about before. The League of Nations and the broadcaster were felt to share the same ideals. As Marconi himself put it, echoing his words of more than twenty years before,[1] 'Communication between peoples widely separated in space and thought is undoubtedly the greatest weapon against the evils of misunderstanding and jealousy, and if my fundamental invention goes some way towards averting the evils of war I shall not feel that I have lived in vain.'[2]

This was high-sounding language. The greatest spur to international agreement about the use of radio was not idealism but self-interest. As the number of radio stations in Europe multiplied, the convenience and comfort of the listener were seriously disturbed. It became apparent that if the radio stations, even stations of low power, operated on the same wavelength or on wavelengths very close to each other, there was liable to be very severe mutual interference in the service area of each station. This interference took the form of the heterodyne whistle, a high-pitched note of 'variable pitch and uncomfortable intensity',[3] and listeners everywhere had an interest in ensuring that wavelengths were allotted by international agreement instead of being left to individual countries or radio companies to exploit as they wished.

It was not until March 1925 that an appropriate international regulating agency was founded and a year later that international agreement on wavelengths was reached. Long before March 1925, however, feelers were put out about possible international arrangements. The first feelers were concerned with wireless in general rather than with broadcasting. In December 1923

---

[1] See above, p. 25.
[2] *The Popular Wireless Weekly*, Jan. 1924.
[3] P. P. Eckersley, *The Power Behind the Microphone*, p. 81.

Carpendale was informed that 'a small committee of experts' meeting the previous month in Geneva had suggested that an International Wireless Conference should be held in 1924 under the auspices of the League of Nations. Not only governments but private undertakings would be invited to attend. F. J. Brown was a member of this 'small committee', which had apparently met for the first time in London in July 1923. Reith was told by Brown that he did not believe the BBC need be represented at the conference, which would not primarily be concerned with broadcasting. Brown stood by this opinion even after Reith wrote to him that 'there is an increasing international aspect in broadcasting'.[1] The Post Office view, as on so many other questions, was expressed in the phrase, 'we cannot commit ourselves at present'.[2] In fact, no League of Nations Conference was held in 1924. And some of the delegates to the League Assembly complained of the failure to convene it. Dr. Nansen, for example, warned that the rapid development of broadcasting services was 'threatening a species of anarchy in the ether'. 'An international wave-length conference is absolutely necessary, and the League of Nations is the body best qualified to carry this through.'[3]

While the League failed, other private interests—some of them located in Geneva—tried to succeed. In February 1924 Lewis received a letter from an official of the Compagnie Française de Radiophonie in Paris about the formation of an international committee—'le Comité International de la T.S.F.'. A month later Reith himself was invited to send BBC representatives to an international conference in Geneva to be sponsored by a Swiss organization, which was as much interested in Esperanto as an international language as in broadcasting itself. Although Reith was informed by a representative of the Marconi Company, who had been in Geneva, that the sponsors of the conference believed that 'if only the BBC could be induced to send out representatives the success of the whole venture would be assured', he decided not to participate. He had no sympathy with the Esperantists and little confidence that the sponsors were the right people to enforce 'order in the

---

[1] *Reith to Brown, 22 Jan. 1924.
[2] *Brown to Reith, 24 Jan. 1924.
[3] *Undated note, 'Anarchy in the Ether'.

ether'. In a pencilled note in the margin of the letter of invitation to the conference, he wrote against one of the references to Esperanto, 'why not spread British thought in English or French which are increasingly understood?'; in a letter to Brown, asking for advice, he expressed the more important objection that 'it is apparently an unofficial conference, so they can only make recommendations, as wavelengths are matters for government sanction'. He wrote formally to Geneva that since there was in existence a 'committee of experts' discussing wavelengths, as there then was, he saw no reason to send BBC representatives to Geneva.[1]

The Geneva Conference of April 1924 was held, therefore, without BBC participation. It was opened by the president of the government of the Canton of Geneva and presided over by a Dutch radio engineer. Thirty-nine organizations were represented. The president of the Swiss Radio-Electric Society, J. Rambert, the man who had corresponded with Reith, was the chief speaker: he described how 'a completely new world had been brought into being by wireless telephony' and went on to advocate the creation of a new organization to regulate it. 'Geneva, which tends to become a centre of internationalism, is best fitted for this first interchange of ideas.' There was a British representative of the magazine *Wireless World* at the conference: like many of the other speakers, he addressed the conference in Esperanto. The most important person present was the Director of the Communications Section of the League of Nations. Little emphasis was placed on technical questions, but when the conference ended the BBC was once again approached to join.

There was a general wish to establish a centre between broadcasting stations for the purpose of exchanging time tables, useful information and suggestions as to common interests. Before taking any steps in this matter, we should like very much to know your opinion on the whole plan and under what form your Company, which plays such an important part in Europe, would be ready to support the proposed organisation. Should it be a union of the broadcasting stations, or only an international office with contributing supporters?

After some delay, Reith replied that the BBC was in general

[1] All these letters are in BBC Archives.

'sympathetic towards the Geneva proposals'. At the same time it wanted to place most emphasis on allocation of wavelengths. This matter was already being discussed at an official level, the appropriate level at which decisions could be reached. A meeting had already been held at the Post Office on 28 May 1924, at which Eckersley had been present. It had been called by Brown to discuss 'the international status of wireless broadcasting', and besides representatives of the Post Office and the BBC there were present serving officers, including the Chairman of the Wireless Sub-Committee of the Imperial Communications Committee, and spokesmen of some of the biggest commercial radio interests. This committee had made definite proposals about wavelengths, which it intended to submit to foreign governments. The most important of the proposals was that the wave-band of 300 to 500 metres should be made an international wavelength for the exclusive use of broadcasting. Eckersley had hailed this proposal as a triumph of broadcasting interests over other radio interests and had described the fact that the British government was willing to make the proposal internationally as 'a considerable feather in our cap'. Neither he nor Reith wished to prejudice international acceptance of this proposal by premature discussions with 'unofficial' bodies.

At the same time they saw that if the principle of this exclusive wave-band were generally accepted, the next step would obviously be 'to allot wavelengths between the various European stations so that between these wavelengths there should be no overlapping among broadcasting stations throughout Europe'. It would be a good idea, therefore, if an international meeting could be held as soon as possible. 'This Conference should be fully representative, and we think that it should be a union of all broadcasting stations, not solely an international office with contributing supporters.'[1]

In September 1924 J. Rambert visited London and was shown round the BBC: he said that he was greatly impressed by the BBC as an organization and hoped that the Swiss would use it as a model in their own broadcasting ventures.[2] During the late summer and autumn of 1924 Reith became convinced that some kind of international organization was urgently necessary.

[1] *Reith to Rambert, 2 July 1924.
[2] *Rambert to Reith, 11 Oct. 1924.

On 1 August he wrote in his diary that there was need for a 'broadcasting association' to examine copyright questions 'and promote the interests of broadcasting generally'.[1] He told Rice to prepare notes on the subject, and discussed it thoroughly with Sir William Bull. On 26 September he prepared a letter to go out to other broadcasting companies in various parts of the world.

The scope and influence of broadcasting [he wrote] are already recognized . . . [and] problems quite peculiar and unique present themselves in the course of the direction of this new art-science. There are many questions on which, we believe, an interchange of views would be helpful. These include the questions of wavelengths, relaying, the interchange of programmes, and licensing. Apart from the definite points enumerated above, we submit that broadcasting in its natural development tends to become an international responsibility, and that it is incumbent on those who direct it to adopt every possible means of co-operation and mutual support, and with this end in view we believe it would be desirable to consider establishing an Association of Broadcasters with perhaps an International Broadcasting Bureau.[2]

He suggested that a conference should be held in London: it should meet on the first of December 1924, and Gainford would preside. Reith secured Rambert's approval of this change in plans at their meeting in London in September.

Events moved slowly and cumbrously, however, and there was a rift between the Swiss and the British which led to much bickering and uneasiness. Having proposed the conference, the BBC had to suggest in October 1924 that the conference should be postponed until the following spring. The reason given for the delay was the need to bring in as many broadcasting interests as possible. It seemed likely that there would be an International Radio-Telegraphic Convention in Washington the following year, and Reith was particularly anxious to strengthen the 'broadcasting interest' by winning the support of the Americans. The Swiss were not impressed with the idea of postponing the conference. Nor were they impressed when Reith proposed that the conference might be held neither in London nor in Geneva but in Paris. They asked instead—with

[1] Diary, 1 Aug. 1924.   *Draft of 26 Sept. 1924.

considerable French support—for a Geneva conference in January
or February 1925.

Their enthusiasm for a conference in Geneva as soon as
possible was not reciprocated in London. Not only did Reith
become increasingly anxious to create a world organization as
distinct from a European organization, but the Post Office,
which he had to consult, was extremely cautious.

I do not think that we would raise any objection to your Company
summoning . . . a Conference [Brown wrote to Reith in December
1924] provided that its scope was clearly defined. We cannot give
you a definite assurance that your Company will be invited to the
International Radio Telegraphic Conference in Washington, but we
propose to lay the facts before the Imperial Communications Committee with a view to their taking action towards this end when the
time is ripe.[1]

There was a long delay before the BBC replied to the pressing
invitation from the Swiss to say whether they would or would
not attend a conference in Geneva at the beginning of February
1925. Finally, a fortnight before the conference was scheduled
to begin, the reply was sent that 'we shall not seek representation at the Conference this year, partly on account of extreme
pressure of business here and partly because we feel that at the
present moment the time is not quite ripe for the kind of Conference which you desire'.[2]

The Swiss offered to change the date to March, and later
shifted it to 3 April. Again the BBC refused the invitation.
Leaving the American question on one side, Reith was genuinely
convinced that unless 'the big concerns' in European broadcasting were represented at the conference it would be of no
value. His pragmatism contrasted sharply with the enthusiasm
of the Swiss. They were very upset, therefore, when the BBC,
having refused to go to Geneva, decided at the end of January to
summon a conference in London for 18 March 1925—without
consulting them about this intention. Moreover one of the items
on the agenda was the creation of an international bureau for
broadcasting, which had already been proposed at the Geneva
Conference of the previous April when no BBC representative

---

[1] *Brown to Reith, 20 Dec. 1924. The first International Conference on Radio
Telegraphy was held in 1906, see above, p. 33.
[2] *Reith to Rambert, 14 Jan. 1925.

had been present. The lines between Geneva and London were becoming tangled, and there were obvious dangers at this time of what Rambert described as 'a useless split' in the international organization of broadcasting.[1] Somewhat surprisingly, there was to be no split. The London Conference created the first international broadcasting organization, the Union Internationale de Radiophonie, and the headquarters of the new organization were located in Geneva.

Delegates from ten countries attended the 'informal' London Conference at No. 2 Savoy Hill on 18 and 19 March 1925. Rambert had decided to attend, constituting what Reith described as 'a sort of opposition',[2] but the scales were weighted in favour of the BBC not only as the host but as the biggest and most powerful broadcasting concern in Europe. As the Czech delegate put it, the BBC was 'the pioneer in this field—with great experience', and it should be left to the BBC to suggest the pattern of organization for a new Bureau.[3] It was eventually decided that the U.I.R. should be founded, that a permanent Bureau should be set up in Geneva, and that Arthur Burrows should be its first Secretary-General. Reith made it clear what kind of man he expected the Secretary-General to be. He must be a 'live man', who at the same time would not exceed his authority, a man who would not make work but would do what was necessary. He must not try to set up 'an enormous organization to keep himself and his satellites in work—which is always rather a danger of bureaux'. Eckersley stressed the technical side of the work of the Bureau. 'The interference which unfortunately goes on a good deal today should be eliminated by one central person who views the problem of Europe as one concrete whole and not as an insular one.'

Other matters discussed were copyright and the exchange of programmes. On the latter Eckersley said that he thought the exchange of programmes in Europe would add enormously to the interest of broadcasting in all countries. The question still remained, however—what was the best way to do it? The BBC broadcast from Brussels in 1924 had shown how many difficulties

---

[1] *Rambert to Reith, 15 Feb. 1925.
[2] Diary, 18 Mar. 1925.
[3] *Minutes of an informal International Conference convened by the BBC on Wednesday, 18 Mar. and Thursday, 19 Mar. 1925.

confronted engineers who were concerned with 'the appalling art of wireless . . . the most inefficient game in the world'. The same difficulties continued in 1925. When in June the Post Office drew the attention of the BBC to a question about to be asked in the House of Commons as to why the BBC did not provide more foreign relays 'to bring the peoples of nations into closer communication', Reith replied that reception was still too bad to make the practice of relaying satisfactory. 'In view of the prominent part we have taken in the recent formation of the International Broadcasting Bureau at Geneva,' he added, 'we hope that the occasional interchange of programmes as between this country and the continent will not be long delayed.'[1]

The constitution of the U.I.R. was drafted in Geneva on 3 April and 4 April 1925. It was then decided that Carpendale should be the first president. He continued to be elected to the office time and time again—in defiance of the constitution—as long as he remained with the BBC. This was another sign of the influence which the BBC exerted within the new organization. The international significance of the BBC was further recognized in July 1925 when David Sarnoff, the titan of American broadcasting, first visited the BBC. 'I believe', Reith wrote too optimistically in his diary, 'that the States are shaping to our system.'[2]

The detailed history of the U.I.R. falls outside the scope of this study. Yet the technical work of the new organization is strictly relevant. At the Geneva Conference in April 1925 it had been decided to form a committee of technical representatives of European broadcasting organizations to draw up a plan to allot wavelengths among sixteen different countries. A meeting of this committee was held at Geneva in July 1925, when it was decided to carry out tests—particularly to establish what could be regarded as the minimum separation between the wavelengths of two adjacent stations. At a further meeting in September 1925 the results of the tests were examined and it was decided to establish a permanent technical committee of the U.I.R. 'to advise the Council on purely technical matters'. The members agreed, first, that the wave-band of 300 to 500 metres, which had been allotted exclusively to broadcasting, was

[1] *Reith to Phillips, 19 June 1923.
[2] Diary, 15 July 1925.

quite inadequate, given merely the number of existing stations; and, second, that 'interference would not cease unless there was complete international agreement for the allocation of wave-lengths'. There was only one possible corollary. 'Certain countries having a large number of wavelengths will have to sacrifice their claims in order to provide channels for countries having none.' At this point agreement always broke down. Detailed proposals drawn up by Eckersley were defeated in September 1925 largely as a result of opposition from the French. Their juridical approach to the international question of broadcasting had nothing in common with the 'functional' approach of the British. This difference was never fully resolved. It bedevilled the later history of the U.I.R.—'a struggle', as Eckersley saw it, 'between realist technicians and those who had legal principles'. The more he talked of the 'ineluctable rights' of anarchy, the more his opponents murmured, *en principe, mais. . . .*[1]

That a measure of agreement was reached in 1925 and 1926 was due to the intervention of a Frenchman, Raymond Braillard, who had made his home in Belgium and was the chief technical expert of Belgian radio. His unusual combination of intelligence and patience was irresistible. 'Braillard seduces his opponents,' Eckersley has written, 'very sound, very eloquent, he stays immovably charming, persuading and cajoling. He is both a master of statistics and analogy. In rare crises he throws off his charm and puts on his indignant act which, being French, he does wonderfully.'[2] The two men worked closely together and evolved a new scheme whereby a number of wavelengths were allotted to each country according to a formula which took account of area, population, and the volume of telephone and telegraph traffic. The formula was accepted first by the French and later, in December 1925, by the Council of the U.I.R. as a whole. Braillard and Eckersley used it as a guide rather than an obligatory injunction.

Further experiments began early in 1926. They were designed not only to test the effects of the rationing of wavelengths but the efficacy in practice of a distinction between two categories of wavelengths—the first, exclusive wavelengths which could be used by one station only and which were to be separated from each other at a frequency interval of 10 kilocycles; the second,

[1] Eckersley, op. cit., p. 26.   [2] Ibid. pp. 90–91.

'ordinary' or 'common' wavelengths which could be repeated several times. The exclusive wavelengths were to be distributed according to the formula; the 'common' wavelengths should be reserved for low-power stations of $\frac{1}{2}$ kilowatt or less. The wavelengths of stations which had been in existence longest should be given the greatest measure of priority in wavelength rationing, and each country should be given the use of at least one wavelength above 250 metres. A committee of technical experts, presided over by Braillard, was to work out a plan along these lines and decide whether it was technically feasible.

The so-called 'Geneva Plan' was the result of this initiative. It was drafted in outline in 1925, prepared in detail during the early months of 1926, and accepted by the Council of the U.I.R. in July 1926. For technical reasons, however, the date of operating the plan had to be postponed twice, first from September to October and then from October to 14 November. The reason at this stage was not lack of goodwill but inadequate 'international wave meters to ensure the maximum of success for the plan'.[1] The countries which agreed to participate in it were Austria, Belgium, Czechoslovakia, Denmark, Finland, France, Germany, Great Britain, Holland, Hungary, Ireland, Italy, Norway, Spain, Sweden, and Switzerland. Each country had, of course, to submit its 'allocation' to its national government for approval.

Before the plan came into effect, the BBC had been using twenty medium wavelengths, some shared with other countries, and one long wavelength. It was now allotted one long wavelength, ten exclusive medium wavelengths, and five 'common' wavelengths below 300 metres. This kind of 'allocation' had been discussed in principle with the Post Office as early as July 1925, when it had provoked strong opposition, particularly from the Services. Although Reith had then explained that it was for the sake of winning international agreement about control of the air that the BBC asked the Post Office to approve the extension of the broadcasting wave-band, the Post Office had not responded favourably. 'We as a Company', Reith said, 'do not desire greatly the expansion of the present national waveband, but it would stultify any sort of international agreement which

[1] P. P. Eckersley, 'Britain's New Wave Lengths', in the *Radio Times*, 12 Nov. 1926.

must come about should we not be prepared to make concessions. . . . There are over 130 stations wishing to transmit
between 300 and 500 metres, and it is obvious that without
mutual concessions chaos is bound to supervene.'[1] The matter
was considered by the Wireless Sub-Committe of the Imperial
Communications Committee, when Eckersley was present. In
the light of his arguments, the sub-committee agreed to the extension of the broadcasting waveband and the allocation of
wavelengths of less than 300 metres to the low-power local relay

43. 'They catch the waves and measure their lengths.'

stations. The Services continued their objections, however, and
the Postmaster-General ruled on 25 July 1925 that 'no extension
of the broadcasting band in this country can be authorised'.[2]

Parallel to the difficult international negotiations in Geneva
between the summer of 1925 and the autumn of 1926, the BBC
was thus engaged in its own difficult negotiations with the Post
Office in London. Experimental use of waves below 300 metres
was reluctantly conceded in August 1925, and on 21 September
four low-power relay stations—Bradford, Nottingham, Stoke,
and Sheffield—were allowed to broadcast on these low wavelengths. 'The Postmaster-General sees no objection to this concession being announced by the Company's representative at
the Geneva Conference', the BBC was told, 'provided that concurrence should be withheld unless other countries are making

[1] *Reith to Sir Evelyn Murray, 16 July 1925.
[2] *Dalzell to Reith, 29 July 1925.

equal concessions with the full consent and authority of their respective governments.'[1] The Services had yielded. Perhaps they had found it impossible to resist the undoubted force of Reith's argument that if Britain was not to be allowed to use a limited number of wavelengths for low-power inland stations, other countries would undoubtedly occupy these wavelengths, probably with stations of far greater power, which would cause far more interference to Services' broadcasting than Bradford, Nottingham, Stoke, and Sheffield.[2] This was Reith's second victory over the Services in the autumn of 1925. They had asked the BBC to suspend all broadcasts from Daventry station during army and air force manœuvres from 6 a.m. on 22 September to 6 p.m. on 25 September. Once again Reith found the right argument for the occasion. 'The Daventry transmissions are already received directly by a large number of listeners on the Continent. . . . We suggest that the suspension of the transmissions from Daventry for three whole days . . . must tend to create an unfortunate impression abroad. . . . It is submitted that the reputation of the Technical Service will not be improved by the tacit admission of their inability to receive [messages] while Daventry is transmitting.'[3]

The Post Office itself fought a dogged rearguard action in 1926. Although Reith and Carpendale assured the Post Office that 'it would have been impossible to secure a better bargain' than had been secured at Geneva,[4] the Post Office pressed the BBC to try as hard as possible to arrange that low-power stations should share the same single wavelength below 300 metres. And when it was recommended that the Birmingham station, which was a main station and not a low-power relay station, should employ a wavelength of 288 metres, the Post Office flatly replied that it would have to operate as before within the 300 to 500 metre band.[5] What could Reith do? He had already urged that permission should not be withheld 'since our position on the Continent will be almost untenable if we, practically alone among nations, are not allowed to make

[1] *Dalzell to Reith, 21 Sept. 1925.
[2] *Reith to Sir Evelyn Murray, 11 Sept. 1925.
[3] *Reith to Sir Evelyn Murray, 28 Aug. 1925. The Post Office replied, giving way to Reith's request, on 10 Sept.
[4] *Carpendale to Dalzell, 24 Apr. 1926.
[5] *Sir Evelyn Murray to Reith, 26 Apr. 1926.

the necessary concessions'.[1] All he could do was to reiterate this case.

It is this desire on the part of all European broadcasting organizations to crowd stations into the 300–500 metre wave band that has been the stumbling block in our negotiations, and we are not a little satisfied in having been able to achieve a solution with but one British main station outside these limits. Suppose now, we, as practically the leading spirits in trying to achieve a just settlement of claims for wavelengths, re-open negotiations on the basis of requiring another wavelength between 300 and 500 metres, we shall quite possibly upset the whole agreement so painstakingly achieved.[2]

Once again the Post Office yielded reluctantly, allowing Birmingham to operate on 288.5 metres 'on the understanding that the question of its continued use will be subject to reconsideration from time to time'.[3] With this concession, there were no official obstacles to the British implementation of the Geneva plan.

All that was left to do was to 'sell' it to the listener, and this Eckersley did in a number of interesting articles in the *Radio Times*. He had his public and he knew how to influence it. He warned some listeners, particularly those who lived in the Aberdeen, Newcastle, and Bournemouth areas, that they might be worse off under the new system, and other listeners in other parts of the country that they would have to retune their receivers. Listeners in London, Cardiff, Glasgow, and Manchester, however, would find no change in the service, and listeners everywhere would benefit from the increased effectiveness of Daventry. The distant listener would benefit at the expense of the local listener. The change was made with an eye to the future. 'To leave European broadcasting to expand unchecked along its present lines would be to court final disaster. Just as an apple tree allowed to grow unpruned produces in the end worse fruit, so broadcasting allowed to expand unchecked will in the end react unfavourably upon the service. Early pruning is essential now if the future of European broadcasting, and with it British broadcasting, of course, is to be assured.'[4]

---

[1] *Reith to Sir Evelyn Murray, 14 Apr. 1926.
[2] *Reith to Sir Evelyn Murray, 4 May 1926.
[3] *Murray to Reith, 26 May 1926.
[4] *Radio Times*, 12 Nov. 1926.

Once again the contrast between the British situation and that in the United States stands out. The BBC had played the most important part in ensuring that not only in Britain but in Europe as a whole there should be no 'chaos of the waves'. It was not until 1927 that the United States Congress passed the Radio Act, which brought into existence the Federal Radio Commission.[1] Despite all the difficulties implicit in European international relations, Europe, one year earlier than the United States, had drafted a plan which if not the best which might have been achieved was certainly the least objectionable.[2] It was a point of departure, an invitation to continue discussion, to modify and to evolve as European broadcasting developed in the future.

Agreement about it certainly strengthened the hands of the 'broadcasting interest' at the Third Radio-Telegraphic Convention in Washington, which was eventually held in the autumn of 1927. Between the drafting of the final agreement and the Washington Conference, broadcasters of the world set about the far from easy task of uniting to protect and extend their influence. There were talks in Paris, and discussions with the Radio Corporation of America. One of the ambitions of Reith and Eckersley had been achieved: they had 'united' Europe on a practical base, and had done it without losing sight of the rest of the world.

Another of Reith's international ambitions was to develop Empire broadcasting. The realization of this ambition falls outside the period covered in this present volume, but the ambition itself had taken definite shape in 1925 and 1926. In addressing the London Conference of March 1925 which created the U.I.R. Reith told the delegates that Britain thought of the regulation of broadcasting not as a European but as a world problem, partly because of the importance of the American broadcasting interest, partly because 'all our colonial concerns are now looking to us to suggest something from which they will benefit'.[3] At the opening of the Daventry station the Postmaster-General

---

[1] See above, p. 67. There is a tidy account of the American situation in C. A. Siepmann, *Radio and Television*, Part I, ch. i, 'Radio in the U.S., Early History 1920–34'.

[2] Report of Braillard to the Council of the U.I.R., 28 June 1926.

[3] *Minutes of an informal International Conference . . . 18 and 19 Mar. 1925.

referred to the development of commercial radio links between Britain, Canada, South Africa, Australia, and India. The Imperial Wireless Telegraphy Committee had recommended in 1924 that effective radio links should be forged between the different countries of the Empire, and the Post Office proceeded with the building of a high-powered long-wave valve transmitting station at Rugby. This was opened for telegraphic transmission on 1 January 1926 and for short-wave telephonic communication with America later in the same year.

Some Colonies and Dominions had themselves started broadcasting before the end of 1926. They included Ceylon, where news and share prices as well as music and talks were being broadcast in 1925,[1] and the municipality of Durban in South Africa, which in October 1924 appointed as its first Station Superintendent G. C. (later Sir Gerald) Beadle, who had joined the BBC in September 1923 and later became Director of BBC Television Broadcasting. A suggestion that the BBC should be directly associated with South African broadcasting had to be turned down because it 'was outside the powers conferred by the BBC Licence'.[2] Nevertheless Reith was responsible for Beadle's appointment in Durban and, once there, Beadle pressed hard for regular relays from Britain. 'You can well imagine', he wrote in April 1926, 'that relays from England, even if they were imperfect technically, would give a tremendous fillip to South African broadcasting.'[3]

Reith was anxious even before Beadle went to Durban to establish close broadcasting links with India. He discussed this subject with Colonel Simpson of the Marconi Company as early as November 1923: 'I should like', he wrote, 'to organise Indian broadcasting from here.'[4] In 1924 after consulting the Board, he approached the India Office on this subject, and in 1925 the Viceroy.[5] He failed. 'There is neither vision', he wrote in his diary, 'nor recognition of the immense potentialities of broadcasting: no ethical or moral appreciation; just commercialism. It is an unparalleled opportunity for service in India, but they

---

[1] Questions on the subject were asked in the House of Commons for the first time in July 1925. *Hansard*, vol. 187, col. 657, 30 July 1925.
[2] *Board Minutes, 14 Nov. 1923.
[3] *Beadle to Reith, 6 Apr. 1926.
[4] Diary, 27 Nov. 1923.
[5] *Into the Wind*, p. 113; Board Minutes, 13 Mar. 1924.

have let the chance go.'[1] Reith was not the only person in the BBC to consider the immense potentialities in India and elsewhere. A memorandum of May 1926 discussed both potentialities and problems: it suggested, among other devices, the 'bottling'—that is to say, the recording—of programmes.

Development of Empire broadcasting was held back before the end of 1926 for both technical and financial reasons. Permission was granted the BBC by the Post Office in May 1926 to set up an experimental short-wave wireless telephony station at Daventry, using power of up to 20 kilowatts, 'to ascertain how far it would be possible—if such a course were found to be desirable—to establish a wireless link for the purpose of transmitting British programmes to the Dominions and Colonies'. Eckersley moved cautiously and deliberately, being compelled to give priority to medium-wave experiments. He did not wish Empire broadcasting to be thought of as an affair of 'stunts' and surprises, but rather as a regular service, properly endowed and efficiently managed. By the time that experiments did begin in November 1927—not from Daventry but from Chelmsford— the BBC could rightly claim, as Reith put it, that the organization was 'in touch with what was happening in pretty well every corner of the world'.[2]

It was certainly known throughout the world as the outstanding institution in broadcasting. As early as October 1923 a Swedish official had been attached to it for training. By 1925 there was a regular stream of visitors, many of them distinguished and influential in their own countries. Almost every writer of books on broadcasting from every country went out of his way to praise what Reith had achieved. 'Favourable reports are heard from all sides concerning the British system', wrote an American professor in 1925. The chief of its advantages was 'the reduction of waste through the elimination of interference, the ability of stations to operate at full capacity, and the proper distribution of broadcasting facilities'.[3]

[1] Diary, 10 Apr. 1925.
[2] *Reith to Lord Clarendon, 29 Apr. 1927.
[3] H. L. Jome, *Economics of the Radio Industry* (Chicago, 1925), p. 245.

VI

FROM COMPANY TO CORPORATION
1925–6

It has been estimated that the growth of
National Institutions is commonly measured
in terms of decades or even centuries. The
Directors of the British Broadcasting Company have had the stewardship of a great public service for only four years, during which
time broadcasting has emerged from nothing
to the position it occupies today — an accepted and essential part of the machinery of
civilization.

LORD GAINFORD
in the *Radio Times*, 24 December 1926

1. The Crawford Committee

THE praise bestowed on the BBC was not showered so universally on the Post Office. 'The attitude of the Post Office towards wireless, in its imperial as well as its domestic aspects,' commented the *Daily Telegraph* in March 1925, 'illustrates very effectively the dangers associated with the nationalisation of industry, and especially an industry of scientific character still in process of development.'[1] Reference was also made to its 'cold, official stereotyped system', which was contrasted with the dynamics of enterprise.

The BBC did not share the burden of this attack, because whatever criticisms could be levied against it, there could be no complaint of lack of enterprise. When Reith gave evidence before the Crawford Committee he emphasized that the success of the Company had depended largely on the choice of men who were capable, possessed plenty of imagination, felt a sense of adventure, and, not least, were endowed with a superabundance of energy. Lord Blanesburgh, a member of the committee, who was anxious to retain the existing company structure, asked him frankly whether this success could be maintained if there were substituted for 'the present shareholding interest' in the company, 'the State or some other body of persons who can derive no profit directly or indirectly from the success of broadcasting'. Reith replied equally frankly that from his experience of the previous three years, 'the idealism and energy and enthusiasm of the staff would carry them through any change of organisation whatsoever, save only this, that we might have imposed upon us such restrictions, if we were to become a Government Department, that it would be impossible by any action or persistency of action on our part to rid ourselves of them. Save only that, I would suggest that the enthusiasm of the present staff would survive any change of constitution whatsoever.'[2]

Reith had long made up his mind that the BBC should be

---

[1] *Daily Telegraph*, 10 Mar. 1925.
[2] *Oral evidence of Reith to the Crawford Committee, 4 Feb. 1926.

both a public institution and an independent institution, as free as possible from interference both by business and by government. He did not consider that service and enterprise were in any way incompatible. Indeed, he went out of his way to show how much care he had taken to further both.

The remarkable fact was that the Post Office completely shared Reith's views on the nature of a future constitution for the BBC. At the beginning of their investigations in November 1925 the members of the Crawford Committee were presented with a memorandum on broadcasting by Sir Evelyn Murray. It upheld the case for what Reith called 'unified control',[1] rejected the opinion that broadcasting should be left to the Post Office or some other government department, and suggested that the best solution might be the setting up of a corporation with a widely representative governing body. The new authority, it went on, could be incorporated by Charter, under the Companies Act, or by Statute. It was Murray and not Reith who stated categorically that 'the Corporation should enjoy a large measure of independence and should not be subject either in its general policy or its choice of programmes to the detailed control and supervision of the Postmaster-General, from which would follow the corollary that the Postmaster-General would not be expected to accept responsibility or to defend the proceedings of the Corporation in Parliament'.[2]

This Post Office document was of fundamental importance, and Sir Evelyn Murray in his evidence to the Crawford Committee merely elucidated its recommendations. He was the first witness examined, and what he said set the tone of the whole of the later proceedings.

The recommendations of the Crawford Committee followed the same lines as these recommendations of Murray, and Murray's recommendations followed the same lines as the thought of Reith, as expressed in his speeches and his writings. If only for this reason, there is far less excitement about the work of the Crawford Committee than about the work of the Sykes Committee. Then, there was an element of doubt: now, there is none. Everything seems to be moving to a predetermined end. Almost all the witnesses before the Crawford Committee,

[1] See above, p. 182.
[2] *Sir Evelyn Murray's Memorandum to the Crawford Committee, para. 27.

however different the interests they represent, generally agree that there shall be a single broadcasting authority subject not to trade but to public control.

Only one man could have effectively challenged this view—Reith himself. Had he urged that the future of broadcasting should remain in trade hands, with the BBC being governed by a similar constitution to that then in being, he might well have won his case. 'I am quite sure', he wrote in his diary in February 1926, 'that if I had been categorically in favour of a continuation of the Company, this would have been achieved.'[1] But instead he was categorically in favour of a public constitution, and there was no one—least of all the members of his own Board—who would or could effectively challenge him. Even the handful of his critics in the radio industry were as adamant as he or Sir Evelyn Murray about the need to perpetuate monopoly authority.

During the hearings of the Sykes Committee, 'monopoly' had been a contentious word: in 1925 it was almost universally accepted. The *Daily Telegraph* might criticize the Post Office, but it was wholeheartedly in favour of a single broadcasting authority.[2] So too were the *Manchester Guardian*, *The Times*, the *Sunday Times*, most of the popular newspapers,[3] and the radio press.[4] The almost unanimous view had been stated by *The Times* on the appearance of Reith's book *Broadcast Over Britain*. 'The worst that can be said of this book', the reviewer noted, 'is that it is an apology, or rather an apologia for monopoly. But in this case we have to consider the alternative to monopoly: it would be, almost certainly, confusion, and quite certainly the debasement of an influence far too permeating to be allowed to be vulgarized. . . . It is now a monopoly, but in generous and humane hands the interest of the majority will probably be in its continuing to be a monopoly.'[5]

Between 1924 and 1926 opinion hardened still further. A further article appeared in *The Times* in March 1925 urging

[1] Diary, 4 Feb. 1926. He made a similar statement even earlier. Ibid., 8 Dec. 1925.
[2] *Daily Telegraph*, 18 July 1925.
[3] An exceptional example of newspaper criticism can be seen in the *Daily Express*, 28 Nov. 1925.
[4] See, for example, the *Wireless World*, 12 Aug. 1925.
[5] *The Times*, 15 Nov. 1924.

that the monopoly should be retained, and Captain (later Sir Ian) Fraser, who was later to be a member of the Crawford Committee, told the House of Commons in July 1925 that whatever changes were made the 'maintenance of unified control' should be continued. 'I believe', he went on, 'that the success [of broadcasting in Britain] is largely due to that point, in which we differ from other great countries which have preceded us.'[1] It is scarcely surprising that the Crawford Committee was unanimously agreed that 'the United States system of uncontrolled transmission and reception is unsuited to this country, and that Broadcasting must accordingly remain a monopoly—in other words, that the whole organisation must be controlled by a single authority'.[2]

The announcement of the setting up of the committee to examine the future of broadcasting was made by the Postmaster-General in the House of Commons on 20 July 1925, the day that Fraser made his statement. Mitchell-Thomson said that the committee would consider the future in the 'widest possible terms'.[3] Later in the debate the Assistant Postmaster-General, Lord Wolmer, added that the Post Office had no desire to behave 'autocratically' in relation to the aspirations of the BBC: all it was concerned to do was to act as a policeman regulating the traffic. Reith was on very friendly terms with Wolmer. They had dined together on 31 March, when Wolmer explained that he was 'anxious to be helpful',[4] and they dined together again between the Postmaster-General's statement that a committee was to be set up and his announcement in the House of Commons on 7 August of the list of names of its members.[5]

The chairman, the 27th Earl of Crawford and Balcarres, had held a variety of government posts and had served as a Cabinet minister in 1916 and 1922: his main interests were in art and music. Lord Blanesburgh was another Scotsman, whom Reith considered to be one of the outstandingly critical, discerning and forceful members of the committee. William Graham, also a Scot, was a Labour member of parliament and Financial Secretary to

[1] *Hansard*, vol. 186, col. 1872, 20 July 1925.
[2] Cd. 2599, *Report of the Broadcasting Committee*, 1925, para. 4.
[3] *Hansard*, vol. 186, col. 1871, 20 July 1925.
[4] Diary, 31 Mar. 1925.
[5] Ibid., 23 July 1925.

the Treasury in the 1924 Labour government. Ian Macpherson, the fourth of the Scotsmen and later first Baron Strathcarron, was an extremely experienced politician. Captain Ian Fraser, the fifth, had been keenly interested in broadcasting long before 1926.[1] The English contingent included a physicist, Lord Rayleigh (who incidentally had an honorary degree from Edinburgh University), Sir Henry Hadow, the distinguished musician and educationist, Sir Thomas Royden, a shipping magnate, Dame Meriel Talbot, and last but far from least, Rudyard Kipling. Unfortunately Kipling had to resign his membership of the committee at an early stage of the inquiry because of illness, and Macpherson, who attended most of the sessions, was ill when the final report was drafted. Reith sometimes regretted that he himself was not a member, as he had been of the Sykes Committee, but he appeared before it on several occasions and was the only member of the Board of the BBC to give full-length evidence.[2]

Reith had first broached the question of the future of the BBC with his own Board at a special meeting on 19 March 1925. Apart from the fact that it was known at that time that a committee would sooner or later be appointed to consider the shape of things to come, there were three other reasons why Reith chose to raise the matter then. First, the debates on the Wireless Bill had revealed considerable anxiety on the part of several members of the House of Commons about the status of the BBC.[3] Second, with the end of the fight to retain protection, Reith was increasingly anxious publicly to divorce the BBC from the radio trade.[4] Third, he was tired of Press magnates refusing to make concessions to the BBC on the grounds that the BBC was an ordinary business enterprise.

On the first of these points Reith—and Gladstone Murray—had gone out of their way to assure Labour members of parliament, in particular, that broadcasting was a 'public service'. When Tom Johnston, the Labour M.P., suggested to Reith on 6 March that there was need for a change in the constitution,

---

[1] He had arranged for a wireless demonstration at the fête for the Blinded Soldiers' and Sailors' Hostel in July 1922. Fraser to F. U. Drury, 15 June 1922. Marconi Company Archives.
[2] W. W. Burnham gave evidence on behalf not of the BBC but of the manufacturers.
[3] See above, pp. 193–4.　　　　　　　　　[4] See above, p. 196.

Reith noted, 'this, of course, is quite true, and I could not disagree with him'.[1] A few days earlier Gladstone Murray had written to J. R. Clynes, the Labour leader, telling him that 'we interpret our functions as essentially a public trust, and if there is to be any change in our constitution at the end of the present Licence, we feel that it should be in the direction of strengthening public control'.[2] Following this letter, a memorandum was prepared, which it was suggested might be sent to all members of parliament urging the case for 'unified control'. 'Any tendency towards commercialisation must be resisted; the public service character [of broadcasting] must be consolidated and perhaps more formally recognised.'[3]

Meanwhile Reith was stating the same case behind the scenes to the Post Office. In December 1924, in one of his last letters about protection, he told Murray that broadcasting policy had never been dictated by the trade, and that there had been many cases of manufacturing policy being adapted to conform to BBC policy.[4] He resented either the Post Office or the Press treating the BBC as if it were an ordinary commercial company. He was annoyed when during the discussions with representatives of the Press, which were held at the Post Office on 13 March 1925, Riddell referred to the BBC not as 'a government service' but as a 'competing commercial company'. 'I do not think Mr. Reith would admit that', the Postmaster-General interposed. Reith nodded and said it was 'unfair' to describe the BBC as an ordinary commercial concern. 'It is a commercial concern', Riddell reiterated, after which the Postmaster-General brought the discussion to a close by saying that the subject 'would be very apt for consideration when it has to be considered by the Government in the fullness of time. I do not think that we had better embark upon it today.'[5]

The Board meeting held only six days later was an interesting one. The minutes are bare. 'The Managing Director briefly explained that the meeting had been called to discuss the advisability of making recommendations to the Postmaster-General in regard to the future constitution of the Company.

[1] Diary, 6 Mar. 1925.
[2] *Gladstone Murray to J. R. Clynes, 23 Feb. 1925.
[3] *Draft of a Memorandum to Members of Parliament, 23 Apr. 1925.
[4] *Reith to Murray, 4 Dec. 1924.
[5] See above, p. 264.

After considerable discussion it was agreed that the Managing Director should write to the Postmaster-General to ascertain if he had any views and to indicate that the Board was prepared to discuss the matter if desired.'[1] Behind this brief statement, there was a considerable amount of drama, everybody talking at once. 'I tried to make them see', Reith wrote, 'how anomalous and absurd the present constitution is, but, of course, they have their own position to think about and mine is one of great difficulty and embarrassment. I wrote a memo. a fortnight ago, but Gainford did not think it would do to send it to the Post Office. The trade are a nuisance so long as they think they can control the BBC, which, of course, they do not do actually, but might do, and so long as other people think they do.'[2]

This was the position in a nutshell—as Reith saw it—and some of the members of the Board, notably Gainford, Bull, Pease, and McKinstry, were in complete agreement with him: others, particularly Kellaway, were less committed. No one, however, questioned the terms of the letter which Reith sent to the Post Office on the Board's behalf. 'I have the honour to inform you that my Board have had in mind since the beginning of this year the Constitution of this Company, and they desire me to write to you, suggesting that you might find it convenient for me to come and see you, in order that I might discuss the matter with you, and let you know what has passed through their minds.'[3]

When the Crawford Committee was constituted, W. E. Weston, the Post Office official who served as its secretary, wrote formally to Reith saying that he assumed that the Company would wish to tender evidence and stating various general points about the kind of evidence which the committee wanted to receive. Reith replied almost at once that the Company did not wish to tender evidence. He made it clear that he did not much like Weston's approach, and added that presumably Weston had thought that since the Company was composed of manufacturers it might wish to make representations about the future constitution. In fact, the Company did not wish to make any such representations, 'believing in view of the manner in which public obligations have been discharged' that their

[1] *Board Minutes, 19 Mar. 1925.   [2] Diary, 19 Mar. 1925.
[3] *Reith to the Postmaster-General, 20 Mar. 1925.

interests would be 'respected'. Instead, he himself would submit a personal memorandum on the 'scope and conduct of the service'.[1]

Reith's written memorandum of evidence for the committee was prepared in November 1925, and circulated to members of the Board later in the month. It was entitled quite simply, 'Memorandum of Information on the scope and conduct of the Broadcasting Service'. It had one avowed aim only—'to show the desirability for the conduct of Broadcasting as a Public Service, for the adoption and maintenance of definite policies and standards in all its activities, and for unity of control'. Reith underlined that it was an 'impartial statement on the conduct of a Public Service' and not an *ex parte* statement in defence of specific interests. 'It is submitted in the interests of Broadcasting, not of the British Broadcasting Company.'

Given this blunt avowal, it is easy to understand why some of the BBC's Directors did not feel 'at all sure' about the memorandum when they first read it:[2] one or two of them felt even less sure when they had pondered on what it meant.[3] It was a shorter version of *Broadcast Over Britain*, expressed rather more starkly and certainly more systematically. 'Rightly developed and controlled,' Reith wrote, 'it [broadcasting] will become a world influence with immense potentialities for good—equally for harm, if its function is wrongly or loosely conceived.'[4] 'It must not be used for entertainment purposes alone.'[5] 'He who prides himself on giving what he thinks the public want is often creating a fictitious demand for lower standards which he will then satisfy.'[6] 'There is neither end nor satisfaction for, no matter what may have been accomplished, there is so much more still to be done.'[7] 'Whilst appreciating the immense potentialities in this opportunity for helping towards the aim of a more informed and enlightened democracy, the BBC have been cramped and restricted towards pressing for its fulfilment.'[8] 'The advent of Broadcasting was regarded with suspicion if not hostility in certain quarters and some definite boycotts were even attempted. Progress was, however, maintained.'[9] The

[1] *Weston to Reith, 19 Oct. 1925; Reith to Weston, 22 Oct. 1925.
[2] Diary, 26 Nov. 1925.   [3] Ibid., 10 Dec. 1925.
[4] *Memorandum of Information*, p. 3.   [5] Ibid., p. 2.
[6] Ibid. p. 3.   [7] Ibid.
[8] Ibid., p. 4.   [9] Ibid., p. 5.

circumstances which had given rise to the 'quasi-commercial constitution' of the BBC had almost been forgotten. Although in practice it was administered as a public service, its constitution was increasingly anomalous. 'Even those who are most definite in their appreciation of the Company's attitude, recognise the desirability of its being a public service not only in deed but in constitution, but not in such a way that the initiative and enterprise through which the present position has been attained shall be fettered unduly.'[1]

The outlines of a new constitution were not set out, but emphasis was placed on unified control and continuity of administrative direction. 'Bureaucratic methods, liable under central control and in monopolies, should be avoided in the future as they have been in the past. . . . The service must, however, have a national conception before either a local or a personal one.'[2] More financial help was needed both for programmes and for capital development. If the community recognized both its opportunities and its responsibilities, broadcasting would finally establish its position as 'part of the permanent and essential machinery of civilisation'.[3]

When he first gave oral evidence on 3 December, Reith reiterated all these arguments about the necessity for public service, standing by the historical record of the Company's policy but refusing to be drawn too closely on what kind of constitution he wanted for the future. 'I may have my own views, my own colleagues on the Board, my own Chairman, may have their views. . . . I do not think it would be quite right for me to give my opinion.' 'We will make up your mind for you', said the Earl of Crawford, to which Reith immediately replied, 'I do not imply that it is not already made up.'[4] When he gave evidence again on 4 February he was equally careful. 'Might there not be a very definite advantage', Captain Fraser asked him, 'from the administrative point of view, and more especially from a research point of view, if you were a little freer of trade control?' 'I can answer the question to this extent,' Reith replied, 'that I consider it certainly an entirely pertinent question. Perhaps I would rather say nothing further than that.'[5]

[1] Ibid., p. 9.   [2] Ibid., p. 11.   [3] Ibid., p. 21.
[4] *Oral evidence of Reith before the Crawford Committee, 3 Dec. 1925.
[5] *Oral evidence of Reith before the Crawford Committee, 4 Feb. 1926.

On 25 February he wrote to Weston that he would be glad to learn whether or not the committee had decided that trade interests in broadcasting should be liquidated. It would make it easier for him to deal with the committee if he felt free of the embarrassment under which he had previously given evidence.[1]

By then the committee had decided. Nearly all the weight of evidence was in favour of a Broadcasting Board or Commission, which, while retaining continuity of executive direction, would include representatives of the public. In particular, the views expressed by the wireless societies pointed to this conclusion. The Wireless Association, for example, described 'monopoly' as 'the only reasonable solution of the [broadcasting] problem' and praised the British broadcasting system as 'superior, both technically and in programmes, to any other Broadcasting Service in the world', but asked for 'nominees drawn from associations acting in the public interest' to sit on the BBC's Board.[2] The Radio Society of Great Britain, which drew attention to the fact that it was the real initiator of broadcasting in Britain, complained that there was no representation of the public on the Board of the BBC although the public supplied almost all the revenue.[3] The Radio Association said that its members showed public disquiet about monopolies, but could not allow a theoretical objection to cause them to ignore obvious facts: the existing monopoly had worked well, and all that was needed in the future was greater public participation through what might be called 'a Board of Broadcasting Control'. 'While, in fact, the directorate of the BBC have acted very wisely in conducting broadcasting as a public service and not as a business run for the private benefit of the manufacturers, there can be no doubt that the impression created on the public by a directorate consisting exclusively of the trade and manufacturing interests is unfortunate. It is desirable to have not more than four manufacturers on a Board of Control consisting of, say, ten members.'[4]

[1] *Reith to Weston, 25 Feb. 1926.
[2] *Prepared evidence submitted by the Wireless Association of Great Britain Ltd. to the Crawford Committee.
[3] *Prepared evidence supplied by the Radio Society of Great Britain to the Crawford Committee, 20 Jan. 1926.
[4] *Prepared evidence supplied by the Radio Association to the Crawford Committee, 21 Jan. 1926. The Radio Association had come round to this view in 1925.

The Wireless League asked for 'some new central authority. . . a specially constituted British Broadcasting Commission instead of a Company. The Postmaster-General would be associated with the Broadcasting Commission by appointing a representative on it, but would not be in control as heretofore, except for the purpose of allocating the broadcasting wave bands.' The Commission should consist of an unpaid chairman, a vice-chairman (a member of parliament), a chief commissioner (the head executive officer), and seven commissioners chosen to represent the Post Office, the radio manufacturers, science, education, the arts, and the opinions of the ordinary listener. The Commission would be somewhat on the lines of the Charity Commission. 'The Government in making appointments would naturally take steps to consult the responsible organisations representing the various interests: for instance, in the case of education the President of the Board of Education: in the case of manufacturers the National Association of Radio Manufacturers and so on.'

In suggesting a commission instead of a company, the Wireless League concluded that it did not wish to make any reflection on the record of the BBC.

We think their pioneer work has been admirable and the standard of their broadcasting extremely good. We think, however, that it is undesirable to continue a monopoly service of this character in the hands of a Company which is in the nature of a private enterprise. We are agreed that the Service must be a monopoly, but monopolies in private hands are always an object of suspicion, and especially in a service of this far-reaching character it is important to provide an administration in which the public interests are represented.[1]

Reith might have submitted most of this evidence himself. He subscribed wholeheartedly to the Crawford Committee's conclusion that 'no company or body constituted on trade lines for the profit, direct or indirect, of those comprising it' could be regarded as adequate for the conduct of broadcasting. He agreed with the corollary that a 'commission' would have to be

The Association had been formed in 1922 to express dissatisfaction about the broadcasting scheme. In May 1925 it came round to support of the BBC. See *Radio Times*, 29 May 1925. The BBC acknowledged the fact that 'the Radio Association had abandoned the "bogeys" of three years ago'.

[1] *Prepared evidence supplied by the Wireless League to the Crawford Committee, 4 Dec. 1925.

set up. More important still—and here he disagreed with some of the radio societies' contentions—he supported the committee's view that the Broadcasting Commission should not consist of representatives of particular interests but instead of 'persons of judgement and independence, free of commitments ... men and women of business acumen and experienced in affairs'.[1] Like the committee, he believed that the place for particular interests was on advisory committees and not on the Commission itself.

Since the Crawford Committee was unanimous in following the general lead given by the Post Office and Reith, the main interest of the evidence offered to it is limited to two aspects. First, some witnesses put forward what in retrospect seem significant suggestions about broadcasting. Second, others among the witnesses revealed that they still thought of broadcasting as an enemy rather than as an ally. The evidence before the committee was not published: in patches, at least, it remains more interesting than the Report itself.

The most significant suggestions were made by the wireless societies. The Wireless League asked for greater variety in programmes. Local needs could be catered for by local programmes; educational needs could be met by the introduction of a separate educational wavelength 'so that the listeners who want this kind of service can tune in for it'. Indeed, in the opinion of the spokesman of the League, 'the policy of allotting special wavelengths might with advantage be adopted for other branches of the Broadcasting Service'. The first of these suggestions contained the germ of a regional scheme, although not of the kind which was eventually introduced in 1929; the latter, a policy with much to be said against it, was introduced even later, after the Reith régime was over and for reasons which certainly did not convince Reith. The Radio Association also urged the need for alternative programmes on different wavelengths. 'The Association believe that this improvement is bound to come. Just as every reader of the newspaper can read what he wishes and omit what he wishes, similarly it should be possible for the listener to tune in to highbrow music if he prefers it or a jazz band if he wishes.'

[1] Cd. 2599, para. 8.

Improvement or not, it was not until 1945 that the Light Programme was introduced, and a year later the Third. The Wireless Association had a further suggestion to make. 'There is no doubt that a considerable income could be obtained from some kinds of advertisement without lowering the tone of broadcasting. The listener is free to cut off the wireless just as the newspaper reader may disregard the printed advertisements.'

Reith chose to comment in particular on two of these points when he submitted his supplementary evidence. Not only, he argued, was the press bitterly opposed to direct wireless advertising—this was a major practical objection—but 'only richer corporations would be able to take advantage of the [advertising] facilities offered on account of the price required'.[1] He admitted the need for alternative programmes. 'The BBC has long since prepared a comprehensive scheme involving the abolition of many low-powered stations and their substitution by fewer stations of much higher power.'[2]

Both the Wireless League and the Wireless Association supported Reith's pleas for greater powers to broadcast news and outside broadcasts and greater freedom to deal with controversial subjects. It was on these two pleas that much of the opposition to the BBC centred. Lord Riddell, Sir James Owen, and H. D. Robertson, the last of whom represented the Scottish press, began by claiming boldly—in defiance of history and logic— that by publishing BBC programmes without payment they had 'been mainly instrumental in popularising broadcasting'. They accepted the fact, which they had accepted far less readily in 1923, that for 'good and sufficient reasons' broadcasting would probably continue to be a 'monopoly'. From this point onwards, however, they restated in full their case for continued restrictions. Many subjects, they maintained, were inherently 'unsuitable' for broadcasting. They ranged from racing and betting news, which 'would be highly objectionable to a large section of the community', to birth control. How improper it would be for a State monopoly to be used for advocating or opposing highly controversial doctrines!

Yet the collection of news should continue to be a monopoly

[1] *Supplementary Memorandum of Evidence arising from statements by other witnesses,* pp. 3, 8.
[2] Ibid. See also below, pp. 395 ff.

of the news agencies. 'Assuming that the effect of disseminating news through the broadcaster was seriously to curtail newspaper circulations, the result would be disastrous. Large numbers of persons would be thrown out of work in the newspaper and allied trades without any corresponding benefit to the public.' No existing industries should be endangered by broadcasting. A limited concession might be made in relation to studio broadcasts. A 'scientific man', such as Lord Rayleigh, might be generously allowed to give a talk on the possible causes of the loss of an airship, but Steve Donoghue should not be allowed to describe the Derby. 'Such an innovation is unnecessary and might injure an industry which has rendered great national services, and upon which, as stated, large numbers of persons rely for their livelihood.' Finally, advertising should be avoided at all costs. 'It would be intolerable if the broadcaster were used to proclaim the merits of so and so's corsets, so and so's pills, or so and so's sausages.'[1]

Reith's pencilled comments on this evidence survive. Against the last point he wrote, 'Nonsense, their own interests affected, only'. Against the reference to Lord Rayleigh he wrote, 'very good of them'. Against the reference to birth control he wrote, 'give both sides'.[2] In his formal supplementary evidence, he gave priority to the need for permission to supply 'narrations from the event', what we now call 'running commentaries'. He rested his case, however, on a broader base. Given the development of broadcasting, surely it was time for the press to make some 'adaptations'. Invention was the mother of necessity. 'Newspapers will tend to become more pronouncedly organs of opinion and comment, and perhaps all the more useful to the public thereby. The efficiency of the modern newspaper in reducing the time-gap between an event and its communication to the public has created such a demand for "red-hot" news that in other countries the Press is already employing the microphone to distribute the news simultaneously with the event.' Adaptation was always necessary when new inventions were brought into general use. It was inevitable that they should create uneasiness. In the press industry itself the invention of the

[1] *Oral evidence of Lord Riddell, Sir James Owen, and H. D. Robertson to the Crawford Committee, 17 Dec. 1925.
[2] BBC Archives.

linotype machine had had this effect. Broadcasting was no longer what the press representatives had suggested it was— a luxury: it was rapidly becoming an essential.[1] Moreover, if it were to be treated as an essential, then it could not merely dispense public platitudes. The ban on controversy must be removed. It retarded progress. 'Whatever be the future constitution, it is hoped that no bureaucratic policies and instructions will be introduced to hinder the development of a service which is still on the threshold of its worth and consequence.'[2]

These statements reveal Reith on the attack: with one section of the press, however, he had to fight a subsidiary defensive battle. By 1925 the 'wireless press', those periodicals dealing specifically with radio, was for the most part controlled by powerful combines—the Berry group, the Amalgamated Press, and Odhams. They complained vigorously about the competition of the *Radio Times*. They objected first to the BBC publishing in its own journal advance information not generally available, and second to the granting of preferential terms to certain categories of advertisers in the *Radio Times*. Their objections went deeper, however. Sir Edward Iliffe gave evidence which was complementary to that of Lord Riddell. 'We are strongly of the opinion that . . . monopoly should not be used to enable such a body as the BBC . . . to compete on privileged terms with the interests of any business community, and we base our belief on public policy and common justice.'[3]

Iliffe did not point out that much information was in fact provided by the BBC to the wireless press; that for two years, to meet the objections of the wireless press, the BBC had voluntarily agreed to exclude advertising of component parts (much against the wishes of the radio industry); and that each week five minutes of listening time were devoted to a review of the technical wireless journals.

Reith was doubtless pleased to turn Riddell's argument on its head and use it against Iliffe. 'While recognising the hitherto friendly attitude adopted by the Wireless Press, and acknowledging the great assistance which it has in many directions

[1] *Supplementary Memorandum*, pp. 3–4.
[2] *BBC Press Release, 4 Feb. 1926.
[3] *Evidence submitted before Broadcasting Committee by the Wireless Press of London and of the Country generally*, p. 2. Oral evidence was given on 28 Jan. 1926.

rendered the Broadcasting Service, it must be remembered that the service itself is in large measure responsible for the success of this press.'[1] He chose to say relatively little in public about the immense value which the BBC attached to the *Radio Times* as its official organ. Gladstone Murray stressed this in an important memorandum which he prepared for Reith. In publishing the *Radio Times*, he stated, the BBC had in mind 'the logical development of our general conception of the service'.[2] Stobart added that the curtailment of the freedom of the *Radio Times* would 'strike a heavy blow at the educational opportunities and ideals of our service'.[3]

Faced with this welter of interests and opinions, the Crawford Committee was eloquent but exceptionally vague and cautious. It recognized that the evidence was bound to be conflicting since 'speculative elements' abounded and 'neither we nor others can predict the reactions of a new and incalculable cycle of scientific resource'. It dismissed some of the forebodings of the critics of broadcasting and stated that the public would in future probably prefer 'original performances' to 'secondhand versions'. Where it might have been tough, however, it was lacking in incisiveness: it placed its hopes chiefly in the healing passage of time, anticipating that problems would 'accordingly solve themselves', and that experience would prove that 'apprehensions, though natural enough at present, will in future be allayed'. Put into concrete terms, these soothing phrases were doubtless an invitation to Reith and Riddell to get together on their own and reach an agreement. This, of course, they did.[4]

The thorny question of controversial broadcasts, which had been examined far more searchingly by the Sykes Committee, was resolved in this manner. 'A moderate amount of controversial matter should be broadcast, provided the material is of high quality and distributed with scrupulous fairness, and that the discretion of the Commissioners in this connection should be upheld.'[5] On the issue of the broadcasting of parliamentary speeches the committee did not 'feel authorised to offer an opinion'. Parliament itself soon did. On 26 March 1926

---

[1] *Supplementary Memorandum*, p. 13.
[2] *Memorandum from Gladstone Murray to Reith, 23 Jan. 1926.
[3] BBC Archives.   [4] See above, p. 267.   [5] Cd. 2599, paras. 12, 15.

Baldwin told the House of Commons that after consulting with the leaders of other parties he had come to the conclusion that 'there was a greatly preponderating body of opinion against broadcasting proceedings of the House'. At this, one member interjected, 'May I thank the Prime Minister on behalf of a long-suffering public.'[1]

It was not only parliament or press, the Third and Fourth Estates, which presented the Crawford Committee with a series of difficult decisions. The Fifth Estate, the entertainment industry, which unlike the press had not been consulted before the BBC was founded, united with the music publishers, the Performing Right Society, and the Incorporated Society of Authors, Playwrights and Composers, in criticizing some of the actions of the BBC. Their case diverged in detail, however, and each of the interests they represented fared somewhat differently in their dealings with the BBC. Precise, practical grievances were mixed together with sultry suspicions of broadcasting as a whole.

Walter Payne spoke for a trio of organizations—the Society of West End Theatre Managers, the Entertainments Protection Association, and the Entertainment Organization Joint Broadcasting Committee. He said that he resented the fact that the protection which had been given to the press had not been given to the interests he represented. It was only after a long struggle that his organizations had reached limited and temporary agreement with the BBC.[2] Grievances still rankled. The advertisement value of broadcasting to artists had been negligible; there had been some depletion of theatre audiences by 'competitive broadcasting programmes' (no reference was made to the cinema); the freshness of West End shows was blunted by the time they reached the provinces; even older shows, like Gilbert and Sullivan operas, would become stale by broadcasting, and for that reason Rupert d'Oyly Carte had not permitted them to be broadcast; finally, variety artists did not like broadcasting and never would. Nor did their managers. 'Offers of the BBC with its vast and growing resources may easily cause chaos in relation to what I may term their market

[1] *Hansard*, vol. 192, col. 866, 22 Mar. 1926.
[2] See above, p. 251–2.

value. Salaries could be raised temporarily to prohibitive heights—only to be followed by complete collapse of the permanent value and freshness of the artistes themselves.'[1] Each of these points was highly tendentious. When questioned, Payne showed no grasp of the fact that wireless presented entertainers with new opportunities. He insisted on treating radio programmes as 'inferior representations' of live performances. 'I cannot think it is satisfactory', he remarked, for example, 'to hear a play without seeing the actors' make-up and their gestures and the scene to make up the performance.' His complaints were economic as well as artistic. He described the wireless licence as a kind of 'entertainment dole for the entire population'. He had no vision of an enormous range of musical and variety programmes being provided directly by the BBC itself, of a complete revolution in what became known as 'show business'.

A. V. Broadhurst spoke for the music publishers. His outlook was quickly and summarily expressed in answer to the first question put to him. 'It is the firm opinion of owners of musical copyright', he said, 'that broadcasting has a deleterious effect upon the sale of music, and consequently upon the earnings of composers and authors.' He gave examples. The life of a popular song was cut down from twelve months to less than six months. Bad reception stopped some good broadcast songs from being appreciated at all. There were fewer concerts. People gave up time to listening-in which they would previously have given up to personal performance. Professionals and amateurs suffered alike. Paid musical performers were already suffering as orchestras in hotels were being replaced by wireless receiving instruments. Having stated these propositions—Sir Henry Hadow rightly described them as inferences rather than facts—Broadhurst passed to a more specific claim for an 'adequate return' to composers, authors, and other owners of copyright. By an 'adequate return', he meant that 10 per cent. of the takings of the BBC should be given over to payments of royalties: this figure, he claimed, was already being given in Australia. At the same time Broadhurst admitted that it had not been necessary to test copyright law in Britain because of 'the conciliatory, even friendly attitude, consistently taken by the Broadcasting

[1] *Oral evidence of W. Payne to the Crawford Committee, 18 Dec. 1925.

Company in their negotiations with the owners of musical copyright'.[1] In fact there was no copyright case until 1927, and the legal, as distinct from the moral, position remained obscure.[2]

William Boosey shared Broadhurst's 'inferences' and added a few more of his own. 'Broadcasting affects the sale of popular sheet music, because a large number of people who listen to Broadcasting absolutely neglect the piano to do so, having neither time nor inclination for both occupations. Broadcasting affects the sale of gramophone records in the same way that it affects the sale of popular sheet music.' These 'inferences' look extremely strange in the light of the subsequent history of the music industry, particularly of the gramophone industry. At the time, indeed, Captain Fraser suggested to the witness that certain gramophone records were being sold by the million because of their constant repetition in wireless programmes. Most of the gramophone companies were co-operating closely with the BBC, the only other 'mass entertainment' industry which did so, and the Gramophone Company (H.M.V.) only a month before had claimed in its annual report that broadcasting and the gramophone industry had not encroached on one another but had been of mutual assistance.[3] The BBC had already tried seriously to co-operate amicably with Boosey himself, as it was to do successfully later on. It was certainly co-operating with some of his artists. 'Mr. Boosey states that he does not allow them to broadcast, but the fact remains that most of them do so regularly.'[4]

John B. McEwen spoke on behalf of the Composers' Committee of the Incorporated Society of Authors, Playwrights and Composers. He put forward a reasonable case for good musical 'production' and equality of contractual treatment. John Woodhouse of the Performing Right Society complained vigorously about the terms his members were offered. On all these matters there was to be scope for further bargaining, much of it hard bargaining. There was also scope for more generous treatment of creative artists by the BBC. The Crawford Committee

[1] *Oral evidence of A. V. Broadhurst to the Crawford Committee, 18 Dec. 1925.
[2] *Messager* v. *British Broadcasting Company Ltd.* (1927) 2 K.B. 543. This problem will be dealt with in the next volume of this history.
[3] *Oral evidence of W. Boosey to the Crawford Committee, 18 Dec. 1925.
[4] *Supplementary Memorandum*, p. 6.

recognized this. 'We should deprecate any cause for grievance amongst those who supply the raw material of Broadcasting and we feel that services rendered to the Commissioners should be adequately rewarded. We hope the Commissioners will maintain and improve their service by allocating ample funds for meeting copyright royalties and for the adequate payment of performers.'[1]

Not all the evidence before the Crawford Committee was innocuously unanimous or heatedly contentious. A number of witnesses dealt not with the control or the terms of broadcasting but with its contents. The British Institute of Adult Education and the National Federation of Women's Institutes praised the educational work of the BBC and demanded that it should be extended. Speaking for the latter, Mrs. Nugent Harris 'refreshed' the committee with her account of how the wireless had encouraged neighbourliness in the villages. People with wireless sets asked their neighbours to drop in and listen with them. Sir Walford Davies gave details about school broadcasts and adult education, confirming the need for a 'special technique at each end'. Professor R. Peers and T. H. Searls described a number of new ways of relating broadcasting and organized adult education, particularly at the local level. Sir Hugh Allen claimed that the opportunities of musical education were almost unlimited but that training in discrimination was needed. Earl Russell spoke up for the 'amateurs', against advertising, and against 'political propaganda for one party only'; on the question of news he declared that he did not think that the BBC should be limited to the 'appallingly jejune farrago now provided by the News Agencies'. Filson Young, formerly editor of *The Saturday Review*, and for a time a paid BBC programme critic, gave a colourful running commentary on the whole work of the BBC. 'I cannot imagine a Government Department alone controlling so intricate and sensitive a thing as an organisation giving the public performances of music for hours every day,' he said, 'nor can I believe that it would be a happy or useful thing for the community if rivalry between different Broadcasting institutions were made possible.' Filson Young nonetheless criticized the BBC on one count. He urged that its

[1] Cd. 2599, para. 12.

artistic policy should be controlled more by artists and less by boards and committees.[1] It was a criticism which was echoed later on by Eckersley, and it clearly contained a substantial amount of truth.[2] The bigger the BBC grew, the greater this danger became.

At the same time most witnesses agreed that the BBC had successfully avoided other and what were thought of as more alarming dangers. Percy Scholes wrote a brief but telling memorandum for the committee on the 'present practice and relative success of broadcasting in Britain and the United States'. It was based on a tour which he had made of the United States from September to December 1925. This memorandum may be compared with F. J. Brown's notes on American broadcasting in 1922.[3] Then it was 'chaos' which concerned Brown most: now it was content. 'It might be thought that the existence of a spirit of competition between stations would produce a constantly rising standard in the type of programme and the manner of performance, but experience shows that this is not so.' Programmes were poor, they were not advertised in advance; artists were either unpaid or badly paid; advertisements, 'more or less subtle', were gaining ground all the time and in all places. Radio was still at a schoolboy level. 'The present attitude of the average American to radio is very much that of the average Briton of three years ago. Radio in America is still a scientific toy. Every boy owns a set, as every boy owns, or hopes soon to own, a motor-car, and the spirit of the "Radio Fan" is, as yet, the spirit of boyhood.' It did not seem fanciful of Scholes to describe the comparative position in Britain as one of 'maturity'. Radio had ceased to be a scientific curiosity: it had become an instrument of culture.[4]

The Crawford Committee accepted this analysis. It welcomed the evidence of those witnesses who had advocated the vigorous and extended employment of broadcasting for education 'in its widest and most liberal sense'. It praised the BBC for having maintained a discreet 'balance' in its programmes between conflicting tastes. Every effort should be made to raise the standard

[1] *Oral evidence of Filson Young to the Crawford Committee, 21 Jan. 1926.
[2] Eckersley, op. cit., pp. 18–19.
[3] See above, p. 68.
[4] *Remarks upon the Present Practice and Relative Success of Broadcasting in Britain and the United States, as a result of observation in both countries.*

of style and performance. 'Special wavelengths or alternative services may provide an escape from the programme dilemma, but we trust they will never be used to cater for groups of listeners, however large, who press for trite and commonplace performances.'[1]

Given this approach, the Crawford Committee followed Reith in demanding that constitutional change should be associated with executive continuity. 'Formed at a moment when Broadcasting was still embryonic—regarded by many as a toy, a fantasy, even as a joke—the Company by strenuous application to its duties, aided by the loyalty of its staff, has raised the service to a degree which reflects high credit on British efficiency and enterprise.'[2] The Commission would be an innovation: the personnel of the Company should stay. 'We attach the greatest importance to maintaining continuity between the old authority and the new.'[3]

2. The Charter

THE Report of the Crawford Committee was published on 5 March 1926: it was not until 14 July 1926, however, that the Postmaster-General announced officially that its main recommendations were accepted by the government.[4] He chose to make his announcement in the course of the debate on the Post Office estimates.

During the interval there had been opportunity to test press and parliamentary reactions. The views expressed in the press continued to be more critical of the Post Office than of the BBC. 'The shadow of the Postmaster-General lies heavy on the scheme', *The Star* complained.[5] Was there not a danger, asked the *Evening News*, that the 'genuine humanity' of the BBC would disappear when the Corporation was formed?[6] The *Westminster Gazette* referred to 'the withering touch of deadhanded depart-

---

[1] Cd. 2599, paras. 13 and 14.   [2] Ibid., para. 2.
[3] Ibid., para. 7.   [4] Hansard, vol. 198, col. 448, 14 July 1926.
[5] The Star, 6 Mar. 1926.   [6] Evening News, 6 Mar. 1926.

mentalism'.[1] Many tears were shed for the Company: many apprehensions were felt about the Corporation. Would not the new constitution be too 'august and autocratic'?[2] 'Complaining to this highborn Commission', *The Referee* maintained, 'will be very much like bombarding St. Paul's with a pea-shooter to influence the Dean and Chapter.'[3]

Some papers saw the new constitution as a move in the direction of socialism: 'Socialism, like the kangaroo, is progressing by leaps and bounds.'[4] The fact that it was 'Conservative Socialism', 'to which the present Government is strongly attached',[5] made it no better. The *Daily Herald* certainly welcomed the Report as 'sensible' and sound.[6] So too, however, did papers with no hint of socialist control. *The Scotsman*, the *Manchester Guardian*, and *The Economist* were all in favour. The last-named, indeed, printed an important article on 'The Finance and Future of Broadcasting' which summed up the issues better than any other newspaper or periodical.[7]

American experience, according to *The Economist*, had proven 'beyond the shadow of doubt' that broadcasting had to be a monopoly. The question was how should the monopoly be controlled? Hitherto it had been controlled by a favoured 'public utility society': now it would pass more directly into public hands. The authors of the Report had unanimously suggested a reasonable compromise. 'They avoid the dangers of bureaucracy in Departmental control; on the other hand, they take what must be a monopoly out of the hands of shareholders who have admittedly a particular interest in the sale of wireless apparatus; and they set up a Corporation, from which all question of private profit is eliminated, to act as a trustee and steward for the public in the maintenance and development of a new element in national life of great social and economic value.'

Perhaps the most interesting section of the article in *The Economist* related to finance, which *The Economist* recognized was of crucial importance. The Company had not been allowed to

---

[1] *Westminster Gazette*, 6 Mar. 1926.
[2] *The Morning Post*, 6 Mar. 1926.
[3] *The Referee*, 7 Mar. 1926.
[4] *G. K.'s Weekly*, 13 Mar. 1926.
[5] *Yorkshire Evening News*, 6 Mar. 1926.
[6] *Daily Herald*, 8 Mar. 1926.
[7] *The Economist*, 13 Mar. 1926.

exploit its monopoly advantage. Not only had its profits been limited to 7½ per cent. but when it disappeared its shareholders would be entitled only to repayment of their capital at par. From the start the Corporation should be ensured by the State all the resources it might require for the economic development of its work, 'a safeguard, which is at once elastic in character and sufficient'. It should be spared 'the raids of even the most predatory Chancellor of the Exchequer'. Surpluses would go to the Treasury only after BBC needs had been met. This should be an arrangement which would both commend itself to the BBC and 'gladden the heart of Mr. Churchill'. *The Economist* concluded by saying that 'in parliamentary circles it is believed that the proposed arrangement is one which will commend itself to the overwhelming majority of the members'.

The prophecy was correct. Most members of parliament were still relatively uninterested in broadcasting. Only a small number of them asked questions on the subject, and an even smaller number took part in the intermittent debates.[1] One member, Sir William Bull, was directly associated with the BBC, and a few others were in close agreement with him. When Reith first addressed a group of members of parliament in the House on 2 March 1925, it was at Bull's invitation and about thirty people were present.[2] At that time in the House there was no 'commercial bloc' with an interest in advocating commercial broadcasting, although there were individual critics of the BBC who spoke up either for the amateurs or occasionally for the press and other interests. Only one member, Colonel Day, Labour member of parliament for Southwark, said openly that he preferred control of broadcasting by 'show business' rather than by public commissioners. '99 per cent. of the people with wireless sets', he contended, 'installed them for the purpose of being entertained':[3] this should be the motive power behind broadcasting.

Few people, however, recognized at that time the opportunities of making large profits out of the control of entertainment.[4]

---

[1] Ian Fraser, 'Why does Parliament take so little interest in Broadcasting?', in *Radio Times*, 31 Dec. 1926.   [2] Diary, 2 Mar. 1926.
[3] *Hansard*, vol. 199, cols. 1563 ff., 15 Nov. 1926.
[4] There was a slump in cinema attendances and profits in 1926, and far from the production of films proving profitable, there were weaknesses in the British industry which led to the protective Cinematograph Films Act of 1927.

Nor was opinion in any of the political parties generally sympathetic to Colonel Day's contention. The Conservative Party contained a large number of members, including business-men, who believed without question in the ideal of 'public service': this was Baldwin's own approach. The Labour Party welcomed any moves made towards 'public ownership': suspic-ious as some of its members often were of the BBC, the general attitude of the party was favourable. A few members of the Liberal Party were concerned about the dangers of 'monopoly', and in the brief debate on the constitution of the new Corpora-tion, E. A. Harvey and L. Hore-Belisha dwelt on the merits of competition in broadcasting. Hore-Belisha, in particular, argued that 'the United States system of free and uncontrolled transmission . . . was more in accordance with the genius and spirit of the English people'. This viewpoint, however, was that of only a small minority of Liberals. Many Liberals were them-selves attracted to the general idea of 'public corporations', and it has been claimed, indeed, that the term was first used in a Liberal Party report. After the Corporation was set up, open criticism of the monopoly by minority Liberals quickly 'died away'.[1] So popular did the case for public corporations become at both ends of the political spectrum that in 1931 no less than 320 members of parliament (including 295 Conservatives) suggested a transfer of the powers of the Post Office itself to an organization of this kind.[2]

Only two questions relating to broadcasting interested more than a handful of members of parliament in 1926—first, the finances of the BBC, and second, the 'controversial programmes' which it occasionally broadcast. During the early months of 1926 nearly all parliamentary questions were concerned with these topics. Pressure was exerted to persuade the Company to publish its full accounts, to record how it was spending 'public funds', to abandon 'secrecy', and make itself accountable to parliament.[3] The pressure came from both sides of the House. There was a division of opinion among the questioners, however, about what was wrong under the existing system. A few members

[1] R. H. Coase, *British Broadcasting, A Study in Monopoly* (1950), p. 135. There is a good general summary of the monopoly debate in Paulu, op. cit., pp. 16–22.
[2] W. W. Robson, *Public Enterprise* (1937), p. 359.
[3] *Hansard*, vol. 189, col. 2025, 21 Dec. 1926.

attacked the Post Office for holding back the 'preposterous' share of one quarter of each licence fee for administrative costs and urged that the BBC should be given more money.[1] Others continued to ask for lower licence fees: their target was not the Post Office but the BBC and 'its innocuous inanities, suitable only for invalids and imbeciles'.[2] On 'controversial' broadcasts each 'side' complained of the advantage given to the other, and both parties had to be reassured by the Postmaster-General (with only a few members expressing uneasiness) that all kinds of political broadcasting were being prohibited.[3]

When the Postmaster-General announced that the government accepted the main proposals of the Crawford Committee his statement was warmly welcomed by almost all the members who took part in the brief debate.

Mitchell-Thomson proposed that on 31 December the service 'at present conducted by the Broadcasting Company should pass over as a going concern' to a new authority. The new authority would be called not the British Broadcasting Commission, as the Crawford Committee had suggested, but the British Broadcasting Corporation. 'It will take over the present business of the Company . . . with all the assets, and I have financial arrangements in hand by which I hope it will be possible for the new body to start with an absolutely clean sheet, clear of all liability.'

The new authority would be set up neither by special statute nor by the Companies Act, as the committee had suggested, but by Royal Charter. The idea of a royal charter had been mentioned in the basic Post Office memorandum, but had subsequently been put on one side by the committee. It had not even been seized upon by the BBC lawyers who drafted a memorandum on the constitution of a new authority in February 1926.[4]

The reasons given by the Postmaster-General for preferring a charter to any other device of incorporation were threefold. First, if a special statute were introduced it would tend to pre-

[1] *Hansard*, vol. 191, cols. 1987 ff., 17 Feb. 1926.
[2] Ibid.
[3] Ibid., vol. 193, cols. 866 ff., 22 Mar. 1926.
[4] *Memorandum on the future Constitution, prepared by Messrs. Steadman, Van Praagh, and Gaylor, 2 Feb. 1926.

judice the position of the new body from the start 'by investing it in the mind of the public with the idea that in some way it is a creature of Parliament and connected with political activity'. Second, if the new body were formed under the Companies Act of 1908 it would 'lack a certain amount of status and dignity'.[1] Third, a company formed under the Companies Act could only do what it was specifically authorized to do by its memorandum and articles, while a corporation incorporated by charter could do anything which the charter did not specifically prohibit it from doing. The BBC's lawyers had suggested incorporation under the Companies Act as simplest, cheapest, and quickest, but naturally Reith preferred incorporation by charter when the method was chosen for the reasons given by Mitchell-Thomson.

As always, however, Reith was cautious. He had privately described parts of the Crawford Committee Report as 'very woolly' and 'liable to misinterpretations of all sorts'.[2] He still remained uncertain of Post Office intentions. The Postmaster-General's acceptance of the principles of the Crawford Committee was excellent, but 'acceptance had to be translated into definite terms in an instrument of incorporation and in a licence from the P.M.G. I knew what to expect of the Post Office. By the time the Civil Service has finished drafting a document to give effect to a principle, there may be little of the principle left.'[3]

Reith had good reasons for expressing himself so cautiously. He knew from experience that dealings with the Post Office were protracted and complicated. He had been given no guarantees about finance. The Postmaster-General specifically reserved the question of finance which he said could be debated in the autumn on the question of a supplementary estimate. Finally, Reith knew nothing about the names of the future 'Governors' of the Corporation. He hoped that Lord Gainford would be the first Chairman, and pressed hard for his selection.[4] Instead Lord Clarendon, Parliamentary Under-Secretary for the Dominions, was chosen. Reith learned this at a dinner party with Lord Wolmer on 13 June.[5] It was not until October that

---

[1] *Hansard*, vol. 198, cols. 448 ff., 14 July 1926.
[2] Diary, 8 Mar. 1926.   [3] *Into the Wind*, p. 104.
[4] Diary, 26 Mar. 1926.   [5] Ibid., 13 June 1926.

the Postmaster-General told the House, and gave members the names of the other four Governors.[1] Lord Gainford, whose claims to be Chairman had perhaps been set on one side because he was a Liberal and a coal-owner[2] (coal-owners were controversial people in the year of the general strike), was appointed Vice-Chairman. The remaining Governors were Sir John Gordon Nairne, formerly Comptroller of the Bank of England (his name had been suggested by the Chancellor of the Exchequer); Dr. Montague Rendall, formerly Headmaster of Winchester (both Mitchell-Thomson and Lord Wolmer were Wykehamists); and Mrs Philip (later Viscountess) Snowden, the wife of one of the most prominent Labour politicians.

The choice both of Lord Clarendon and of Mrs. Snowden was unfortunate. She was thought of as conveniently uniting the claims of Labour and Womanhood. Ramsay MacDonald, however, did not approve of the choice, holding her accountable for 'most of Philip's stupidities'.[3] She was to be a thorn in Reith's side, and it is unfortunate for the historians that she has not left her own account of what happened in the BBC between 1926 and 1932, when her governorship came to an end. Reith was unhappy even at their first meeting. 'Met Dr. Rendall and Mrs. Snowden for the first time. Both very cordial, but I could not understand the latter at all.'[4]

Before the names of the Governors were announced in the House of Commons, Reith had had several abortive talks about finance at the Post Office. He was anxious to have an increasing supply of income which would not be diverted to the Post Office at the whim of the Postmaster-General. The Crawford Committee had recommended that only after BBC needs had been met should the surplus accrue to the Post Office. This left the question open, however, of what the needs of the BBC really were. Reith wanted both better programmes and a technical reorganization of the service.[5] In July 1926 he took the highly unorthodox course of sending out a memorandum to all members of parliament clearly stating his case.

The BBC feels that the Service cannot stand still. If it does not go

---

[1] *Hansard*, vol. 199, col. 542, 25 Oct. 1926.
[2] *Into the Wind*, p. 105.
[3] Diary, 3 Oct. 1926; *Into the Wind*, pp. 114-15.
[4] Diary, 25 Oct. 1926.   [5] See below, pp. 395-7.

forward, it must decline. The saturation point of productive and efficient expenditure on the Broadcasting Service is not yet within sight. Moreover, if it is desirable to make Broadcasting a permanently supplementary source of public revenue, much more satisfactory results may reasonably be anticipated if the Service is more fully developed, particularly in research, equipment and improved quality and variety of programmes, before its financial resources are curtailed.[1]

This memorandum secured a considerable amount of parliamentary support, several members, notably Captain Fraser and Lt.-Commander Kenworthy (on other counts a frequent critic of the BBC), arguing that it was quite iniquitous to treat licence fees as a form of concealed taxation.

The Post Office did not welcome this parliamentary pressure. Wolmer was very sympathetic both to the BBC and to Reith personally, but Sir Evelyn Murray was intransigent on financial questions. And it was Murray rather than Wolmer who exercised the preponderant influence on Mitchell-Thomson.[2] Reith did his best to reassure Mitchell-Thomson that he looked upon him as an ally, not as an opponent.

We have all along, as I think you will agree, acted loyally by the Post Office and have never sought to defend ourselves at their expense. I hope you have not felt in our recent discussions that I was in any way obstructive. I am motivated solely by a genuine desire to see the Service under the new Constitution maintain the same rate of progress that we have maintained, and by a real alarm that the present proposed provisions are absolutely inadequate to take care of its normal developments, still less of the new ones which must come.[3]

Matters came to a head in October 1926 soon after the new Governors had been chosen. The Postmaster-General formally proposed on 28 October, at a meeting which lasted for several hours and was concerned with the draft Charter, that the BBC's share of licence revenue should be determined according to a sliding scale. After deducting $12\frac{1}{2}$ per cent. of gross licence revenue to cover expenses, the Post Office would pay the Corporation 90 per cent. of net revenue on the first million licences, 80 per cent of the net revenue on the second million, 70 per cent.

---

[1] *The Broadcasting Service* (July 1926).
[2] *Into the Wind*, p. 106.
[3] *Reith to Mitchell-Thomson, 19 July 1926.

on the third million, and 60 per cent. on the fourth and each subsequent million. Borrowing powers of up to £500,000 would also be granted to the new Corporation, provided that the Corporation's auditors were satisfied that proper provision was made for depreciation and a sinking fund.

This proposal was an improvement on previous proposals made by the Post Office, but Reith regarded it as 'still inadequate'.[1] 'The position is most unsatisfactory', Reith wrote, 'and the new body is not getting any more autonomy than the old, which is a deliberate ignoring of the Crawford recommendations, apart from anything else. The treatment of finance is abominable.'[2] To make matters worse, Reith believed that the Post Office was being parsimonious without bothering adequately to consult the Treasury. Indeed, the Treasury had been told that the BBC was quite satisfied with what had been proposed.[3]

The more Reith examined the draft Charter, particularly its financial proposals, the more unhappy he became. He persuaded the new Governors to protest against the terms on 29 October and went back to the Post Office to see Mitchell-Thomson and Murray. He stayed there for 2½ hours. During the discussion the Postmaster-General hinted that if the new Governors did not like the financial proposals he would have to find another five people. 'Why?' asked Reith. 'Because', Mitchell-Thomson replied, 'it looks as if they wouldn't sign the agreement.'[4]

On the following day Mitchell-Thomson sent for Clarendon and more or less told him that if the draft Charter were not approved, new Governors would be appointed. According to Reith, Clarendon yielded. He paid no attention to a memorandum prepared by Reith and accepted the Postmaster-General's terms. To Reith this was 'appalling weakness'.[5] His opinion of Clarendon fell even further during the next few days when Reith felt that he (Reith) was battling with the Post Office all alone. 'The proposed financial provision', he affirmed time and time again, 'will enable the Service to be maintained in its present state, and will even admit of a certain improvement. I believe,

[1] Diary, 20 Oct. 1926.
[2] Ibid., 28 Oct. 1926.
[3] Ibid.; *Into the Wind*, p. 106.
[4] *Ibid.*, p. 115. Pencilled account of the proceedings by Reith, 29 Oct. 1926.
[5] Diary, 1 Nov. 1926.

however, that the Corporation will be able to avail itself of comparatively few of the opportunities which will present themselves for progress with respect to standard, variety and distribution, and that it will early and continually find itself seriously handicapped.'[1] The only concession he could wring from the Post Office was that the financial provisions would be reviewed again in two years' time.

When the Post Office published the Charter on 12 November and the Postmaster-General told the House that it was an 'agreed' document, Reith's indignation was unrestrained. 'I cannot express my opinion of the way that the Post Office has treated us; they have been unfair, arbitrary and quite dishonest. They have printed outside the document that the terms were mutually agreed. . . . The constitution was to be changed to admit more scope and more autonomy, but none of these has materialised.'[2] He sent a telegram to Gainford asking him whether he considered that the statement printed on the Parliamentary White Paper that the terms of Charter and Agreement had been 'mutually agreed' was fair. 'No,' Gainford replied, 'but acceptance is some justification. Suggest Clarendon might publish letter to P.M.G. remove misunderstanding.'[3] No letter was published.

In this inauspicious way the British Broadcasting Corporation received its first Charter. Letters Patent under the Great Seal were duly forwarded to Clarendon on 29 December. They were acknowledged a day later, and the Charter lay on the table at the first formal meeting of the new Governors in January 1927.

The ringing terms of the Charter give no hint of this last chapter of doubts and disillusions.

WHEREAS it has been made to appear to Us [it begins] that more than two million persons in Our Kingdom of Great Britain and Northern Ireland have applied for and taken out Licences to instal and work apparatus for . . . the purpose of receiving Broadcast programmes AND WHEREAS in view of the widespread interest which is thereby shown to be taken by Our People in the Broadcasting Service and of the great value of the Service as a means of education

---

[1] *Reith to Clarendon, 3 Nov. 1926.
[2] Ibid., 15 Nov. 1926.
[3] The telegrams are in BBC Archives.

and entertainment, We deem it desirable that the Service should be developed and exploited to the best advantage and in the national interest . . . [by] a Corporation charged with these duties . . . [and] created by the exercise of Our Royal Prerogative.[1]

The Corporation was created for a period of ten years from 1 January 1927.

The five Governors were each appointed for five years, but they were all eligible for reappointment. Reith was formally named with a new title of Director-General. The powers and duties of the Chairman and Governors were formally set out. So too were their salaries. The Chairman was to receive £3,000 a year, the Vice-Chairman £1,000, and the other Governors £700. Reith did not like these relatively large salaries, which he feared would make the new Governors devote too large a part of their time to 'interference' with the executive.[2]

Among the provisions of the Licence, the Postmaster-General took care to restate his own position in relation to broadcasting. He retained authority to approve the location, wavelength, power, and height of aerials of the broadcasting stations. The stations were always to be open to Post Office engineers for supervision or inspection. He also had to approve the hours of broadcasting. He could take over the stations completely in case of emergency. As far as programmes were concerned, the Corporation was called upon to 'send [out] efficiently. . .programmes of broadcast matter'. If government departments wished it to make official announcements, it was compelled to do so. Mitchell-Thomson explained that this provision was designed to cover such announcements as police messages, gale warnings, and outbreaks of foot-and-mouth disease. 'If any Government oversteps the line,' he added, 'and goes beyond this I have no doubt they will be brought to book and properly brought to book, in the House of Commons.'[3] In addition it was specified that 'the Postmaster-General may from time to time by Notice in writing to the Corporation require the Corporation to refrain from sending any broadcast matter (either particular or general) specified in such Notice'.[4]

[1] Cd. 2756 (1926). This White Paper had as its title 'Wireless Broadcasting'. It contained both the Draft of the Royal Charter and the Draft Licence.
[2] *Undated notes on the Crawford Committee Report.
[3] *Hansard*, vol. 199, col. 1579, 15 Nov. 1926.
[4] Licence, clause 4, Cd. 2756.

The Postmaster-General at once specified a continued restriction on the freedom of the BBC. He informed the House of
Commons on 15 November that he had instructed the Corporation that, when it began operations, it was not to broadcast its
own opinions on matters of public policy nor was it to broadcast
on matters of political, industrial, or religious controversy.[1]
Reith's plea for controversial broadcasting, powerfully restated
to the Post Office in July 1926,[2] had been rejected. It was not
until 1928 that the ban on controversial broadcasting was withdrawn 'experimentally' and what to broadcast or not to broadcast was left to the discretion of the Director-General and the
Governors.[3]

In part-compensation for the failure to meet Reith's wishes in
1926, restrictions on the broadcasting of news were officially
withdrawn. One of the objects of the Corporation was stated in
its Charter to be 'to collect news of and information relating to
current events in any part of the world and in any matter that
may be thought fit and to establish and subscribe to news-
agencies'.[4] The prohibition against the receipt of payment for
the broadcasting of programmes was not withdrawn. It is
interesting to note that an early list of BBC objections to the first
draft Charter included as one of its points of disagreement the
'no advertising' clause. 'Should not the Corporation', Reith
asked, 'have liberty with regard to advertising as a supplementary source of revenue in case of need?'[5]

Reith wished also to have a specific monopoly clause inserted, one which would formally lay down that the Postmaster-
General should not license any other body for broadcasting.[6]
The Post Office refused, but it no longer made mention, as it
had done in the revised Licence issued after the Sykes Committee Report, of the Postmaster-General's right to license new
broadcasting authorities. When Sir Harry Brittain, who was
extremely interested in broadcasting and a good friend of the
BBC, asked the Postmaster-General why there was no specific
monopoly clause, Lord Wolmer replied that there was practically general agreement that there had to be a monopoly in

[1] *Hansard*, vol. 199, cols. 1580–1, 15 Nov. 1926.
[2] *Reith to Mitchell-Thomson, 6 July 1926.
[3] *Into the Wind*, p. 128.
[4] Charter, clause 3 (*e*), Cd. 2756.
[5] *Undated list of contentious points.   [6] Ibid.

broadcasting and that once you were committed to monopoly, you were also necessarily committed to government control. Like the Postmaster-General himself, however, he pleaded for genuine independence under the new Charter. 'I want to make this Service not a Department of the State, and still less a creature of the Executive, but as far as is consistent with Ministerial responsibility, I wish to create an independent body of trustees operating the Service in the interest of the public as a whole.'[1]

3. The General Strike

THE debate on the Charter was perfunctory and unilluminating. For most people in 1926 a more important milestone in the history of broadcasting than the Crawford Committee was the general strike of 3 May to 12 May. It took place between the publication of the Crawford Committee's Report and the decision of the Postmaster-General to implement the committee's decisions. Its chronological placing is significant, therefore, in relation to the development and formulation of attitudes towards broadcasting both of the government and of the public. Equally significant to the historian, however, is the influence of broadcasting on the course of the general strike. If there had been no BBC, the national course of events might well have been different. By providing a steady and regular supply of news and announcements for all parts of the country, the Company greatly assisted the government of the day. It also served to check the application of more drastic measures which a minority within the government was seriously prepared to contemplate.

At the same time the BBC itself—with great difficulty—maintained a precarious measure of independence throughout the strike: it could never be completely identified with the government, at least by those who knew the 'inside story'. Reith was anxiously vigilant to retain this measure of independence. He even succeeded against the odds in using the strike to strengthen

[1] *Hansard*, vol. 199, cols. 1563 ff., 15 Nov. 1926.

the position of the BBC. 'I do not welcome crises', he wrote at the time, 'but admit to welcoming the opportunities which crises bring.'[1] The period of the strike was one of 'unprecedented strain, with the situation changing several times a day, with all manner of movements and counter-movements', but at the end Reith could report that the consequence he most feared—'namely that BBC prestige and tradition might suffer'—had not occurred.[2]

Most accounts of the role of the BBC in the general strike are over-simplified, although Julian Symons's recent study is neat, well-balanced, and supported both by documentary and oral evidence.[3] The constitutional position of the BBC was plain. The government had the legal authority not only to order the BBC to broadcast whatever messages it chose to provide, but, if it wished, to commandeer the BBC. The 'diplomatic' position was much more complicated. The Cabinet itself—and the Strike Committee of the Cabinet—included at least two sections of opinion. One, led by Winston Churchill, the Chancellor of the Exchequer, was prepared to resort to extreme measures to put down the strike, which it thought of as a political and constitutional crisis: this section was ready and willing completely to take over the BBC and to mobilize broadcasting as a direct agent of government. The other section regarded the strike as an unfortunate and irresponsible industrial dispute which had better be brought to an end as quickly as possible: the members of this section, who included Sir Samuel Hoare (later Lord Templewood), believed—doubtless for reasons of temperament as much as of policy—that it would be wiser to leave the BBC a measure of independence or at least of 'semi-independence', as Hoare has described it.[4]

Baldwin, who was not a member of the Strike Committee of the Cabinet and seemed singularly detached from its decisions, undoubtedly took the latter view. He knew, liked, and trusted Reith, whose views on the strike were not dissimilar from his own. Reith saw him after breakfast on 6 May. 'He said he entirely agreed with me that it was far better to leave the BBC with

---

[1] Diary, May 1926; *Into the Wind*, p. 107.
[2] *Reith's report to the Directors, 18 May 1926.
[3] J. Symons, *The General Strike* (1957), pp. 177–82.
[4] BBC Programme, *The General Strike* by Julian Symons, 24 Feb. 1960.

a considerable measure of autonomy and independence. He was most pleasant.'[1] In the middle of the strike Baldwin broadcast a message from Reith's house, which Reith himself amended. It was on Reith's suggestion that these words were inserted: 'I am a man of peace. I am longing and working and praying for peace, but I will not surrender the safety and the security of the British Constitution.'[2] It was impossible for the listener to tell that these words which created a great impression were not Baldwin's own: Baldwin said he was grateful to Reith for coining them. They were completely in character, focusing the image of an honest and sympathetic Prime Minister, more moderate and far-sighted than some of his more belligerent colleagues.

On this occasion as on other occasions during the strike the BBC was sharply differentiated from the *British Gazette*, which Churchill edited and managed from 11 Downing Street. The *Gazette* was a piece of straight government propaganda, treated by strikers with distrust and derision, but appealing to the militant opponents of the strike who were alarmed by what seemed to them to be its revolutionary implications. It soon became an object of bitter controversy. At the beginning of the strike the editor of the *Gazette* tried to treat the BBC as an 'offshoot'. 'I told him', Reith wrote in his diary, 'that I was not going to have that at all.'[3] He added later, 'Davidson [J. C. C. (later Viscount) Davidson, Deputy Chief Civil Commissioner] is very pleased with the first copy of the *British Gazette* ... but I told him I did not think much of it.'[4]

Davidson was the 'contact man' between Reith and the government throughout the strike. They were near neighbours, and had long discussions in which they by no means always agreed. During the weekend before the strike Reith tried to impress three points on Davidson—first, that consultation between government and BBC was preferable to giving orders; second, that if the BBC were branded as completely 'partisan', a mere organ of government, the strikers could paralyse the whole broadcasting service; and third, that, given the right occasion, the BBC could play a positive role. 'In the end conciliation of some kind must supervene and ... the BBC could

---

[1] Diary, 6 May 1926.   [2] Ibid., 8 May 1926.
[3] Ibid., 4 May 1926.   [4] Ibid.

act as a link to draw together the contending parties by creating an atmosphere of good will towards its service on both sides.'[1]

Once the strike had started, Reith reiterated that although the BBC had to be 'for the Government in the crisis'—he never doubted the necessity of this—it was essential that it should 'be allowed to define its position to the country'. Unless it retained public confidence, 'its pioneer work of three and a half years will have been undermined [and] as an influence of almost unlimited potency . . . shaken'.[2] Reith himself refused either to suspend his conscience or his judgement throughout the strike. His battle for the independence of the BBC was something more than a battle for the neutrality of a medium. He had a standpoint of his own. He had no sympathy with the coal-owners, but he had little sympathy with organized labour either and disliked the very idea of a general strike. He preferred mediation to showdown. If his views had coincided with those of the sponsors of the *British Gazette*, he would have had fewer qualms about allowing the BBC to fall directly into the hands of the government. As it was, his personal convictions gave strength to his insistence on constitutional proprieties.

The 'diplomacy' was complicated in other ways too. The Cabinet Committee was vague about what it wanted to do with the BBC. The picture of a resolute and efficient governmental machine confronting an enthusiastic labour movement, irreso- lutely led, is quite misleading. When Reith first visited David- son's office at the Admiralty he wrote 'things are very mixed up . . . and Davidson with no clear ideas at all of what he wants me to do, nor what he is supposed to be doing himself'.[3] When he attended his first meeting of the Cabinet Strike Committee on 6 May, he had the same impression. Joynson-Hicks, the Home Secretary and former Postmaster-General, with whom Reith had previously had so many disagreements on BBC matters, was in the chair. He told the committee that Baldwin wished the BBC to retain its autonomy. Churchill 'emphatically ob- jected and said it was monstrous not to use such an instrument to the best possible advantage'. To Reith's great surprise, Joynson-Hicks replied cautiously that if anybody felt strongly

[1] *See *Suggestions for the Policy of the Broadcasting Service During the Emergency.*
[2] *Reith to Davidson, 6 May 1926.
[3] Diary, 4 May 1926.

about the matter it had better be discussed at a full Cabinet meeting.[1] The point was dropped, and officially the position of the BBC was never fully clarified during most of the period of the strike. It was not until 11 May, just before the strike ended, that the Cabinet decided formally not completely to take over the BBC. The uncertainty placed the organization and Reith personally in what by an uncharacteristic understatement Reith described as 'an awkward position'.[2] 'When it was all over I wondered', he has written, 'if it would have been better had the BBC been commandeered. My conclusion was that it would have been better for me, worse for the BBC and the country.'[3]

Immediately the strike was over, Reith described his decisions and his dilemmas extremely candidly in a confidential letter to Heads of Departments, Station Directors, and Superintendent Engineers. It is a revealing document of basic importance and it deserves to be quoted extensively.

The responsibility of keeping the country in touch with the progress of events, as practically the sole means of general communication, was an onerous one, and that it has been discharged with almost no error of judgment or failure of any kind is, in view of the multiplicity of interests and the extent of the operations, a conclusive achievement in itself. I feel that some explanation is due to the staff with regard to our position during the Emergency. Under the Emergency Regulations, the Government would have been within its powers if it had taken over our organization literally, making Broadcasting an official medium comparable with the Government newspaper. There were indeed considerable efforts from some quarters to have this done. I felt it would be unfortunate from every point of view, the Government's, the country's and our own. By the terms of our Licence, even apart from Emergency Regulations, we were bound to broadcast official announcements, but, largely due to the sympathetic and enlightened attitude adopted throughout by the Deputy Chief Civil Commissioner, Mr. J. C. C. Davidson, in charge of official news, the B.B.C. was not definitely commandeered. We were given direct access to all official news, allowed to exercise editorial discretion with regard to it, and were also permitted to preserve, apart from this, an appreciable degree of impartiality in the broadcasting of general news. I may say that the Prime Minister and the Home Secretary in particular approved of our being left with a considerable measure of independence. This indicated a gratifying trust in the Company's loyalty and judgment.

[1] Diary, 6 May 1926   [2] *Into the Wind*, p. 108.   [3] Ibid., p. 109.

There could be no question about our supporting the Government in general, particularly since the General Strike had been declared illegal in the High Court. This being so, we were unable to permit anything which was contrary to the spirit of that judgment, and which might have prolonged or sought to justify the Strike. The broadcasting of official communiqués issued by the Government would have been expected and demanded irrespective of its political complexion. But as it was we were able to give listeners authentic impartial news of the situation to the best of our ability.

The arguments used against definite commandeering included the following: that we had secured and held the goodwill and even affection of the people; that we had been trusted to do the right thing at all times; that we were a national institution and a national asset; that if commandeered or unduly hampered or manipulated the immediate purpose of such action would not only have been unserved but actually prejudiced; that it was not a time for dope, even if people could have been doped; that those hostile to the Government would only have been more hostile; that if we had suppressed news of any unfortunate situation arising, it might only have led to the panic of ignorance, which is more dangerous than a knowledge of facts. But, on the other hand, since the B.B.C. was a national institution, and since the Government in this crisis were acting for the people, apart from any Emergency powers or clause in our Licence, the B.B.C. was for the Government in the crisis too; and that we had to assist in maintaining the essential services of the country, the preservation of law and order, and of the life and liberty of the individual and of the community.

It was unfortunate that we were unable to define our position. The matter was discussed several times at Cabinet meetings, but, embarrassing as the situation was, it was less undesirable than a definite commandeering. Had we been commandeered we could have done nothing in the nature of impartial news, nor could we have in any way helped inspire appreciation of the fact that a prolongation of the stoppage was a sure means of reducing the standard of living, which it was the avowed intention of the Trade Unions to improve. Nor could we have initiated or emphasized statements likely to counteract a spirit of violence and hostility. We felt we might contribute, perhaps decisively, to the attitude of understanding without which goodwill could not be restored.

It was urged therefore as cardinally important even during the crisis, to maintain the B.B.C. tradition and preserve its prestige, and as for the future when the trouble was over, that it would be a calamity if public confidence in the B.B.C. had been dissipated through actions, negative or positive, during the Emergency. Its pioneer work for nearly four years might have been undermined and its great influence shaken.

From the above you will realize that the position was one of extreme delicacy and embarrassment throughout. It was impossible to give the lead which we should have liked, but it is a satisfaction to find an almost universal appreciation and recognition of the services rendered, and it may be only ourselves who feel that we might have done more with a freer hand.

The only definite complaint may be that we had no speaker from the Labour side. We asked to be allowed to do so, but the decision eventually was that since the Strike had been declared illegal this could not be allowed.

This is a highly confidential document, but I shall be glad if you will read the contents or such part of them as you consider necessary or advisable, to those under you.[1]

This memorandum begs a certain number of questions—notably contentious questions about the legality of the strike[2]—but it reveals much about motives and judgements. It clarifies the desire of the BBC to convey 'authentic impartial news', while at the same time remaining in every sense of the word 'an organisation within the constitution'.[3] It is a useful prelude to a brief narrative account of what happened to the organization of the BBC as a whole during the strike.

This country first learned from the BBC that there was a strike: it also first learned from the BBC that the strike was over. At 1 a.m. on Monday 3 May Davidson told Reith that negotiations between the government and the T.U.C., which had been in progress throughout Sunday, had been broken off, and that the general strike which had been announced for 3 May would definitely take place. This message was broadcast at 1.10 a.m. It was followed by other messages to the same effect throughout Monday.

[1] *Reith to the senior staff of the BBC, 15 May 1926.
[2] Reith, like many other people, was particularly impressed by Astbury's judgment on 11 May in the Chancery Division of the High Court that 'the so-called General Strike by the T.U.C. is illegal'. Sir John Simon expressed the same view in Parliament (*Hansard*, vol. 195, cols. 584-5, 6 May 1926) and in his *Three Speeches on the General Strike* (1926). The view was challenged later. See A. L. Goodhart, 'The Legality of the General Strike in England', in the *Yale Law Journal*, Feb. 1927. See also, Symons, op. cit., pp. 121-4; W. H. Crook, *The General Strike* (1931), pp. 401 ff.
[3] *This phrase was used privately on several occasions and publicly in a broadcast of 12 May referring to the Astbury judgment.

A few days earlier, on Friday 30 April, the BBC had inter-rupted its late-night programme of Jack Payne's dance music to announce that a coal strike had been called for midnight on Monday 3 May. The failure of the talks between the T.U.C. and the government had converted the coal strike into a general strike. This was an emergency which the government had anti-cipated and prepared for during several months. At least once during that period of preparation the BBC had refused to broadcast a speech by a representative of the unofficial Organiz-ation for the Maintenance of Supplies which was formed in the late summer of 1925 (with the Home Secretary's approval) to 'mobilise the resources of the community' in time of need. 'We feel it would prejudice our reputation for being non-political', Reith wrote, 'unless we allowed a prominent Trade Unionist to make his observations on the O.M.S.'[1]

On the eve of the strike the BBC made its own plans for action. Of its central staff, 247 men and girls lived near enough to Savoy Hill or had private transport facilities to enable them to reach their work in any emergency. Forty-six other people, it was decided, were to be provided with special transport, and fifteen men and twenty-seven girls were not to be required to come to work. A special transport system was organized with two charabancs and two motor cars. The BBC had been de-clared an 'essential service' by the government so that no one on the staff could volunteer for any other duties. Station Directors were warned to take extra care in the scrutiny of visitors and to cease the practice of showing people around the studios. Daventry was to be protected by twelve plain-clothes men.

The decision of the T.U.C. to bring out the printers along with other workers automatically meant that most of the great national newspapers ceased publication in the regular and reliable form to which their readers were accustomed. Only a cer-tain number of provincial newspapers and *The Times* were issued daily with a reasonable coverage of news and these had strictly limited circulations. The *British Gazette* and the T.U.C.'s official organ the *British Worker* did not appear until 5 May.[2] This state of affairs gave special importance to the broadcasting of

[1] *Reith to the Post Office, 20 Oct. 1925.
[2] Symons, op. cit., pp. 154 ff.

news by the BBC. The news agencies temporarily abandoned all the restrictions placed on the content and timing of BBC news bulletins, and on the morning of 4 May the BBC set up an emergency news staff, which worked in three shifts. The day shift included Major C. F. Atkinson, Miss Milnes, Miss Waller, D. H. Clarke, and J. S. Dodgson, the last of whom was seconded from the London station. Later on two others were added. The night shift which took over in the late evening was headed by R. Gambier Parry and included Mrs. Kidson and G. S. Strutt. Everyone worked in one room only fifteen feet by twenty feet with five telephone lines and four typewriters in constant use, but there was astonishingly little confusion.[1]

Most of the news came in from Reuters and Davidson's office at the Admiralty, linked to the BBC by two direct lines. Miss Shields and W. Fuller of the BBC staff were installed in the Admiralty at the beginning of the strike, and were soon joined by Gladstone Murray who received, filtered, and passed on news material, including his own 'appreciation of the situation', which was broadcast as a 'leading article' each day. This 'appreciation' was vetted by Davidson. One or two BBC employees actually went out collecting news, a task which had been expressly forbidden by the press agencies in normal conditions. P. W. Darnell, a member of Gladstone Murray's staff, was the most active of these: he was sometimes joined by B. B. Chapman.[2]

News bulletins were broadcast at 10 a.m., 1 o'clock, 4 o'clock, 7 o'clock, and 9.30 p.m. each day. The first of them Reith described frankly as 'pretty rotten': this he attributed to inefficiency in the Admiralty Office.[3] 'The public should understand', listeners were told in the first morning bulletin, broadcast at 10 o'clock on 4 May,

that the sudden change from the bulky newspaper to the short bulletin cannot be perfected in an instant. Moreover, the world has been asleep and not active for the last eight or ten hours and therefore there is bound to be comparatively little news in the first bulletin. In co-operation with Reuters, we are endeavouring to secure that at

---

[1] There is a graphic account of the arrangement by Miss Shields, Reith's secretary, in *St. Martin's Review*, June 1926.

[2] *C. F. Atkinson, *Memorandum on the Work of the Emergency News Staff*, 18 May 1926.

[3] Diary, 4 May 1926.

any rate a bare minimum of information essential to the community
shall be available in spite of the suspension of ordinary means of communication. The B.B.C. fully realizes the gravity of its responsibility
to all sections of the public, and will do its best to discharge it in the
most impartial spirit that circumstances permit. In the last issue of
the newspapers allusion is principally made to the possibility of wholesale oscillation. As to that, we express no opinions, but we would ask
the public to take as serious a view as we do ourselves of the necessity
of plain objective news being audible to everybody. Nothing is more
likely to create a panic than the complete interruption of authentic
news. This would only leave the field open to wild rumour and the
consequences would be very serious. We shall do our best to maintain
our tradition of fairness, and we ask for fair play in return.[1]

As the strike continued, a more effective routine was established. Transport material was separated out in special bulletins
from 7 May onwards; a sub-division of subjects was evolved, the
material relevant to each sub-division being pasted on separate
sheets; the Managing Director personally examined most of the
bulletins from 6 May onwards before they went on the air; and,
in a number of cases, matters of exceptional importance were
broadcast in the course of ordinary programmes and not in the
bulletins. In their final form the regular news bulletins included
special messages and announcements, official notices, full reports
of parliamentary proceedings, Murray's 'appreciation of the
situation', and a weather report as well as news items. When
the strike was over, the press criticized the arrangement of the
BBC news bulletins, but journalists admitted that the service
improved. 'The early difficulties showed', wrote the *Manchester
Guardian*, 'what a specialised faculty the "news sense" is and
how it could not be mobilised at a moment's notice.'[2] The
writer did not add that the improvement between 3 May and
12 May showed what could be done to develop that sense in a
remarkably short space of time. The BBC had not been allowed
to exercise it before 4 May because of restrictions imposed by
the press. It had to develop the sense in the most difficult conditions when the collection even of routine news was a major
problem in itself.

The reference to oscillation in the first bulletin relates to

---

[1] *News Bulletin, 4 May 1926.
[2] *Manchester Guardian*, 17 May 1926.

threats made by the strikers to interfere with BBC programmes. The General Council of the T.U.C. had published a statement on 1 May warning its members that since the BBC would be in the hands of the government during a strike its members should not pay attention to wireless statements. In some parts of the country instructions were given to interfere with programmes. Once the strike started, however, strikers listened to news bulletins as much as non-strikers, however much they found them distasteful, and very few attempts were made to interfere with reception. Some of the local lock-out committees were very hostile to 'public wireless broadcasting', but pictures soon came in from all parts of the country of strikers and non-strikers alike clustering round their radio receivers.

The public was informed that it was admissible and desirable to spread the news in every possible way, and in many places wireless bulletins were copied out by hand and posted up in public places. Sometimes, indeed, it was the local newspaper office which served as the meeting point. This was the case, for example, at Dover.[1] More usually it was the local radio shop. 'Broadcasting to the Fore' was a heading in the *Brighton Herald*. It showed 'Gallier's Electric Shop, where the usual large crowd was listening to the broadcast news'.[2] Beatrice Webb noted in her diary that 'the sensation of a general strike, which stops the Press, as witnessed from a cottage in the country, centres round the headphones of the wireless set'.[3] Certainly many people listened to radio programmes during the general strike who had never listened before: they included the Bishop of Winchester who, after 'manfully resisting the numerous appeals of wireless' before 1926, had a set installed specially to hear the news.[4] The London Clubs bought sets for the first time,[5] and in the House of Lords the Lord Great Chamberlain arranged for copies of each news bulletin to be circulated not only to members of both Houses of Parliament but to the press

[1] *Dover Express*, 14 May 1926.   [2] *Brighton Herald*, 8 May 1926.
[3] Quoted Symons, op. cit., p. 181.
[4] *Southern Daily Echo*, 19 May 1926.
[5] *Bristol Times and Mirror*, 8 May 1926. The results, this paper claimed, were a little surprising. At one club in St. James's Street 'all the members wanted to hear the news bulletins, but not everyone cared to listen to the musical programmes, so there was at first much friction between old fogies who hated the tango and the jazz, but wanted the news, and the younger members who quite appreciated a little enlivening syncopation'.

gallery.[1] In several parts of the country enterprising people (including schoolboys) printed news sheets based almost exclusively on BBC information. The General Radio Company in Regent Street, London, for example, distributed over 80,000 printed copies of bulletins within thirty minutes of broadcasting.[2] During the reading of the news bulletins the BBC engineers resorted to over-modulation so that the transmissions could reach crystal-set users more easily. After the strike ended many complaints were sent to the BBC that reception had become weaker again, and Eckersley had to explain publicly that stronger signals had been used during the strike.

On the whole the programmes were impartial. The nickname BFC (British Falsehood Company) which the BBC knew was being employed in some parts of the country[3] was by no means generally used: a more frequent comment was of the kind collected by Julian Symons, who heard from an old-age pensioner in the 1950s that he still had amongst his junk 'the little home-made crystal set, which worked lovely with the iron bedstead for aerial and the gas stove for earth, and which told me and my wife (each with one earphone to the ear) what was really happening'.[4] Symons rightly picks out the phrase 'what was really happening' and puts it into italics. While the strike was in progress messages poured in to the BBC. There was a fairly constant dribble of criticism, but there was also a lavish showering of praise. Announcers were treated as major public personalities. 'Rapidity of one o'clock announcer very exasperating to long suffering public' ran one message; 'splendid—never been so well done' ran another.[5] On 11 May a large box of kippers and haddock arrived at Savoy Hill. They were from a trawler owner who thought that the staff might be running short of food.[6]

A perusal of all the news bulletins sent out by the BBC during those hectic nine days suggests that what was included was usually right, although much news was excluded. There was no fabrication, no attempt to twist or to distort. It was only when the popular newspapers came back again that the public

[1] *The Newspaper World*, 26 May 1926.
[2] *Letter to the BBC, 8 May 1926.
[3] *C. F. Atkinson, *Memorandum*.
[4] Symons, op. cit., p. 181.
[5] BBC Archives.
[6] Hibberd, op. cit., p. 20.

was confronted with headlines like 'Revolution Routed', 'Surrender of the Revolutionaries'.[1] One of the first BBC bulletins on 4 May began with the T.U.C.'s statement that 'we have from all over the country from Land's End to John o'Groat's reports

Whatever inconveniences may have been caused by the cessation of the taxi-cabs - and this was not easily apparent - there were scores of people who, if they could afford to be selfish in their personal considerations in these days, derived satisfaction from the fact that at all events the cab ranks were empty.

Other good uses were found for these empty spaces in the centre of the streets, and Kingsway from one end to the other was soon converted into a car park such as any American city might be proud.

Every available inch of space was utilised. Owners of motor-cycles had stacked their machines in compact masses where it was most needful they should be placed, but the big and little cars were jostled together, cross-ways to the pavements and according to the direction in which their owners will go home. The narrower thoroughfares gave up half their space and the principal road-ways - even Old Broad Street - had an unending line of stationary cars against the kerbs on each side of the road. Yet the City of London was doing those things for which it is traditionally known the world over.

In many shop windows the broadcast bulletins were displayed

44. Corrected Script of a News Bulletin

that have surpassed all our expectations'. Messages from the General Council, which were explicitly excluded from the *British Gazette*, continued to be broadcast throughout the strike. Speeches of trade-union leaders inside and outside parliament were quoted freely: of a labour demonstration on 10 May it was stated that it took place 'with no disorder and no inflammatory speeches'. The opinions of critics of the government, like Lloyd George, were summarized, as were articles in the *British Worker*.

[1] *Daily Mail*, 13 May 1926.

Occasionally, however, misleading reports were broadcast, probably because of failures in the news collecting and checking system. Typical examples were accounts on 7 May of engine-men and firemen returning to work at Oxford, of the break-down of the strike at Salisbury, and of the discharge of food ships near Grimsby. Each of these reports was corrected by the unions in the areas concerned, and the *British Worker* sometimes published such corrections. Although the BBC was informed of

45. A Cartoon by Low.

these mistakes, the corrections were not broadcast.[1] Provincial Station Directors were warned from the start to exercise great care in the 'censorship of local news'. 'When in doubt about any particular item, and unable to refer it to London, you are to delete it. You are not, however, to exclude items from T.U.C. sources provided that they are objective and you are convinced of their truth.'[2] The one limiting factor—and it was a most important one—was that 'nothing calculated to extend the area of the strike should be broadcast'.[3]

There is little doubt that BBC news assisted the government against the strikers. Above all, it had a steadying effect on opinion. It helped more than any other factor to dispel rumours.

[1] Symons, op. cit., p. 179.
[2] *Directive to Station Directors, 6 May 1926.
[3] *Directive to Station Directors, 7 May 1926.

Among the rumours in circulation were that four police inspectors or sergeants or constables had been killed at Canning Town or Poplar or Stepney; that two Divisions of the Red Army were on their way from Archangel to Wick; that armed blue-jackets were guarding the corridors of the House of Commons; and that there had been a riot at Hyde Park Corner when a number of society women had been involved, some being hit over the head with milk bottles.[1] Just before the strike took place the BBC itself had given a good though inadvertent example of rumour-mongering. On 16 April Father Ronald Knox's famous broadcast on a fictitious riot of the unemployed in London had alarmed people all over the country, although it included such unlikely details as the roasting alive of a well- known philanthropist in Trafalgar Square.

Apart from the negative task of dispelling rumours, the BBC tried more positively to spread 'good cheer'. 'Anyone who is suffering from "Strike Depression" can do no better than to pay a visit to "R.S.V.P." at the New Vaudeville Theatre', one blatant advertisement stated. 'The theatre was opened last night to all Special Constables. Last night was the first under this new arrangement, and there must have been about half-a-dozen rows of "Specials"—of whom seventy-five per cent. were undergraduates.' There were frequent words of uplift, like 'at the close of the first week of the greatest strike in history, one of the most encouraging features is the cheerfulness and confidence maintained by Londoners'.[2] There was almost a war-time note underlying broadcasts of this kind. No attempt was made, however, to depict the realities of working-class life, the sense of solidarity, struggle, and occasional triumph which the strikers felt. The side of the general strike which still attracts the historian of labour was unrepresented. There was no doubt, as an early message to the Station Directors put it, that there was a 'certain natural bias towards the Government side'.[3] There was equally no doubt that the straight facts of working-class life were not well known to most members of the early BBC.

The announcements were both official and unofficial. They included appeals for civil constabulary reserves in London, warnings against abuses of picketing, details of movements of

[1] BBC Archives.   [2] Ibid.
[3] *Directive to Station Directors, 7 May 1926.

trains, buses, and voluntary transport, conditions in hospitals, and cancellations of functions ranging from the annual meeting of the British Spiritualists' Lyceum Union to the Primrose League. 'The droning of the train times', one newspaper later noted, 'proved as soothing as the blessed word "Mesopotamia".'[1] It was back to Ditcham and his list of trains in 1920—with a difference.

The last announcement was the most dramatic of all. The strike ended on 12 May. Reith himself was reading the 1 o'clock news, since he had heard that a meeting had been arranged between the Prime Minister and representatives of the T.U.C. for 12 noon that day at 10 Downing Street. It was he who had broken into the dance-music programme to announce the impending strike: it was he who was in the right place at the right time to announce its ending. While he was reading the news, Stuart Hibberd, who was acting as liaison officer between G. S. Strutt and Reith, received a message on the tape to say that the strike was over. He ran down to the studio with it, exactly as it had come through, and after Reith had reached the end of the paragraph he was reading, pushed it in front of him at the microphone. Reith paused, read it through and reflected, then signed to Hibberd for a pencil. Quickly he scribbled on the paper 'Get this confirmed by 10 Downing Street'. Some ten minutes later Hibberd obtained the necessary confirmation, and Reith announced the end of the strike to the whole country. 'At a meeting with the Prime Minister at 10 Downing Street, Mr. Pugh announced on behalf of the General Council of the T.U.C. that the general strike is terminating today.'[2]

Special consideration must be given to three other points of interest during this brief but hectic period in the history of broadcasting—first, the failure to put on the air a labour or trade-unionist speaker; second, the delaying of news of an important announcement by the Archbishop of Canterbury; and third, the contentious question of the BBC's own 'editorials' or 'appreciations of the situation' which caused difficulties even when the strike was over.

In the summary of events which he prepared for the staff

[1] *The Nation and Athenaeum*, 29 May 1926.
[2] Hibberd, op. cit., pp. 20–21.

after the strike was over, Reith referred to complaints that there had been no labour speaker, and said that his attempts to arrange such a broadcast had been vetoed by the government. This was true. He had met a deputation of the Parliamentary Labour Party on the morning of 5 May, and was directly approached on 7 May by William Graham, the Labour member of parliament who had served on the Crawford Committee, with a request that 'one of their people' should be allowed to speak.[1] The idea was frowned upon by Davidson, and Reith in person explained his difficulties to Trevelyan and Hugh Dalton on 8 May. 'I thought', he wrote, 'I made them understand the position.'[2] Naturally the Labour Party persisted, particularly when Viscount Grey broadcast a speech on behalf of the Asquithian Liberals on 9 May which included some bitter strictures on the actions of the trade unions.[3]

The same day Graham formally wrote to Reith asking him to allow 'a representative Labour or Trade-Union leader to state the case for the miners and other workers in this crisis',[4] and the next day Ramsay MacDonald telephoned Reith twice to ask permission to broadcast. Reith finally got in touch with him during the early evening.

He was reasonable enough [Reith wrote at the time]. He said he was anxious to give a talk. I said that we were not entirely a free agent, but that he might send the manuscript along. I got it at No. 6 with a friendly note offering to make any alterations which I wanted. . . . I sent it at once to Davidson for him to ask the Prime Minister, strongly recommending that they should allow it to be done. I do not think that they treat me altogether fairly. They will not say we are to a certain extent controlled and they make me take the onus of turning people down. They were quite against MacDonald broadcasting, but I am certain it would have done no harm to the Government.[5]

A letter from MacDonald, written immediately after the telephone conversation, survives. It urged that since so much was being said which was hostile to labour it was felt that 'the fair minded and reasonable public ought to have a different note

[1] Diary, 5, 7 May 1926.   [2] Ibid., 8 May 1926.
[3] This speech was made on 9 May and not, as Lord Reith states in *Into the Wind*, pp. 111-12, on 10 May.
[4] *Graham to Reith, 9 May 1926.   [5] Diary, 10 May 1926.

BROADCASTING THE NEWS.
LISTENING TO THE STRIKE BULLETINS—

IN TOWN

[*Sport and General.*]

AND COUNTRY.

[*Dell and Wainwright.*]

46. News Bulletins during the General Strike, 1926

47. Miners and Railwaymen waiting to hear a News Bulletin, 1926

48. The BBC's Post Bag

49. A Group at Daventry

Sir William Bull, P. P. Eckersley, Lord Gainford, Sir W. Mitchell-Thomson, J. C. W. Reith

50. A Broadcast of Speeches by the Prince of Wales and Winston Churchill from a Banquet in the House of Lords

struck'.[1] Reith agreed with this, and attributed the government's refusal to pressure from Churchill. It was not until the strike was over that a labour leader was allowed to broadcast, and the first person who did so on 14 May was at that time the most unpopular of all the labour leaders—J. H. Thomas.

There were recriminations later. Reith wrote to both Graham and MacDonald on 14 May explaining how his hands had been tied during the strike and hoping they would not attribute BBC actions entirely to him. What he had been able to do, he said, was to make news bulletins as authentic and reliable as they could have been in the circumstances and to include a considerable amount of T.U.C. news. He added that he was 'concerned that broadcasting should not lose in influence and prestige by any misunderstanding or misconception of our action or lack of it during the Emergency'.[2] Neither Graham nor MacDonald was predisposed at this stage to forgive and forget. Graham complained of 'hopelessly one-sided matter' being broadcast; MacDonald stated that the BBC was a 'biased agency . . . misleading the public'. Similar views were expressed in the *Radio Times* by Philip Snowden and Ellen Wilkinson. The latter was particularly angry. 'The attitude of the BBC during the crisis', she exclaimed, 'caused pain and indignation to many subscribers. I travelled by car over two thousand miles during the strike and addressed very many meetings. Everywhere the complaints were bitter that a national service subscribed to by every class should have given only one side during the dispute. Personally, I feel like asking the Postmaster-General for my licence fee back.'[3] Ordinary trade-unionists and members of the Labour Party also wrote in complaint. 'Whilst admitting that there was very little said against the miners,' wrote one, 'I would like to ask what was said in their favour? . . . My opinion is that to be fair in such a thing as broadcasting it should be independent of either Government, politics or class, and if news in a crisis like we have just passed through must be broadcast, please let the leading spokesmen on both sides have so many minutes or hours each.'

The only possible reply to these complaints was given in the

[1] *MacDonald to Reith, 10 May 1926.
[2] *Reith to Graham, 14 May 1926.
[3] *Radio Times*, 28 May 1926.

Radio Times, both by the editor and by Reith. The BBC had lacked 'complete liberty of action' during the strike. Within the limits set from outside, the trade-union case had been stated. 'We do not believe that any other Government, even one of which Mr. Snowden was a member, would have allowed the broadcasting authority under its control greater freedom than was enjoyed by the BBC during the crisis.'[1] It was a grim comment, but a true one. Nor is it likely that any differently constituted broadcasting authority would have been able to behave differently in 1926, unless a commercially-sponsored authority had sided openly with the coal-owners.

Graham, MacDonald, and the other Labour Party leaders soon got over the annoyance which they felt in May 1926. They probably came to realize not only that the BBC had been placed in a difficult position but that any broadcasting authority in such circumstances would have been unable to act freely. MacDonald was writing in more friendly fashion by early June, but explaining that he was unable to see Reith to talk matters over because he was 'worried out of his life just now with engagements and things to be done'.[2] He still did not appreciate the potentialities of broadcasting as Baldwin did. Graham's postscript was written in November. 'You will readily understand how acutely many of us felt the events of the general strike, and the manner in which, as we thought, it was aggravated by the use of the broadcasting system and other devices. I had a talk with Trevelyan; so far as I am concerned, not one trace of feeling remains; and I certainly appreciate the great difficulty in which you must have been placed.'[3]

Just as controversial as the refusal to allow a labour leader to broadcast was the delaying of news concerning a 'peace appeal' put out by the Archbishop of Canterbury and other churchmen on 6 May. The churchmen asked for a resumption of negotiations between the government and the trade unions based upon three points to be put into effect 'simultaneously and concurrently'—the cancellation of the strike, renewal of government subsidy to the coal industry for a short, definite

[1] *Radio Times*, 21, 28 May 1926.
[2] *MacDonald to Reith, 2 June 1926.
[3] *Graham to Reith, 11 Nov. 1926.

period, and withdrawal by the mine-owners of their suggested new wage scales. The Archbishop telephoned Reith on 7 May, asking to be allowed to broadcast this appeal to the whole country. He told Reith that he had already communicated with the Prime Minister and that the Prime Minister would not prevent its being broadcast although he preferred that it should not be. 'A nice position for me to be in between Premier and Primate,' Reith wrote much later, 'bound mightily to vex one or other; at thirty-six years of age.'[1]

Reith asked the Archbishop to send him the draft of the appeal. Reith read it through and consulted J. C. C. Davidson, who told him, whatever he thought of it, not to broadcast it, on the grounds that it would provide Churchill and his group with just the opportunity they had been wanting to take over the BBC. This was at an early stage in the strike, and the likelihood of the BBC being taken over was still considerable. Reith decided to accept Davidson's advice, and telephoned accordingly to Lambeth Palace, telling the Archbishop that he could not broadcast the statement. The Archbishop, a little perplexed, replied that he supposed that the responsibility for not allowing him to broadcast was Baldwin's, to which Reith had to say no, it was his.

I explained [Reith stated in writing in a letter posted next day] that we were in a position of considerable delicacy at the moment. We have not been commandeered, but there have been strong representations to the effect that this should be done. I think it would be regrettable from every point of view. We have maintained a certain degree of independence hitherto and the matter is still *sub judice*. It would therefore be inadvisable for us to do anything that was particularly embarrassing to the Government, by reason of the fact that it might lead to the other decision that we are hoping to obviate.[2]

This was the low-water mark of the power and influence of the BBC. The Company existed on 8 May by sufferance, and Reith realized this. Protests from listeners poured in immediately: they continued to be made after the strike was over. The Labour Party was as much worried by the case of the Archbishop as by the refusal to allow MacDonald to broadcast. Both Reith and the

---

[1] *Into the Wind*, p. 109. The Archbishop's point of view is described in Bell, op. cit., vol. ii, ch. lxxx.
[3] *Reith to the Archbishop of Canterbury, 8 May 1926.

Archbishop felt the same. 'Had a long talk with the Archbishop in the afternoon', Reith wrote in his diary on 8 May. 'He is still worried and so am I.'[1] On Sunday 9 May the Archbishop was scheduled to broadcast a sermon from St. Martin-in-the-Fields. Reith said he did not want to look at the notes of the sermon. 'Apparently Lane-Fox, Secretary for Mines, was not so confident of his discretion; he had also been to see the Archbishop, fearful of what he might say.'[2] On 10 May Lloyd George raised the question in the House of Commons as to why the Archbishop's appeal had not been broadcast or published in the *British Gazette*. It was broadcast at last the following day, the day when the government formally decided not to take over the BBC. The *British Gazette* still did not print it. Churchill had to admit in his reply to Lloyd George's question in the House that there was a basic difference between the BBC and the *British Gazette*. 'I cannot answer any question about broadcasting for which I have not even a general responsibility. . . . As far as the Government newspaper is concerned, it is used to give the country information as to what is proceeding in all parts of the country and also to sustain the nation in the difficult period through which we are passing.'[3] In other words, Churchill's responsibility was limited. Baldwin is said to have remarked to G. M. Young that the 'cleverest thing' he had ever done was 'to put Winston in a corner' and tell him to edit the *British Gazette*.[4] His powers evidently did not stretch as far as Savoy Hill. Churchill only met Reith once during the strike, and it was the first time they had ever met. He was polite but critical. At the end of the meeting he went out to the car with Reith. 'He said he had heard that I was badly wounded in the war. I said that was so, but that had no bearing on my actions at present, which embarrassed him.'[5]

BBC 'editorials' posed different problems. The first of them was broadcast on 4 May. It was a radical departure in broadcasting policy, as radical as the frequent supply of news. 'Many of you', the announcer began, 'will be missing the editorial chat

[1] Diary, 8 May 1926. [2] *Into the Wind*, p. 110.
[3] *Hansard*, vol. 195, col. 707, 10 May 1926.
[4] Symons, op. cit., p. 154.
[5] Diary, 9 May 1926; *Into the Wind*, p. 112.

in your favourite newspapers, and I hope you will not think we are presuming if we venture to supply its place with a few words of advice to the ordinary good citizen. You will not expect from us any comment on the merits of the present controversy.' This was hardly tough talk or controversial talk, but it was new. It followed an idea put out by Nicolls in April 1926: at that time it was suggested that speakers from outside might give these brief statements and that they should include labour leaders like Clynes.[1] The conditions of the strike made such an adventurous idea impracticable. The later 'editorials' during the strike were always non-controversial, largely consisting of appeals to people to keep calm.

When the general strike ended, however, and the coal strike continued, the 'editorials' began to deal with more serious matters and to approach controversial questions. From 19 May they were confined to the late-night news bulletin, but they were slightly increased in length. On 21 May the question 'lockout or strike?' was posed, and the announcer urged that some urgent way of reaching agreement about the miners' claim was imperative. On 22 May the title was 'Coal and Countryside': the speaker compared the fortunes of holiday-makers and strikers and warned his listeners not to yield to the temptation 'to push old King Coal and his Fiddlers Three off the stage for one golden moment of relaxation'. On 24 May a deliberate attempt was made to construe the recent utterances of the miners' leaders to suggest that they were moving in the direction of a settlement. A further editorial on 25 May began, 'It will hardly be denied that the great social problem of the twentieth century is how to reconcile or rather how to combine economics with humanity'.[2]

After the editorial on 24 May, which, like the others in the series, was essentially a plea for moderation and social justice, the Postmaster-General, who was also Chief Civil Commissioner, telephoned Atkinson and protested against the whole policy of editorials. The following day he told the House of Commons that the editorials would be suppressed if they became avowedly controversial. He insisted that they should be read either by himself or by Davidson. This decision pleased many of the newspapers, which had included several articles of protest against BBC 'usurpation' of their powers. '2 LO-QUACIOUS' was one

[1] *Nicolls to Reith, 26 Apr. 1926.   [2] BBC Archives.

headline.[1] It also pleased many members of parliament who disliked the line of argument which seemed implicit in the BBC's statements.[2] From 25 May onwards the editorials changed their name to 'editorial reviews', and later they became plain 'reviews'. As they had to be submitted to Davidson or the Postmaster-General, there was a long delay and sometimes the drafts were never returned. Ironically, in view of the continuing coal strike, the last 'review' to be broadcast on 2 June had as its subject 'oil fuel'.[3]

Behind the scenes the story of the editorials was more interesting. Gladstone Murray was extremely anxious to retain the 'reviews'. He was close to Davidson, and wished to use the reviews to put forward views which he knew were shared by Davidson. He felt that the government was anxious for the BBC to preach the doctrine of co-operation even, if necessary, '*ad nauseam*'.[4] Not all members of the government agreed with this policy, nor did all the members of the Board of the BBC. One of them, indeed, wrote to Reith referring to the editorials as 'an unjustifiable imposition on the public'. 'I recognise', he stated, 'that the composition of the editorial is a matter of individual opinion, but the policy of introducing the editorial, and particularly of introducing it in its present position, namely between the weather forecast and the news bulletin, is a question on which I think every Director has a right to express an opinion; and more than this it is, I think, a question on which the Directors should have been consulted.'[5]

Reith replied tactfully, attributing public disquiet about the editorials to a press campaign. 'Through no fault of ours we had to exercise the functions of the Press, or at any rate all the relevant and essential functions of the Press during the strike.' The attack was a sign that things were back to normal again.[6] In the meantime, Reith had approached the Post Office in vain to relieve the Company from the ban on controversy. 'The recent Emergency proved conclusively, if proof were required, how important a factor broadcasting can be in the

[1] *Evening News*, 25 May 1926.
[2] See a letter in *The Times*, 2 June 1926.
[3] BBC Archives.
[4] *Murray to Atkinson, 21 May 1926.
[5] *Binyon to Reith, 27 May 1926.
[6] *Reith to Binyon, 28 May 1926.

life of the community, and we have, as you know, long felt that it is much to be regretted that the influence of the Service should be so restricted.'[1] A series of talks in connexion with industry and industrial relations was long overdue. The Post Office would not budge, and it was the BBC which had to yield. Sir Evelyn Murray did not care about anything that his name-sake and Davidson might be saying behind the scenes: he coldly stated that 'the Postmaster-General considers it right that the existing policy of avoiding the broadcasting of controversial matter should be maintained during the remaining period of the Company's Licence'.[2] The 'reviews' ceased forthwith.

All this was negative. In August 1926 Churchill approached Reith to ask him to allow Havelock Wilson, a right-wing trade unionist who had bitterly opposed the general strike, to broadcast an appeal for industrial peace. Havelock Wilson was one of the most controversial characters in British Labour politics, and this time it was the BBC which turned him down. Later in 1926 it also turned down attempts made from behind the scenes to put on broadcasts by members of the Industrial Peace Union of the British Empire.[3]

The inability to introduce regular controversial broadcasting by a backstairs route was a curious epilogue to the strike. On the controversial question of how fair and effective the BBC had been during the strike, an enormous majority of the vocal listeners, new and old, were full of praise. The Programme Correspondence Department collected statistical details: 3,696 people had written to say how much they appreciated BBC news during the strike, 176 had written to say that they were critical.[4] The views of the 176 have already been quoted; the 3,696 had a distinguished spokesman in Sir Oliver Lodge.

The universal feeling [he declared] is one of gratitude to the BBC for the admirable part their organization has played during the recent happily-ended strife. Had it not been for this possibility of prompt and broadcast communication, the country might have become more uneasy, and been perturbed far more seriously than it has been. By the sending out of trustworthy news, and by the prompt

[1] *Reith to Dalzell, 27 May 1926.
[2] *Sir Evelyn Murray to Reith, 2 June 1926.
[3] BBC Archives.
[4] *Note by R. Wade for Gladstone Murray, 14 June 1926.

denial of false rumours, the pulse of the country was kept calm and healthy. . . . Both sides of the dispute ought to be grateful to the organizers of this new means of spreading intelligence.[1]

As we have seen, one side had more reason to be grateful than the other. The BBC not only spread intelligence during the strike: it reinforced authority. Broadcasting could no longer be regarded as a toy. It was a force in national life with enormous possibilities for good or ill. Again it was Baldwin who recognized this most clearly. He warmly congratulated Reith and his staff who deserved, he said, 'the greatest credit' for all they had done.[2] Two months later, when the events of May were beginning to fall into place, he added that 'the power of broadcasting triumphantly showed itself in a searching test'.[3]

4. The Last Year of the Old Régime

AMONG the people who congratulated Reith most warmly in May 1926 was Lord Gainford. He told his Managing Director that the policy he had followed would certainly have been the policy followed by the whole Board 'had we had the chance of indicating our views concerning it'.[4]

The Board withered away during the last few months of 1926. When the Report of the Crawford Committee was considered on 11 March, the Directors simply recorded on Reith's advice that they felt that 'whilst there were recommendations in regard to the future constitution which they did not approve, no action as a Board should be taken on the Report'.[5] Reith did not even bother to refer to this item in his diary. The next meeting was not held until 10 June. Bull presided in the absence of Gainford, and business was brief. At the short meeting on 8 July the only business was the discussion of the Chairman's speech

---

[1] *Radio Times*, 28 May 1926.
[2] *Baldwin to Reith, 17 May 1926.
[3] Baldwin to Reith, 16 July 1926. This letter is in Lord Reith's possession.
[4] Gainford to Reith, 15 May 1926. This letter is in Lord Reith's possession.
[5] *Board Minutes, 11 Mar. 1926.

to be delivered at the Third Annual General Meeting of the shareholders:[1] for the first time at a Board meeting there was no agenda and no Managing Director's report. The next meeting on 9 September lasted for only eleven minutes, Binyon arriving just in time to sign his name at the end of the meeting.[2] At the meetings of 21 October and 12 November liquidation was the chief item which was considered. The announcement of the names of the new Governors of the British Broadcasting Corporation was a sign that the old régime was drawing to a close. Indeed it needed only an appropriately hushed BBC voice to announce it.

There was evidence, however, that with the demise of the Company some of the old issues of 1922 were re-emerging in the relations between the constituent companies which made up the BBC. At the meeting of 12 November Kellaway on behalf of the Marconi Company argued that the British Broadcasting Company was in no way obliged to transfer the use of its patent rights to the new Corporation. The question of patents remained troublesome and complicated long after the new Corporation was founded, although the Corporation itself escaped serious difficulties:[3] it was fortunate that its sole concern was with broadcasting.

As far as broadcasting itself was concerned, some of the members of the old Board made a last effort in December 1925 to concern themselves with programmes. W. Burnham wrote to Reith on 7 December complaining that as long as he had been a Director the question of programme policy had never been considered by the Board. He asked that it might figure on the next agenda. He said that he did not wish to echo criticisms made in the press, but there were many plausible complaints of weakness in the structure of programmes—'too much education, too many lectures and matters of that sort'; 'too much talk by the announcer'; 'no continuity of programmes'; 'too many uninteresting items, such as Elizabethan music, newfangled songs, weird quartettes and quintettes, groaning chamber music, quite unappreciated by the public, readings from unknown

---

[1] At this meeting, which was held on 8 July 1926, some apprehension was expressed at the imminent transfer to what some shareholders described as 'government control'.

[2] Diary, 9 Sept. 1926.

[3] See Sturmey, op. cit., ch. xi.

poets etc. . . . also talks on subjects which are of no interest to 99% of the listeners'; 'too short a programme on Sunday evenings'; and 'no alternative programmes from Daventry'. He described the Programme Board as 'somewhat complacent and self-satisfied' and offered two ideas of his own—all educational talks to be given before 7 p.m. and the immediate introduction of an alternative service from Daventry.

Burnham sent copies of this letter to his fellow Directors and the Board considered the matter at its meeting on 10 December. As a result Burnham and Binyon were both invited to attend the meeting of the Programme Board on 22 December 1925, and Binyon also attended the meeting on 5 January 1926. Their case was substantially the same, and it was very strongly supported by letters from wireless retailers.[1] Binyon urged that there should be 'a larger proportion of purely recreative items as opposed to those items demanding sustained concentration', and that Saturday evening in particular should be livelier and more attractive; Burnham was more modest than he had been in his letter, and asked that there should be a greater variety in the persons conducting the London Orchestra, more musical programmes devoted to single composers, and more studio engineers with musical knowledge.[2] Binyon set out some of his views on paper in a letter of 23 December after he attended his first Programme Board. He said that he believed that despite what he had been told, programmes were not well balanced and that there was too great a variation from night to night. He no longer shared, however, if he ever had shared, Burnham's criticisms of the membership of the Programme Board. 'I was much impressed by the meeting yesterday,' he wrote, 'and I do not think it would be possible to collect a more competent staff to frame programmes. One thing that surprised me is the fact that they seem to be able to stick, day in and day out, this exacting work and yet still create in one, as they did yesterday, the impression that everyone was enthusiastic.'[3]

Reith must have treasured this letter, for he himself had been anxiously concerned about both people and programmes during the last few months of 1925. Yet welcome though Binyon's

---

[1] *Letters to this effect are to be found in the Binyon Papers.
[2] *Programme Board Minutes, 22 Dec. 1925.
[3] *Binyon to Reith, 23 Dec. 1925.

opinion was, Reith did not welcome the intrusion of the Board
into what had previously been an exclusively executive territory. He wanted it to remain such, not because things should
for ever remain the same but because there was a great opportunity at that time of making them very different. The direction
of programmes had been in the hands of C. A. Lewis since
Burrows left to take up his post in Geneva in March 1925:
Lewis, however, had not inherited Burrows's title of Director
of Programmes, and his interests were concentrated on drama.
In September 1925 Roger Eckersley, brother of Peter, was
appointed as Organizer of Programmes, and a central booking
department was set up within the Programme Department.
Rex Palmer was in charge of it under Eckersley's direction.[1]
'Programme re-organization is the biggest thing on hand', Reith
wrote in his diary about this time; he also expressed his opinion
that Roger Eckersley, whose personal talents were conspicuous
but very different from those of his brother, should be marked
out for 'greater responsibility'.[2] As part of the reorganization,
the Control Board was re-created as a separate entity after
having been merged with the Programme Board for a few
months since March 1925. When Burnham's letter reached
Reith, all these changes had been very recently made: Reith
saw no reason why they should not be allowed to work themselves out.

The 'new management' prepared a detailed reply to the
uneasy Directors, and apart from sharp criticism of BBC programmes in Burnham's evidence before the Crawford Committee[3] and a number of complaints from the Board as a whole
about 'editorials',[4] the initiative of December 1925 and January
1926 was the first and last the Directors took. The reply set out
the guiding views of the programme planners inside the BBC.
While there were modifications in administrative arrangements
later in 1926, these views remained unchanged.[5]

The reply had a number of headings and concluded with a

---

[1] BBC Archives.   [2] Diary, 3 and 7 Sept. 1925.
[3] *W. Burnham's written and oral evidence before the Crawford Committee,
26 Jan. 1926.
[4] *Board Minutes, 10 June 1926: 'The policy of these and topical talks was discussed and it was thought that any expression of the BBC on topics should be dis-
couraged and avoided.'
[5] *The memorandum is undated. It can be found in the Binyon Papers.

statistical digest. Daventry was not supplying a full alternative programme because only about 10 per cent. of the total number of listeners could receive both Daventry and London. Originally three programmes a week from the Daventry transmitter had been different from the London programmes: this figure had been reduced to one. In future it would be increased to two. This was hardly a bold suggestion, but behind the scenes arrangements were being worked out for a radical transformation of BBC technical policy. More high-powered stations were to be the order of the day. More outside broadcasts were to be put on at once, although 'we are often prevented from doing many more things owing to the impossibility of finding a suitable hall'. A new conductor was to be appointed, new arrangements were to be made to ensure 'musical balance and control', and there would be more orchestral accompaniments and fewer gramophone records. No apology was made, however, for sixteenth-century and 'futurist' music: 'a certain amount of this should be included, and the Programme Board does not feel it is being overdone in any way'.

Experiments would be made to improve studio arrangements. Indeed, all sorts of experiments had already been made by the Research Department without much success, 'except that for plays the problem is being successfully handled by using one studio for speech, an adjoining room for noise effects, and a microphone in the corner for echo'. Knowledge of acoustics had not been highly developed before the advent of broadcasting, and the practical experience of BBC engineers had been more useful than the theory of scientists. The work would continue.[1]

Care would also be taken to choose better artists. That care was needed is shown in the figures given in the note relating to the number and proportion of artists receiving different ranges of fees in the quarter ending 30 September 1925 (see p. 389). It was with such statistics in mind that Reith prepared his argument for a larger BBC income from the Post Office. The news-

---

[1] *An interesting report was prepared by A. G. D. West at almost exactly the same time as this letter was written headed *Report on Experiments Carried Out by the BBC Research Department in Connection with Studios and Halls* (Binyon Papers, File 125. 1). It described American experiments on 'reverberation' and said that in Britain the whole technique of broadcasting from outside halls had been very much modified by experiments made in connexion with the broadcast of a service from York Minster in May 1925.

papers could scarcely contradict the logic of this demand. And
when Clara Butt returned to Britain from a tour of Australia
and New Zealand in June 1926, she urged on behalf of 'really
great artists' a policy of greater enterprise. If the only way to
get 'really great artists' to the microphone was to raise more

	Number	Percentage
Under £5 .	5,237	82·81
£5 to £10 .	854	13·50
£10 to £20 .	146	2·31
£20 to £50 .	84	1·33
£50 to £100 .	3	0·05

revenue for broadcasting, then the 10s. licence should be raised
to £1 and the extra income used to pay 'star artists adequate
fees'.[1]

The programme analysis for two months late in 1925 had some
interesting, provocative, and low-brow sub-headings (p. 390).
Whatever criticisms may be made of this programme balance,
the table shows how broadcasting had progressed during its first
few years from Godfrey Isaacs's original suggestion in 1922 that
it would be a good thing to set up 'a wireless broadcasting company with the object of sending out music, bed-time stories and
jokes'.[2]

The last year's programmes of the 'old BBC' were more
carefully polished than those of any previous year and a number of them stood out above the rest. What was generally described as the greatest musical achievement in the history of
the Company was the broadcast from the Royal Opera
House, Covent Garden, on 30 March 1926 of the first (concert)
performance in Britain of Rimsky-Korsakov's opera *Kitesh*. On
20 September the first Gilbert and Sullivan opera was broadcast, *The Mikado*: it was the opening performance of the d'Oyly
Carte Company's London season. A performance on 21 November of James Elroy Flecker's play *Hassan*, with incidental music
by Delius, is said to have displayed considerable improvement
in wireless dramatic technique, which none the less, as has been
shown, was still imperfect at the end of the year.[3]

[1] *Weekly Dispatch*, 20 June 1926.
[2] *The Financier and Bullionist*, 15 Aug. 1922.
[3] See above, p. 282.

Category	Details	October Hours	October %	November Hours	November %
EXOTIC MUSIC	Ancient or Futurist	0·03	0·03	0·09	0·09
CLASSICAL MUSIC	Opera	3·2		3·13	
	Orchestra (Symphony Concerts, &c.)	2·9		1·97	
	Chamber Music	3·3	12·02	2·76	9·93
	Song Recital	2·0		0·89	
	Violin, 'Cello, Piano, &c., Recital	0·62		1·18	
MEDIUM MUSIC	'Music which may please all tastes'	7·42	7·42	11·86	11·86
POPULAR MUSIC	Orchestra or Band, with songs, entertainers, instrument solos, &c.	16·9		11·21	
	Musical Comedy	0·6		1·58	
	Revue	0·3		1·08	
	Star Entertainers, Celebrity, &c.	1·5	30·7	1·18	23·96
	Ballad Recitals	1·9		0·21	
	Restaurant and Cinema Music, popular but unclassified	9·5		8·7	
DANCE MUSIC		6·62	6·62	11·51	11·51
DRAMA	Plays	1·7		1·69	
	'Stunts', Descriptive episodes and features	0·8	2·5	1·67	3·36
SPEECH	News	5·05		4·65	
	Society, &c., Bulletins	1·04		0·73	
	Lecture Talks	15·0	22·09	14·51	20·84
	Poetry and Prose Readings	1·0		0·95	
GRAMOPHONE RECORDS	Unclassified	10·2	10·2	5·8	5·8
RELIGIOUS SERVICES	Organ, Bells, Musical Services and Address	1·2	1·2	2·18	2·18
CHILDREN'S CORNER	Stories and Music	8·12	8·12	7·4	7·4
THEATRE CEREMONY SPEECHES	} Outside Broadcasts	nil nil nil	nil	0·39 0·49 1·19	2·07

TOTAL HOURS BROADCAST	October 31 days 248·75	November 30 days 253·25	Increase 4·5 hrs.

Among the 'stunts' were broadcasts by a diver from the bottom of the Thames near the buildings of the London County Council and an outside broadcast from the Gaumont Studios of a scene in the filming of *Whirlpool*. The Changing of the Guard at Buckingham Palace was also broadcast for the first time, as was the Ceremony of the Keys at the Tower of London.

The year began on 7 January with the first broadcast test for shorthand writers. The first broadcast dancing lesson was given on 5 April. In a feature programme called 'The Wheel of Time, Yesterday, Today and Tomorrow', Osbert Sitwell read his own poems 'in a manner irresistibly suggestive of a machine-gun barrage'.[1] Soon afterwards Alan Cobham was given a 'radio welcome' on his return from his flight to Australia. Finally, as a gesture to the critical public, a series called 'My Programme' was broadcast by prominent men. They were designed in part at least to find out what types of programme were popular and to look for new ideas. The Programme Board was often as critical about programmes as the public. In a note prepared by Nicolls for Roger Eckersley in January 1927, Nicolls stated frankly that in his view although 'we may have progressed during the year 1926 in the direction of more artistic presentation (e.g. in the refinement of effects) I personally do not feel that we have got much forwarder in the choice of material'.[2] The more enthusiastic listeners were far less critical than this. One listener wrote happily to the *Radio Times* in October 1926 that the time was approaching when as much respect would be paid to a 'date with the radio' as to a 'night at the opera'.[3]

Behind the scenes there were considerable changes in the administrative arrangement of programmes during 1926. Lewis ceased to be chairman of the Programme Board in May 1926 and at the same time left the permanent staff. He continued to be employed as a Programme Adviser until March 1928. George Grossmith continued to act as a Programme Adviser, and Filson Young was appointed to a similar post in September 1926. With Lewis's resignation, Roger Eckersley took over the chairmanship of the Programme Board. At that time the members of the Board who attended most regularly were Lewis, who continued

[1] B.B.C. Year Book (1930), 'The Old B.B.C.', p. 150.
[2] *Report of Feb. 1927.   [3] *Radio Times*, 1 Oct. 1926.

to serve as an ordinary member, Pitt, Stobart, Nicolls, and Grossmith. Peter Eckersley, Gladstone Murray, Rex Palmer, Jeffrey, and Gambier Parry also were present frequently. Carpendale occasionally was present. Reith very seldom attended, although in April 1926 he made out the new organization chart himself, a job 'which I quite liked doing'.[1]

The organization of the BBC as a whole was considerably tightened up at this time. Rice ceased to be Secretary of the Company in April 1926 and was transferred to the Publicity Department as Business Manager of the *Radio Times* and other Company publications. His old post was abolished altogether, and a completely new method of planning expenditure on programmes was subsequently introduced. Hitherto all matters of programme expenditure had been referred to Rice, who was responsible under Reith for dealing with them. It was Rice who dealt with the 'programme allowances' which were made to the various stations, the only exception being that Stobart had a strictly limited sum of money to distribute for educational 'talks'. By the terms of the new arrangement the Chief Accountant, T. Lochhead, who was to have a long and distinguished career of service in the BBC, was to allocate annually to the Programme Department a sum which it was expected would cover the entire programme expenditure for London and the provincial stations. This sum was to be administered by the Organizer of Programmes, Roger Eckersley, who was given complete control over its allocation.

In the summer of 1926 the Programme Department had five sections—Music, Education, Drama, London Executive, and Administration; and the Administration section alone was divided into five sub-sections—Central Booking, directed by Rex Palmer, Copyright, Provincial Outside Broadcasts and Liaison with Stations, Programme Accounts and Simultaneous Broadcasting, and the Co-ordination and Publication of Programmes. There was a further regrouping in November 1926 when the title 'Programme Executive' was adopted. The five sections of the Programme Executive at Savoy Hill were concerned with Central Booking, Copyright, Programme Finance, Simultaneous Broadcasts, and Programme Correspondence, the last of which became closely associated for the first time not

[1] Diary, 19 Apr. 1926.

with publicity but with planning. The programme side of the *Radio Times* had been managed since 1924 by the Programme Executive as part of the work of the section dealing with Simultaneous Broadcasting.

This administrative rearrangement was part of a bigger set of changes which affected the whole organization. At the end of the old régime five Assistant Controllers were subordinate to Carpendale and to Reith. Peter Eckersley was in charge of Engineering, Gladstone Murray in charge of Information, Roger Eckersley in charge of Programmes, V. H. Goldsmith, formerly Assistant to the Controller, in charge of the Secretariat, and T. Lochhead in charge of Finance. Together with Carpendale and Reith, these five men constituted the Control Board, which met regularly and took all major decisions on broadcasting policy. For the first time within the organization there was beginning to be a clear-cut distinction between 'them' and 'us'.

Two of the decisions taken by the Control Board during the last few months of the Company's life were to sort out the Company's papers, discarding everything that was 'useless',[1] and at the very last meeting on 21 December to reorganize the filing system, taking in an expert on a temporary basis to evolve a new system.[2] Reith was doing his best to withstand the operation of Parkinson's Law. He informed the Control Board (for instance) that as a matter of principle he would rather tear up ten letters and lose one which might be of possible use than keep them all including the nine which would never be wanted.[3] In practice, however, the consequences of growth begin to be traceable in internal communications in the course of 1926. A new style can be discerned in documents which read as follows: 'It will considerably simplify the sorting of memos at Head Office if Station Directors will address memos for sub-sections 2, 3, 4, and 5 of the Admin. Section directly to the person concerned, i.e. to the Organiser of Programmes, for the attention of Mr. . . .'[4]

More important, it was recognized in 1926 that improved

---

[1] *Control Board Minutes, 23 June 1926.
[2] Ibid., 21 Dec. 1926.   [3] Ibid., 23 June 1926.
[4] *Memorandum of 21 June 1926. A year before that a system of reference letters had begun to be used on internal memoranda (ibid., Memorandum of 23 May 1925).

liaison with the provincial stations was necessary. Visits of
Station Directors to London were inadequate. Scotland had had
a liaison officer since March 1926. In October 1926 a Northern
Area Director was appointed, and in December 1926 the post of
Station Liaison Officer was created. The task of the new officer,
D. H. Clarke, was to provide a link between the Programme and
Administrative Departments at Head Office and the Stations.
He was expected to spend four days at Head Office for every ten
days away.[1]

Reith certainly made every effort to control the size of the
staff. In September 1926, for example, he sent round a memorandum to all Station Directors warning them to make a full
survey of their staffs before the new constitution came into
effect. 'Is the work that is being done all absolutely necessary,
and are the people who are doing it thoroughly efficient in
every sense for that work? I do not want Station staff to be overworked, but on the other hand we cannot afford to carry what
might be termed "reserves" at all stations.' The detailed replies suggest that none of the stations was over-staffed: they
almost all ended with the words, 'I honestly consider that all
members of the staff here are worthy of transfer to the Corporation'.[2]

The better side of expansion was the increased concern for
the social security of members of the BBC's staff. Although it
was not until 1929 that there emerged the idea of a regular
'Establishment', a Provident Fund was started in October 1925.
Originally it had been intended to set up a Company Pensions
Fund, but soon after the first deductions from current salaries
had been made, the Postmaster-General instructed the Company to delay the beginning of a pension scheme until after the
future constitution of the BBC had been decided. Although the
Post Office would accept no responsibility for the details of a
scheme, which it claimed was 'a matter entirely for the Company', it added that it had to be understood that 'no contributions to such a Fund should be made from revenue accruing
from licence fees'.[3] In a memorandum of November 1925 the
staff were told of this, and the name Provident Fund was agreed

[1] BBC Archives.
[2] Ibid.
[3] *Dalzell to Reith, 31 Oct. 1925.

upon. It was not until 1931, however, that a properly constituted Pension Scheme was instituted.[1]

There was one interesting feature of early staff policy. The
principle of eligibility of women for any posts had been maintained from the start;[2] it was reaffirmed in striking language in
April 1926. 'I wish all such titles as Woman Organiser, Chief
Aunt, and so on', Reith told the Station Directors, 'to be completely abandoned. Apart from their being cumbersome and
rather stupid, they convey a limited conception of the responsibilities of women. The class of women whom we are now employing (or ought to be employing) is such that they should rank
on the same footing as men assistants.'[3]

The one section of the BBC which employed no women in
posts of executive responsibility was the Engineering Department. It was that department which in the course of the last year
of the old régime prepared the way for the biggest of the changes
of the future—the introduction of high-power regional broadcasting. Regional broadcasting did not start until several years
later, but the foundations of future technical policy were decided before the Company disappeared.

An interesting internal memorandum of July 1925 went
farther than the critics of the BBC in advocating 'variety of
programmes'. The public, it stated, would soon demand 'the
universal possibility of a *choice* of programmes'. The possibility
of such a choice rested on a new set of technical developments.
There were three possible ways of providing choice: first, by
abandoning all the relay stations and replacing them by a few
stations of high power; second, by creating groups of three
stations located at single points near large towns and cities and
transmitting alternative programmes; and third, by getting rid
of all the existing stations, main as well as relay, and erecting two
or three national high-power stations. All these schemes were
described as technically possible, but the social disadvantages of
the first and third were acknowledged. If either were to be im-
plemented, there would be a loss in 'local interest'. 'Those who
have not been much in the Provinces cannot assess the extra-

[1] BBC Archives.
[2] *Control Board Minutes, 16 Nov. 1926.
[3] *Reith to the Station Directors, 30 Apr. 1926.

ordinary value placed upon the local station by provincial listeners.' These social disadvantages were thought to outweigh all technical advantages, and the argument was consequently advanced for what was called a 'multiple scheme'.

The scheme as suggested had four features—the increasing of the power of at least four of the main stations, the erection of a new and additional London station, the erection of a new high-power long-wave station, and an increase in the power of the relay stations. The additional London station would be able to provide genuinely 'different' programmes. While the first London station would put on educational talks, news bulletins and so on, the second would transmit dance music from 9 o'clock to 1 o'clock in the morning. One station could be confessedly 'high-brow' (Reith put an exclamation mark in the margin against this suggestion): the other would be—and it was a curious word—'cosmopolitan'.[1]

This memorandum should be examined in the light of what subsequently happened in 1925—the opening of the new Daventry station and the technical discussions at Geneva associated with the U.I.R. Neither Reith nor Eckersley was content with Daventry; they wished to experiment with two London stations 'to test the practicability of alternative programmes from the average listener's point of view'.[2] They were irritated when in their evidence before the Crawford Committee the National Association of Radio Manufacturers and Traders criticized BBC 'power policy' on the grounds that the provision of 'low power main stations and trifling power relay stations' was 'absolutely wrong'. They were as unwilling to perpetuate existing policy as the N.A.R.M.T. was, and were already thinking along the lines of a number of high-power transmitters in six or seven regional 'zones'. A note in Gladstone Murray's handwriting against the radio trade's memorandum reads: 'This is all wrong. They are putting up a scheme as if *they* had thought of it, which was really initiated by us and circulated to them.'[3]

Eckersley himself has written that he first got the idea of the

---

[1] *Internal memorandum (undated, but probably July 1925), *Reorganization of Power and Wavelength of BBC Stations*.

[2] *Reith to Dalzell, 26 May 1926.

[3] *A Trade View on the Broadcasting Service* (1926).

regional scheme 'in about 1924'; he has added that from Reith he received consistent support, which was invaluable in view of substantial and internal opposition. He has described in detail the form that opposition took and the technical problems which had to be solved.[1] In July 1926 he was putting the whole question before the readers of the *Radio Times*. 'What is the right policy for the distribution of a broadcast service? A lot of little stations? Fewer medium-powered stations? Or few high-power stations? Or is it to be a combination of all three types?'[2] He already had his own answer prepared—broadcasting from regional centres each of which would be given two wavelengths. 'In combination, and with their much higher power, the transmitters would spread their dual programmes all over the territory to be served.'[3] He could publicize the questions more than the answers—and he was an excellent publicist—for the Post Office was reluctant to allow any publicity on the problem of power. When, for instance, in November 1926 the Postmaster-General gave the BBC permission experimentally to increase the power of Daventry to 30 kilowatts, he stated at the same time that the use of increased power should not be advertised in the public press.[4]

The old régime did have its last moments of triumph in the public press. Indeed, as Reith wrote, it went out 'in a blaze of glory'.[5]

On the morning of 16 December Carpendale went into Reith's office and to Reith's great surprise summoned him to a meeting. Reith was presented by his colleagues with four silver candlesticks and a flower bowl. 'Everybody in the company had apparently contributed to the presentation on a regular scale and I had known nothing about it.'[6] The candlesticks had a special significance. Reith had recently played the part of the thief in the play *The Bishop's Candlesticks*, and Carpendale had played the part of the Bishop. When Carpendale said he had a present for Reith and produced the Georgian candlesticks, there was plenty of opportunity for association of ideas. In the even-

[1] Eckersley, op. cit., p. 116.
[2] 'Daventry Calling', *Radio Times*, 23 Sept. 1926.
[3] Eckersley, op. cit., p. 118.   [4] *Phillips to Reith, 4 Nov. 1926.
[5] *Into the Wind*, p. 116.   [6] Diary, 16 Dec. 1926.

ing of the same day a valedictory dinner party was held at the Hotel Metropole in honour of the Prime Minister, the retiring Directors of the Company, and the Governors-designate. About one hundred members of the London staff were at the dinner along with the twenty Station Directors. Also present were the Postmaster-General, the Assistant Postmaster-General, the Secretary of the Post Office, and several principal officials of the Post Office.

Reith was in the chair, and he described the occasion as a family party. In his opening speech he emphasized that there was to be no break in continuity. He chose military metaphor. 'In the past by forced marches we have advanced through unknown and dangerous country, with adversities and conflicts which will never in like degree beset us again; some of us feel the effects of the campaign more than we dare to admit, but we know the expedition is not yet near fulfillment.' He restated his philosophy of broadcasting and his assessment of its social consequences. 'We have tried to found a tradition of public service and to dedicate the service of Broadcasting to the service of humanity in its fullest sense.' It was the 'fundamental policy of public service' which the outgoing Board of Directors had approved and permitted Reith to follow which itself determined the change in constitution which was coming.

Bull, speaking on behalf of the Directors, chose similar terms. So did Gainford and Mitchell-Thomson, the Postmaster-General, who declared that not the least of the advantages which the new Corporation would enjoy would be that of unbroken continuity of management on the administrative and the technical side. Lord Riddell, who had been arguing for about two hours about business with Reith that afternoon, quipped jovially about the success of the enterprise having been ensured by the press. Walter Payne spoke on behalf of the entertainment industry, and promised that he and Lord Riddell together could and would tell the new Broadcasting Board 'what the public wants'. All this was in the mood of a very friendly family party, and doubtless Marconi, who was present, was pleased when a letter from Ramsay MacDonald moved away from family matters and linked science with the BBC in a way that none of the other speakers chose to do. MacDonald recalled that in the beginning was the invention. 'I should like to be able to say by word of mouth what revolutionary significance of an elevating kind I attach to the wonderful discoveries in physics which have brought the British Broadcasting Company into being.'

Baldwin, as always, was both eloquent and practical. Puffing at a pipe given him by Edgar Wallace a few months before, he compared ironically the distinguished guests, 'the lovers of the limelight and the darlings of the Press', with the 'far more distinguished, silent, anonymous, obscure people' who had created broadcasting. He saluted the fact that they had not been actuated merely by mercenary and 'get-rich-quick' motives. He noted how young were the men who had made the key decisions during the previous few years, and he praised them for sticking at all times to the 'bare, uncoloured truth'. 'We shall follow with immense interest your progress, sympathise with your struggles and rejoice in all your triumphs.'[1]

Four days later Reith learned that he was to be given a knighthood. He accepted it only after hesitation.[2] On the last day of the old year he paid a visit to Magnet House and recalled the forlorn occasion when he had first arrived there four years ago. For him too the wheel might have turned full circle. He was to stay with the BBC until 1938, but he was asked on that last day of the old four years whether he was interested in an important and lucrative new post in a large national organization. Without hesitation he said no. He was tired with the labours of the previous few months, but he could hardly leave the BBC 'the beginning of the new régime'.[3]

5. Prospect and Retrospect

THERE were, in fact, no sharp breaks. The new Governors were already studying 'the multifarious and delicate operations of this

---

[1] *A verbatim report of all the speeches is in BBC Archives.

[2] He wrote to his mother on 30 Dec. 'I delayed replying for over a week as I did not feel *at all* anxious for such a thing. I consulted Dean Bell, Woodward, Ramsay MacDonald and Carpendale, and they all urged it, so eventually I accepted. I am not happy about it.' This letter is in Lord Reith's possession.

[3] Diary, 31 Dec. 1926.

great organisation'.[1] The staff had to be specifically told to remember the change 'and not to refer [over the air] to the Company instead of the Corporation by inadvertence. Artists and speakers who may speak at the microphone should also be advised. It is, however, preferable that the abbreviation "BBC" be used at the microphone.' Only one title within the organization was to be changed. Reith was now Director-General. The symbolic changes had a curious element of ritual about them. On Friday night 31 December, for instance, when the last Company programmes were going out over the air, staff in Head Office were told to leave all stationery bearing the name of the British Broadcasting Company Ltd. on the tops of their desks. 'On Saturday, staff (coming specially for the purpose) will remove this and replace it by Corporation stationery.'[2]

It proved quicker and easier to bring the new Corporation into existence than to liquidate the Company. Reith added to his titles that of 'Liquidator' on 9 December 1926.[3] Surprisingly enough he was still serving in this capacity in 1929. It was not until 12 December 1929 that the old Company finally ceased to exist.[4] The chief reason for this was the unwillingness of the new Corporation to abandon the old BBC trade mark. Since the Corporation did not 'traffic in goods or merchandise', there were difficulties in securing a new trade mark, and after long correspondence between the BBC solicitors, the Board of Trade, and the Trade Marks Branch of the Patent Office, it was decided to cling to the old trade mark as long as possible. The Corporation feared that the mark might be used by unauthorized persons to mislead the wireless trade and the public.[5] The mark was renewed again in 1938 after the Trade Marks Branch of the Patent Office had written a letter reminding the BBC that after fourteen years the original trade mark was due to expire. With a magnificent lack of knowledge of what was happening in the world outside, the letter was addressed to the British Broadcasting Company Ltd., 2 Savoy Hill, Victoria Embankment, London W.C. 2.[6]

By this time many of the members of the old Board had died,

[1] Lord Clarendon, 'The New BBC' in *Radio Times*, 31 Dec. 1926.
[2] *Memorandum to Station Directors and Head Office, 31 Dec. 1926.
[3] *Board Minutes, 9 Dec. 1926.   [4] BBC Archives.
[5] *Memorandum to the Post Office, Feb. 1928.
[6] *Letter of 8 Mar. 1938.

and broadcasting was completely divorced in the public mind from its commercial origins. Only in the light of post-war controversies has new point been given to old stories.

Without the initiative of business enterprise there would have been no BBC: without a concept of public service there would have been no Corporation. Reith saw the Corporation as the logical successor to the Company. Not all the members of the Board accepted the logic. Binyon, for example, complained of a passage in the BBC memorandum which was circulated among members of parliament in July 1926. It read, 'the policy of the British Broadcasting Company, during its stewardship of the service, has led logically and indeed inevitably to the creation of a Public Corporation'.[1] 'I take strong objection to this statement', Binyon declared, 'which I think is not only an unwise statement but an untrue statement. Had the British Broadcasting Company abused its period of stewardship, I could then understand that it might inevitably lead to the creation of some different organisation.'[2] Reith did not withdraw his statement. He wanted public safeguards to protect the conception of public service: he was not prepared to leave future control to the 'accident of management'.

In retrospect the company shell in which broadcasting was so successfully developed between 1922 and 1926 appears at best as temporary, something to be discarded when the organization grew and when the radio industry had ceased to have a compelling motive for continuing to sponsor broadcasting. In the words of the Crawford Committee, the manufacturers of radio apparatus were prepared in 1922 to conduct a broadcasting service without cost to the taxpayer, and they had at their disposal technicians of the highest order. . . . The scheme had the advantage that it tided over the initial period when the finance of broadcasting was highly speculative and established a system under the best technical auspices with a guarantee of adequate financial backing by responsible firms and a strict limitation of the operating Company's profits. . . . It was not intended to be more than a temporary arrangement, and the currency of the Licence was deliberately limited . . . in order that the organisation might be open to review when sufficient practical experience had been acquired.[3]

[1] For the Memorandum, see above, p. 334.
[2] *Binyon to Reith, 10 Aug. 1926.
[3] Cd. 2599 (1925), para. 3, Appendix II.

Between 1922 and 1926, while the radio industry developed on business lines, the BBC grew as a kind of 'mixed' institution, commercial yet public, independent yet, as the experience of the general strike showed, 'within the Constitution'. The structure and powers of the Company would not have been the same as they were had there not been initial regulation by the Post Office. This framework of regulation, which has been carefully described and analysed, was acceptable to the radio manufacturers because they expected sufficient profits from the sale of radio sets to make them willing to take on their own shoulders the task of broadcasting. Yet they made little money out of broadcasting itself: as Baldwin said at the valedictory dinner, they had not been mercenary. He might have added that they were not allowed to be. Not only was dividend restricted to 7½ per cent., but no capital gains were allowed. When the Company's assets were transferred to the Corporation, the new public body acquired a going concern unencumbered by capital liabilities. Permanent assets to the extent of £334,788 had been acquired entirely out of revenue, and liquid assets had been reserved which sufficed to pay all liabilities in full, including issued share capital.

The enterprise, as we have seen, was not without its risks. It became an institution not through universal acceptance but through struggle. Most of those risks were borne by the so-called 'Big Six'. When the Company was wound up, about 1,600 manufacturers held between them only about 11,000 £1 shares: the remainder was held by the 'Big Six' and by about eighty wireless dealers who had joined the Company later. Apart from the 'Big Six', none of the shareholders was responsible for even the smallest fraction of the expenses of the Company. For bearing these risks the 'Big Six' received no concessions. Together they made up a monopoly, but it was a monopoly which enjoyed no monopoly profits and few monopoly advantages.

It was the Post Office which did best financially out of the deal. The surplus income accruing from licences was far greater than could be justified as a payment for administrative costs. When the government decided to pay a fixed sum to the BBC each year, *The Financial Times* commented in a leader headed 'Grab', it was apparently the intention of the Post Office to regard 'listening in' as nothing but a means of obtaining revenue for a department which 'did nothing in return'.[1] Even the sliding-scale arrangement which was arrived at later gave the new Corporation only a limited share in the fruits of broadcasting progress. 'Broadcasting is still only in its infancy', the Wireless Retailers' Association complained. 'The BBC has done wonders, but the possibilities, which are enormous, will never become realities as long as the Post Office has the power to make such arbitrary raids on licence revenue.'[2]

The Directors of the BBC themselves were treated with little generosity when the Company was wound up. Some of them did not approve of the names of the newly appointed Governors and they must have resented the fact that the Governors were to be paid three times as much as they had been: they must have found it difficult to retain their enthusiasm during the last few months of 1926. Yet the Post Office queried their entitlement even to one year's honorarium of £200. It was Reith who was left to point out that they had made no protest against the change in constitution and that throughout the whole of their period of office they had 'subordinated their trade interests and permitted the Company to be run as a public service. Perhaps I alone can realise how different things might have been.'[3] In any case, the total cost of such honoraria would be met entirely out of the profits of the Publications Department: the honoraria would not be paid by licence-holders at all. The Treasury accepted Reith's arguments 'with some reluctance',[4] and it was hardly surprising that one of the retiring Directors refused to take the honorarium at all. 'The real value of such, if paid,' he said, 'would rest in the knowledge that it was a gratuitous and spontaneous recognition of their work in establishing broadcasting in this country and conducting it as a public utility service rather than in the narrower interests of those concerns which took the financial risk in forming the Company.'[5]

If Reith had had different Directors, the story of broadcasting might have been very different, but then Reith in his early thirties was a man who would have stood out in any company.

---

[1] *The Financial Times*, 7 Sept. 1926.
[2] *Evening Chronicle* (Newcastle), 4 Sept. 1926.
[3] *Reith to the Postmaster-General, 3 Feb. 1927.
[4] *Dalzell to Reith, 7 Feb. 1927.
   *Letter of 10 June 1927.

Wireless was invented, but as Mary Agnes Hamilton has said, Reith could not have been invented. 'He was markedly and patently out of the common run . . . an original.'[1] Given that the constitution of the British Broadcasting Company was the ephemeral product of a unique meeting between enterprising business men and vigilant Post Office officials, the outlook of the Company was the external expression of Reith's abiding principles. He wanted the Company to be converted into a Corporation: it was so converted. Why was the change necessary? 'Because, in view of the magnitude of the public obligations involved, a commercial institution of any sort, and however slight, appears invidious . . . more particularly because such large sums of money were accruing from the licence revenue that it appeared desirable to have a different constitution, with public representatives instead of trade representatives on the Board.'[2]

So firm was Reith's grasp that he will inevitably be the leading figure in the second volume of this history, as he has been in this. In him was the strongest guarantee of continuity. A fascinating letter survives which he received from Lord Blanesburgh in October 1926. Blanesburgh had been prepared as a member of the Crawford Committee to urge the continuation of the Company at least for a further spell. He had questioned Reith extremely searchingly on this matter.[3] But he capitulated to Reith's arguments, and when Reith felt a little uncertain about his own future in the autumn of 1926, reassured him.

I don't think that you have anything to fear at the hands of the new authority [Blanesburgh wrote]. Your influence will have to be exercised in a different way perhaps. The new Commissioners will be much keener on the artistic and educational side than the old Board; they will want to justify themselves in the eyes of the public by reason of their interest in that side of the work. Your influence accordingly and especially at first, while it may be as real as ever, will have to be more subtly exercised. But with a little tact I feel sure it will not grow less: nay more, it will increase. . . . Everyone knows the part you have played in making broadcasting in this country what it is.[4]

[1] BBC Programme, *The BBC Story*, July 1958.
[2] *Radio Times*, 5 Nov. 1926.
[3] See above, p. 327.
[4] Blanesburgh to Reith, 19 Oct. 1926. This letter is in Lord Reith's possession.

Everyone did, and everyone knew Peter Eckersley's part also. The part played by others, as this volume has shown, was often decisive and always significant. Broadcasting is a collective achievement. Its success depended upon many voices and many hands. Some of the voices were very different from that of Reith. In this pioneer period, however, most of the hands were working for the same purpose and with the same enthusiasm. It was a shrewd and kindly remark of Baldwin to refer to the anonymous and to the obscure.

Not only was broadcasting a collective achievement: it had a collective impact. It affected the life of the community. Its controversial qualities have already been described. It could be blamed for anything and praised for what it did not do. It could be held responsible not only for every kind of moral, intellectual, and social vice but for depressions off the coast of Iceland. It could be satirized in *Punch* and sanctified by the Archbishop of Canterbury. By the end of 1926 if it was not part of the Establishment, whatever that then was, the BBC was certainly established. *Punch* and the Archbishop of Canterbury were both in agreement about it.

Broadcasting [the Archbishop declared in December 1926] is now a well-assured factor in our national life—a uniquely widespread influence. The fact that upwards of two million people in this country hold wireless licences means, I suppose, that several more millions of people are constantly listening to the broadcast programmes. There is no stratum in our social life, no place of recreation, no educational centre into which the influence of broadcasting does not already penetrate. I hear of loud speakers now in constant use all over England—in hospital wards, in union workhouses, in factory dining-rooms, in clubs, in the servants' halls of the great houses, and even among the workers in the fields.

It is a curiously dated list of places, which reminds us sharply that this was 1926 not 1956. More significant, however, than the list was the Archbishop's emphasis on the suddenness of what had happened. 'We woke, so to speak, to find it present in our midst and affecting us all.'[1] *Punch* believed that there was still something magical about it. A poem by 'Algol' published in *Punch* in 1926 ends with the word 'necromancy':

[1] *Radio Times*, 17 Dec. 1926.

Gaunt pole that rises into upper air,
  High o'er my clumps of holly and genista,
How my whole soul revolts to see thee there,
  Bisecting what was once a high-class vista.
Not—oh, believe me—not from whim or choice
  Would I maintain an object so appalling,
But lo! from thy slim apex comes the Voice
  That nightly tells me 'This is London calling'. . . .

. . . Wherefore stand on, O eyesore unalloyed,
  Seeing thou bearest that so potent cable
That snares all news, all knowledge, from the void
  And drops it neatly on my study table;
Ay, and the Voice, that disembodied tongue,
  That I so oft have sought in playful fancy
To add a face to, shall not go unsung
  While I've a voice to praise thy necromancy.[1]

[1] Quoted Hibberd, op. cit., p. 21.

BIBLIOGRAPHICAL NOTE

THE main source used in the writing of this history has been the voluminous BBC Archives. There are approximately 6,500 items in the BBC Archives relating to the period covered in this volume. The items are well catalogued with cross-references in a number of files divided in terms of subject-matter. The foundations of the Archives were laid when the Central Registry was formed in 1927, and compilation was continuous between 1930 and 1939. Summaries were made of what were thought to be the most significant developments.

The first set of files covers the Minutes and correspondence of the 1922 Broadcasting Committee of Manufacturers. The files of the Company proper contain full records of correspondence and internal memoranda on such topics as the drawing up of Articles of Association, negotiations with the Post Office relative to the terms of the Licence, the issue of receiving licences, protection, technical matters, finance, and liquidation. Verbatim accounts of shareholders' meetings and the Company's reports and balance sheets conclude this section.

A large number of files relate to the work of the Sykes and Crawford Committees. Many of these files duplicate material in the Post Office Archives with which they must be studied in conjunction. Particularly useful in this collection are the BBC glosses on evidence supplied by individuals and organizations. There are also files of the meetings of the Broadcasting Committee.

Board Minutes of the BBC may be supplemented by Minutes of the Control Board and the Programme Board. All these formal Minutes are complete. In addition there are (in some cases fragmentary) Minutes of some of the trade advisory committees and advisory committees concerned with programmes of a special nature such as opera. The records of some of the regional advisory committees also survive.

There are invaluable files which are concerned with dealings with outside individuals and bodies including politicians, the press, government departments, and radio and listeners' organizations. A large volume of material relating to the *Radio Times* is neatly and tidily catalogued.

The daily programme sheets giving details of the programmes as broadcast are complete from the first day of broadcasting, the amount of detail varying considerably over the years. Only a few of the actual scripts of programmes broadcast before 1927 are still in existence.

About 350 items comprising internal memoranda, letters between the Director-General, the Prime Minister, and others, and news bulletins have survived from the time of the general strike of 1926. Many of the letters preserved are from listeners expressing their opinions of the broadcasting service during the strike.

Public opinion over longer periods is well expressed in a comprehensive collection of volumes of press cuttings in the BBC Library. There are nineteen volumes covering this period. They are divided by subject, covering such topics as Programmes, Education, the Regional Scheme, Wavelengths, and the General Strike.

Among the early books on broadcasting, which now have the commanding authority of early sources, four are indispensable:
(1) BURROWS, A. R. *The Story of Broadcasting.* Cassell, 1924.
(2) LEWIS, C. A. *Broadcasting from Within.* Newnes, 1924.
(3) REITH, J. C. W. *Broadcast Over Britain.* Hodder & Stoughton, 1924.
(4) 'The Old BBC', in the *BBC Year-Book (1930)*. This illuminating, anonymous article was, in fact, written by D. H. Clarke.
Later volumes, including autobiographies which are illuminating and helpful in relation to the period, are:
(1) ECKERSLEY, P. P. *The Power Behind the Microphone.* Cape, 1941.
(2) ECKERSLEY, R. *The BBC and All That.* Low, Marston, 1946.
(3) GIELGUD, Val. *Years of the Locust.* Nicholson & Watson, 1947.
(4) — *British Radio Drama, 1922–1956.* Harrap, 1957.
(5) GORHAM, M. *Sound and Fury.* P. Marshall, 1948.
(6) HENRY, L. *My Laugh Story.* S. Paul, 1937.
(7) HIBBERD, S. *This—is London.* Macdonald & Evans, 1950.
(8) MASCHWITZ, E. *No Chip on My Shoulder.* Jenkins, 1957.
(9) PAYNE, J. *Signature Tune.* S. Paul, 1947.
(10) — *This is Jack Payne.* Marston, 1932.
(11) REITH, J. C. W. *Into the Wind.* Hodder & Stoughton, 1949.

The key official sources for the period, apart from *Hansard*, which has been very fully used, are:
(1) Cd. 1822 (1923), Wireless Broadcasting Licence: Copies of (1) Licence by the Postmaster-General to the British Broadcasting Company Limited. . . . (2) Agreement with respect to the Broadcasting of News and General Information. 24 pp.

(2) Cd. 1951 (1923), Broadcasting Committee Report [The Sykes
Committee Report].
(3) Cd. 1976 (1923), Wireless Broadcasting Licence: Copy of
Supplementary Agreement . . . to Cmd. 1822 of 1923.
(4) Cd. 2599 (1925), Report of the Broadcasting Committee.
(5) Cd. 2755 (1927), Wireless Broadcasting Service: Copy of Agreement between the Postmaster-General and the British Broadcasting Company, providing for the transfer of the broadcasting
service on the 1st January 1927.
(6) Cd. 2756 (1927), Wireless Broadcasting: Drafts of (1) Royal
Charter . . . for the incorporation of the British Broadcasting
Corporation; and (2) Licence and Agreement . . . between
H.M. Postmaster-General and . . . the British Broadcasting
Corporation.

Among later books on the BBC and its setting, which are relevant to the period covered in this volume, the following stand out:

(1) COASE, R. H. *British Broadcasting: a Study in Monopoly*. Longmans, 1950.
(2) GORDON, L. *The Public Corporation in Great Britain*. O.U.P., 1938.
(3) GORHAM, M. *Broadcasting and Television Since 1900*. Dakers, 1952.
(4) O'BRIEN, T. H. *British Experiments in Public Ownership and Control*. Allen & Unwin, 1937.
(5) PAULU, B. *British Broadcasting: Radio and Television in the United Kingdom*. O.U.P., 1957.
(6) ROBSON, W. A. (ed.) *Public Enterprise*. Allen & Unwin, 1937.
(7) SIEPMANN, C. A. *Radio, Television and Society*. New York, O.U.P., 1950.
(8) STURMEY, S. G. *The Economic Development of Radio*. Duckworth, 1958.

Other books are cited in the footnotes, which include frequent
references to general histories, histories of American radio, studies of
technical development, and the writings of significant critics of radio
such as Gilbert Seldes in the United States and Raymond Williams
in Britain.
Among the periodicals which have been consulted for the period
discussed in this volume, the following have proved especially useful—the *Radio Times*, the *Scientific American*, *Economist*, and *Wireless
World*. The files of *The Times*, the *Daily Express*, and the *Daily Mail*
have also been carefully consulted.

APPENDIX I

AT the 'Conference on Wireless Telephony Broadcasting' held on 18 May 1922 at the General Post Office the following were present:

1. *Representing the Post Office*

Sir G. Evelyn P. Murray, K.C.B. (Secretary to Post Office), Chairman
Mr. F. J. Brown, C.B., C.B.E.
Mr. J. I. de Wardt, O.B.E. (Secretary's Office)
Mr. E. H. Shaughnessy, O.B.E. (Engineering Dept.)
Major A. J. Lee, M.C. (Engineering Dept.)
Cmdr. F. G. Loring, R.N. (Inspector of Wireless Telegraphy)

2. *Representing Interested Companies*

Mr. Godfrey C. Isaacs Col. Adrian Simpson Major H. MacCallum	Marconi's Wireless Telegraph Co. Ltd.
Major W. W. H. Burnham Mr. Frank Phillips	Messrs. Burndept Ltd.
Mr. D. Sinclair Mr. H. H. Harrison	Automatic Telephone Manufacturing Co. Ltd.
Mr. S. G. Brown	Messrs. S. G. Brown Ltd.
Mr. F. Gill Mr. V. Wright Mr. H. M. Pease Mr. G. H. Nash	Western Electric Co. Ltd.
Mr. R. C. Clinker	British Thomson-Houston Co. Ltd.
Mr. J. W. S. Prior Mr. G. Z. Aukland	G. Z. Aukland & Son
Mr. H. Powell Rees	Messrs. H. P. R. Wireless Ltd.
Mr. A. W. Wright	Messrs. Mitchells Electric & Wireless Ltd.
Mr. E. Gambrell	Messrs. Gambrell Bros. Ltd.
Mr. H. Hirst Mr. Charles F. Tripps	Messrs. General Electric Co. Ltd.
Mr. H. R. Rivers-Moore	R. M. Radio Co. Ltd.
Mr. Charles J. Close Mr. R. N. Cunningham	Messrs. Cunningham Ltd.
Mr. H. D. Butler	Messrs. Butler & Co.
Mr. B. Mittell	Messrs. C. F. Elwell Ltd.
Mr. B. Binyon	Radio Communication Company.
Mr. A. P. M. Fleming	Metropolitan-Vickers Electrical Co. Ltd.
Mr. S. H. Smith	A. W. Gamage Ltd.

APPENDIX II. Finance

BRITISH BROADCASTING COMPANY, LTD.

(i) Balance Sheets Statistics

	31.3.24	31.3.25		31.3.26		31.12.26		Valuation of transfer to Corporation	
	Amount	Amount	Increase or Decrease	Amount	Increase or Decrease	Amount	Increase or Decrease	Amount written off	Valuation transferred
	£	£	£	£	£	£	£	£	£
Reserves									
Depreciation and Capital	14,411	48,443	34,032	159,463	111,020	334,788	175,325	159,850	174,938
Revenue Account	718	79,685	78,967	1,110	−78,575	..	−1,110	..	..
	15,129	128,128	112,999	160,573	32,445	334,788	174,215	..	..
Income carried forward—Tariffs	81,579	62,457	−19,122	..	−62,457	..	..	..	..
(a)	96,708	190,585	93,877	160,573	−30,012	334,788	174,215	..	..
Liabilities									
Share Capital	67,858	69,915	2,057	71,532	1,617	71,536	4	..	..
(b)	164,566	260,500	95,934	232,105	−28,395	406,324	174,219	..	..
Sundry Creditors	69,631	84,275	14,644	123,714	39,439	175,030	51,316	..	..
Dividend	3,093	5,172	2,079	5,308	136	4,026	−1,282	..	..
	£237,290	£349,947	£112,657	£361,127	£11,180	£585,380	£224,253	£159,850	£174,938
Assets									
Capital Expenditure (c)	70,493	177,339	106,846	271,448	94,109	334,788	63,340	159,850	174,938
Debtors, Investments, and Cash	166,797	172,608	5,811	89,679	−82,929	250,592	160,913	..	..
	£237,290	£349,947	£112,657	£361,127	£11,180	£585,380	£224,253	£159,850	£174,938
Surplus Reserves: (a)−(c)	26,215	13,246	..	..	..	nil	..	..	..
Deficient Reserves: (c)−(a)	..	..	..	110,875	..	..	..	..	..
Surplus Reserves and Capital: (b)−(c)	94,073	83,161	..	..	..	71,536	..	..	..
Deficient Reserves and Capital: (c)−(b)	..	..	..	39,343	..	..	..	..	..

BRITISH BROADCASTING COMPANY, LTD.

(2) *Revenue and Expenditure Accounts*

	15.12.22 to 31.3.24	Year to 31.3.25		Year to 31.3.26		Nine months to 31.12.26		
	Amount	Amount	Increase or Decrease	Amount	Increase or Decrease	Amount	Annual rate equivalent	Increase or Decrease
	£	£	£	£	£	£	£ £	£
Income								
Licences	176,934	488,881	311,947	500,000	11,119	601,869	*$\frac{4}{3}$ of 530,333 707,111	207,111
Tariffs	25,378	35,689	10,311	61,020	25,331	..	..	−61,020
Publications, &c.	4,662	13,959	9,297	9,872	−4,087	44,598	59,464	49,592
	206,974	538,529	331,555	570,892	32,363	646,467	766,575	195,683
Balance brought forward	..	718	718	79,685	78,967	1,110	say to balance 6,161	−73,524
	£206,974	£539,247	£332,273	£650,577	£111,330	£647,577	£772,736	£122,159
Expenditure								
Programme, Engineering and Administration Exs.	179,788	377,352	197,564	511,023	133,671	464,776	619,702	108,679
Provident Fund	..	10,000	10,000	4,916	−5,084	3,289	4,385	−531
Directors' Fees	3,364	4,606	1,242	3,200	−1,406	3,672	4,896	1,696
Capital and Depreciation Reserves	14,411	34,032	19,621	111,020	76,958	175,325	*$\frac{4}{3}$ of 103,789 138,385	27,365
Income Tax	5,600	28,400	22,800	14,000	−14,400	−3,511		−14,000
	203,163	454,390	251,227	644,159	189,769	643,551	767,368	123,209
Dividend	3,093	5,172	2,079	5,308	136	4,026	5,368	60
	206,256	459,562	253,306	649,467	189,905	647,577	772,736	123,269
Balance carried forward	718	79,685	78,967	1,110	−78,575	..	..	−1,110
	£206,974	£539,247	£332,273	£650,577	£111,330	£647,577	£772,736	£122,159

* Less share capital included £71,535.

APPENDIX III

Union Internationale de Radiophonie

Statutes
submitted to the General Assembly Meeting at the League of Nations
on the 4th April 1925

1. *Formation*

An International Union of Radiophonie is formed, governed by the present statutes, to which are admitted all societies or associations exploiting public broadcasting enterprises.

Its centre of action is: 'Office Internationale de Radiophonie', with the office at Geneva.

2. *Object*

(1) To establish a liaison between the various European broadcasting enterprises which have adhered to the present dispositions, without excluding a future extension to enterprises of other continents;

(2) To protect the particular interests of these enterprises;

(3) To centralize the study of all questions of general interest arising and to arise from the development of wireless telephony;

(4) To pursue the realization of all schemes or all desires in connection with broadcasting in a sense favourable to broadcasting enterprises.

3. *Admission*

Applications for admission must be sent to the Office of the Union, which will be accepted under reserve of ratification by the next Council.

4. *General Assembly*

The General Assembly of the delegates of all adhering enterprises are convened at least once a year by the President of the Council of the Union, who will fix at the same time the place of the meeting.

5. Administration

The Union is controlled by a Council of 5 to 9 members. Of these, three members will be representatives of the countries in which the broadcasters exploit the stations using the greatest total power, calculated as power is defined hereafter, and one representative of the broadcasting company of the country where the registered office of the Union is established. The other members are chosen each year by the General Assembly from among the representatives of other participants.

The administrative year comprises the period from April 1st to March 31st of the following year.

[6. Council

For the first year ending 31st March 1926, the constitutional assemblies met at London and Geneva, from which the following were appointed as members of the Council:

Germany: M. Heinrich Giesecke: Representing the German broadcasting companies.

France: M. Robert Tabouis, Director of the French Broadcasting Company.

Great Britain: Admiral Carpendale, B.B.C.

Switzerland: M. Maurice Rambert, Ad.: Radio-Genève.

Belgium: M. A. Hubert, Ad.: Radio-Belgique.

Spain: M. Garcia, Chief Engineer of Radio-Barcelona.

Norway: M. Skottun, President of the Norwegian Broadcasting Company.

Holland: M. A. Dubois, Director of Ned. Sentoestellen.

Czechoslovakia: M. E. Svoboda, Radio-Journal, Prague.]

7. Committee

The Council is to meet at least every six months at the place indicated in the convening notice.

The Council elects each year, after the General Assembly, a committee which comprises:

A president

2 vice-presidents

It designates at each meeting a secretary who may be chosen outside the members of the Council.

The Council to nominate a delegate to establish a permanent liaison between the Council and the Director of the Office to ensure the execution of Council decisions.

8. *Direction*

The Direction of the Office may be confided to a director appointed by the Council outside that body, the latter to fix his powers, attributions and emoluments. The Direction to be able to fix all personal remuneration under reserve of ratification by the Council or its delegate.

9. *Subscription*

The annual subscription of each member to be fixed each year by the General Assembly on the proposition of the Council with a minimum of 500 Swiss francs per member.

[In pursuance of this article, the Council fixed for the year 1925–26 the sum of 700 Swiss francs per kilowatt of the feed of the plate circuit, on the basis of the power of the different stations at the 1st April, 1925.]

By power is meant the high tension voltage applied to the anode of the oscillating valves multiplied by the anode current of these valves. After calculating the total nett power, fractions of 1 kilowatt less than $\frac{1}{2}$ kilowatt will be counted as $\frac{1}{2}$ kilowatt.

Every member who erects a new station or increases the power of the existing station during the course of the administrative year, will pay an additional subscription fixed on the basis of the annual subscription pro rata the increase of the power and the remaining months.

Payment of the subscription must be made as soon as application for admission has been accepted.

10. *Resignation*

Should a member desire to leave the Union Internationale de Radiophonie, he will have to make his decision known to the President of the Council before 31st December of each year, this resignation taking effect at the end of the current administrative year.

INDEX

PRINTED IN GREAT BRITAIN
AT THE UNIVERSITY PRESS, OXFORD
BY VIVIAN RIDLER
PRINTER TO THE UNIVERSITY